Unquiet Lives: Marriage and Marriage in England, 1660–1800

Based on vivid court records and newspaper advertisements, this book is a pioneering account of the expectations and experiences of married life among the middle and labouring ranks in the long eighteenth century.

Its original methodology draws attention to the material life of marriage, which has long been dominated by theories of emotional shifts or fashionable accounts of spouses' gendered, oppositional lives. Thus it challenges preconceptions about authority in the household, by showing the extent to which husbands depended upon their wives' vital economic activities, household management and child care. Not only did this forge co-dependency between spouses, it undermined men's autonomy. The power balance within marriage is further revised by evidence that the sexual double-standard was not rigidly applied in everyday life. The book also shows that ideas about adultery and domestic violence evolved in the eighteenth century, influenced by new models of masculinity and femininity.

JOANNE BAILEY is a Junior Research Fellow at Merton College, Oxford.

Cambridge Studies in Early Modern British History

Series editors

ANTHONY FLETCHER
Professor of English Social History, *Institute of Historical Research, University of London*

JOHN GUY
Visiting Fellow, Clare College, Cambridge

JOHN MORRILL
*Professor of British and Irish History, University of Cambridge,
and Vice-Master of Selwyn College*

This is a series of monographs and studies covering many aspects of the history of the British Isles between the late fifteenth and the early eighteenth century. It includes the work of established scholars and pioneering work by a new generation of scholars. It includes both reviews and revisions of major topics and books, which open up new historical terrain or which reveal startling new perspectives on familiar subjects. All the volumes set detailed research into broader perspectives, and the books are intended for the use of students as well as of their teachers.

For a list of titles in the series, see end of book.

UNQUIET LIVES

Marriage and Marriage Breakdown in England, 1660–1800

JOANNE BAILEY

Merton College, Oxford

CAMBRIDGE
UNIVERSITY PRESS

CAMBRIDGE UNIVERSITY PRESS
Cambridge, New York, Melbourne, Madrid, Cape Town, Singapore, São Paulo, Delhi

Cambridge University Press
The Edinburgh Building, Cambridge CB2 8RU, UK

Published in the United States of America by Cambridge University Press, New York

www.cambridge.org
Information on this title: www.cambridge.org/9780521810586

First published 2003
This digitally printed version 2008

A catalogue record for this publication is available from the British Library

ISBN 978-0-521-81058-6 hardback
ISBN 978-0-521-09311-8 paperback

In memory of
my father Giovanni Begiato
and my grandfather Stanley McDermott

CONTENTS

ACKNOWLEDGEMENTS

This project has been part of my life for several years. It started out as a Ph.D. thesis at the University of Durham in 1995. My supervisor Christopher Brooks has been my mentor and I owe him several debts of gratitude for his assistance, encouragement, and good humour. I am also indebted to Christopher and his wife Sharyn Brooks for their friendship and hospitality to me and my family. I met my good friends and fellow graduates Rebecca King and Adrian Green at Durham and I thank them for discussing and reading my work, and for their insights and enthusiasm. I must also thank the British Academy and the Institute of Historical Research for funding me with, respectively, a three-year scholarship and a Scouloudi Fellowship.

I have turned this thesis into a book while a junior research fellow at Merton College, Oxford, and I am sincerely grateful to the Warden and Fellows for this privileged position and the opportunities it has given me. Steven Gunn, Olwen Hufton, and Michael Baker have been particularly helpful and I thank them for their interest and help. Where else but in the collegiate system at Oxford could I have benefited from a physicist's informed comments on my work? Joanna Innes has also given me much advice and kind encouragement.

I would like to thank numerous other people for reading my work, offering advice or useful references: Helen Berry, Elizabeth Foyster, Perry Gauci, Tim Hitchcock, Ian McBride, Toby Osborne, Tim Stretton, and Keith Wrightson. The archivists in the libraries and county record offices in which I have worked have been helpful, particularly the team at the Centre for Buckinghamshire Studies, Joe Fewster, Margaret McCollough at the University of Durham, and Christopher Webb at the Borthwick Institute of Historical Research.

I must also thank Anthony Fletcher for his tireless encouragement and guidance over the course of my research. In addition, his role as one of the editors of this series has been invaluable to me, boosting my confidence and providing me with just the right mix of support and incentive to finish my book.

Finally I owe my family everything. My parents-in-law Sheila and Tony Bailey have been interested in my work, kindly read various pieces of my writing, and given me hospitality during my research. My grandparents gave me the gift of the computers that I relied on while studying. This book owes much to my husband, Mark Bailey. I thank him for his invaluable belief in my abilities, his support, and his comments on my writing. I began writing my book just after our son Gabriel was born. Its production is therefore intangibly bound up with him and I will never think of writing it without being reminded of the joy he brings us. Lilian Begiato, my mother, has looked after him while I work, and for that as well as her selfless emotional and material support, I thank her. This book is for her.

ABBREVIATIONS AND CONVENTIONS

All dates are in the old style, but with the new year beginning on 1 January

ABBREVIATIONS

Published works

Bailey, 'Favoured or oppressed?'	J. Bailey, 'Favoured or oppressed? Married women, property and "coverture" in England, 1660–1800', *Continuity and Change* 17, 3 (2002), 1–22
Bailey, 'Voices in court'	J. Bailey, 'Voices in court: lawyers' or litigants'?' *Historical Research* 74, 186 (2001), 392–408
Clark, *Struggle for the Breeches*	Anna Clark, *The Struggle for the Breeches: Gender and the Making of the British Working Class*, London, 1995
Erickson, *Women and Property*	A. L. Erickson, *Women and Property in Early Modern England*, London, 1993
Gowing, *Domestic Dangers*	L. Gowing, *Domestic Dangers: Women, Words, and Sex in Early Modern London*, Oxford, 1996
Hunt, 'Marital "rights"'	M. Hunt, 'Wives and marital "rights" in the Court of Exchequer in the early eighteenth century' in P. Griffiths and M. S. R. Jenner (eds.), *Londinopolis: Essays in the Cultural and Social History of Early Modern London*, Manchester, 2000, pp. 107–29.

Kent, 'Gone for a soldier'	D. Kent, '"Gone for a soldier": family breakdown and the demography of desertion in a London parish, 1750–91', *Local Population Studies* 45 (1990), 27–42.
O'Hara, *Courtship and Constraint*	D. O'Hara, *Courtship and Constraint: Rethinking the Making of Marriage in Tudor England*, Manchester, 2000
Shoemaker, *Gender*	R. B. Shoemaker, *Gender in English Society, 1650–1850: The Emergence of Separate Spheres?* London, 1998
Snell, *Annals*	K. D. M. Snell, *Annals of the Labouring Poor: Social Change and Agrarian England, 1660–1900*, Cambridge, 1985
Stone, *Divorce*	L. Stone, *Road to Divorce, England 1530–1987*, 2nd edition, Oxford, 1990
Stone, *Family, Sex, Marriage*	L. Stone, *The Family, Sex and Marriage in England 1500–1800*, abridged edition, London, 1977
VCH	*The Victoria County History of the Counties of England*
Vickery, *Gentleman's Daughter*	A. Vickery, *The Gentleman's Daughter: Women's Lives in Georgian England*, London, 1998

Archival sources

BIHR:	Borthwick Institute of Historical Research
Chanc.CP.	Chancery cause papers
Cons.CP.	Consistory cause papers
CP.	Cause papers
D/C.CP.	Dean and Chapter cause papers
Trans.CP.	Transmitted cause papers
CBS:	Centre for Buckinghamshire Studies
Q/SM/	Quarter sessions minute books
Q/SO/	Quarter sessions order books
QS Rolls	Quarter sessions rolls

DRO: Durham Record Office
    DPR/   Durham Probate Records
    EP/   Church of England parish records
    Q/S/OB   Quarter sessions order books

NCAS: Northumberland County Archives Service
    QSB/   Quarter sessions bundles
    QSO   Quarter sessions order books

NYA: North Yorkshire Archives
    PR/   Parish records
    QSB/   Quarter sessions rolls and bundles
    QSM   Quarter sessions minute and order books

OA: Oxfordshire Archives
    Mss.D.D.Par/   Parish collections
    Mss.Oxf. dioc.papers   Diocesan papers, consistory and
                              archdeaconry court
    Par   Parish
    QS/   Quarter sessions records

TWA: Tyne and Wear Archives
    QS/   Quarter sessions order books

UOD: University of Durham, University Library, Palace Green section
    DDR/EJ/CC   Durham diocesan records, ecclesiastical
                        jurisdiction, court books
    DDR/EJ/CCD/   Durham diocesan records, ecclesiastical
                        jurisdiction, Consistory court documents
    DDR/EJ/PRC/   Durham diocesan records, ecclesiastical
                        jurisdiction, Proctors' correspondence
    DDR/EJ/PRO   Durham diocesan records, ecclesiastical
                        jurisdiction, probate records

GM   *Gentleman's Magazine*
JOJ   *Jackson's Oxford Journal* (1753–1800)
N.Ad   *Newcastle Advertiser* (1788–1800)
N.Chron   *Newcastle Chronicle* (1764–1800)
N.Cour   *Newcastle Courant* (1711–1800)
N.Jour   *Newcastle Journal* (1739–88)
NCJ   *North Country Journal* (1734–8)
Y.Chron   *York Chronicle* (1773–1800)
Y.Cour   *York Courant* (1728–1800)
Y.Her   *York Herald and County Advertiser* (1790–1800)

1

Introduction: reassessing marriage

In 1675, Grace Allenson, reflecting on her unhappy marriage, told her servant 'that if she might have but bread and water to live on she were happy if she could but be quiet with it'.[1] Charles Pearson, a merchant tailor, also echoed *The Book of Homilies*' sentiment that quiet in marriage should be prized above houses, servants, money, land and possessions.[2] In the advert that he placed in 1756 in the *York Courant*, announcing his and his wife's mutually agreed separation, he mused 'What is all the World without Quietness?'[3] More than tranquillity, quiet evoked peace of mind and body, undisturbed by rage or passion. This study reconstructs the types of behaviour that constituted a quiet or unquiet life in England in the long eighteenth century. It is based on fragments of information from over 1,400 marriages that were in difficulty between 1660 and 1800 (Appendix 1), ranging in length from a few formulaic lines to hundreds of detailed pages. Much of this was written by a clerk of court or typeset in a provincial newspaper, although occasionally a surviving letter in a spouse's own hand poignantly conveys the intimacies of wedlock across the centuries.[4] The evidence that is produced about the nature of married life is elusive and inscrutable. After all, the reality in sources is difficult to pin down, for the 'truths' that they contain are diverse, contradictory and dependent upon the teller.[5] Despite this, it is important for the historian not to treat these moments of extreme marital tension as abstracts. These events, invariably sad, sometimes uplifting and touching, often brutal and callous, had great meaning for the people involved. This book is about more than the ideology of marriage and marital roles. It conveys something of marriage as it was lived in England from the perspective of the middling

[1] BIHR, CP.H/3264, *Allenson c. Allenson*, 1675, Cruelty Separation, Margaret Green's deposition.
[2] *Book of Homilies, The second Tome of Homilies, of such matters As were Promised and Entituled in the former part of Homilies* (London, 1633), p. 247.
[3] *Y.Cour*, 21 September 1756, p. 3.
[4] UOD, DDR/EJ/PRC/: Correspondence received by proctors or lawyers, and letters that were submitted as evidence.
[5] See Bailey, 'Voices in court'.

sort and wage labourers. Reconstructing a set of national expectations about married life, it shows how these altered in a period of great social, economic and cultural change.

It is vital to understand married life in the past. Marriage mattered in much the same ways as it matters today. Governments attempted to control it, the church tried to retain some hold on it, pundits bemoaned its state, and most proclaimed it the key to social order. Matrimony has always been at once a public and a private institution. The pre-modern household, a social and economic institution, linked to other households in a chain of credit, often had the conjugal couple at its centre.[6] Marriage shaped the lives of most adults, whether they entered informal or formal versions of it, or did not marry through choice or circumstance. It marked physical, emotional and economic maturity and – depending upon sex – wealth, status and participation in civic and social duties and rights.[7] It is hardly surprising that historians have used it to explain demographic shifts and to explore kinship, parenting, economics, work, law, property ownership, violence, sexuality and reputation. Though matrimony is frequently discussed by historians, few historical studies are entirely devoted to it. The formal rules and informal customs associated with its making and, to a lesser extent, its breaking have received some attention. Reflecting the way that marriage was rooted within its social, economic, demographic and cultural environment, it is usually considered as a discrete section or chapter in a diverse body of work. When this literature is used to trace the development of marriage over the centuries, it becomes apparent that there are only a few key interpretative debates, which have been determined by the available source material. It also highlights the areas where more research and new interpretations are necessary.

Information about the experience of late medieval marriage is limited. In this period matrimonial cases that came before the church courts were mostly about the formation of marriage rather than its breakdown, providing little detailed information about married life.[8] Even elite experience of

---

[6] C. Muldrew, *The Economy of Obligation: The Culture of Credit and Social Relations in Early Modern England* (London, 1998), pp. 9, 97, 148–72; K. Wrightson, *Earthly Necessities: Economic Lives in Early Modern Britain* (London, 2000), pp. 30–4, 300–3. The contemporary understanding of 'household-family' was flexible and did not necessitate that it was formed around a married couple; nonetheless they still retained the hierarchical form, with heads of household and dependent members (N. Tadmor, 'The concept of the household-family in eighteenth-century England', *Past and Present*, 151 (1996), 111–40).

[7] For examples of such rights, see D. Cressy, *Birth, Marriage and Death: Ritual, Religion and the Life-Cycle in Tudor and Stuart England* (Oxford, 1997), p. 287; S. Mendelson and P. Crawford, *Women in Early Modern English Society, 1550–1720* (Oxford, 1998), p. 131.

[8] M. Ingram, 'Spousals litigation in the English ecclesiastical courts c. 1350–1640' in R. B. Outhwaite (ed.), *Marriage and Society: Studies in the Social History of Marriage* (London, 1981), p. 36; P. Rushton, 'The broken marriage in early modern England: matrimonial cases from the Durham church courts, 1560–1630', *Archaeologia Aeliana*, 5, 13 (1985), 191.

marriage is less accessible than in later centuries, given the scarcity of personal records like letters, memoirs and diaries.[9] The most useful surviving sources relate to work.[10] Inevitably this shapes the questions that are asked about marriage, centring on a debate about what wives' contributions to the domestic economy and household meant in terms of relative power between spouses. The consensus among historians is that late medieval spouses worked equally hard to ensure the efficient functioning of their households. Elite wives hired and fired domestic servants, and in their husbands' absence managed estates and acted unilaterally to protect their land or goods.[11] Rural and urban couples of lower social status formed economic partnerships and their work is described by historians as complementary. Thus while wives' productive labour varied according to locality, was less specialised than their husbands' and adapted to their reproductive life-course, it contributed to a successful household.[12] Where historians disagree is about how far this translated into any type of power within marriage. Alice Clark, writing in the early twentieth century, personifies the traditional approach with her argument that wives' contributions to their husbands' enterprises rendered them mistresses of the business as well as domestic sphere. Their work was so important that young unmarried people did the 'menial' domestic tasks usually associated with married women. Not only did wives gain public value from this 'family enterprise', husbands could be fruitfully involved in parenting.[13]

The view that joint labour caused some practical equality between spouses still has its supporters, but on the whole the idea that the pre-industrialised world was a 'golden-age' for women has been adapted or rejected.[14] The revised version demonstrates that women's overall status fluctuated. For example, following the Black Death they enjoyed increased work opportunities and improved wages. Pertinently, it is proposed that this allowed them to defer matrimony or exercise a wider choice of marriage partner.[15] In turn, the economic recession and increase in labour supply by the late fifteenth century

---

[9] Notable exceptions include N. Davies (ed.), *Paston Letters and Papers of the Fifteenth Century*, 2 vols. (Oxford, 1971, 1976), Vol. I.

[10] For example, administrative records such as tax records and manorial court rolls relating to fines imposed on regulated areas of employment.

[11] M. Mate, *Women in Medieval English Society* (Cambridge, 1999), pp. 65–6.

[12] H. Jewell, *Women in Medieval England* (Manchester, 1996), pp. 69–71, 93; B. Hanawalt, *The Ties that Bound: Peasant Families in Medieval England* (Oxford, 1986), pp. 141–7; J. Bennett, *Women in the Medieval English Countryside: Gender and Household in Brigstock before the Plague* (Oxford, 1987), p. 118.

[13] A. Clark, *Working Life of Women in the Seventeenth Century*, 3rd edition (London, 1992), p. 157.

[14] For an example of a fairly traditional view, Hanawalt, *Ties that Bound*, p. 153. For an overview of the debate see S. H. Rigby, 'Gendering the Black Death: women in later medieval England', *Gender and History*, 3, 12 (2000), 745–54.

[15] On the other hand, the terrible mortality may simply have reduced the numbers of men available for marriage.

reduced women's opportunities, making marriage their only economic option. It is inferred that the former state granted wives more independence and value, while the latter caused a hardening of gender divisions, relegating women to a more passive role in marriage formation, and, one imagines, within married life itself.[16] The theory is rejected, on the other hand, by historians who insist that there was continuity in women's status in both marriage and work and who question the link between the two. They point out that female subordination was unaffected by changes in the availability and remuneration of labour because both failed to improve women's social power or legal rights.[17] Thus, whatever work wives did, husbands controlled material resources, the work that was done and the profits that labour brought.[18]

Historians of early modern marriage do not resolve the debate. Having found little evidence that wives achieved formal power as a result of their contributions to the domestic economy, the question has in some sense become less urgent and its serious analysis is left to medievalists. Historians who investigate early modern marriage continue to be interested in questions of relative power and authority, but their approach is framed by the nature of the sources, which shift the basis of the debate from work to emotion. In the first place, personal records are more widely available. The way historians have used these sources has varied. Thus Lawrence Stone's controversial account of an emotional transition from cold distant marital relationships in the sixteenth century to initially more patriarchal, but ultimately closer relations between spouses in the seventeenth century has been replaced by case-studies which reveal the affectionate, dynamic nature of specific marriages from several social ranks.[19]

Secondly, the increase in advice literature for married couples after the Reformation helps structure the debate about marriage around patriarchy. Thus, it often turns on how far this ordering principle of the household, with men as heads of household exercising authority over their subordinate wives, children and servants, was mitigated by love, personal character or, occasionally, wives' material contributions.[20] There was a tendency to propose that

[16] P. J. P. Goldberg, *Women, Work, and Life Cycle in a Medieval Economy: Women in York and Yorkshire c. 1300–1520* (Oxford, 1992), p. 361; Jewell, *Women in Medieval England*, p. 114.
[17] Mate, *Women in Medieval English Society*, pp. 30, 96–100.
[18] Bennett, *Women in the Medieval English Countryside*, pp. 115, 139; Mate, *Women in Medieval English Society*, p. 34.
[19] Stone, *Family, Sex, Marriage*, pp. 88–9, 145–6; A. Fletcher, *Gender, Sex and Subordination in England 1500–1800* (London, 1995), pp. 154–72; K. Wrightson, *English Society 1580–1680* (London, 1982), pp. 95–8, 101–4; R. A. Houlbrooke, *The English Family 1450–1700* (Harlow, 1984), pp. 102–6.
[20] For example, Fletcher, *Gender, Sex and Subordination*, p. 191.

these factors rendered most early modern marriages companionate. Recently, a rather less cosy image of wedlock has been offered. Laura Gowing's reconstruction of sixteenth- and seventeenth-century London marriage is very different. These couples shared few activities, goals or expectations because their social and cultural lives were gendered to such an extent that they were entirely oppositional. In spite of the female agency that she demonstrates, the conjugal power relationship was depressingly skewed in favour of men.[21]

Thirdly, litigation concerned with conjugal breakdown, which replaced disputes in the church courts about marriage contracts from the sixteenth century, also shapes analysis of marriage. The most detailed suits were separation from bed and board, which was sought by couples on the grounds of adultery and cruelty, and it is noticeable that most work about married life actually considers wife-beating and extra-marital sex.[22] Male violence can provide evidence about the exercise of male power within the early modern household. Detailed information about wife-beating in matrimonial litigation, its legal status, the advice supplied to husbands about correcting their wives, and references to domestic violence in popular literature have all inspired studies of wife-beating. The evidence is ambiguous, however, and has resulted in two positions. In one view, male violence was an accepted, or at least, expected, feature of married life, and considered a rational response to female disobedience.[23] There is, nevertheless, evidence that husbands' potential to beat their wives was legally, socially and culturally controlled. Wife-beating paralleled public violence in that it was tolerated when it corrected inappropriate actions, was exercised in a limited way and monitored by neighbours, friends and family.[24] In the light of these restrictions on male tyranny, therefore, other historians argue that contemporaries viewed wife-beating as abnormal, irrational behaviour, which represented unmanliness.[25] Both views about wife-beating infer an unchanging male desire to use violence against women. Similarly, work on the sexual double-standard prevalent in literary, prescriptive and legal writings, and studies of the numerous defamation cases in the church courts relating to sexual slander, privilege chastity as the key to single, married and widowed women's

---

[21] Gowing, *Domestic Dangers*, pp. 4–5, 180–231.

[22] In a 22-page section about marriage, 8 pages are devoted to wife-beating and sexual behaviour, with several more about men's authority and how women dealt with it, in Mendelson and Crawford, *Women in Early Modern English Society*, pp. 126–48.

[23] R. Phillips, *Untying the Knot: A Short History of Divorce* (Cambridge, 1991), pp. 97–100; Gowing, *Domestic Dangers*, pp. 219–20.

[24] S. D. Amussen, '"Being stirred to much unquietness": violence and domestic violence in early modern England', *Journal of Women's History*, 6, 2 (1994), 70–89.

[25] E. A. Foyster, 'Male honour, social control and wife beating in late Stuart England', *Transactions of the Royal Historical Society*, 6th series 6 (1996) 214–24; Wrightson, *English Society*, p. 94.

reputations.[26] For example, defamation cases imply that wives needed to avoid any behaviour that raised suspicion, because it would lead to marital conflict and damage their standing in the local community.[27] In this context, the fact that most adultery separation cases were brought against wives leads to the conclusion that men's extra-marital sexual behaviour was unlikely to be punished within or outside marriage, and consequently had little effect on their reputation.

The influence of the source material is striking when we consider the marriages of wage labourers. The lack of personal records means that discussion about their unions is often restricted to the mechanics of the making and breaking of matrimony. Stone speculated, for example, that the poor's lack of property permitted freedom of choice regarding who and when to marry, and made it easy for poorer men to abandon unsatisfactory marriages.[28] Similarly, sources such as parish poor-relief records, settlement papers and prosecutions of vagrants, all of which reveal evidence of desertion, highlight the instability of the marriages of those vulnerable to poverty and form a bleak picture of callous male deserters and their pitiful starving wives.[29] This approach has been counter-balanced recently by more perceptive work that shows that the lower ranks were subject to constraint in making marriage. For example, in periods of social, economic or demographic stress, parish authorities frequently prevented the marriages of the poor.[30] Even more significant is Diane O'Hara's reassessment of the making of marriage in the sixteenth century, which reveals the extent to which poorer people themselves exercised caution on entering marriage. Her conclusions that men's and women's choice of marriage partner was influenced by material calculation, rather than personal attraction, raise many questions about married life itself.[31]

It is not easy to characterise marriage between 1660 and 1800 because the secondary literature is so fragmentary and the same sources as those in studies of earlier periods tend to be used, in spite of a wider range of available evidence, like newspapers, better surviving quarter sessions records, and the plethora of related cases in the equity courts and civil suits. Stone's *Road to Divorce* and Leah Leneman's account of separation and divorce in Scotland

---

[26] The classic text on the former is K. Thomas, 'The double standard', *Journal of History of Ideas*, 20 (1959), 195–217; the range of work for the latter is substantial, but for a recent interpretation see Gowing, *Domestic Dangers*, p. 3.

[27] Gowing, *Domestic Dangers*, p. 230.

[28] Stone, *Family, Sex, Marriage*, p. 89, and *Divorce*, p. 141.

[29] For instance, Snell, *Annals*; Kent, 'Gone for a soldier'.

[30] M. Ingram, *Church Courts, Sex and Marriage in England, 1570–1640* (Cambridge, 1987), p. 131; S. Hindle, 'The problem of pauper marriage in seventeenth-century England', *Transactions of the Royal Historical Society*, 6 (1998), 71–89.

[31] O'Hara, *Courtship and Constraint*.

are useful, but catalogue the formal methods of leaving marriage rather than exploring the nature of married life itself.[32] Amanda Vickery's convincing chapter on married life in Georgian England and Margaret Hunt's work on middling-sort marriage in the early eighteenth century use wider sources, but they only provide a picture of five provincial gentry and professional marriages and a handful of middling-sort London relationships. Moreover, in Hunt's opinion the female agency that she uncovered was unorthodox and probably unique to London.[33] Analyses of nineteenth-century marriage provide little retrospective information on its eighteenth-century counterpart. Influenced by industrialisation and modernisation, these accounts view the last quarter of the eighteenth century as a precursor to later developments. Late eighteenth-century marital roles, for instance, are investigated in studies exploring the role of gender in the formation of the middle and working classes.[34]

It is also problematic that people writing about nineteenth-century married life have preconceptions about the eighteenth century. One claim that needs to be tested, for example, is that working conditions in the pre-industrial household fostered conjugal friendship and harmony.[35] This hypothesis is linked to escalating industrialisation, which reopens the question of the relationship between the economic role of wives and their power status within marriage. Anna Clark, for instance, proposes that shifts in employment patterns and different working conditions influenced the quality of relationships between spouses.[36] This approach recalls that of Alice Clark, by centring on whether women's employment opportunities were declining, forcing them to depend on their husbands, or increasing, creating independence, and how husbands reacted in terms of violence.[37] Issues about gender, class and shifts

[32] Stone, *Divorce*; L. Leneman, *Alienated Affections: The Scottish Experience of Divorce and Separation, 1684–1830* (Edinburgh, 1998).

[33] M. R. Hunt, 'Wife Beating, Domesticity and Women's Independence in Eighteenth-Century London', *Gender and History*, 4 (1992), 10–29; Hunt, 'Marital "rights"'; also see J. Hurl-Eamon, 'Domestic violence prosecuted: women binding over their husbands for assault at Westminster Quarter Sessions, 1685–1720', *Journal of Family History*, 26, 4 (2001), 435–54.

[34] Clark, *Struggle for the Breeches*; L. Davidoff and C. Hall, *Family Fortunes: Men and Women of the English Middle Class, 1780–1850* (London, 1987).

[35] J. Tosh, *A Man's Place: Masculinity and the Middle-Class Home in Victorian England* (London, 1999), p. 26.

[36] Clark, *Struggle for the Breeches*, p. 75.

[37] For example, it is argued that enclosures, the switch to pastoral agriculture and mechanisation of the textile industry in Somerset made male labourers increasingly dependent on their spouses. The resulting tensions found expression in their physical abuse of their wives (P. Morris, 'Defamation and sexual reputation in Somerset, 1733–1850', Ph.D. thesis, University of Warwick (1985), p. 393). Also see N. Tomes, 'A "Torrent of Abuse": crimes of violence between working-class men and women in London, 1840–1875', *Journal of Social History*, 11, 3 (1978), 328–45. A less stereotyped view is provided by S. D'Cruze, 'Care, diligence and "Usfull Pride" [*sic*]: gender, industrialisation and the domestic economy, c. 1770 to c. 1840', *Women's History Review*, 3, 3 (1994), 315–45.

in working conditions coalesced in literature about separate spheres for men
and women and a new emphasis on the ideology of domesticity.[38] Both in-
form another problematic claim, which is that men's role as husbands only
came under sustained criticism in the Victorian era.[39] It is an argument that
is surely shaped by the proliferation in legislation pertaining to divorce, wife-
beating and married women's rights to property and children, which places
much emphasis on male cruelty, the class aspects of wife-beating, and the
sexual double-standard.

This overview of work on marriage across five centuries reveals that, regardless of the period under consideration, historians seem to be divided
into two views about marriage, which can be described as pessimistic or
optimistic.[40] For example, pessimistic medievalists concede that married
women might have contributed equally to their household, but insist that
their work was different, controlled by their menfolk and rated secondary
to men's.[41] Since it never altered the dominant ideology about women or
their legal, economic or political standing, their state in marriage remained
one of dependence. In public terms, the lives of married men and women
were particularly divergent with few common experiences.[42] For pessimistic
early-modernists, the sexual double-standard ensured that wives' lives were
shadowed by their sexual reputation, which restricted their personal and
public activities. Husbands, in contrast, bathed in the sunshine of permis-
siveness, for their wives turned a blind eye to infidelity, and their personal
sexual behaviour had little impact on their reputation.[43] All are sure that
wife-beating was common and not abnormal.[44] In sum, pessimists tend to see
spouses' experiences as oppositional.[45] Optimists propose that marriage was
more mutual and complementary, whether they define it as a partnership or
companionate, depending on the period in which they specialise.[46] They argue that the pre-industrial household encouraged harmony between spouses
because they often worked together in the same trade, craft or occupation.

[38] For a comprehensive overview, see L. Davidoff, M. Doolittle, J. Fink and K. Holden, *Family Story: Blood, Contract and Intimacy 1830–1960* (London, 1999), pp. 3–15.
[39] A. J. Hammerton, *Cruelty and Companionship: Conflict in Nineteenth-century Married Life* (London, 1992).
[40] The same point can be made about medieval women's history (Rigby, 'Gendering the Black Death').
[41] Bennett, *Women in the Medieval English Countryside*, pp. 115–39; Mate, *Women in Medieval English Society*, p. 100.
[42] Bennett, *Women in the Medieval English Countryside*, pp. 139–40.
[43] Stone, *Family, Sex, Marriage*, pp. 81, 146, 315–17; Gowing, *Domestic Dangers*, pp. 1, 3, 8, 229–31.
[44] Mendelson and Crawford, *Women in Early Modern English Society*, pp. 128, 140.
[45] For example, ibid., p. 147.
[46] Hanawalt calls medieval peasant marriages partnerships, specifically rejecting the term companionate (*Ties that Bound*, p. 219).

Such economic partnerships caused wives' contributions to be socially valued and led to shared goals and less likelihood of domestic violence.[47] Optimists invoke the formal and informal restrictions on male tyranny, the recommendations in most advice literature that husbands be affectionate, and the cultural demands that men employ self-control, along with wifely 'non-confrontational' tactics, to emphasise the extent to which the potential in marriage for men's oppression was tempered. Furthermore, spouses' complementary social interests and joint economic endeavours led to some shared components of reputation, which softened the blow of the sexual double-standard.[48]

The two views are partly explicable because contemporary culture itself, whether sermon, pamphlet, ballad or newspaper, promoted an idealised view of harmonious relations between spouses while simultaneously demanding female subjection. Historians have offered a range of explanations for this contradictory state of affairs. Some differentiate between a restrictive ideal and a permissive reality. Keith Wrightson concludes that patriarchal and companionate marriage were 'poles in an enduring continuum in marital relations', but that most were the latter form because the potential for very authoritarian relationships was mitigated by the demands of daily life.[49] Tim Stretton observes that it was the gap between reality and prescription that facilitated patriarchy's success, by ensuring that if women could not live up to the positive images that were promoted, they tried not to live down to the negative ones.[50] Another view is that early modern people saw no inconsistency between male authority and affectionate partnership. Anthony Fletcher, for example, argues that protestant conduct-book writers and their male audience saw little discrepancy in their twin values. While they were eager to experience the strong bonds of mutual marital love, they wanted to maintain social and gender order in uncertain times.[51] Sara Mendelson and Patricia Crawford nonetheless note that male writers stressed subjection, while female writers emphasised companionship.[52] Other historians have argued that the inconsistency in the advice about marital relations was recognised. Thus Linda Pollock comments that the sexes were reared and socialised to

---

[47] Ibid., pp. 153–5; Houlbrooke, *English Family*, pp. 106–10.

[48] Wrightson, *English Society*, pp. 91–104; Vickery, *Gentleman's Daughter*, pp. 85, 86; Houlbrooke, *English Family*, p. 119.

[49] Wrightson, *English Society*, p. 104; Shoemaker, *Gender*, p. 112.

[50] T. Stretton, *Women Waging Law in Elizabethan England* (Cambridge, 1998), pp. 10–11, 229.

[51] A. Fletcher, 'The protestant idea of marriage in early modern England' in A. Fletcher and P. Roberts, *Religion, Culture and Society in Early Modern Britain* (Cambridge, 1994), pp. 161, 180–1.

[52] Mendelson and Crawford, *Women in Early Modern English Society*, p. 135; K. Davies, 'Continuity and change in literary advice on marriage' in Outhwaite (ed.), *Marriage and Society*, p. 60.

deal effectively with the dual demands made on them of subordination and competence.[53] What is clear is that one of the reasons for the patriarchal system's longevity was that it allowed flexible behaviour. Fletcher has shown how it was adapted, as a gender system, in order to ensure its success.[54] Pollock has concluded more recently that patriarchal power was not simply mitigated, but that the structural conditions of the system limited its fullest expression. She critiques any simplistic categorisation of family relations as either affectionate or oppressive, observing that they could be many things at different times because relationships changed over a lifetime according to circumstances and priorities.[55]

Nonetheless, the pessimistic and optimistic models are problematic for several reasons. The discrepancies between them cannot be explained by variations in regional economics and industries, or the couples' rank, wealth and life-course. Marriages from a similar period, social status and local environment, whether rural or urban, have been characterised by both approaches. Both views of marriage are largely from a male perspective and, given the sources, even that perspective is restricted to an educated elite male opinion. Optimists and pessimists alike tend to take it for granted that husbands either implemented their power over their wives to its full extent, or benevolently lessened it at their own whim. Yet this fails to take account of recent findings about manhood, reputation, patriarchy and the experience of the common law doctrine of coverture. Men did achieve status from their position in their household and domestic economy. Nonetheless, many had difficulties in achieving economic mastery, occupational independence, and full or unquestioned authority within the household and family, and their credit status was contingent upon many factors.[56] Equally, it ignores evidence that women's reputations rested upon a broader foundation than just chastity, drawing on their position as housewives, as well as their occupational status and charitable works.[57] It is also becoming clear that married women were less restricted in their daily lives than their status under coverture would indicate. Amongst other limitations, this left married women unable to own or manage personal and real property and prevented them from entering contracts. Yet numerous ordinary married women have been discovered organising their own property and participating in the commercial

[53] L. A. Pollock, '"Teach her to live under obedience": the making of women in the upper ranks of early modern England', *Continuity and Change*, 4, 2 (1989), 233.

[54] Fletcher, *Gender, Sex and Subordination*.

[55] L. A. Pollock, 'Rethinking patriarchy and the family in seventeenth-century England', *Journal of Family History*, 23, 1 (1998), 20.

[56] A. Shepard, 'Manhood, credit and patriarchy in early modern England c. 1580–1640', *Past and Present*, 167 (2000), 83–6.

[57] G. Walker, 'Expanding the boundaries of female honour in early modern England', *Transactions of the Royal Historical Society*, 6 (1996), 235–45.

world.[58] Such women would seem to have had greater control over their own lives than the pessimistic and optimistic models of marriage suggest. It is time, therefore, to reassess husbands' and wives' experiences of married life and their understandings of marital roles.

This book explores what marriage meant for husbands as well as wives and offers a new and more integrated model of married life. Chapter 2 describes the social and occupational diversity of the married couples in this study and the diverse urban, rural, industrial and agricultural conditions of the counties in which they lived. This provides useful information about marital experience outside London, which is all too readily considered unusual or atypical. Chapter 2 also outlines the book's methodology, which focuses on 'secondary complaints', instead of the primary accusations of cruelty or adultery, which provide the key to understanding everyday married life. The wide range of informal and formal methods of resolution that were on offer to couples experiencing marital difficulties are outlined in chapter 3 to reveal that many types of marital conflict were considered to be normal, not deviant, in order to facilitate reconciliation. As a result, records of marital difficulties provide invaluable evidence for historians to assess married life in all its forms. Chapters 4 and 5 turn to the central thesis of this book, which is that spouses' experiences were not wholly gendered, differing according to their sex, and that extensive co-dependency existed between them. Chapters 6 and 7 illustrate that both the marital power balance and the sexual double-standard were far more nuanced in practice than stereotypes might suggest. Finally the book turns to the previously unexplored issue of how spouses of different ranks, occupations and levels of wealth dealt with life after their marriages had collapsed. Chapter 8 reveals that while marital separation caused social dislocation and/or poverty for women, whatever their original social status, it also caused disruption to men's socio-economic status, which underlines the extent to which marital co-dependency extended its grip to husbands as well as wives.

[58] Bailey, 'Favoured or oppressed?'; Erickson, *Women and Property*; M. Finn, 'Women, consumption and coverture in England, c. 1760–1860', *Historical Journal*, 39, 3 (1996), 702–22; Shepard, 'Manhood, credit and patriarchy'.

2

'To have and to hold': analysing married life

In order to reappraise marriage in the seventeenth and eighteenth centuries, it is vital to use sources that include a wide range of social and occupational groups and reflect both sexes. Correspondence, memoirs and autobiographies are rewarding sources for the study of married life, but they only provide an insight into elite marriage. The best way to investigate the marital behaviour of the middling sort and wage labourers is to analyse evidence from matrimonial conflict. This study examines matrimonial and correction suits, for which cause papers survive, that came before Durham, York and Oxford ecclesiastical courts. As well as dealing with the administration of the Church, these courts maintained the spiritual discipline of the clergy and their parishioners. Court business involving the laity was conducted in two ways. In disciplinary cases (office cases), church courts brought people before them to be corrected for a range of offences, of which immorality is of interest here. Secondly, people sued each other (instance cases), and this study examines litigation concerning marriage.[1] Church courts offered a range of solutions to people suffering from marital difficulties, including: annulment, where specified impediments dissolved marriage, allowing spouses to remarry; separation from bed and board on the grounds of adultery and cruelty, which permitted couples to live apart but not remarry; and restitution of conjugal rights, ostensibly a way to force a spouse to return or to accept the other back into the marital home, but commonly used to settle problems about financial maintenance. Matrimonial litigation was dealt with by the church courts throughout the early modern period until 1857.

Though often detailed, one of the shortcomings of this evidence is that the people who used the courts were from a narrow range of social status largely because the costs of their services were fairly high. In 119 cases it is possible

---

[1] For a description of the courts and their business see A. Tarver, *Church Court Records* (Chichester, 1995).

to determine the income or occupation of the husbands who came before the three ecclesiastical courts, which can be used as a rough indicator of the couples' social status (Appendix 5). Some 41% of the couples were titled or of gentry rank. The majority of the rest were from the more financially secure sections of the middling sort, with 23% relatively high-status manufacturers, shop owners, innkeepers or master mariners, and 17% professionals, often attorneys and clergymen. Only 15% of the men were of a lower social group than middling sort, and most of them earned around £25 0s 0d per annum in building and textile trades. Only one servant and one labourer were recorded.

In order to extend the analysis to marriages of lower middling-sort couples and wage labourers, therefore, records of the courts of quarter sessions of Northumberland, Newcastle, Durham, North Yorkshire, Buckinghamshire, and Oxfordshire were also examined. In their dealings with criminal offences and administrative business, justices both in and out of session came into contact with a number of marriages that were either in difficulty or had collapsed, usually instances of desertion, separation and domestic violence. The third main source of evidence, public announcements made by husbands using town criers, printed leaflets or local newspapers, also includes people from a broad section of society and occupations. Husbands used the announcements to refuse to pay their wives' debts. Married women were denied any separate legal existence by the common law doctrine of coverture, so that they could not enter economic contracts in their own right and in order to make basic purchases (necessaries) on credit had to do so in their husband's name. The right to pledge their husband's credit was granted by the law of agency.[2] Marital disagreement, elopement and mutual separation lie at the heart of these financial declarations. The announcements were common in the seventeenth century, but their analysis is only possible from the 1720s when they were placed as advertisements in newspapers. Thirteen newspapers from Newcastle, York and Oxford were sampled to build a picture of this largely unexplored phenomenon.

In contrast to the church courts, only 2% of the husbands considered by the quarter sessions and 5% of the advertising husbands were gentlemen (Appendices 6 and 7). Only a handful were professionals, 6% of the advertising husbands and 2% of those before the quarter sessions, including attorneys, clergymen and surgeons. The majority in both cases (57% of the advertising husbands and 47% of those who appeared at the sessions) were tradesmen, craftsmen and retailers (including blacksmiths, butchers, carpenters, cordwainers, tailors and weavers), with some unskilled workers

[2] L. Holcombe, *Wives and Property: Reform of the Married Women's Property Law in Nineteenth-Century England* (Oxford, 1983), pp. 27–30; Finn, 'Women, consumption' (she calls it the law of necessaries).

and soldiers, militia-men and sailors or mariners. Extending the range of occupations still further to include rural and agricultural workers, 16% of the advertising husbands and 20% of the husbands at the quarter sessions were yeomen, farmers and husbandmen. Another 14% of the former and 26% of the latter were wage labourers. It is also likely that a substantial number of the men whose occupations were not recorded in the quarter sessions material were poor, because many were deserting husbands. This does not always hold true and some were lower middling sort, since men who left their wives and families chargeable were automatically categorised as vagrants, regardless of their trade or craft.[3]

The newspaper advertisements also have the benefit of providing some gender balance. Women dominated the majority of matrimonial cases dealt with by the church courts and courts of quarter sessions. They initiated 70% of 114 selected separation, restitution of conjugal rights, annulment and jactitation suits (Appendix 2). Wives (53%) and parish authorities (46%) initiated nearly all wife-beating and desertion cases before the quarter sessions (Appendix 3). Specifically, wives brought most of the cruelty prosecutions and were responsible for at least 14% of desertion cases coming to public attention, through their petitions for relief. It is also likely that some of the 83% of the desertions that enter the records through the actions of parish officers were initially brought to their notice by the abandoned wives themselves. The public announcements, in contrast, were almost all male: 94% were placed by husbands and only 3% by wives (Appendix 4). Consequently they provide a unique glimpse into lower middling-sort male views of marriage from a different perspective to that of conduct writers or diarists.

The combination of records draws in married couples from a broader geographical area, for each of the sources covers different parts of the counties. People who lived near a main road that led to a town where a court convened were more likely to litigate than those with poorer access.[4] For example a large number of litigants at the York ecclesiastical courts came from the city of York and the larger towns of the North Riding, which had reasonable communications with the city. The higher levels of wealth of those who used the church courts may have allowed them to travel further, for a significant minority came from the expanding industrial areas of the West Riding, including Leeds and Saddleworth. A few litigants were prepared to take their litigation to its extreme, regardless of distance; in addition people living distant to the church courts used lawyers to act as intermediaries between them

---

[3] Chapter 8, pp. 173–4.
[4] The same applied to York ecclesiastical courts in the fourteenth century (F. Pedersen, 'Demography in the archives: social and geographical factors in fourteenth-century York cause paper marriage litigation', *Continuity and Change*, 10, 3 (1995), 410–11).

and the proctors in the town where the court was held.[5] Included in the causes from the church courts at York are forty suits transmitted from the archdeaconries of Nottinghamshire, Northumberland and Richmond and consistory courts of Chester, Carlisle, Durham and the Isle of Man. Advertising husbands were mostly from a region's more highly populated areas, but include those not represented by the ecclesiastical or quarter sessions courts. For instance, couples that appeared in the York newspapers extend the coverage of this study to the East Riding.[6] People who came before the quarter sessions were also mainly from the towns where the sessions were held, or were concentrated in areas that had routes to sessions' towns. The courts were relatively peripatetic for most of the period studied, meeting in boroughs and market towns, which allowed people from supposedly peripheral or less accessible areas to be within travelling distance of a sessions at least once or twice a year. Thus the data includes couples from areas that are not represented by users of the ecclesiastical courts. For example, users of Durham church courts came from the more populous eastern side of the county, and from Newcastle, as well as some of the main towns in Northumberland. The inclusion of Northumberland quarter sessions, however, draws couples from other Northumberland market towns and villages into the study, like those along the northern coastal routes, in the south of the region, and along the main lines of communication to Hexham, and even Haltwhistle in the west.

REGIONAL CONTEXT

To analyse married life more fully, it is also necessary to explore understandings of marriage outside London. It is all too easy to assume that the metropolitan experience was so different from provincial urban and rural experiences that it also made London spouses' experiences of marriage somewhat unusual.[7] This is not necessarily the case. Studies of material consumption, literacy and architecture, for example, suggest that the metropolitan experience should not be seen as entirely unique. A national culture developed further in the eighteenth century. Moreover, the transmission of ideas, influence and innovation was a dynamic two-way process between the capital and other parts of England. Joyce Ellis observes that market towns and county centres, for instance, acted 'as a vital interface between national urban developments and the large majority of the population still living in

---

[5] Bailey, 'Voices in court', 395.

[6] The West Riding of Yorkshire was not represented because the Leeds press catered for advertisers.

[7] For the effect on litigation of the unusual characteristics of life in London see Gowing, *Domestic Dangers*, pp. 13–22.

the countryside'.[8] Another generalisation is that the urban environment, especially that of the capital, allowed women to exercise more autonomy, ultimately leading to proposals that London wives were better able or more likely to assert or defend marital rights.[9] Yet Vivien Brodsky Elliot's study would suggest that London wives' independence cannot be taken for granted. For example, she discovered that London-born women married earlier than migrant women, to older husbands. This type of marriage is generally viewed as likely to create a more patriarchal relationship, surely conditions that were unlikely to allow such independent attitudes to develop. Migrant women on the other hand had more 'equitable' marriages, in terms of age, status and, following this line of argument, power relations. Such marriage patterns were not unconventional, or only achieved because they lived in London. Thus the model of more biddable wives who held 'conventional' views about marital relations in villages and small towns is questionable.[10]

A study of provincial urban and rural couples is therefore essential, to establish just how unusual London spouses' attitudes were. Five counties with distinct social, economic, rural, urban, agricultural and industrial contexts have been selected. Topographically, the north-eastern counties are similar in that they all include harsh upland areas, with more populous fertile valleys and long coastal regions. Northumberland is low and flat near the coast, hilly in the centre, and mountainous towards the west. Most of the population was in the south-east and south-west corners, near the coalfield, as well as in the seaports.[11] County Durham is divided into two: the more populous lowland areas in the east and the less inhabited western upland areas.[12] The North Riding consists of the Pennine hills in the west and the North York Moors in the east. Settlement was concentrated in the rich Vale of York that divided the two areas of moorland and in the areas circling the North York Moors to the north and south.[13] Both southern counties are landlocked, fairly flat regions. The land rises in the south of Buckinghamshire

---

[8] L. Weatherill, *Consumer Behaviour and Material Culture in Britain 1660–1760* (Cambridge, 1988); J. Ellis, *The Georgian Town 1680–1840* (Basingstoke, 2001), pp. 2, 137–41.

[9] Gowing notes that urban women were more autonomous (*Domestic Dangers*, p. 265), and this is taken further by Hunt to propose that London women were even more so ('Marital "rights"', pp. 123–5).

[10] V. Brodsky Elliot, 'Single women in the London marriage market: age, status and mobility, 1598–1619' in Outhwaite (ed.), *Marriage and Society*, pp. 86, 89.

[11] C. J. Bates, *The History of Northumberland* (London, 1895), pp. 4–11; W. Weaver Tomlinson, *Comprehensive Guide to the County of Northumberland* (London, 1888), p. v.

[12] M. Knight, 'Litigants and litigation in the seventeenth-century palatinate of Durham', Ph.D. thesis, University of Cambridge (1990), p. 26.

[13] M. Barker, *Yorkshire: The North Riding* (London, 1977), p. 13; J. S. Cockburn, 'The work of the North Riding quarter sessions in the early eighteenth century', Master of Law thesis, University of Leeds (1961), pp. 4–5.

to the Chilterns, a chalk escarpment which also forms Oxfordshire's boundary in the south-east. The limestone Cotswolds form the latter's boundary in the north-west.[14] Oxfordshire's population was settled in the river valleys.[15]

The regions had diverse agricultural and industrial experiences. The north-east of England combined agriculture with early and extensive industrialisation.[16] Mixed husbandry was practised in Northumberland and County Durham. The former was still poor in the later seventeenth century, the legacy of its position as a border area between England and Scotland, but by the eighteenth century it contained industrial areas in the south such as North Shields.[17] Due to its coal deposits County Durham was highly industrialised, with industries such as shipbuilding, the salt trade, iron foundries, potteries, glass making and textiles.[18] The coalfield also had an impact on agriculture, providing bigger markets, and therefore more intensive production and specialisation.[19] In contrast, the rural North Riding of Yorkshire, Buckinghamshire and Oxfordshire were predominantly agricultural. Roads in all three counties were poor until the later eighteenth century, though the North Riding had outlets to the sea at ports like Whitby, and some areas of the southern counties had fairly efficient water communications.[20] Manufacturing only took off in the nineteenth century in the North Riding of Yorkshire, although some areas were involved in the alum industry

---

[14] I. F. W. Beckett, *Shire County Guide 13: Buckinghamshire* (Aylesbury, 1987), pp. 3–4.

[15] H. L. Turner, *Oxfordshire: A Look at the Past* (Derby, 1997), pp. 5–7.

[16] Historians rarely categorise the counties in the same way. Durham, Northumberland and the three ridings of Yorkshire have been classified as the north-east of the 'Highland' area of England (R. Adair, *Courtship, Illegitimacy and Marriage in Early Modern England* (Manchester, 1996), p. 51). Another study makes Northumberland and Durham a different cultural province from the three ridings (C. Phythian-Adams (ed.), *Societies, Cultures and Kinship, 1580–1850* (Leicester, 1993), pp. 10–11). Others are struck by the similarities of the northern counties with Scotland (G. Morgan and P. Rushton, *Rogues, Thieves and the Rule of Law: The Problem of Law Enforcement in North-east England, 1718–1800* (London, 1998), pp. 9–26).

[17] E. Hughes, *North Country Life in the Eighteenth Century, The North-East, 1700–1750* (London, 1952), p. xvi. While there were troubles during the 1715 Jacobite Rebellion, the county was not particularly affected by the 1745 rising (Bates, *History of Northumberland*, pp. 257–63; R. Simpson, *North Shields and Tynemouth* (Surrey, 1988), pp. 2–5). For regional agriculture, see J. Thirsk (ed.), *The Agrarian History of England and Wales* (Cambridge, 1967), Vol. IV, *1500–1640*.

[18] For a case-study of a parish in the Durham coalfield, D. Levine and K. Wrightson, *The Making of an Industrial Society: Whickham 1560–1765* (Oxford, 1991). See also W. Page (ed.), *The Victoria County History of the Counties of England, A History of Durham* (London, 1968 edition), Vol. II, pp. 275–326.

[19] Knight, 'Litigants', pp. 34, 20.

[20] W. Page (ed.), *The Victoria County History of the Counties of England, Buckinghamshire* (London, 1969 edition), Vol. II, p. 104; W. Page (ed.), *The Victoria County History of the Counties of England, Oxfordshire* (London, 1907), Vol. II, p. 206. Canals were a feature of the very last years of the eighteenth century.

in the eighteenth century.[21] The two southern counties were less affected by industrialisation because they had no mineral resources that industry could exploit.[22] The few industries that existed were small-scale and those that could be supported by water power, like weaving and paper making. In Oxfordshire there was blanket making, quarrying, glass making, malting and brewing.[23] Lace making was important in Buckinghamshire and straw plaiting took off after 1750 in the east of the county. Both counties had brick, tile and pottery works.[24] Nonetheless Buckinghamshire and Oxfordshire experienced agrarian developments and market specialisation.[25] Thus their populations were largely involved in pastoral and arable agriculture or the trades supplementary to it.[26]

The urban experiences of the counties were also disparate. Applying Peter Borsay's categories of settlement, it is noticeable that the northern area under analysis contained two 'provincial capitals': Newcastle and York.[27] Newcastle was a borough, with a sphere of influence that extended into Scotland. It had no one predominant trade or industry, with the main employment divided between maritime, clothing, food and drink, building, and metalwork trades.[28] York was the ecclesiastical centre of the diocese as the seat of the archbishop, it had the court of the Northern Province, and a regional communications and distribution centre for the agricultural area of the North and East Ridings.[29] As with Newcastle, in York most people were employed in service industries involved in the preparation and retail of food, drink, dress and apparel.[30] Newcastle and York were commercial, social and political centres, with assembly rooms and theatres, a leisure industry and a burgeoning press.[31] Oxford, Durham and Buckingham and

[21] Barker, *Yorkshire*, pp. 24–9, 92, 121; A. Armstrong, *Stability and Change in an English County Town: A Social Study of York 1801–51* (London, 1974), pp. 16–27, 31.

[22] Turner, *Oxfordshire*, p. 8.   [23] Page, *VCH, Oxfordshire*, Vol. II, p. 225.

[24] Page, *VCH, Buckinghamshire*, Vol. II, pp. 83–4.

[25] Thirsk (ed.), *Agrarian History*, Vol. IV, p. 50; Vol. V, I, pp. 319–20.

[26] Page, *VCH, Buckinghamshire*, Vol. II, p. 37; Page, *VCH, Oxfordshire*, Vol. II, pp. 200–1; Turner, *Oxfordshire*, p. 8. For regional farming in the area see Thirsk (ed.), *Agrarian History*, Vol. IV, pp. 49, 50, 64–7, and Vol. V, I, pp. 317–27.

[27] P. Borsay, *The English Urban Renaissance, Culture and Society in the Provincial Town, 1660–1770* (Oxford, 1989), p. 4.

[28] R. Howell, *Newcastle upon Tyne and the Puritan Revolution* (Oxford, 1967), pp. 1, 353.

[29] For a description of provincial courts, see C. R. Chapman, *Ecclesiastical Courts, Their Officials and Their Records* (Dursley, 1992), pp. 25–6. The West Riding tended to use Leeds as its market for agricultural produce (Armstrong, *Stability and Change*, pp. 16–18).

[30] Armstrong, *Stability and Change*, pp. 28–31.

[31] Literacy rates were higher than in other parts of England (Morgan and Rushton, *Rogues, Thieves*, p. 10). A study of the social profile of County Durham based on house size implied in the 1674 hearth tax shows that the mean average for hearth ownership was comparable with the midlands and the north-west, but lower than the south-east and the home counties (A. Green, 'Houses and households in County Durham and Newcastle-upon-Tyne, c. 1570–1730', Ph.D. thesis, University of Durham (2000), pp. 89–92).

Aylesbury in Buckinghamshire were 'regional centres'. Still, the first two were major provincial centres. In Oxford's case this was due to its university, and many of the city's inhabitants were employed in the university's paper-making, printing and publishing industries and in servicing the institution.[32] Oxford also shared many of the social features of the two provincial capitals, with town walks, coffeehouses, scientific societies and various drama and music venues.[33] Durham's prominence was increased because it was the legal centre of the Palatinate, which covered the area between the rivers Tyne and Tees and had its own legal system.[34] While Buckingham and Aylesbury were small-scale county towns, providing markets for their hinterland, and various trades and services, even they offered cultural and leisure facilities.[35]

By the later seventeenth century, none of the counties were culturally isolated or backwards, despite their different contexts. For example, most of the regions had some inter-action with the capital. On a personal level, the counties' gentry visited London and kept up consistent correspondence with their friends and suppliers.[36] For the ranks below the gentry, there are several references in the sources to them seeking temporary work in London, or visiting for legal cases. In Buckinghamshire and Oxfordshire, roads and rivers headed to London, and London citizens travelled through the towns and villages.[37] The local newspapers in Newcastle, York and Oxford devoted much space to London news, both political and social. Retailers' advertisements in these papers demonstrate that shops offered goods for sale from London, as well as keeping readers up-to-date on fashions in everything from clothes to food.[38] All were connected to London by trade. Newcastle, for example, gained its population and wealth from the coal trade that forged vital links with the capital.[39] Buckinghamshire and Oxfordshire had a thriving trade in supplying London with wheat, malting barley and dairy products. Indeed, most of London's corn was shipped along the Thames from Buckinghamshire, Oxfordshire and Berkshire.[40] Oxfordshire also supplied

[32] T. Allan (ed.), *Philip's County Guide: Oxfordshire* (London, 1994), pp. 6–7.
[33] Borsay, *English Urban Renaissance*, pp. 137, 145, 147, 162.
[34] Knight, 'Litigants', p. 21.
[35] For example, Buckingham had an assembly rooms from 1670, and Aylesbury had horse-race meetings from at least the later seventeenth century (Borsay, *English Urban Renaissance*, pp. 150, 356).
[36] H. Berry, 'Prudent luxury: the metropolitan tastes of Judith Baker, Durham gentlewoman' in P. Lane and R. Sweet (eds.), *'On the Town': Women and Urban Life in Eighteenth-Century England* (forthcoming, 2003), 130–54, 149. My thanks to Dr Berry for letting me read her chapter before publication.
[37] Thirsk (ed.), *Agrarian History*, Vol. IV, p. 49.
[38] Provincial shops stocked a wide range of such goods (Berry, 'Prudent luxury', p. 149).
[39] Knight, 'Litigants', p. 34; Berry, 'Prudent luxury', p. 136.
[40] Thirsk (ed.), *Agrarian History*, Vol. IV, p. 508.

20 *Unquiet Lives*

cattle and sheep and Buckinghamshire sent lace, and wood for fuel and building.[41] This could make for direct contacts between town and capital. The Rigbys from Newport Pagnell were dealers in bone lace in the 1740s and '50s, carrying on their trade in London and the country. Susannah Rigby organised, and supplied her husband Robert with, the lace, which he took to London and other places to sell.[42] If nothing else, local farmers and suppliers dealt with the drovers and merchants who visited the London markets. Of course the movement of goods to sell in London created a return trade. This meant, for instance, that the north-east had a very high proportion of middling-sort ownership of goods.[43] Equally, in the eighteenth century the Durham gentry had luxury items from London delivered via coastal transport.[44]

It would be interesting to explore how far local industrial and agricultural conditions affected the quality of married life. Unfortunately the scattered spread of cases and their variety of origins makes this difficult. We know that both had a social impact. The escalating urbanisation related to industrial developments in the north of England during the eighteenth century, for example, led to certain towns becoming heavily populated and criticised for their dirtiness and poverty.[45] Although the two southern counties escaped these problems, they faced others caused by agrarian development. The agricultural improvements that were implemented in the early eighteenth century led to prosperity for some Oxfordshire farmers.[46] Inevitably, however, enclosures caused economic distress for poor landholders and agricultural workers. The difficult economic conditions of the late eighteenth century had harsh consequences for such people in Oxfordshire and Buckinghamshire.[47] Such regional variations were reflected in the records of marital difficulties, albeit in an ambiguous manner. For instance, there are several wife-beaters from South Shields. It is not clear whether this was due to the unusual conditions of this dynamic town and its effects upon wives and husbands, or more simply to the nearness of a magistrate. After all, as we have seen, other factors brought marital conflict to public attention, such as proximity to a court or justice of the peace and the degree of personal wealth, which dictated the level of prosecution. Equally, Buckinghamshire quarter sessions dealt more harshly than the other counties with deserting husbands in the later eighteenth century. But it is difficult to show whether this was because

[41] Wrightson, *Earthly Necessities*, p. 234; L. W. Hepple and A. M. Doggett, *The Chilterns*, 2nd edition (Sussex, 1994), pp. 135–40.
[42] CBS, QS Rolls Michaelmas 1755.   [43] Weatherill, *Consumer Behaviour*, pp. 51–2.
[44] Berry, 'Prudent luxury', p. 136.
[45] Morgan and Rushton, *Rogues, Thieves*, pp. 11–13.
[46] Turner, *Oxfordshire*, pp. 54, 80–1.
[47] Page, VCH, *Buckinghamshire*, Vol. II, p. 85; Page, VCH, *Oxfordshire*, Vol. II, pp. 203–4.

more families were splitting up in the difficult economic conditions, or because the authorities were eager to use these men as examples, in the hope of relieving the pressing problems of poor-relief provision.[48] What can be said with certainty is that people in all the counties shared the same expectations about acceptable and unacceptable marital behaviour. Just as most English people used the marriage service in the Book of Common Prayer to enter matrimony, there was a national understanding of the basic criteria that constituted a good or bad marriage.[49]

It is worth considering how far these collective expectations were shaped and informed by cultural representations of marriage, widely available in sermons, religious texts, conduct books and advice written by religious and secular authors, and humorous epistles, tales and ballads. It is possible to trace some basic themes common to both this literature and the language used to express marital difficulties. While prescriptive models of household and marriage affected the expression of marital roles and experience, practice was no mirror of ideals. Current research about the relationship between the reader and the text, the viewer and the image is growing more sophisticated. It is clear that, whatever authorial intention, sex, occupation, status, wealth, age and experience influenced the way that people interpreted what they saw, read and heard. Lady Sarah Cowper's use of advice literature makes an insightful case-study. Her numerous commonplace books, written between 1670 and 1700, and seven volumes of diaries from 1700, show that while Cowper had appropriated the view of ideal female marital behaviour from fashionable advice texts, she manipulated it to suit her own situation. Thus Anne Kugler demonstrates that she used the texts to vindicate rather than direct her behaviour.[50] This complex and subtle process of adaptation, avoidance and reinterpretation led contemporary readers to extract different meanings from the representations of married life. Thus, though spouses certainly assimilated them, they were subject to much adjustment in everyday life. Indeed, this very flexibility had the potential to create severe tensions between wives and husbands when the inconsistency between gender roles and everyday life could not be accommodated.

This material has a less ambiguous aspect, whose effect is easier to interpret. Whatever the genre, whether serious, bawdy, satirical or sentimental, most images of married life offered ways to avoid or deal effectively with conflict. It has been proposed that by bringing marital incompatibility, which

---

[48] Chapter 8, pp. 174–8.

[49] Even couples who contracted betrothal or entered irregular unions read out loud from the Book of Common Prayer. The form of words often appears in disputes over the validity of such unions.

[50] A. Kugler, 'Constructing wifely identity: prescription and practice in the life of Lady Sarah Cowper', *Journal of British Studies*, 40 (2001), 291–323.

was categorised as a deviance, to public attention, it was 'possible to reinforce the social norms of marital stability' in eighteenth-century America.[51] In England, images of marital difficulties served a very different purpose. In effect the very ubiquity of the images of marital conflict made it unsurprising and unexceptional. As a result, they are excellent sources for people's perceptions and experiences of married life in the long eighteenth century, though they are not without problems.

INTERPRETING MARRIAGE: A METHODOLOGY

This book uses a combination of sources in order to resolve some of the problem areas associated with the individual ones, and therefore build as broad and diverse a picture of married life as possible. Problems of interpretation arising from husbands' public announcements are least obvious, because they have rarely been explored in any depth to date. Analysis of their use is limited to the press advertisements (seven church court suits make passing reference to announcements made through bellmen). A sampling of every fifth year of twelve newspaper titles from Newcastle, Yorkshire and Oxfordshire provides 278 examples.[52] Using the conventional style of advertisements, they appear consistently but irregularly in the provincial newspapers. In some cases, the placement of an advert appears to have stimulated a flood of others, which followed close on its heels and used similar wording, only to dry up again a few weeks later. The announcements uncover more than a denial of female credit. The flexibility of advertising as a genre, and its tendency to use a prose style similar to the newspaper reports, allowed significant variation in content. Consequently, the backgrounds of the financial denials were sometimes detailed, and descriptions of elopement, separation and quarrels were common. Obviously, only one side of the conflict was presented and as wives' advertised responses show, husbands' and wives' versions could be very different. In order to explore the range of issues that might underlie or prompt these announcements, therefore, some of the couples have been traced outside of this medium.

Quarter sessions records can seem at first to be unrewarding sources of information about married life. They do, however, offer more than a set of depressing statistics about abandoned women or men bound over to keep the peace towards their wives. Admittedly, the record-keeping in order books is frequently brief and formulaic, which can be frustrating. For example, recognizances, which bound over wife-beaters, are sometimes recorded in

---

[51] H. R. Lantz, *Marital Incompatibility and Social Change in Early America* (Beverly Hills, 1976), pp. 36–7.
[52] Another 58 adverts were placed by parish authorities seeking the whereabouts of absconded husbands.

the order book with the name of the wife-beater and victim, without specifying their relationship. Others fail to state the victim's name. Likewise, in settlement papers, women are recorded as 'wife of', as opposed to 'widow' or 'single woman', and their children are noted, but the whereabouts of the husbands are not mentioned. Fortunately, valuable cross-referencing and missing information can be provided by calendars of prisoners and the more enlightening quarter sessions bundles, where they survive. In these cases, details about lone wives can be cross-referenced, to show that some of them were indeed deserted. Crucially, the bundles include informations, depositions, petitions, presentments, and poor-law papers, and thus put flesh on the bare bones of conflict recorded in the order books. It should be noted in addition that the couples who appeared before the quarter sessions courts were those who had reached a certain level of prosecution. The work of justices of the peace outside of session, occasionally recorded in journals and diaries, is therefore invaluable for tracing the antecedents of such prosecutions.

The use of the church courts varied but the legal process itself only altered slowly from the medieval period. All evidence was provided in written form (cause papers) rather than verbal, so that the suits are often lengthy with extensive documentation. Ironically it is this level of detail that makes ecclesiastical court records of matrimonial dispute so problematic. Though this evidence is fascinating and powerfully direct, it is misguided to assume that it reflects ordinary conjugal life. Indeed it is questionable how far these suits were representative. After all, the survival of records is dictated by chance, and the lengthier and therefore more detailed cases were atypical because litigants usually abandoned their suits at an early stage. The factual basis of the records is itself debatable, considering that the cases were adversarial. Correspondence received by Durham ecclesiastical court proctors from their clients uncovers just how dramatically different the public and private sides of litigation could be. In fact, there were often at least two quite distinct versions of events.

Historians of records of litigation have further revealed their elusive nature by explaining that they were mediated through the legal profession, who shaped a suit's format, direction and evidence.[53] While this stress on the multi-vocal nature of court records has important implications for historical interpretation, we must not lose sight of the individuals who are represented in them. The letters that the Durham proctors received make it possible to hear separate voices. They show the ways in which litigants of both sexes were directly involved in their own litigation; for example, how court documents were constructed from the information provided by plaintiffs and defendants. The letters even show that litigants could influence the

---

[53] For different approaches to analysing litigation see Bailey, 'Voices in court', 406–8.

progress of a suit through court. This personal insight brings us no closer to any unifying truth, unfortunately. Though certain events obviously occurred, litigants viewed them in different ways. In sum, litigants' own, often inscrutable, motives obscured the reality underlying a lawsuit as much as the legal process.[54] Nonetheless, such records remain an invaluable source when used with sensitivity. It is wise, for example, to follow up some of the couples for which most information survives, in order to track their behaviour following the court appearance, and compare it with the claims made in the legal record. Perhaps most significantly, the ambiguous nature of the allegations makes it even more imperative to pay attention to the other layers of information that are available.

Far too often these incidents of marital conflict are reduced to the two issues of adultery and cruelty. It is possible to see the logic behind this approach. After all, separation was available to both sexes on the grounds of cruelty and adultery, but it was wives who sued their husbands for cruelty and mostly husbands who brought adultery suits against wives.[55] Of the twenty-five adultery separation suits studied, twenty-three were brought by men and two by women (Appendix 2), although in addition numerous women sued their husbands for a combination of cruelty and adultery. When the historian is not vigilant, this sexual division in suing can dictate the interpretation of marriage. Dangerously, the pleading, structure and language of records of litigation come to symbolise the meanings of gender and its impact on spouses.[56] Thus, to take one example, since adultery cases often focus on the alleged infidelity, whereas cruelty accusations frequently include details about the marriage itself, it is argued that the requirements of proof were less ambiguous and subjective for female adultery than for male violence.[57] In turn this is seen as emblematic of gender relations in society. Thus the sexual division in separation suits apparently reflects a profound double-standard in sexual behaviour, marital power balance and spouses' experience. This finds its most extreme expression in Laura Gowing's declaration that '[e]ffectively, only women could be penalized for extramarital sex and only men could be guilty of violence'.[58]

---

[54] The correspondence is discussed in detail in ibid., 392–408.
[55] For similar breakdown of separation cases in other church courts, see Gowing, *Domestic Dangers*, p. 180; Stone, *Divorce*, p. 193. For less gendered results, see D. M. Turner, 'Representations of adultery in England c. 1660 – c. 1740: a study of changing perceptions of marital infidelity in conduct literature, drama, trial publications and the records of the Court of Arches', Ph.D. thesis, University of Oxford (1998), pp. 184–6.
[56] Gowing, *Domestic Dangers*, pp. 8–9, 180–4.
[57] S. D. Amussen, *An Ordered Society: Gender and Class in Early Modern England* (Oxford, 1988), p. 128; Gowing, *Domestic Dangers*, p. 184.
[58] Gowing, *Domestic Dangers*, p. 180.

One of the problems of this approach is that it fails to explain the re-lationship between the ideology of gender and its application in everyday life. Moreover, when large numbers of matrimonial cases are available for comparison, their variety in detail, length and format shows that suits were influenced by several factors, not just the sex of the plaintiff. For instance, the degree of information varied according to whether the case was defended, how far it progressed through court, how easy or difficult an allegation was to prove, and the litigants' own aims. Admittedly, some adultery cases did fo-cus only on a wife's illicit behaviour. In general, however, these were initiated after a lengthy separation, which the adultery post-dated. These suits were less likely to be defended because the wife was living or had lived with a lover and for that reason were unlikely to provide much information about the marriage. Cases where wives were accused of adultery while living with their husbands were often longer, and provided most detail about the marriage.[59] Equally, some cruelty separations were brief. Brought by a wife as a warning to an abusive husband, or to force agreement on maintenance, and aban-doned if their aim was achieved, they provide little information about the unions outside the violence. Moreover, legal handbooks recognised that both types of marital offence could be difficult to prove and recommended caution in making judgements. Richard Burn noted that 'matrimonial causes have been always reckoned and reputed amongst the weightiest, and therefore require the greater caution when they come to be handled and debated in judgement'. He wisely advised that 'good circumspection and advice be used, and that the truth may (as far as is possible) be sifted out by the deposition of witnesses and other lawful proofs'.[60]

In fact the only way to get a nuanced picture of married life is to give the same weight to all the layers of information in records of marital difficulties. Crucially, there is a framework of acceptable and unacceptable marital be-haviour, which I have called 'secondary complaints', underlying the 'primary' allegations of adultery, cruelty, desertion and refusals of credit in each of the three sources. In all of them, spouses of both sexes used a series of similar complaints, which served to support or contextualise the primary accusation or defence.[61] These secondary complaints can be divided into twelve separate categories (Appendix 8). Women complained that their husbands refused to

---

[59] For an example of the former see BIHR, *Siddall* c. *Siddall*, 1708; BIHR, *Wentworth* c. *Wentworth*, 1756. For the latter see BIHR, *Manwaring* c. *Manwaring*, 1761; BIHR, *Surtees* c. *Surtees*, 1745.

[60] R. Burn, *Ecclesiastical Law* (London, 1763), Vol. II, p. 41.

[61] This is not unlike the 'multiple-complaint pattern' in modern divorce records (R. Chester and J. Streather, 'Cruelty in English divorce: some empirical findings', *Journal of Marriage and Family*, 34 (1972), 710).

provide for them, kept their property from them, denied them their right
to manage their households, and inverted household government by replacing the wives' command with that of servants.[62] Husbands charged their
wives with conveying away goods from them or the marital home, financial
and domestic extravagance and mismanagement, and inadequate household
care. Both spouses complained about financial matters, often about the assignment of various types of personal or real property, and alleged that the
other was failing to fulfil their requisite obligations to their children and
step-children. Couples also accused each other of infidelity and violence as
secondary charges, regardless of the primary accusation, and charged each
other with drunkenness and jealousy. To reiterate, the widespread use of
the same categories of grievances throughout all the sources, and by both
sexes, and a range of social and occupational groups, indicates that, both
legally and culturally, they were intended to reflect recognised standards of
marriage.

Although secondary complaints were expressed in all the sources, ecclesiastical separation and restitution suits often provide the most detailed descriptions, simply because they tend to be more informative in general. They
appeared in articles alongside the primary allegation in these suits, but were
often described in separate articles, and several could be stated in one case.
Deponents expanded on the complaints and sometimes reported additional
grievances. Pertinently, the same charges were made as either accusations or
counter-accusations in defences, so that they arise from all detailed matrimonial disputes before the ecclesiastical courts. Indeed, secondary complaints
had an important legal function in cruelty separation suits and help us to
understand why the suits often contained contextual detail about the marriage. Husbands did not always attack their wives in front of witnesses, so
beaten wives listed their husbands' daily misdemeanours in order to demonstrate that the men were temperamentally suited to committing frequent acts
of violence, and to confirm that the women's existing and future well-being
was threatened.[63] Secondary complaints also often occur in cruelty cases
because they were most detailed and numerous in defended suits. Husbands
defended themselves more frequently than women, due to men's superior
economic position as much as any gender bias in the requirements of proof.

[62] Some law handbooks suggested that a husband taking apparel or necessaries from his wife
was a cause for divorce on the grounds of cruelty, see Anon., *Baron and Feme. A Treatise of
Law and Equity, concerning husbands and wives*, 3rd edition (London, 1738), p. 433; Anon.,
*The Laws Respecting Women, as they regard their natural rights, or their connections and
conduct* (London, 1777), p. 96. More commonly these acts were acknowledged to constitute
cruelty in particular circumstances (J. P. Bishop, *Commentaries on the Law of Marriage and
Divorce and Evidence in Matrimonial Suits* (London, 1852), p. 476).
[63] J. M. Biggs, *The Concept of Matrimonial Cruelty*, University of London Legal Series, 6
(London, 1962), p. 22; Bishop, *Commentaries*, pp. 456, 462.

Nevertheless, the additional grievances also appear in adultery cases when wives had enough financial and/or familial support to mount a defence, or when the alleged infidelity was more difficult to prove because it happened within a functioning marriage, when the couple were not separated.

CONCLUSION: A HOLISTIC VIEW OF MARRIED LIFE

This methodology offers the historian several fresh insights into the emotional and material aspects of married life. Essentially, the secondary complaints indicate that both spouses were concerned about the other's affection and respect for them, their treatment of their own and each other's children from previous marriages, and the allocation, management and ownership of material resources and property. The grievances highlight the extent to which parenting influenced married life.[64] Studies of society and the family include valuable research on maternity, child-rearing and parent–child relationships, but these experiences are often discussed separately from marriage, as if the relationship between spouses was isolated from that between them and their children. Although children were rarely mentioned in the formal parts of court cases because fathers had legal custody, substantial supplementary evidence exposes their role in marital conflict.[65] Most obviously, pregnancy and child-birth were sites of extreme tension, and it is possible that infant mortality damaged marital harmony. Spouses also quarrelled over their children's upbringing, and both children and step-children were blamed as emotional and financial catalysts in marital difficulties. We already know that the strains of having several infant children in poor households were a factor in male desertion.[66] It should also be recognised that parenting had an influence upon spouses remaining together, most obviously when women stayed with violent husbands because of their children.

The secondary complaints are perhaps most significant in evoking the material side of marriage. Indeed it is this study's awareness of the material aspects of marriage that makes it unusual. It cannot be too strongly recommended that the material life is as important to consider as the emotional life of wedlock given the context of everyday life for the middling sort and labouring poor. Work by Christopher Brooks and Michael Mascuch has exposed that it was not social mobility that concerned the middling sort, so

---

[64] This point has been made about analyses of nineteenth- and twentieth-century families (Davidoff, *et al., Family Story*, p. 43).

[65] Some of these issues are considered in E. Foyster, 'Silent witnesses? Children and the breakdown of domestic and social order in early modern England' in A. Fletcher and S. Hussey (eds.), *Childhood in Question: Children, Parents and the State* (Manchester, 1999), pp. 57–73. I am grateful to Dr Foyster for this reference.

[66] Chapter 8, pp. 170–2.

much as the urge to secure their financial and social position and ensure that their children would be able to maintain a household, provide for a family and avoid poverty.[67] Wage labourers also sought to secure their economic status and sometimes simply to survive in the face of the contingencies of life in the seventeenth and eighteenth centuries. It is not intended, however, to fall into the trap of economic determinism, and suggest in any way that economic self-interest was the prime motive for marriage or the prime factor in married life.[68] Diane O'Hara has persuasively argued that 'any dichotomy drawn between love and individual autonomy, as opposed to parental and community control, is oversimplistic' in her attempt to shake off the Stone/anti-Stone position about the making of marriage.[69] A similar point can be made about married life. It was not determined by either pragmatic material factors or emotional ones, because the two were not mutually exclusive. Most people believed that marriages must be based on love. Personal correspondence and diaries provide excellent case-studies of the deep affection spouses felt for each other.[70] Matrimonial litigation supplies evidence of marital love among those of lower social ranks. In 1684 William and Frances Thorold were presented to the church courts, probably for pre-marital sex, although, in fact, the two servants had married secretly in order to keep their positions until the end of their contracts. A love letter written in 1683 from Frances to William was exhibited as proof of their marriage:

My dear,
thy well-being is the joy of my heart, when two hearts are one they both repose together as ours did. I found myself to be very weary but thy cordial hath refreshed me, one hug with thee my dear would set all to rights. I now find that satisfaction leads to true content, which God grant, we both enjoy to Gods glory heart, and the eternal happiness of our souls hereafter is the faithful Prayer of, my dear. Thine to the end of days.[71]

Successful cohabitation depended upon love. The cleric of Wadworth, in Yorkshire, describing his failed attempts to get John Laughton to live with his wife, in 1721, remembered that John 'fell into a violent passion and said God Damn her he neither would nor could lead his Life with her adding

[67] C. Brooks, 'Apprenticeship, social mobility and the middling sort, 1550–1800' in J. Barry and C. Brooks (eds.), *The Middling Sort of People: Culture, Society and Politics in England, 1550–1800* (Basingstoke, 1994), p. 52; M. Mascuch, 'Social mobility and middling self-identity: the ethos of British autobiographers, 1600–1750', *Social History*, 20, 1 (1995), 45–61. For the precarious nature of early modern life, see Wrightson, *Earthly Necessities*, chapters 2 and 8, pp. 308–20.
[68] W. Coster, *Family and Kinship in England 1450–1800* (London, 2001), p. 10.
[69] O'Hara, *Courtship and Constraint*, p. 237.
[70] Houlbrooke, *English Family*, pp. 103–5; Vickery, *Gentleman's Daughter*, pp. 39–86.
[71] The case is indexed as 'matrimonial', but no libel survives, therefore the exact reason for presentment is uncertain (BIHR, CP.H/3589 *Office c. Thorold and Collins*, 1683/4).

that he did not Love her'.[72] The absence of love in marriage was so serious that those who experienced mental distress cited this as a reason for their suffering.[73]

As these examples illustrate, marital breakdown had profound repercussions for people's emotional lives. The secondary complaints provide much-needed information about the way that it disrupted the material lives of spouses, husbands as well as wives. The next chapter explains that marital harmony or 'quiet' had wider implications than personal satisfaction in the long eighteenth century, which, along with the unavailability of divorce with remarriage to the vast majority of the population, ensured that couples were offered several ways and means to deal with their difficulties.

[72] BIHR, CP.I/631, *Laughton c. Laughton*, 1721.

[73] Female patients of Richard Napier often complained that their marriage was unhappy because their husbands lacked love and affection for them (M. MacDonald, *Mystical Bedlam: Madness, Anxiety, and Healing in Seventeenth-century England* (Cambridge, 1981), pp. 102–3).

3

'For better, for worse': resolving marital difficulties

DEFINING MARITAL DIFFICULTIES

'Marital difficulties' is a term applied in this study to describe collectively any conflict between wives and husbands. It encompasses isolated incidents and lengthy periods, whether they resulted in the continuance or restoration of cohabitation, an agreed separation, or went unresolved. It also acts as a simplified term for the range of specific expressions employed by people in the long eighteenth century, which covered the spectrum from disagreements between partners to the irrevocable collapse of a relationship. When contemporaries discussed the former, they usually referred to spouses 'having some words', or 'quarrels', 'contests', 'disputes' or 'misery'. More particularly, wives and husbands 'ill-treated' their spouses, behaved 'unbecomingly', or in men's cases 'barbarously'. Breakdown was carefully divided into separation and desertion. Accounts of separation used this term, though it was more commonly stated that a couple had 'parted', followed by a phrase that showed it was a mutual, consensual decision to live apart. Desertion and elopement, however, were unilateral decisions by one partner to leave. Such spouses were described as 'leaving', 'absconding' or 'absenting' and 'withdrawing' themselves. Gender-specific terms were applied, so that it was mostly wives who eloped and men who either 'ran-away' or 'turned-out' wives and children.

People in the long eighteenth century did not think of these types of marital difficulties as separate phenomena, but stages of the same process that could occur at any time in the life of the marriage. This makes historians' distinctions between marital conflict, breakdown, separation and divorce somewhat artificial.[1] Of course people recognised that there were escalating degrees of conflict, but resolution was perceived to be a possible outcome of most of them. The link between conflict and resolution marked nearly all forms of assistance given to conflictual couples. When a separation from bed

---

[1] For instance, distinctions made between breakdown and divorce/separation in Phillips, *Untying the Knot*, pp. 93–7.

and board was decreed, it was ostensibly only until the couple could settle their differences.[2] Private deeds or contracts of separation, which organised the financial circumstances of spouses who lived apart, were essentially transitory and could be ignored or discarded. Even desertions were not seen as final. In the eighteenth century, many parishes offered absconded husbands the chance to return to providing for their wives and families without incurring punishment.

Individual and institutional concerns to resolve marital difficulties, preferably before separation was necessary, are best understood in the context of the absence of divorce with remarriage, which was only available to a very few wealthy men.[3] This encouraged efforts to ensure the survival of existing unions, because unresolved marital problems were recognised to have profound consequences. On an intimate level they could lead to mental instability and even suicide.[4] Where economic status was concerned, the personal shaded into the public. At worst, marital difficulties caused familial poverty, which became a concern of parish authorities in the distribution of poor relief. This was not just caused by desertion. Disorder in any household relationships could result in credit being refused or restricted, since economic life depended upon trust and the belief that debts would be paid.[5] Marital conflict may have had wider implications for a community than preventing single households from purchasing necessaries or making business transactions, because households were linked together in what Craig Muldrew calls a chain of credit.[6] In a more abstract fashion, social order was linked to stability within marriage, whatever the political context: whether hierarchical relationships were considered to be divinely ordained, or when it was argued that authority rested on the consent of the individual.[7] Since personal, economic and social well-being depended upon stable marital relationships,

---

[2] Tarver, *Church Court Records*, p. 90.

[3] For a history of parliamentary divorce see Stone, *Divorce*, pp. 301–46.

[4] Marital problems were the second most frequent type of stress suffered by Richard Napier's mentally disturbed patients (MacDonald, *Mystical Bedlam*, pp. 75, 98–105); they were also considered a motive for suicide (M. MacDonald and T. R. Murphy, *Sleepless Souls, Suicide in Early Modern England* (Oxford, 1990), pp. 261–4).

[5] Muldrew, *Economy of Obligation*, pp. 124–5.

[6] The pervasiveness of the credit system and links between households are a central theme of Muldrew, ibid., particularly pp. 95–8, 150–1.

[7] For an account of the way seventeenth- and eighteenth-century political theories were interpreted with relation to marriage, see Amussen, 'Being stirred', 72–3, 82–3; A. Clark, 'Humanity or justice? Wifebeating and the law in the eighteenth and nineteenth centuries' in C. Smart (ed.), *Representing Womanhood: Historical Writings on Marriage, Motherhood and Sexuality* (London, 1992), pp. 188–92. The two theories were not chronological. The plurality of middling-sort and professional political thought is described by C. Brooks, 'Professions, ideology and the middling sort in the late sixteenth and early seventeenth centuries' in Barry and Brooks (eds.), *The Middling Sort*, pp. 113–40.

unresolved conflict was considered dangerous and 'apparent harmony' in marriage was promoted.[8] Thus much effort was channelled into solving conjugal difficulties. This chapter describes the network of solutions offered to wives and husbands, which covered the spectrum from ad-hoc to organised, informal to formal, mediatory to interventionary, passive to active, any of which cut across each other. It will explain that spouses could seek help from relations, friends, neighbours, servants, clergymen, parish officials and justices of the peace, as well as using the services of the ecclesiastical courts, attorneys and newspapers.

INFORMAL INTERVENTION IN MARITAL DIFFICULTIES

Husbands and wives who could no longer effectively manage their own conflict turned first to their families, friends, neighbours, servants and clergymen for assistance.[9] The goal of this intervention was to integrate spouses back into a working marriage. Its frequency is difficult to quantify, but the traces that survive in more detailed sources suggest it was common and wide ranging, as do findings that most inter- and intra-familial conflict was dealt with through informal channels.[10]

John West, the 54-year-old neighbour of Robert and Barbara Dobby, of York, was standing at his door in 1718 when he heard Robert shout insults at Barbara. He entered their house to investigate, and he and the Dobbys' maid, and Robert's parents who had just arrived, managed to prevent Robert from attacking his wife. John reported that he did not leave the house until the Dobbys were friends again.[11] It is such dramatic evidence of intervention that best survives. Of the 136 references to the involvement of other people in the affairs of couples, 28% described direct assistance for a wife who was being attacked or threatened by her husband (Appendix 9). The Dobby account illustrates that it was neighbours and servants who provided this help, because one or the other was closest at hand, depending on the status, wealth, occupation and type of residence of the couple. While family or friends participated when present, their usual role, particularly for fathers and brothers of the beaten wife, was to warn husbands against future bad behaviour. As Ann Watson complained in 1801, her husband had

---

[8] O. Hufton, *The Prospect Before Her: A History of Women in Western Europe, 1500–1800* (London, 1995), p. 152.

[9] For an account of parents' involvement in their adult children's lives, see E. A. Foyster, 'Parenting was for life, not just for childhood: the role of parents in the married lives of their children in early modern England', *History*, 86, 283 (2001), 313–27.

[10] Wrightson, *English Society*, p. 157. See examples of early seventeenth-century neighbourly attempts to mediate in marital difficulties in Amussen, *An Ordered Society*, p. 127; Amussen, '"Being stirred"', 78–80.

[11] BIHR, CP.I/581, *Dobby c. Dobby*, 1719.

continued his cruelty 'notwithstanding the Interference and Remonstrance of their friends'.[12]

Another type of assistance (21%, Appendix 9) gave wives a place of refuge from conflict. Families were most likely to provide this help, especially in the shape of long-term lodgings. Following an agreed private separation, Dorothea Wentworth stayed with her sister near York for a year from 1749, until she lodged independently in the city of York and in Knaresbrough.[13] After escaping her husband's tyranny, Catherine Ettrick lived at her father's house in Durham from 1765 until she died in 1794.[14] The proximity of neighbours made them an ideal temporary refuge for wives avoiding further conflict or escaping violence. When Ursula Knowles was violently beaten in 1739, 'she was obliged to Escape out of a Window in this bloody Condition' to a neighbour's house.[15] Material aid was also offered to wives (15%, Appendix 9) whose husbands refused to contribute to the domestic economy, withheld cash, credit and property, or locked away food. Typically food and clothes were provided for wives and their children, and, occasionally, direct financial aid. It was normally families who helped, though one or two servants, a few neighbours, and some friends also did so.

Not all help was directed at women. One way to identify those involved in marital difficulties on men's behalf is to analyse the sureties of bound-over husbands. People who were prosecuted by recognizance had to find two sureties who were each bound to pay half the sum promised by the defendants if they failed to keep its conditions.[16] Of those husbands who succeeded in persuading individuals to stand surety for them, 189 men have been selected because details about the names, occupations and places of residence of one or more of their sureties were available. One third of them were probably related to one or more of their sureties because they shared the same name; the same place of residence linked 32% of them and their sureties; and 34% of the husbands had one or more sureties who shared the same occupation, or occupations that indicate that the men knew each other as work colleagues, or through providing services to each other (Appendix 10) – for example, those who followed different trades, but were all involved in building work, or a tailor and a cutter.

---

[12] UOD, DDR/EJ/CCD/3/1801/15, *Watson c. Watson*, 1801. There is no evidence that women were more inclined than men to intervene to assist beaten women. The evidence can sometimes seem to suggest this, but the ratio of male to female assistance depends on where the violence occurred.

[13] BIHR, CP.I/1376, *Wentworth c. Wentworth*, 1756.

[14] Probably with her brother, as her father had died before this (J. W. Summers, *The History and Antiquities of Sunderland, Bishopwearmouth, Bishopwearmouth Panns, Burdon, Ford, Ryhope, Silksworth, Tunstall, Monkwearmouth, Monkwearmouth Shore, Fulwell, Hylton, and Southwick* (Sunderland, 1858), Vol. 1, p. 186).

[15] UOD, DDR/EJ/PRC/2/1740/8, *Knowles c. Knowles*, 1740.

[16] Several men had only one surety who was bound for the same sum as the defendant.

These defendants seem to have been more likely to have a relative stand surety than in other types of cases. Shoemaker's study of London and rural Middlesex quarter sessions, between 1660 and 1725, found that only 5% of 2,361 defendants shared the same name as their sureties. Concluding that defendants were unlikely to be relatives, neighbours or co-workers of their sureties, he proposes that justices favoured distantly connected sureties because they were 'more likely to try to get their financial liability discharged by demanding that defendants fulfil their obligations [the conditions of the recognizance]'. Such sureties were able to apply pressure on the defendants to appear at the sessions in order to discharge their recognizances and to arrive at informal settlements with their plaintiffs.[17] This theory is relevant to the 10% of husbands who were of lower social status than one or more of their sureties. While these husbands were sometimes simply categorised as labourers, their sureties' occupations suggest that they were their employers. Intriguingly, 3% of the husbands were of higher social status than one or more of their sureties, which might imply that they were unable to get sureties of their own status (Appendix 10). If relationships between the bound-over husbands and their sureties were closer than usual, it might be because distantly connected people were reluctant to become personally and financially involved in the peculiar complications involved in settling disputes between spouses and simply did not trust the husbands to keep their obligations. After all, standing surety had direct consequences. Early in 1693, John Parker of Tetsworth, Oxfordshire, was forced to petition the quarter sessions for relief for him, his wife and his five small children. He had become bound for his father and was then forced into poverty by having to sell everything to pay the sum for which he was bound.[18] The relationship between aggressive husbands and their sureties had to be fairly close or secure in order to make such a leap of faith.

Mediation, in the form of advice and reconciliation, was offered equally to husbands and wives (25%, Appendix 9). This was provided by friends rather than family. For example, Mary Ferman had an affair with a spirit merchant in Newcastle and eloped from her husband in February 1789. It was the 'intercession' of Mrs Crawford, the wife of a neighbouring grocer, which persuaded John Ferman to take Mary back.[19] However, families had additional means to encourage spouses to be reconciled. Robert Dobby's grandfather refused to leave him anything in his will because of the differences between Robert and his wife.[20] Relatives were well placed to negotiate separations, particularly those in which financial or maintenance issues had

---

[17] R. B. Shoemaker, *Prosecution and Punishment, Petty Crime and the Law in London and Rural Middlesex, c. 1600–1725* (Cambridge, 1991), pp. 107–9.

[18] OA, QS Ep 1693 10.   [19] UOD, DDR/EJ/CCD/3/1801/4, *Ferman c. Ferman*, 1801.

[20] BIHR, CP.I/581, *Dobby c. Dobby*, 1719, Robert Dobby's personal response.

ramifications for property inheritance. Spouses also turned to local clergy-men for advice and assistance in getting them back together. Clerics had lo-cal knowledge, provided free advice, and were suitably authoritative figures. The fact that their remit included reconciling warring couples is highlighted by the church court prosecution of the curate John Turner in 1706, which claimed that '[you] doth breed strife and sedition amongst your Neighbours and very often between Man and Wife by adviseing them to part from one another (whereas by your holy office you should be a peace maker...)'.[21]

Of course spouses viewed the intervention of other people in contrasting ways, some claiming that it worsened marital difficulties (10%, Appendix 9). For instance, Edward Bearparke complained that the inadequate curate John Turner had endeavoured to widen a breach between him and his wife, by telling her to procure a warrant from a justice of the peace against him.[22] She probably saw this somewhat differently. It was common for a spouse to accuse other people of exacerbating marital problems. In 1740 Francis Gomeldon blamed his wife's best friend and her attorney for inciting her to leave him.[23] Moreover, it was sometimes a relative or a servant who informed a husband that his wife was unfaithful. Most ambivalence was expressed about family members, including children and step-children. They were regularly blamed for causing or continuing conflict, often by supporting one spouse against the other. Francis Spence of Ripon, who was sued for separation on the grounds of cruelty in 1782, dramatically claimed in his defence that he was:

very Cruelly used by his said Wife and four of his eldest children but particularly by his said wife and his Sons Francis and Henry who by the Advice and Direction of his said Wife have taken all the Pains in their Power to make him unhappy and thereby to render his Life Miserable and by shortening his Days thereby to come sooner at his Estate and Effects.[24]

The negative aspects of family intervention are all too clearly demonstrated by the few cases where relatives of the husbands physically helped to beat the wives.[25]

FORMAL INTERVENTION IN MARITAL DIFFICULTIES

Local parish officers

Formal intervention and assistance in marriage difficulties were diverse and began at the level of local parish officials. These unpaid officers, who were

[21] BIHR, CP.I/2732, office c. Turner, 1706.   [22] BIHR, CP.I/2732, office c. Turner, 1706.
[23] UOD, DDR/EJ/PRC/2/1740/6, Gomeldon c. Gomeldon, 1740.
[24] BIHR, CP.I/2013, Spence c. Spence, 1782, Personal answer of Francis Spence.
[25] For example, DDR/EJ/PRC/3/1717/2, Bowes c. Bowes, 1717.

intended to be available in each village and township, frequently came into contact with marital conflict.[26] Not all of this attention was invited. Until the mid eighteenth century, after which the practice largely disappeared, church-wardens occasionally presented adulterers of both sexes (Appendix 1), and more rarely couples who lived apart, to the church courts for correction. This type of disciplinary case and ensuing public penance was aimed at halting the sinful or inappropriate behaviour and reconciling couples, as well as providing cautionary examples to the rest of the community.[27]

Parish officers' execution of settlement and vagrancy laws included intervention that was probably not always welcome either. Nearly 14% of the 608 desertion cases (Appendix 1) collected in this study involved deserted wives who came into contact with the settlement laws because they were chargeable or likely to be so in the future (86, Appendix 11). At least 60% of the desertions concerned individuals who were categorised as vagrants. Eighteen of them were abandoned wives who were moving around in order to find their husbands or to get a living, but, typically, absconding husbands were at the receiving end of the implementation of vagrancy laws. Parishes actively sought to find such men; though wives also initiated the search for deserting husbands, since warrants committing men to the house of correction were sometimes issued on the oath of the wife as well as the complaint of the overseers.[28] From the mid eighteenth century, poor-law officers placed adverts in local newspapers using a similar format to other 'hue and cry' advertisements seeking criminals or deserted soldiers.[29] They stated the husband's occupation, sometimes suggested where he might be working, often described his age, appearance and clothing, and offered a reward of one or two guineas for the man's apprehension or information leading to his whereabouts. They aimed to prevent husbands finding other work, which would force them to return home, contribute to their wives' and families' upkeep and reimburse the parish for costs to date. Several announced that if the men would return to their financial obligations, they would not be prosecuted.[30] It is difficult to tell whether these adverts were successful. Some were repeated, but it is impossible to know what proportion of the rest delivered the husbands into their parish officials' hands. Those who refused to return, as well as those who threatened to leave their wives, were prosecuted as vagrants when the authorities caught up with them. Upon conviction they were publicly whipped and incarcerated with hard labour

[26] Overseers were appointed to townships within very large parishes, which included Yorkshire, Northumberland and Durham (R. Burn, *The Justice of the Peace and Parish Officer*, 15th edition, 4 vols. (London, 1785), Vol. III, pp. 316–17).
[27] Disciplinary cases are analysed by Ingram, *Church Courts*, pp. 238–81.
[28] CBS, QS Rolls 1756, Q/SM/4, p. 76, Henry Lacey.   [29] Fifty-eight in total.
[30] For instance, advert about Daniel Harris, *Jackson's Oxford Journal*, 6 April 1765, p. 3.

in houses of correction, and in Buckinghamshire repeat offenders could be transported.[31]

Another 16% (100, Appendix 11) of these desertion cases came to the public notice through poor-law officers' administration of the poor laws on behalf of deserted wives. Mostly this was in response to the women's direct request. Anyone who needed to supplement his or her income with poor relief had to approach a parish overseer, whose reactions to abandoned wives varied. Notoriously, some refused to pay an appropriate relief or halted it too early, forcing wives to petition their justice of the peace to have the support paid or restored.[32] In many cases wives and their children could be relieved with one-off or regular aid. Thus, the account book of the overseer of the parish of St Nicholas, Newcastle, from 1787 to 1794, records a single payment in 1789 of 1s to a poor woman whose husband had left her, and weekly sums paid from 1789 to 1790 to Jane Scott and Jane Bee, whose husbands had left them and, respectively, their seven and five children.[33] Deserted wives also contacted parish officers when their husbands had not disappeared, but simply refused to contribute towards their maintenance. They provided the poor-law officers with detailed knowledge of the men's property, to enable officials to seize the men's goods, or profits from land, to pay towards their families' upkeep.[34]

Constables also came into contact with marital problems in their role as community peace-keepers. Their regulatory duties included executing warrants upon deserting husbands and wife-beaters and in their policing function they responded to beaten wives' requests, or those of people acting on their behalf, for them to intervene in domestic violence (Appendix 1). This is difficult to quantify because so much of the evidence is anecdotal.[35] Moreover, constables had an informal conciliatory role in the localities, settling village conflicts without formal presentment, and this applied to domestic violence too. In 1688 Robert and Ann Shaw both called on George Wintringham, the constable in Wistow, Yorkshire, during a very conflictual phase of their marriage. Following a violent dispute, Ann left the house and Robert visited

[31] For punishment of vagrancy see Shoemaker, *Prosecution and Punishment*, pp. 36, 37, 39. For committal to the house of correction see J. M. Beattie, *Crime and the Courts in England 1660–1800* (Oxford, 1986), pp. 492–500.
[32] R. Connors, 'Poor women, the parish and the politics of poverty' in H. Barker and E. Chalus (eds.), *Gender in Eighteenth-Century England: Roles, Representations and Responsibilities* (London, 1997), pp. 135–9.
[33] NCAS, EP.86/118, Overseers' Account Book, St Nicholas, Newcastle, 1787–94.
[34] Husbands were under a statutory obligation to reimburse poor-law authorities for the upkeep of their wives and families (G. Nicholls, *A History of the English Poor Law*, 2 vols. (1898 edition), Vol. II, pp. 5–6).
[35] The frequency of their use also depended upon the availability of constables to a spouse. In the 1730s in Newcastle there were about sixty constables, one for every 340 inhabitants (Morgan and Rushton, *Rogues, Thieves*, p. 27).

George at about two or three in the morning, requesting that he make a search for her. In the early hours of yet another morning during another struggle, Ann shouted for her servant Ellinor to get the constable. Ellinor did, but when she returned with him found that the door was bolted, preventing them from gaining access.[36] Ann's experience illustrates that constables' powers were limited. In general, they could not directly intervene in wife-beating except in the most extreme cases. They were only allowed to break into a house to keep the peace when an affray was underway, which was categorised as such when weapons were drawn or a stroke given or offered.[37] Therefore incidents usually came to attention because a deadly weapon was involved or when a wife called out 'murder'. Jonathan Cade, for example, a constable in York in 1711, recalled hearing Margaret Sayer cry out 'murder' three times in the year after she was married. Each time he went into the house 'as being Constable fearing some harme might be done to some p[er]son, but when he went in he found noe disorder'.[38] No doubt his presence served to bring her husband's violence to an immediate stop, but it is likely that women used constables for long-term help as much as short-term aid, to warn off husbands from future aggression.

Justices of the peace in and out of session

In 1765, Jane Allison of North Shields asked her friend to go to Squire Collingwood, the local justice of the peace, to ask his advice whether 'she [Jane] was to putt up with that Ill usage' from her husband. His reply was that she might 'overcome Him, meaning her Husband, with Love if Possible, and if that woud [sic] not Do, that then the Law woud [sic] give her a separate Maintenance'.[39] Jane's expectations of guidance and support from a justice of the peace were not unfounded. As well as their judicial presence in the courts of quarter sessions, justices were intended to be available to people outside of the quarterly meetings of the courts, and they possessed powers that allowed them to act singly or in pairs.[40] In their judicial and administrative work they provided a range of services for people with more persistent or severe forms of marital difficulties. Quarter sessions justice offered four types of prosecution for misdemeanours and breaches of the peace, which spouses were able to use: arbitration, binding over by recognizance to keep the peace, summary conviction, and indictment.[41] Responsible for

---

[36] BIHR, Trans.CP.1697/2; D/C.CP.1696/3, *Shaw* c. *Shaw*, 1696.

[37] G. Meriton, *A Guide for Constables*, 6th edition (London, 1679), pp. 15–17.

[38] BIHR, CP.I/291; CP.I/187, *Sayer* c. *Sayer*, 1711, Cade's deposition.

[39] UOD, DDR/EJ/CCD/3/1765/2, *Allison* c. *Allison*, 1765.

[40] For the various powers of justices see N. Landau, *The Justices of the Peace 1679–1760* (Berkeley, Calif., 1984); T. Skyrme, *History of the Justices of the Peace*, Vol. II, *England 1689–1989* (Chichester, 1991), pp. 62–7.

[41] For descriptions, see Shoemaker, *Prosecution and Punishment*, pp. 19–41.

the poor laws, justices also approved requests and issued orders to have husbands' goods seized to reimburse parishes, adjudicated in appeals from wives about their inadequate poor relief and in parish disputes over pauper settlements. As Jane Allison's experience shows, their remit was wider: not only in offering advice, which may have been rendered more useful by their local knowledge, but in setting maintenance payments for separated wives and in negotiating separation agreements.

The most commonly used form of prosecution in cases of marital difficulties was justices' mediation, usually between wives and violent husbands or husbands who refused to contribute to the domestic economy.[42] It is, however, impossible to quantify because much of it occurred outside of the sessions with only more severe forms of marital difficulties going to court. Some information about justices' work outside of sessions is available from a few surviving journals or notebooks, and a survey of the out-of-sessions activities of Edmund Tew (1750–64, rector of Boldon, County Durham), Henry Norris (1730–41, a Hackney magistrate), Richard Wyatt (1767–76, Surrey), and William Hunt (1744–9, Wiltshire), shows that they spent around 3% to 6% of their time with incidents relating to marital difficulties.[43] The differing times taken in dealing with people experiencing marital difficulties were probably a consequence of the proximity and accessibility of justices to their users. At various periods, some areas were not well served by justices because they did not have a resident magistrate or because not all those on the commission for each county were active; these problems were somewhat alleviated by the appointment of clerical magistrates from the mid eighteenth century.[44]

It is important to emphasise that mediation was not peculiar to those suffering from marital difficulties. For instance, in a study of the north-east quarter sessions, Peter Rushton and Gwenda Morgan found that informal settlements were far more common than formal punishments. Contestants frequently agreed and discharged cases, so that complainants outnumbered prosecutions.[45] Mediation was diverse and adapted to fit the occasion. On 17 January 1760 Edmund Tew recorded 'Wrote to Mrs Jackson of Shields ab[ou]t her husb[an]d's quarrel with her.' Less ambiguously, he noted 'Agreed

---

[42] One of the prescribed roles of a justice of the peace was to reconcile quarrels and differences (Beattie, *Crime and the Courts*, p. 268).

[43] DRO D/X 730/1; R. Paley (ed.), *Justice in Eighteenth-century Hackney: The Justicing Notebook of Henry Norris and the Hackney Petty Sessions Book*, London Record Society (London, 1991); E. Silverthorne (ed.), *Deposition Book of Richard Wyatt, JP, 1767–1776*, Surrey Record Society, 30 (Guildford, 1978); E. Crittal (ed.), *The Justicing Notebook of William Hunt 1744–1749*, Wiltshire Record Society, 37 (Stoke-on-Trent, 1981).

[44] For activity of justices on the commissions of the peace, see B. Webb and S. Webb, *English Local Government from the Revolution to the Municipal Corporations Act: The Parish and the County* (London, 1929), p. 321. Clerical magistrates are discussed in Skyrme, *Justices of the Peace*, pp. 6–7, 26, 30.

[45] Morgan and Rushton, *Rogues, Thieves*, p. 31.

betwixt them' in his entry relating to the appearance of Robert Crisp of Jarrow on the complaint of his wife.[46] Such arbitration was often backed up by the husband's verbal promise or written note not to re-offend, as well as by the payment of costs.[47] Mediation was not an easy option; it was intended to humiliate and punish husbands. A wife's complaint usually resulted in the issue of a warrant summoning the husband. This was executed by a constable and the justice would reprimand the husband when he appeared, prior to negotiating a compromise. Furthermore, as we have seen, the action often carried some financial penalty. This prosecution was the cheapest means for wives to achieve formal intervention. Judging its efficacy, however, is not straightforward. In the course of the information that Elizabeth Davis of Steeple Claydon gave about her husband in 1765, she commented that, after previously being warned by Earl Verney, William 'had behaved something better'.[48] Clearly this was short-term, since she was complaining about him again. A count was made of the number of times that husbands reappeared before the four justices sitting out of session. Of the husbands they dealt with, 21% reappeared, but it can only be speculation to suppose that the prosecutions succeeded in their aims in the other instances.[49]

A more severe form of prosecution was to bind over a spouse by recognizance. Authorities used recognizances to ensure the appearance at court of men who failed to contribute to their family's maintenance, leaving them chargeable, in order to prosecute them under the vagrancy laws. It was also used as a form of prosecution in its own right. Like other victims of assault, or those who feared future violence, wives and husbands visited the justice and swore on oath that they were in danger. They requested articles of the peace against the defendant who was obliged to enter a recognizance to keep the peace, or to appear before the court to answer objections and in the meantime to keep the peace. While articles of the peace were granted simply on the threat of violence, they were usually used for more serious forms of violence.[50] Most of the men who came before Tew, Norris, Wyatt and Hunt out of session, for example, were dealt with by warrant and mediation, and several of these prosecutions were granted on the complaint that the husband threatened to kill his wife, rather than for specific injury.

[46] DRO D/X 730/1, Journal of Edmund Tew, unpaginated, 19 March 1761.
[47] Crittal (ed.), *Justicing Notebook of William Hunt*, p. 52.
[48] CBS, QS Rolls Michaelmas 1765, Information and Complaint of Elizabeth Davis, 1 August 1765.
[49] Two of the fourteen husbands before Edmund Tew reappeared (DRO D/X 730/1); three of the eleven husbands before William Hunt (Crittal (ed.), *Notebook of William Hunt*); seven of the seventeen before Henry Norris (Paley (ed.), *Justicing Notebook of Henry Norris*); no husbands reappeared before Wyatt (Silverthorne (ed.), *Deposition Book of Richard Wyatt*).
[50] Burn, *Justice of the Peace*, Vol. IV, p. 248. Margaret Hunt's contention that articles of the peace were only available for very serious cases is misleading (M. Hunt, 'Wife Beating', 18).

Therefore recognizances were a form of prosecution that was mainly dealt with by the courts of quarter sessions. Although both wives and husbands could request articles of the peace against each other, it was usually wives who made such a request. Only eleven husbands prosecuted their wives for violence (Appendix 1): one of them was discharged, seven were prosecuted by recognizance, although four of them failed to get sureties, and three were indicted. Women were inclined to use recognizances against their husbands because they were relatively cheap. Importantly, however, they were not perceived to be a lenient form of prosecution. Legally, binding over was not a punishment in itself, although the spouses involved saw it as such. The defendant had to pay a fee for the recognizance and was obliged to appear at the quarter sessions where the articles of the peace were read out and he could be reprimanded.[51] If he broke its conditions he was forced to pay a considerable sum to the crown.

The length of time that husbands were bound over by recognizance is unknown in 32% of the 207 cases where it is known that individuals entered a recognizance (Appendices 12 and 13). The duration of recognizances in 84 instances can be estimated either when the date of discharge was recorded or when the recognizance was specified for a set amount of time. The latter ranged between one and three years; but the majority of recognizances were discharged at the next sessions, which in itself suggests that the tensions were, at least temporarily, resolved.[52] In 5 cases it was explicitly recorded that wives gave their consent to the discharge, or requested it themselves, and another 4 defendants were discharged because no complaint was made at the sessions, probably a decision taken by the plaintiff not to proceed further. Around 22% of the recognizances were continued or respited at the next sessions, in what was an ongoing assessment of the likelihood that the defendant would be violent again. Occasionally there are glimpses into this process. In 1730 Thomas Plumbe wrote to Mr Parr, a justice of the peace, about his brother-in-law Thomas Holderness, who was bound over to keep the peace towards his wife Elizabeth and her mother Ann Wattes:

Upon consideration of the kind advice you was pleas'd to give us on Sunday last My Mother Sister and my self join in one Request that if possible you woud do us the favour to continue Mr Holderness on his Recognizance... Sister has just receiv'd a Line from him by which we understand, he will soon be the same man if not restrain'd by some superior power.[53]

---

[51] Landau, *Justices of the Peace*, p. 207.

[52] This was the recommended duration (Burn, *Justice of the Peace*, Vol. IV, pp. 252–3).

[53] The letter, included in the sessions roll, is not dated, and it is difficult to tell whether it referred to the sessions in which it was enclosed. Thomas Holderness' recognizance was discharged at the Easter sessions, but it is not clear if he re-entered a further recognizance (CBS, QS Rolls 110/23; QS Rolls 110/64).

Another 98 wife-beaters were probably initially prosecuted by recognizance, but were imprisoned because they failed to find sureties. The men were discharged once they were able to find sureties and enter a recognizance, or if their wives requested it.[54] It is difficult to estimate how long these husbands spent in the house of correction because the information does not always come from calendars of prisoners, which stated the date of committal. Where it is known, husbands spent anything from a day to more than eight months there. One very troublesome individual spent one year in a solitary cell, but it is likely that many were discharged at the next sessions. The men's failure to get sureties has three possible explanations. Shoemaker has shown that it was often the poor who were summarily convicted and sent to the house of correction.[55] No doubt this method was a tool used against troublesome, poor husbands as hinted in a letter from one justice to another, contained in the quarter sessions rolls from Bedfordshire. In 1786 T. Potter wrote to Jeremy Fish Palmer:

A few days since, I committed to Bedford gaol one William White . . . for not finding security for the peace. The complainant is his wife Mary whom I have directed to call upon you either to exhibit articles of the peace against him or to make it up with him. I have not taken a formal recognizance as she is a femme couverte and a pauper. The man seems to have a savage stupid idea that he may beat his wife as much as he pleases, provided he does not kill her. Perhaps a little confinement may show him his error.[56]

It is, however, not the only reason. Although only 20 of the husbands have their occupations recorded, they cover a very wide range from paupers and labourers to an attorney and gentleman. It is plausible perhaps that the men who failed to find sureties were simply the most violent and were unable to find sureties who believed that they would adhere to the recognizance's condition that they keep the peace.

A third related possibility is prompted by Cockburn's conjecture that justices set exorbitant sums for recognizances so that sureties could not be found, ensuring that the defendant was committed.[57] Unfortunately it is difficult to tell if this applied in the case of wife-beaters who ended up in the house of correction, because the suggested sum is not recorded. Nonetheless it is possible to test the theory by examining the sums of money pledged by husbands who found sureties. Theoretically, a recognizance was tailored to suit the litigants' rank and there is a rough correlation between the sums and

---

[54] Fourteen husbands were specifically recorded as discharged at their wives' request or with their consent or because their wives had not gone on to lodge a complaint.

[55] Shoemaker, *Prosecution and Punishment*, pp. 166–97.

[56] *Bedfordshire County Records. Notes and Extracts from the County Records comprised in the Quarter Sessions Rolls from 1714 to 1832* (Bedford, 1902), Vol. I, p. 59.

[57] Cockburn, 'Work of the North Riding Quarter Sessions', p. 63.

the social rank or occupation of the husbands.[58] The bulk of violent men were bound over for £20 or £40. Many of these men were from the lower reaches of the middling sort. The greatest sums of £100 and £200 were applied to higher-ranking men, including a few gentlemen and a hostman of Newcastle. Cockburn's idea may be correct, since bond sums were not always dependent upon rank. It is not unreasonable to suppose, for example, that the labourers bound over for £40 struggled to get their social peers to pledge £20 each. Equally, though a schoolmaster and two innkeepers were bound over for £100, others of their rank may not have been able to find sureties prepared or able to pledge £50. It is therefore feasible that men who were particularly violent were set higher bond sums than their social status would normally recommend.

As well as committing those who failed to get sureties, justices of the peace also had powers to convict an offender summarily, without a jury or the corporate backing of the bench of justices, during a sitting of the quarter sessions, and they were consistently used against husbands who had deserted their wives.[59] Conviction entailed a fine or committal to the house of correction.[60] At the sessions following their committal the bench might consider the individual's case and either order a specified time for incarceration, or discharge him. The length of committal of half of 158 men who deserted their wives and families, or refused to assist in their support, is unknown. Of the rest, most were in the house of correction for one week to one month. Some faced between two months and eight months, and two men were probably imprisoned for one year. Those who threatened to leave their wives and children were also imprisoned until they gave security to indemnify the parish from the costs which it would incur from maintaining the offender's family if they absconded.[61] It was intended that the recalcitrant husband would return to contributing to his wife and family after his punishment.

Indictment was a more rigorous type of prosecution than being bound over, because the defendant was tried in court and formally convicted and fined if found guilty. In the case of marital difficulties it was authorities rather than individuals who used it most. Of 126 known indictments, parishes brought 63% of them against husbands for deserting their families and leaving them

[58] William Shephard advised justices of the peace that the sum bound, and the number of sureties, was at their discretion. He recommended that the principal should be bound at £20 and the two sureties at £10 each (W. Shephard, *A Sure Guide for his Majesties Justices of the Peace* (London, 1663), p. 204).

[59] Apparently two justices were necessary to convict absconded husbands and those who threatened to do so. Yet some of the men in this study seemed to have been placed in the house of correction with only one justice's name entered.

[60] Webb and Webb, *Local Government*, p. 298; Shoemaker, *Prosecution and Punishment*, p. 35.

[61] For example, CBS, Q/SM/2, and Q/SO/13, p. 177, Thomas Bayley.

chargeable to the parish, and individuals brought 32% against marital violence (Appendix 14).[62] It is possible that incomplete record-keeping masks additional defendants who were bound over to appear at court in order to be indicted.[63] Nevertheless, when a detailed and fairly complete set of quarter sessions records is available, like that for Buckinghamshire, it is clear that indictment was the least popular form of prosecution. Wives, however, were not discouraged from indicting their violent husbands by higher rates of failure in their indictment bills than other complainants. One third of the outcomes of indictments against wife-beaters are unknown, but 34% of them were found guilty or had their indictment repeatedly respited; another 31% were found innocent (Appendix 15). This figure cannot be directly compared with Cockburn's findings that a little over half of all indicted defendants at the North Riding Quarter Sessions between 1699 and 1750 were convicted; although it is suggestive that Cockburn's figure corresponds with the conviction rate of all indictments relating to marital difficulties, where 56% were found guilty (Appendix 16).[64]

In fact wives did not indict their husbands because this form of prosecution provided them with few extra benefits. Indicted defendants did spend some time in gaol or the house of correction, which may well have been a deterrent to future ill-behaviour. Yet imprisonment was a double-edged sword for wives, who required their husbands to continue contributing to the domestic economy in addition to stopping their violence. Ultimately, however, convicted indicted wife-beaters were merely fined and bound over. Therefore the same end result could be achieved by the other forms of prosecution for far less cost, in less time and with less disruption to the domestic economy. Compare 1s 0d for a warrant with from 2s 4d to 4s 4d for a recognizance, and £1 0s 0d for indictment.[65]

Justices of the peace also played a role in private separations. To some extent, magistrates legitimised separations whenever they ordered that a husband pay towards his wife's upkeep. For example, James Brown was ordered to pay maintenance at Epiphany, 1754, for 'so long time as the said James Brown and Ann his Wife shall live separate'.[66] Often this was a pragmatic way to prevent further violence. At Ann Taylor's complaint in

---

[62] They were indicted either for misdemeanour or for felony. The latter seems to have occurred when they had been absent for some time and owed the parish for the upkeep of their families. Husbands who failed to provide for their families were also bound over by recognizance for 'public wrongs', specifically increasing the number of people dependent on poor relief (Shoemaker, *Prosecution and Punishment*, p. 99).

[63] R. Shoemaker, 'Using quarter sessions records as evidence for the study of crime and criminal justice', *Archives*, 20, 90 (1993), 147, 155–6.

[64] Cockburn, 'Work of the North Riding Quarter Sessions', p. 74.

[65] For costs, Beattie, *Crime and the Courts*, p. 41; Shoemaker, *Prosecution and Punishment*, p. 117.

[66] NYA QSM/ Vol. 22, 1754, p. 109; also see QSB/1750, film 137.

1722 that her husband had been cruel to her and left her for another woman, the quarter sessions simply ordered him to pay maintenance to her and his child.[67] Similarly, when Penelope Roberts sought articles of the peace from her husband and her parents-in-law, in 1758, the Oxfordshire bench ordered that her husband be discharged 'on Condition he allowes his wife £1 6s a week and furnishes a room properly for her soe long as she does not disturbe her husband'.[68] Yet justices also took a direct part in the arrangements of separations of couples with some means.[69] For example, the mayor of Hull, a justice of the peace, presided with other witnesses over Elizabeth and William Idelle's separation, when William gave a bond that he would pay Elizabeth maintenance of £50 per annum.[70] They also set conditions. The Newcastle quarter sessions order book noted at the Epiphany session in 1768 that William and Jane Wrangham were 'willing and desirous and have mutually agreed to live separate'. The justices accepted this upon seven financial and legal conditions that were listed in detail and made an order of the court.[71]

In conclusion, it is worth considering whether quarter sessions justice treated spouses with marital difficulties differently from other people who came before them. There is no evidence that deserted wives seeking relief fared any better or worse than other lone women. Certainly, some justices were sympathetic towards them when they had been denied relief by their local parish officials.[72] Equally, absconding husbands offended justices as much as any vagrant whose refusal to work made them a burden on the parish. It is sometimes suggested, however, that beaten wives were not well served by courts of quarter sessions. For example, Margaret Hunt proposes that justices of the peace believed men had the right to beat their wives.[73] There is little evidence to support this, for wife-beaters were prosecuted by the same methods as anyone else who broke the peace or committed assault. The use of mediation and recognizances in preference to indictment was typical. Like other defendants, they were committed to the house of correction when no sureties were available and when convicted they were fined similar amounts.[74] Actually, quarter sessions authorities aimed at a

---

[67] NCAS QSB 58, 1722, fol. 40, and QSO 6, Various orders, pp. 212, 220, 227, 241.

[68] OA, QS/1758/Mi/11–13, Minute Book XI, p. 36.

[69] Magistrates handled at least four of the eighteen private separations referred to in the records.

[70] BIHR, CP.I/154; CP.I/241; CP.I/2735, Idelle c. Idelle, 1706.

[71] TWA, QS/NC/1/7, p. 391.

[72] This is explored by Connors, 'Poor women' in H. Barker and E. Chalus (eds.), Gender, p. 144.

[73] Hunt, 'Wife beating', p. 18. Neither justices' notebooks nor quarter sessions records give any indication of such an opinion.

[74] Husbands received fines of between 6d and 1s in Oxfordshire. In Essex quarter sessions between 1748 and 1752 the main punishment for those convicted of assault was a nominal fine of 1s or less (P. King, 'Punishing assault: the transformation of attitudes in the English courts', Journal of Interdisciplinary History, 27, 1 (1996), 49).

working balance between punishing the husbands and protecting the wives, while ensuring that the men continued to contribute to the support of their wives. They offered forms of prosecution that wives, who had less access to cash, found useful. Of course, this is not to say that the system worked, flexible though it was, or was used by disputants in the same way. For instance, while recognizances encouraged couples to continue cohabiting by controlling the husband's violence, some believed that the prosecution ended a relationship. When she was advised to return to her husband, in the 1760s, Catherine Ettrick replied, 'How can I go home to a Man that I have swore the peace against in open Court?'[75] Her rejection of cohabitation was, no doubt, influenced by the security of being able to live with her wealthy father. Not many women had alternative incomes or lodgings.

The ecclesiastical courts

For those who could afford them, the church courts offered legal solutions to marital difficulties that had become intolerable. We have seen that the disciplinary arm of the courts imposed correction cases upon adulterous spouses in the later seventeenth century. Fifty-five have survived with their cause papers and the majority were mere office cases, which were promoted by the judge. Nonetheless individuals promoted sixteen of them (Appendix 17). Two promoters were fathers of the women involved, and one a neighbour, but in several cases the relationships between the promoter and the individuals accused of adultery are unclear. It is possible to offer some suggestions for the promotion of four cases, since, although categorised as corrections of adulterers, they actually dealt with men who had allegedly attempted rape or sexual assault. The female victims' husbands were the promoters in three of these cases and it is possible that this was one way to seek redress.[76] Another two husbands promoted suits against the lovers of their wives. Surviving cause papers are not detailed, so it is unclear why they would do this instead of instigating a separation suit; perhaps they wanted to remain with their wives, but nevertheless publicly punish and humiliate them and their lovers.[77] Spouses were also disciplined for having married within the prohibited degrees of consanguinity or affinity. Between 1660 and 1741, York and Durham ecclesiastical courts brought thirty-seven of these cases. Over

---

[75] BIHR, CP.I/1475, *Ettrick c. Ettrick*, 1765, Sarah Beadnell's deposition.

[76] One case was complicated by the defendant's claim that the accusation was caused by a quarrel begun when the couple's pigs trespassed on his land and he set his dog on them (OA, Mss.Oxf.dioc.papers c.91, fol. 80, *Rutters v. Smith*, 1665).

[77] It is not clear whether the men also acted against their wives, because the only surviving cause papers are against the lovers.

35% were against people who had married their deceased spouse's sibling, usually the deceased wife's sister.[78]

The bulk of the courts' dealings with conflictual spouses in the eighteenth century, however, came in the form of instance cases related to marriage breakdown. Ostensibly, ecclesiastical law offered long-term solutions for marital problems. In practice, however, this was most applicable to annulment cases, which dissolved an existing marriage on account of some pre-existing impediment and allowed the spouses to marry again. Marriages could be declared null and void for several reasons including frigidity, impotence, lunacy, prohibited degrees, bigamy and minority. Considering the difficulty of proving some of these grounds it is hardly surprising that nullity suits were very rare, and only eleven came before York and Durham ecclesiastical courts between 1660 and 1800 (Appendix 1). Six were brought on the grounds of minority, by one of the spouses or their family members. Before the mid eighteenth century such cases tended to involve minors who were manipulated into marriage for financial gain, or were attempting to escape the financial depredations of their guardians upon their estate.[79] Marriages of expediency did occur, but they were clearly unusual, not least due to their lack of success. After the mid-century, such cases were often occasioned through irresponsible behaviour by the minors themselves, which they or their parents sought to rectify. Annulment was occasionally used several years after a marriage took place, in ways that suggest the spouses were happy to escape what had become an unsuitable union. Sarah Pattison of Berwick upon Tweed brought an annulment suit against her husband in January 1788. She had married her husband, John Gray, a wool comber, in 1781, when he was nineteen and she was fifteen years old. She waited until she was twenty-one years old and had come into her father's inheritance before launching the suit, although the marriage had clearly broken down much earlier. Her father's cousin, Mary Shell, deposed that since July 1787, 'being the last time that...Sarah Pattison eloped from the said Defendant', she had allowed her a small sum of money weekly towards her support.[80]

The most common suits were separations from bed and board on the grounds of adultery and cruelty, which permitted couples to live apart legitimately. Although this was a potential outcome, 28% of the suits were abandoned or agreed before reaching the final sentence. Indeed, at least 28% of all annulment, separation and restitution suits did not reach sentence

---

[78] These have not been included in Appendix 1 because they have not been discussed in detail in this study. For a discussion of prohibited degrees and incest see S. Wolfram, *In-Laws and Outlaws: Kinship and Marriage in England* (New York, 1987), particularly pp. 21–7.

[79] For example, BIHR, Trans.CP.1667/2, *Henry and William Bunbury c. Henry Davies and Margaret Manley*.

[80] UOD, DDR/EJ/CCD/3/1788/5, *Pattison c. Gray*.

(Appendix 18). Judges' arbitration between wives and husbands in order to get them to reach some compromise might have precipitated an early resolution. Unfortunately, this is difficult to quantify because it is most noticeable when it failed. During Elizabeth Finch's separation suit against her husband, Samuel, in 1779, on the grounds of his violence, Durham consistory court's judge consulted with both parties to see whether Samuel would take Elizabeth back and treat her as a husband ought, according to his circumstances.[81] Samuel agreed to the judge's proposal, but Elizabeth refused, fearing further cruelty. In response, the judge rejected Elizabeth's petition for alimony and costs, causing her proctor to appeal the case to York. This case prompts one to wonder whether other cases, which were resolved at this point, involved judicial discrimination against the women, especially since the majority of cases that did not reach sentence had a female plaintiff. Just over half of all the annulment, separation and restitution suits brought by husbands reached a sentence in their favour (52%), whereas only 15% of wives' did (Appendix 19).[82]

Nonetheless, this is a superficial judgement.[83] For one thing, another 27% of wives' suits were probably favouring them, since the male defendant appealed or was excommunicated for failing to carry out the court's decree (Appendix 19).[84] In the main, the sex-ratio of the outcomes of cases reflected economic inequity. An early resolution was a practical solution to women's economic disabilities. Initiating a suit at the ecclesiastical court was not particularly expensive or difficult, but each step thereafter accumulated costs. One of the cheapest cruelty separations lasted for a year, from July 1745 to July 1746, and cost £4 4s 0d. In general, costs were much higher and a deterrent to women taking the legal process as far as it would go.[85] Few claimed the right to be admitted *in forma pauperis*, which allowed litigants who were worth less than £5 to sue at a lower fee. Thus wives used separation suits to achieve specific goals while simultaneously avoiding excessive costs. These included attempting to stop husbands' violence, arranging financial maintenance or simply forcing some private agreement. When these ends were achieved they would abandon or agree the case.

---

[81] BIHR, Trans.CP.1779/1, *Finch c. Finch*, 1779.

[82] Only 26% of women's separation suits alleging their husband's violence at the London consistory court in the late sixteenth and early seventeenth centuries received a final sentence (Gowing, *Domestic Dangers*, pp. 39, 181).

[83] It has been observed that the weaker side in an adversarial relationship often started legal proceedings as a 'recognised tactical manoeuvre' (O. Anderson, 'State, civil society and separation in Victorian marriage', *Past and Present*, 163 (1999), 181).

[84] Some excommunications were for failing to appear (contumacy).

[85] Defended cases could be astronomically expensive. The Ettrick cause (appealed to York in July 1767) reached a staggering £355 before it was appealed to the Court of Delegates early in 1768.

While wives often used separation suits to restore or continue their husbands' financial contributions to their livelihood, husbands frequently used them to escape their financial commitment to wives. To some extent this is evident from the stage in marriage at which some separation suits on the grounds of adultery were initiated. Seven suits were brought after a period of separation, during which financial assistance had been paid, so legitimate separation was not always the desired outcome. A suit was brought once proof of a subsequent affair was gathered. Some suits voided the conditions of a private separation deed for similar reasons. For the wealthiest men an adultery suit was part of the process of achieving a parliamentary divorce that permitted them to remarry. Economic motivation might also partly explain why so many of the adultery suits brought by men were continued to the final decree. Husbands sued twenty-three of the twenty-five adultery suits and fourteen of them obtained a decree in their favour, with another four heading that way since their wives appealed (Appendices 2 and 18). This is the consequence of men's greater access to capital, which helped them amass proof and pursue the case when it was defended, but it was also due to the benefits gained from winning the suit. Proven adulterous wives were denied the right to their husbands' financial support and use of the law of agency, as well as custody of their children.[86]

Not all men were economically motivated in these cases. Some simply sought legitimate separation from the wife whose affair had caused them distress and, perhaps, in the process, to punish them and restore their own reputation. Still, it is noticeable that in these cases the men continued to provide their wives with financial support. John Greenwood, a mill owner from Dewsbury Mills, Yorkshire, sued his wife for adultery in 1796. After fourteen years of marriage and six children, he found out that she had been unfaithful for a year or so with a twenty-year-old saddler. John's death at only thirty-five years old brought an abrupt end to this very sad case, in which the pain that the couple felt is quite evident. His last will and testament, made the year before he died, in the midst of suing his wife, contained the clause:

Whereas Mary my wife hath for some time last past conducted herself in such a Manner towards me that it is become impossible any longer to cohabit with her and also makes it necessary for me to obtain a Divorce in which case I apprehend she will be only entitled to Alimony during my life and no longer but in order to prevent her being under the Necessity of conducting herself improperly for want of a subsistence ...

---

[86] Burn, *Ecclesiastical Law*, Vol. II, p. 43. Interestingly, the alimony allotted in private separation contracts was not always dependent upon the behaviour of the wife since adulterous women could negotiate maintenance from estranged husbands (S. Staves, 'Separate maintenance contracts', *Eighteenth-Century Life*, 11 (1987), 82).

He went on to give her an annuity of £100 and a £50 legacy.[87] In November 1788, Eleanor Smith confessed to her husband, William, a Northumberland clergyman, that she had been unfaithful and that their youngest child was in fact fathered by her lover. Eleanor and the little boy went to live with her mother and by November 1790 William had gained a separation. Yet he paid maintenance to Eleanor and 2s a week towards the child's support. Interestingly, when William died in 1812, nearly twenty-two years later, he left no will and Eleanor, described as his widow, was appointed as administrator.[88]

A further suit available to both spouses was restitution of conjugal rights. Theoretically used to force one spouse to cohabit with the other, or to permit a wife to return home after being turned out, its use in practice was more ambiguous. The reasons that some defendants gave for living apart, for example, would make the restoration of cohabitation unlikely. The outcomes of cases do not clarify matters. It is impossible to tell what living arrangements resulted from suits where defendants (seven husbands) appealed during the proceedings or from the eight cases which were abandoned or agreed (Appendix 18). Though five plaintiffs (four wives and one husband) succeeded in getting a sentence in their favour, it is still not known whether they lived with their partner afterwards. One explanation for restitution suits is that they were used to trigger a separation suit. The defendant would explain why he/she refused to live with his/her spouse, usually by accusing them of cruelty or adultery, and this would lead on to them launching a separation suit. Only a few of York's and Durham's cases followed this pattern and it is likely that most of the wives, the majority of plaintiffs (Appendix 2), used such suits to organise financial support.[89] Jane Allison's private letter to her proctor in November 1765 advised him that she 'intend[ed] to persist in the suit till he [her husband] either allow me more or take me home the...latter I dont want to come to pass'.[90] The church courts tacitly acknowledged this practice. Referring to a cause begun by Margaret Leighton against John Leighton in Durham in 1770, the legal opinion was expressed to the Chancellor of York that 'Matrimonial Causes of this nature have always been Favoured with particular Privileges to Enable the Wife to Obtain

---

[87] This is confusing because separation by bed and board did not deny a widow the right of dower, whereas a divorce, ecclesiastical (annulment) or parliamentary, meant that the wife had her goods returned to her but was unable to claim any inheritance rights as a widow (Anon., *Laws Respecting Women*, p. 200; Burn, *Ecclesiastical Law*, Vol. II, p. 502).

[88] BIHR, CP.I/2486, *Greenwood c. Greenwood*, 1796; John Greenwood, Pontefract, May 1797. UOD, DDR/EJ/CCD/3/1789/4, *Smith c. Smith*, 1789; DPR William Smith, Ilderton, 1812.

[89] The same was true of nineteenth-century plaintiffs, see O. Anderson, 'State, civil society', 173.

[90] Ironically, later letters show that this *was* what she wanted (UOD, DDR/EJ/PRC/2/1765/3, *Allison c. Allison*, 1765). For a detailed account of the Allisons see Bailey, 'Voices in court'.

Justice (vizt.) the Allowance of Alimony Pending the Suit'.[91] Wives probably hoped that any maintenance would continue after the suit. Interestingly, one of the few men who sought restitution may also have had economic reasons. Arthur Sayer, a Durham joiner, relied on his wife's property and income to keep his head above water; indeed she accused him of marrying her for that reason.[92]

In summary, it is unwise to make too many generalisations about spouses' use of the church courts. Firstly, we cannot assume anything from the outcomes of suits. Abandonment could mean that the plaintiff ran out of money and was unable to continue; it could mean that she or he achieved a satisfactory compromise or agreement, whether this was a privately agreed separation, negotiated maintenance or, indeed, restored peaceful cohabitation. Where additional evidence reveals events after the legal proceedings, they are so utterly unexpected that they belie any of the usual platitudes about gender bias.[93] All that is clear is that spouses, who were motivated to initiate a suit in the church courts by a variety of physical, economic, reputational and emotional reasons, achieved both short- and long-term solutions for their matrimonial difficulties. Secondly, although the ecclesiastical courts tended to attract clients of a higher social profile than the other venues that dealt with marital difficulties, and were more expensive to use, people of relatively modest means did use them. The high cost of suing a case through to sentence, however, did lead to bias in their use. Husbands' greater access to capital meant that they could use the appeal process for their own ends, and overall 73% of the cases that were appealed had male appellants. An appeal could be used to delay a case, or push wives into abandoning their case because they ran out of money; it even allowed one husband to avoid paying alimony to his wife in the interim.[94] Nonetheless, ecclesiastical court procedure was relatively flexible, and though women were limited by the high costs, it would be a mistake to see them as its victims. Wives with fairly limited resources used ecclesiastical courts, achieving their ends by initiating a cause, which was not too expensive, and then abandoning it when appropriate. There is evidence that even women of lower middling rank and narrow means felt in control of their activities in the church courts and satisfied by the results. Jane Allison sued her husband on two separate occasions for separation and restitution, respectively, in the 1760s. Her correspondence with her proctor shows that she viewed the court as a convenient and beneficial forum for

[91] For the Leighton suit see BIHR, CP.I/573; CP.I/1691; Trans.CP.1773/3, *Leighton* c. *Leighton*, 1770. This quote is taken from the information upon the answers of the defendant John Leighton to the libel and allegation of faculties, which is contained within material that remained at Durham after the case was transmitted (DDR/EJ/CCD/3/1770/10).

[92] BIHR, CP.I/291; CP.I/187, *Sayer* c. *Sayer*, 1711.

[93] See Bailey, 'Voices in court'.   [94] Ibid., 399.

the resolution of her marital difficulties. She did not bring multiple cases because she felt that the courts had failed, but because they were successful in helping her solve problems as they arose.[95]

Local attorneys

Attorneys provided several services for couples suffering from marital difficulties. They were widely available in most market towns; in 1790, Hexham in Northumberland had ten attorneys, Malton in Yorkshire one, and Newcastle twenty-nine.[96] This made them relatively accessible even to people who had to travel from more remote rural areas. Their services were quite expensive, but not as costly as some of the other avenues for the resolution of marital conflict. George Draper's casebook, dating from 1669, illustrates that charges for drawing up instruments ranged between 13s 4d and £1.[97] If such sums were charged for drawing up a private separation contract, which spouses would hope was a once-and-for-all cost, this made the procedure more accessible to those of limited means. Indeed Christopher Brooks has shown that early modern attorneys' services were far from restricted to the gentry or professional ranks, since 70% of their clients consisted of yeomen, husbandmen, merchants and artisans.[98] Middling-sort wives and husbands were just as ready to use their services.

In the main, provincial attorneys' business came from providing non-litigious services to their clients, and spouses sought advice from them about relieving marital problems. This may have been fairly common, but tends to escape notice, only coming to attention when referred to incidentally, or because something went wrong. Margaret Lees of Manchester sought advice from the attorney Thomas Jones about leaving her horrifically violent husband, who began to abuse her immediately after their marriage in 1796. Jones mistakenly told her that leaving her husband would be a bar to seeking judicial relief. Following his advice she endured further violence from James Lees until 1802, and she and Jones were obliged to explain this delay in the separation suit that she brought against him.[99] Interestingly, despite his poor advice, Jones acted as an intermediary between Margaret Lees and her proctor at Chester Consistory Court until his death in 1804. This was

---

[95] Ibid., 400–6.

[96] Drawn from the Law Lists of 1790 and 1800 in R. Robson, *The Attorney in Eighteenth-Century England* (Cambridge, 1959), Appendix 4. Also see C. Brooks, *Pettyfoggers and Vipers of the Commonwealth: The 'Lower Branch' of the Legal Profession in Early Modern England* (Cambridge, 1986), pp. 113, 184, 264.

[97] Brooks, *Pettyfoggers and Vipers*, pp. 240–1.   [98] Ibid., p. 264.

[99] BIHR, Chanc.CP.1803/3, *Lees c. Lees*, 1803, Exhibits in proof of libel and position additional.

quite common, probably because it was convenient for most users of the church courts. Proctors were based in the cities where consistory courts sat, so those who lived further afield called on their local attorney who then dealt with the proctor. Thus an attorney in Hexham bridged the considerable gap between one woman who lived in Simonburn, Northumberland, and her proctor in Durham city. Attorneys either took on all communications, or simply provided more formal assistance when required.[100]

Attorneys' primary work was in drawing up legal instruments. Spouses used them, therefore, to organise and finalise their private separation agreements (Appendix 1), which Susan Staves calls 'quasi-legal collusive self-divorce'.[101] These contracts were particularly useful for people whose marriage had irretrievably broken down, without any cruelty or adultery. If successful, they tend to remain hidden to historians. For example the agreement between Ralph Carr of Cocken and his wife would have gone unnoticed, except that Thomas Gyll, variously the solicitor-general of the County Palatine of Durham in 1733 and the recorder of the city of Durham in 1769, commented on it in his diary, in 1762.[102] Some come to light because they were superseded by other legal actions. For example, a defendant might bring a deed of separation as an exhibit in a court case to explain why the plaintiff should not be permitted to initiate it. Private separations included fairly 'low-key' contracts for people of small means, as well as elaborate versions, which organised the living and property arrangements of the very wealthy.[103] In January 1766 Charles and Jane Allison, respectively a master mariner and a mantua maker of North Shields, decided to visit an attorney for assistance in negotiating maintenance and property ownership, and in drawing up a security whereby Charles would honour his obligations and would forfeit a sum if he disobliged his wife in future. Charles first sent to Mr Letteney, an attorney at North Shields, to come and draw the security. Finding that he was away, they sent instead to Mr Barker, another attorney. When they discovered that he was ill, they took a coach to Newcastle to Mr Widdrington, yet another attorney, who failed to get them to compromise on the settlement.[104]

[100] UOD, DDR/EJ/PRC/2/1726/15, *Wear c. Wear*, 1726. Elaborated in Bailey, 'Voices in court', 395.
[101] The origin and development of private separation contracts are described in Staves, 'Separate maintenance contracts', and Stone, *Divorce*, pp. 149, 189. The reasons for the popularity of private deeds of separation (civil separation) over judicial separation (state separation) in the nineteenth century are explored in O. Anderson, 'State, civil society', 161–201.
[102] 'The diary of Thomas Gyll' in J. C. Hodgson (ed.), *Six North Country Diaries*, The Surtees Society, 118 (Durham, 1910), p. 212.
[103] A similar range of social ranks used private separation in the nineteenth century (O. Anderson, 'State, civil society', 163).
[104] UOD, DDR/EJ/CCD/3/1765/2, *Allison c. Allison*, 1765, Jane Allison's positions additional to the libel.

Couples with complicated property and inheritance issues needed legal expertise to settle them in contracts between the husband and the wife's trustees. These contracts had several common features. Typically they arranged alimony and the rights of the spouses with regard to an existing marriage settlement. The deed of separation, dated 9 September 1749, between Godfrey Wentworth and his wife's brothers committed him to pay his wife Dorothea £420 for her alimony, and, if she survived him, to settle an annual sum of £150 as an increase of her jointure of £250 a year. Deeds usually stipulated that a wife could possess certain goods and money for separate use without the interference of her husband. Thus Godfrey Wentworth promised not to meddle with his wife's annuity, interfere with any money paid to her or her trustees, or claim any of her clothes, goods or chattels. Dorothea was to retain separate use of certain lands, could make her own will, sign acquittances and discharges, and dispose of her money as she wished.[105] In effect, agreements allowed a wife to act as if she were unmarried and not under coverture. Deeds also therefore included conditions that protected a husband against his wife's debts. Finally, contracts often denied spouses the right to sue the other in court thereafter. This condition, as we have seen, was broken; an action that the ecclesiastical courts permitted.[106]

Attorneys also acted on behalf of husbands in criminal conversation cases, which flourished between 1680 and 1800, accelerating from the 1760s.[107] The action allowed a husband to sue his wife's lover to obtain satisfaction through the award of financial damages. Occasionally it was a precursor to an ecclesiastical separation suit and ultimately a parliamentary divorce. Research into this action often concentrates on the most notorious cases that were based in London, gathered from bills for parliamentary divorces, printed pamphlets about criminal conversation actions or adultery trials, newspaper reporting and the *English Law Reports*. Thus the evidence is somewhat self-selecting of the most scandalous cases, wealthiest participants, or metropolitan couples. There is evidence, however, of provincial cases (Appendix 1). Suits were started in the central court of King's Bench and, if the case went to trial before a jury, were heard at a county assize court. For instance, John Carr's case against his wife's lover was heard at

---

[105] BIHR, CP.I/1376, *Wentworth c. Wentworth*, 1756.

[106] H. C. Coote, *The Practice of the Ecclesiastical Courts* (London, 1847), p. 362.

[107] Stone, *Divorce*, p. 430, table 9.1; S. Staves, 'Money for honor: damages for criminal conversation', *Studies in Eighteenth-Century Culture*, 11 (1982), 281. For an account of the actions in the first half of the eighteenth century see D. M. Turner, 'Representations of adultery in England c. 1660 – c. 1740: a study of changing perceptions of marital infidelity in conduct literature, drama, trial publications and the records of the Court of Arches', Ph.D. thesis, University of Oxford (1998), chapter 6.

York assizes in 1797 where the jury awarded him £1,000 damages.[108] Such cases were reported in provincial newspapers, from both the locality and other counties, ensuring that people were familiar with criminal conversation. Indeed it was so well known that its use was threatened in order to obtain an out-of-court settlement from the lover, without dragging the affair into public in a court case. In June 1791 William Burton received £50 from Edward Milbanke as damages for a 'criminal intercourse', which took place between him and William's wife. Burton released Milbanke from any future suits on account thereof.[109] It was attorneys who negotiated this procedure. In August 1744, George Surtees applied to John Widdrington, the Newcastle attorney, to bring an action against George Coulson, his wife's alleged lover. The attorney then contacted Coulson and informed him about these directions. Following negotiation, Coulson paid £51 5s and the attorney drew up a release between the parties.[110]

There was another version of this action, whereby husbands sued for the loss of their wives' household services rather than their sexual relations.[111] In this case the law of consortium was popularly known as the law of harbouring. A couple of cases came before the quarter sessions. For instance, John Ward, a yeoman, was prosecuted by John Moone of Newton Mulgrave, Yorkshire, for entertaining, keeping and lodging Margaret Moone and 'thereby createing and fomenting Differences' between the Moones.[112] Interestingly, this action rarely seems to have got as far as the legal profession because, instead, husbands tended to threaten to use it (Appendix 1). Thirty advertisements placed by husbands in the local press, for example, threatened to use the law against people harbouring or entertaining their wives.

The threat seems to have served two purposes. It allowed husbands, maliciously, to prevent their wives finding a place to live or to work, while simultaneously denying them the marital home and financial assistance. The information that Anne Tomlinson, of Knarsdale, gave to a justice of the peace in 1719, is telling. About three years before, as a widow, she brought livestock, an annuity and household goods to her marriage with Robert Tomlinson, a weaver. Soon after, he disposed of her goods, cattle and personal estate,

---

[108] *Y.Cour*, 27 March 1797, p. 3. Carr asked for £10,000 damages. My thanks to Chris Brooks for explaining this procedure to me.

[109] UOD, Baker Baker, vouchers, ref. 92/83. My thanks to Dr Fewster for this reference.

[110] BIHR, Trans.CP.1748/1, *Surtees c. Surtees*, 1745. As with John Widdrington, the names of attorneys and proctors who dealt with couples with matrimonial problems appear several times. It is possible that they specialised in this service.

[111] P. S. James with D. J. L. Brown, *General Principles of the Law of Torts* (London, 1978), pp. 333–4.

[112] NYA, QSB/1708, film 158.

finally turning her out of doors with the vow that he would starve her. Being 'willing and able to work for her living' she went to work for the parson of Knarsdale, but he had to let her go when Robert brought an action against him for entertaining her. Anne ended up destitute because Robert threatened to sue any person that entertained her.[113] By the late eighteenth century, the very act of threatening to use the law without reason was included in allegations of cruelty. Catharine King was granted articles of the peace against her husband, a dairyman in Steeple Claydon, in 1796. Her articles of the peace stated that Thomas King had placed a newspaper advert that he would prosecute anyone who harboured her, and since then she had become increasingly afraid of being removed by force from her father's house, where she had escaped her husband's violence.[114] The second reason to threaten to use the law of harbouring was to try to coerce a wife into returning home. John Sander of Unthank of Kirkoswald (Cumberland) advertised in 1756 that his wife had left him without reason. He warned people not to supply her or harbour her, so 'that she may thereby be oblig'd to return to her said Husband'.[115] Pertinently, several of the occasions when its use was threatened involved wives who had taken their children with them.[116]

Public announcements

Public announcements by spouses were sometimes used to resolve marital difficulties. Robert Renwick, an engineman of Newcastle, advertised in 1787 that the 'family Differences' which had recently happened between him and his wife and her mother had been 'happily Agreed to the mutual Satisfaction of all Parties'. He went on to warn that he would prosecute anyone spreading false reports injurious to his and his wife's character, under the pretext of these difficulties.[117] Mostly the announcements dealt with the aftermath of conflict and disagreement, since the majority were placed by husbands refusing to pay their wives' debts (Appendix 1). Wives had little reason to place such adverts, and only occasionally placed adverts in response to their husbands'. Nonetheless, women regularly placed the same sort of advert as business owners denying credit to their business partners. Ann Salmon, of Scarborough, for instance, warned merchants and traders not to give credit to her son-in-law, as she would not pay for any goods contracted in her name.[118] Announcements were placed in a variety of ways to reach the maximum audience. John Styles has shown that the media used

[113] NCAS, QSB 50, fols. 57, 79.
[114] CBS, Q/SO/24, QS Rolls 96, Catharine and Thomas King.
[115] *N.Jour*, 4–11 September 1756, p. 3.
[116] For example, *N.Chron*, 8 October 1768, p. 3; ibid., 18 November 1796, p. 3. Men had sole legal right of custody over their children in the event of separation.
[117] *N.Chron*, 27 January 1787.   [118] *Y.Chron*, 23 September 1785, p. 3.

for them varied in price and served different audiences. Bellmen cried out the announcement in the church yard on a Sunday, or in the market place on market day. Their services were fairly cheap, costing, for example, 6d in Sheffield in 1764, and 1s in Manchester in 1772, and reached an audience in a concentrated urban area. Handbills, which were pasted and distributed, served rural areas where newspaper circulation was limited.[119] Newspaper advertising was most costly: the basic rate in the 1720s, for instance, was 2s 6d, and in the 1790s, 5s, to which a duty of perhaps 2s or 3s had to be added.[120] This expense was justified, however, since newspaper advertisements captured a broad, distributed audience, sometimes covering several counties. Before the advent of provincial newspapers, in 1697, Elizabeth Pighells' husband 'ordered severall Bel-men in severall markett towns to give notice to and forbid all tradesmen and others to trust her for any goods, wares, meate, drinke, washing or lodging'.[121] The same could be achieved with one newspaper advert. Naturally, spouses made use of several media to capture the widest audience. In 1769 an advert about the Wranghams' mutual separation was placed in the *Newcastle Chronicle* as well as cried out by the bellman.[122]

At one level, husbands' announcements were simply attempts to ensure that they did not end up with debts beyond their means. As Daniel Ottie of York explained in 1685, he had placed an advert about his wife 'for his own security and to p[re]vent her from running him into debt'.[123] They sought security because the use of the law of agency enabled wives to bypass the rules of coverture and participate in consumption largely at their own discretion. However, it was a qualified right. It only applied to the purchasing of necessaries (defined as food, lodging, clothing, medical attendance and medicine) suitable to the couple's station in life.[124] A wife's agency arose from her husband's consent, either explicit or implied: he could authorise his wife to act as his agent, or more typically consent was inferred from their cohabitation and the wife's management of the household.

Thus husbands could limit the scope of their wife's role as agents and even forbid it if they were inclined by demonstrating that they had already

[119] J. Styles, 'Print and policing: crime advertising in eighteenth-century provincial England' in Douglas Hay and Francis Snyder, *Policing and Prosecution in Britain, 1750–1850* (Oxford, 1989), pp. 69–73.

[120] J. J. Looney, 'Advertising and society in England, 1720–1820: a statistical analysis of Yorkshire newspaper advertisements', Ph.D. thesis, Princeton University (1983), p. 36.

[121] BIHR, CP.H/4505, *Pighells c. Pighells*, 1697.   [122] *N.Chron*, 14 January 1769, p. 3.

[123] BIHR, CP.H/5734, D/C.CP.1685/8, *Ottie/Ottey als. Awtie/Awtey c. Ottie/Ottey als. Awtie/Awtey*, 1685.

[124] The law of agency is outlined in L. Holcombe, *Wives and Property: Reform of the Married Women's Property Law in Nineteenth-Century England* (Oxford, 1983), pp. 27–30, and Finn, 'Women, consumption'.

supplied the household with necessaries, had paid the wife enough money
to purchase the goods without resort to credit, or that the articles were
beyond the couple's social status.[125] In practice this meant that a husband
could legitimately deny his wife the use of his credit within marriage, as
25% of the advertisers did (Appendix 20). As we have noted, however, this
had to be justified, so all of them stressed that their wives had acted in
ways that economically endangered them. The advert of Daniel Felldon, a
tailor from Oxford, is typical. He announced in *Jackson's Oxford Journal*,
in April 1761, that Susanna, his wife, had contracted diverse debts to his
prejudice, so he forbade anyone from giving credit to her on his account.[126]
Another 57% of the adverts made it clear that the wife had eloped without
provocation, because such wives automatically lost eligibility to invoke the
law of agency, as did those who were adulterous. Only wives forced out of
the marital home by their husbands' cruelty, or turned out by them, were
entitled to maintenance and to continue to use the law of agency.[127] Finally,
when a couple agreed to live apart, the husband was expected to continue
contributing to his wife's support and, having arranged a specific sum, was
not obliged to pay debts that she contracted. Hence 12% of the press adverts
were placed by men who notified retailers that they would not settle their
wives' debts because they had mutually agreed to separate, and carefully
referred to an indenture, bond or deed, which committed them to providing
a separate maintenance for their wives.

It is apparent, on closer study, that the announcements served wider purposes, both defensive and offensive, than to avoid extra debt. As we have
already seen, husbands sometimes used them to force a wife to return home
by threatening to use the law of harbouring. They also used the adverts to
ask their wives directly to come back. Approximately 10% of the advertising husbands offered to take back their eloped wives, often emphasising that
they would be kindly, affectionately or humanely received, and occasionally offering to forgive their former faults. When George Roper, a wright of
Lanchester, County Durham, notified the public in 1771 that his wife had
eloped without provocation, and ill-treated him in ways he did not wish to
reveal, his advert still concluded, 'He will put up with all the ill Treatment
he has received by her, if she will return again, and be kindly received by
her said Husband.' If not, he refused to pay her debts.[128] One man even
offered to receive his wife after an absence of ten years.[129] Most attached
conditions, stipulating that their wives must return by a certain date, return
to their duty or behave as became a wife.[130]

[125] Holcombe, *Wives and Property*, pp. 30–1.
[126] *JOJ*, 11 April 1761, p. 2.   [127] Burn, *Ecclesiastical Law*, pp. 43–4.
[128] *N.Chron*, 30 March 1771, p. 3.   [129] *N.Cour*, 20 August 1763, p. 3.
[130] See *N.Chron*, 30 April 1763, p. 3; *N.Cour*, 14–21 September 1751, p. 3.

The adverts were also a means by which men sought to protect their credit in the sense of their character as well as their financial status. In stabilising their own reputation, husbands attacked their wives' credit. Their announcements, especially those that hinted at or described their wives' scandalous economic and sexual behaviour, were intended to damage the women's chances of acquiring goods on credit and their reputation. This is why Rebecca Whatmore described her husband's advertisement, which stated she had eloped and refused to be accountable for her debts, in 1788, as an attempt to 'defame' and 'misrepresent' her in the eyes of the public.[131] The link between the adverts and personal reputation is clear in the way that spouses used them to set the record straight. Joseph Fleming's advert blamed his wife for his marital problems, for any financial shortcomings to which his customers had been exposed, and attempted to secure his future economic security by asking his neighbours in Sunderland to 'encourage me in School Teaching to help to get my Bread'.[132]

In some cases women were driven to place adverts offering their own versions of their marital difficulties. The six wives who did so (Appendix 20), in styles that varied from injured to forthright, sarcastic and aggressive, derided their husband's account, detailed their shortcomings, and appealed to the 'World' to decide who was right.[133] Francis and Jane Gomeldon used the newspapers to give their own, very public, version of their marital problems. In 1740 the gentleman Francis Gomeldon placed an advert in the *Newcastle Journal* announcing that his wife, Jane, had left him and asking for her return. A remarkable set of claims and counter-claims followed in two newspapers, when Jane promptly responded with an advert in the *Newcastle Courant* explaining that she had left because he was cruel to her and was intermeddling with the fortune that her mother had bequeathed her, secured for her sole and separate use.[134] Elizabeth Bowie was of lower social status than Jane Gomeldon, but her response to her husband's advert was equally forthright, ending: 'And whereas I did not elope from him, but was kicked out of Doors, even to the Danger of my Life had I continued. Therefore, tis referred to Common Sense and the matrimonial Law, whether my said Husband, Archibald Bowie, can prove or make good this Allegation against me, his Wife, he being the principal Aggressor.'[135]

---

[131] BIHR, CP.I/2221, *Whatmore c. Whatmore*, 1788, libel.
[132] *N.Chron*, 4 February 1769, p. 3.
[133] See C. Hall's response to Soloman Hall's advert, *JOJ*, 18 June 1774, p. 3; for a particularly cutting example, Phillis Dimery's advert, *JOJ*, 1 December 1781, p. 3.
[134] Francis' adverts: *N.Jour*, 5 July, 19 July, 2 August 1740. Jane's adverts: *N.Cour*, 12 July, 26 July 1740.
[135] *N.Jour*, 31 January – 7 February 1756, p. 3; and 7–14 February 1756, p. 3.

CONCLUSION

Reconciliation was the goal of many forms of resolution offered to couples with marital difficulties. Though early modern people sought marital stability, it had a number of forms, of which one was simply that couples were in agreement and unlikely to attack each other, physically, financially or emotionally.[136] Perhaps unexpectedly, for example, even female elopement could be acceptable. In 1771 the *Newcastle Courant* lamented the death of Mrs Grizzel Ross. Stating that she was 100 years old, and born of noble parents, it commented matter-of-factly that she had 'eloped from her husband about 45 years ago', and settled at Hepple, Northumberland, where she 'gained the love and esteem of all her neighbours'.[137] Since marital difficulties were not universally considered deviant, they are thus an excellent way to understand married life holistically, in all its forms, both good and bad. The next four chapters turn to the complaints spouses made during marital conflict, which reveal what people considered the most important features of married life in the long eighteenth century.

[136] This follows Susan Amussen's observation that in marital arrangements stability was favoured over strict legality (Amussen, *An Ordered Society*, p. 128).
[137] *N.Cour*, 9 March 1771, p. 2.

4

'An honourable estate': marital roles in the household

The extensive secondary complaints made by spouses with marital difficulties offer a holistic view of rural and urban seventeenth- and eighteenth-century married life, in the context of the household and its economy. 'Household' is used in the broadest sense as the place of residence of a married couple, sometimes with children and/or servants. It is not, however, intended to suggest that a household can only be considered as such when it was based upon a nuclear family, with a property-owning husband as an authoritative figure to whom other household members were subordinate. Contemporary perceptions of family were much wider and the existence of households was not dependent upon the conjugal unit, since lone men and women frequently headed them.[1] Moreover, the matrimonial cases demonstrate that authority did not always reside only in the male and that households were not tied to specific types of property or social ranks. For example, married couples from the poor to the gentry lodged in lodging houses, and they too formed households. The chronology of marriage and life-course often influenced both the type of residence, with some couples living in lodgings or with parents in the early years, and the number of residents within the household. Children came and went according to age and situation, second marriages introduced step-children, and siblings, cousins and parents temporarily resided, as did lodgers, servants and apprentices.[2] As the latter indicate, household residents carried out a range of paid and unpaid activities, servicing it and contributing to the domestic and business economies.

[1] Tadmor, 'The household-family'. For examples of households headed by lone people see S. J. Wright, 'The elderly and the bereaved in eighteenth-century Ludlow' in M. Pelling and R. M. Smith (eds.), *Life, Death, and the Elderly, Historical Perspectives* (London, 1991), pp. 104, 115, 121–3; A. M. Froide, 'Old maids: the lifecycle of single women in early modern England' in L. Botelho and P. Thane, *Women and Ageing in British Society Since 1500* (Harlow, 2001), pp. 24–95; S. Ottaway, 'The old woman's home in eighteenth-century England' in Botelho and Thane, *Women and Ageing*, pp. 116–20.
[2] For a case-study that demonstrates the flexibility and mutability of households, although of a slightly later date, see D'Cruze, 'Care, diligence'.

For all the diversity in the composition of households, the married couples in them had common ambitions: to manage their households and economies efficiently and to protect their individual and household credit and creditworthiness. These goals offered a measure of security in a precarious physical environment. Indeed the middling sort responded to life's contingencies with an ethos in which sustaining one's family's socio-economic situation by avoiding decline was more important than improving it through social-climbing or amassing wealth.[3] These were not solely middling-sort preoccupations. Labouring people depended on credit because their incomes were irregular, and their creditworthiness could be the key factor that prevented them from resorting to poor relief in difficult times.[4] Such factors are reflected in nearly three-quarters of the secondary complaints, which focused on the provision, government, distribution and ownership of material resources (Appendix 8).[5] Their analysis opens up seventeenth- and eighteenth-century people's views about spouses' roles with regard to their financial obligations to each other, their children and their households, the management of the household and its economy, and attitudes to property ownership.

MANAGING THE DOMESTIC ECONOMY

Married women's disabilities under the common law's doctrine of coverture are notorious. They lost ownership of personal property and the management of their real estate unless it was protected by a separate settlement. Law handbooks described coverture, however, as a reciprocal legal relationship. So, ostensibly in return for the property benefits that they gained, men shouldered a number of financial obligations on entering marriage, of which the most profound was to provide for their wives and children. Wives were unable to make economic contracts or to purchase goods on credit in their own name and therefore had the right to be maintained by their husbands and to use the law of agency.[6] As *The Laws Respecting Women* stated: if 'a woman cohabit with her husband, he is obliged to find her necessaries, as meat, drink, clothing, physic, [etc.] suitable to his rank and fortune. So if he runs away from her, or turns her away, or forces her by cruelty or ill-usage to go away from him.'[7]

---

[3] Mascuch, 'Social mobility', 53, 55.   [4] Wrightson, *Earthly Necessities*, p. 315.

[5] The categories relating to property ownership, household hierarchy, male provision, female extravagance and financial mismanagement, general financial conflict, and spouses' drinking were added together, forming a percentage of 72%.

[6] For the legal responsibilities that men took on when they married see Anon., *The Laws Respecting Women*, pp. 148–84; Anon., *A Treatise of Feme Coverts: Or, the Lady's Law containing all the Laws and Statutes relating to Women* (London, 1732); Anon., *Baron and Feme*; Holcombe, *Wives and Property*, pp. 26–7, 30–1.

[7] Anon., *Laws Respecting Women*, p. 66.

Male provision emphasised the ideal of male economic autonomy, protection, responsibility and fair-dealing, and was thus closely linked with middling-sort manhood. Indeed these standards of male behaviour permeated most advice for married men. In 1716 William Fleetwood advised them that one element of the love they owed to their wives was 'in taking care of and making all due Provision for them'.[8] The *Newcastle Chronicle* explained in 1765 that all the good husband's 'care and industry are employed for [his wife's] welfare; all his strength and power are exerted for her support and protection'.[9] A variety of evidence indicates that men assimilated and aspired to this powerful ideology. Early in his marriage Ralph Josselin ruminated: 'a man is bound to provide for his family, and lay up for them, this Scripture alloweth, commendeth, requireth'.[10] Michael Mascuch's review of early modern autobiographers illustrates that, when considering marriage, many men considered whether they could afford to maintain a family. Thomas Gent, a printer of York, recalled, 'I was not very forward in my love, or desire of matrimony, till I knew the world better, and, consequently, more able to provide...a handsome maintenance'.[11] The ideal shaped male self-defences in marital difficulties. For example, in 1696, Robert Shaw presented himself as a good husband, observing that since his marriage he had 'always kept a very good and plentifull House as to meate and drink' and went on that his wife 'was maintained with very good Cloaths suitable to her rank and quality'.[12]

The ideal of provision was culturally enforced through its use as a favourable sign of manhood. In *The History of Myddle*, for instance, Richard Gough judged men's success in marriage by their hard work and ability to keep their household fed.[13] To suggest otherwise was to discredit a husband. Alexandra Shepard's work, based on debt and injury litigation that came before the Cambridge University Courts in the late sixteenth and first half of the seventeenth centuries, shows that some men responded to accusations that they neglected their wives and their children by initiating actions for injury.[14] Similar concerns are evident in the eighteenth century. Ben Clark was forced to place an advert in *Jackson's Oxford Journal* in 1773, explaining 'I have circulated a false and scandalous report that Joshua Tyson, foreman to Mr Townsend, mason, Oxford had ran away from Maidenhead-Bridge' on account of his wife and child coming to him from the north of

---

[8] W. Fleetwood, *The relative duties of parents and children, husbands and wives, masters and servants; consider'd in sixteen practical discourses with sermons upon the case of self-murther*, 2nd edition (London, 1716), pp. 236, 260–2.
[9] *N.Chron*, 31 August 1765, p. 1.   [10] Cited in Mascuch, 'Social mobility', 58.
[11] Ibid., 56–7.   [12] BIHR, Trans.CP.1697/2; D/C.CP.1696/3, Shaw c. Shaw, 1696.
[13] Cited in Fletcher, *Gender, Sex and Subordination*, p. 268.
[14] Shepard, 'Manhood, credit and patriarchy', 83–6.

England. In return for Ben's apology and statement that the rumour was un-
true Joshua agreed to stop his action at law against him.[15] Shepard explains
that men were damaged by such allegations, since diverting resources from
the household was equated with idleness and neglect, amounting to dishonesty, because it jeopardised both individual families and other men's credit.[16]
Indeed, men's refusal to provide could contribute to behaviour that was categorised as a misdemeanour. The quarter sessions grand jury at Morpeth,
for example, presented Robert Trumble, a maltster, at Easter 1715 because,
along with his reckless violence and threats, he had reduced his family to
beggary and 'will neither work himselfe nor suffer his wife to work to get a
mentenance for the famelly'.[17]

It is conceivable, however, that not all men saw male provision positively.
Obviously, some husbands simply abandoned the ideal during marriage.
It was not unusual to describe this as an explicit act of rejection by the
husband in question. In 1682 Samuel Clyatt, of Gray's Inn, the brother
of the plaintiff Martha Brooke, recalled that her husband Timothy Brooke
visited him in London and instructed him to write to Martha on his behalf.
Somewhat surprisingly, Samuel wrote the letter in which she was ordered to
leave Timothy's house, and warned that he would cut her throat if she were
still there when he returned. Samuel deposed that Timothy's demand was
'craftilie made on purpose to gett ridd of his wife and to ease himselfe of
the charge of maintaineing of her'.[18] In 1710 Rebecca Clark complained to
Buckinghamshire quarter sessions that her husband, a maltster, fraudulently
made over all his stock, cattle and personal estate to the value of £400 to his
son by a former marriage in order to avoid keeping her and paying some few
debts of hers.[19] Even those who promoted the ideal described it as a burden.
A 'poetical essay' in the *Gentleman's Magazine* of 1733, entitled 'Woman's
Hard Fate', bemoaned female subjection first to a father, then a brother and
finally a husband, naming the latter as a sovereign, and describing marriage
as a 'fatal bondage'. A 'Gentleman's' response observed that men simply safe-
guarded women, who after all had the better deal in the conjugal bargain
because: ''Tis *man's*, to labour, toil and sweat, / And all his care employ, /
Honour, or wealth, or pow'r to get; / 'Tis *woman's* to enjoy.'[20]

Wives from most social ranks and all regions claimed that their husbands
refused to provide for their household in 21% of all the secondary complaints (Appendix 8).[21] In her cruelty separation suit, for example, Ann Shaw

[15] *JOJ*, 29 May 1773, p. 3.   [16] Shepard, 'Manhood, credit and patriarchy', 83–6.
[17] NCAS, QSB/42, fol. 1.   [18] BIHR, CP.H/3516, *Brooke c. Brooke*, 1683.
[19] CBS, W. Le Hardy and G. L. Rickett (eds.), *County of Buckingham Calendar to the Sessions
Records*, 4 vols. (Aylesbury, 1933, 1939, 1951), Vol. III 1705–1712, pp. 30, 46–7.
[20] GM, 3 (July 1733), 371.
[21] A divorce *causa saevitae sive Metus* is mentioned in some eighteenth-century law books
aimed at women, in addition to the usual divorce *a vinculo* and divorce *a thoro et mensa*.

responded to Robert's flattering self-portrait with a firm rebuttal: he was miserly, allowed the milk of only one cow for the household, 1s for house-keeping, kept food under lock and key, and her clothing was tattered.[22] This complaint took two main forms. Firstly, some wives accused their husbands of denying them common necessaries (food, drink and clothing) during co-habitation by failing to provide them, removing them or locking them away. It is clear that these acts, and threats to starve wives and children, were categorised as a form of abuse because the complaint was listed alongside accounts of physical cruelty in twenty-seven of the forty-seven cruelty separation cases and it was also mentioned in detailed cases of wife-beating that came before the quarter sessions.[23] In a sworn information heard by the Northumberland Quarter Sessions at Morpeth in 1687, Margaret Story of Bedlington described both her husband's brutal beatings, and his habit of hiding victuals from her and their child in the fields, or leaving her without money to buy food when he went on long drinking bouts.[24] Emphasising that these men also neglected their children exacerbated the complaint's force. Their duty began at the child's birth, since they were expected to maintain their wives in the crucial period of their lying-in. Ralph Rand deposed with disgust that his daughter Elizabeth Day was forced to go to his house to lie-in because her husband failed to provide for her.[25] Elizabeth Stradling's separation suit on the grounds of cruelty, against her husband Thomas, a gentleman, called equal attention to his beatings and to his lack of care for her and their two children. Thus, for example, she reported that when she 'with tears desired something for the maintenance of herself and two Children . . . he said to her God damne You and Your cubbes', forcing them to eat 'a mean and poor dyett not fitt for Christians' for four years.[26]

Men's responsibilities for provision extended to their step-children (Appendix 8).[27] In many cases men gained control over their step-children's inheritance, since the property that a widow brought to marriage included her previous husband's estate unless he had bequeathed portions to his children.[28] This could be dangerous. Jane Currer, for example, responded to her husband's restitution suit in 1673 by accusing him of both cruelty and

Its grounds was a husband taking necessaries from his wife, as well as one or other spouse fearing poisoning. Anon., *Baron and Feme*, p. 433; Anon., *The Laws Respecting Women*, p. 96.

[22] BIHR, Trans.CP.1697/2; D/C.CP.1696/3, *Shaw c. Shaw*, 1696.

[23] The complaint was made in 41% of cruelty separations and restitution suits.

[24] NCAS, QSB/5, fols. 14–15, Information of Margaret Storey.

[25] BIHR, D/C.CP.1699/1, *Day c. Day*, 1699, Ralph Rand's deposition.

[26] BIHR, CP.I/291, *Stradling c. Stradling*, 1713.

[27] For some of the problems associated with remarriage see E. Foyster, 'Marrying the experienced widow in early modern England: the male perspective' in S. Cavallo and L. Warner (eds.), *Widowhood in Medieval and Early Modern Europe* (London, 1999), pp. 108–24.

[28] Erickson, *Women and Property*, p. 132.

refusing to pay the portions that her children's father had provided for them, which caused the children's trustee to sue the couple.[29] Ensuring children's financial well-being was a principal consideration in the decision whether or not to remarry. The curate James Currie told his friends that he had re-married in 1727 for the preferment and advancement of his four children.[30] When Thomas Haswell courted Elizabeth Dodgshon, he promised to make her children equal to his own and offered £40 0s 0d in order to bind her son out as an apprentice.[31] Consequently, on remarrying, women sought to pro-tect their children's interests by getting their new husbands to enter a bond obliging them to pay the portions of children from previous marriages.[32] Henry Moor, for example, entered into articles in which he covenanted not to meddle with either the real or personal estate of his wife's first husband or her father. Rents or profits for the use of her five children were to be re-ceived by trustees appointed by their father. Henry broke all these promises, retaining the lands and the rents.[33] Mary Giles placed an advert in 1744 that 'being desirous of robbing the Infants of' their provision, her second husband had 'incessantly pressed her to give up' the articles he had entered, which secured the money left by her first husband to her two children.[34] The women presented these acts as cruelty and went on to show that their husbands' actions were starving them and their children.

The second form of the complaint was made by wives who were turned out of the marital home or forced to flee because of their husbands' cruelty. They explained that maintenance was denied during the ensuing separation. This category of secondary complaint is separate to the primary allegation that their husbands had abandoned them. Failure to provide in separation was still often linked with male cruelty. For example, wives who petitioned their justices of the peace for poor relief made it clear that their husbands offered only physical abuse when asked for maintenance.[35] Husbands' obligations towards their wives in separation were determined by women's behaviour.

---

[29] Restrictions imposed in bequests on widows remarrying were primarily to ensure that prop-erty remained in the hands of the chosen heirs, and could not be dissipated by a new husband (ibid., pp. 168–9).

[30] BIHR, Trans.CP.1730/6, *Currie c. Currie*, 1729. Jane Ballantine told him that having four children was the reason not to marry again (her deposition).

[31] By contrast, Elizabeth's twenty-year-old son deposed that Thomas warned him in 1725 that if he and his sister were not pleased that their mother was Thomas' wife, he would take her away and leave them to fend for themselves (BIHR, Trans.CP.1729/10, *Haswell c. Dodgshon*, 1727, Robert Motley's deposition, personal answer of Elizabeth to Thomas' allegation and exhibits).

[32] Bonds were made obligatory in the 1670 Act for the Better Settling of Intestates' Estates, which required that any person having charge of an estate for the benefit of minor children had to give bonds for the children's portions (Erickson, *Women and Property*, pp. 131–3).

[33] BIHR, CP.I/2741 *Moor c. Moor*, 1707.

[34] *N.Jour*, 19 May 1744, p. 3, and 2 June 1744, p. 3.

[35] See OA, QS/1694/Mi/17; NCAS, QSB/42, Petition of Ann Eades, 1716.

Maintenance was unavailable to wives who eloped without provocation or were adulterous.[36] Deserted wives were unable to use the law of agency for the simple reason that creditors could not pursue their husbands. Even otherwise entitled estranged wives were denied it if they tried to keep their children without their husbands' consent. When Grace Featherstone sued her husband for restitution, her husband's proctor sought advice about whether Grace could demand maintenance for their child, since she had taken their daughter against her husband's will. The legal adviser responded that while Grace refused to let Ralph Featherstone have his daughter she could neither pledge his credit nor demand maintenance for herself or the child.[37] Furthermore, wives had limited legal means to enforce maintenance.[38]

Margot Finn has proposed that such problems led separated wives to manipulate the law of agency in two ways in the late eighteenth and nineteenth centuries. Firstly, she cites examples of women using it profligately to blackmail their husbands into restoring or starting maintenance.[39] Secondly, she uses five nineteenth-century court cases to illustrate that judges and juries frequently upheld wives' right to pledge their separated husbands' credit, allowing them to gain maintenance in goods for which their husbands would be forced to pay.[40] Court cases reported in the Newcastle, York and Oxford newspapers from the mid eighteenth century indicate, however, that this was no guaranteed outcome. Only one husband paid his wife's debts, in 1793, out of six randomly selected cases, and even then he paid the creditors half the sum required.[41] One woman, a coffee house keeper, was required to pay her own debts in 1787, after failing to prove that her husband was reconciled to her and therefore liable.[42] Another suit was decided against the wife with costs, in 1783, because her husband was in Ireland and thus too far away to be pursued by creditors.[43] Two cases in 1753 and one in 1773 were decided in the husbands' favour because it was proven that their wives had eloped before pledging their credit.[44] Legal handbooks were equally pessimistic about separated women's opportunities to force their husbands to support them

---

[36] Anon, *Laws Respecting Women*, pp. 68–9; Burn, *Ecclesiastical Law*, Vol. II, pp. 43–4.

[37] UOD, DDR/EJ/CCD/3/1776/2, DDR/EJ/PRC/2/1776/2, *Featherstone c. Featherstone*, 1776.

[38] Chapter 8, pp. 181–3.   [39] Finn, 'Women, consumption', 710–12.

[40] The five cases that Finn uses are not straightforward and most fall within loopholes (ibid., 712–14).

[41] *Y.Chron*, 18 July 1793, p. 2.

[42] *N.Cour*, 30 June 1787, p. 4. Susan Staves found that, from around 1675 to 1778, a wife with a separate maintenance allowance could be sued as though she were a *feme sole*, because by making the contract she had relinquished her entitlement to her husband's support (Staves, 'Separate maintenance contracts', 86).

[43] One would expect the ruling to have been given simply because she had a separate maintenance (*N.Chron*, 8 February 1783, p. 2).

[44] *Y.Cour*, 18 September 1753, p. 2 (also reported in *JOJ*, 15 September 1753, p. 1); *JOJ*, 15 December 1753, p. 2; *JOJ*, 27 February 1773, p. 1.

by using the law of agency. Richard Burn discussed four court cases under his entry for 'wife' in *The Justice of the Peace and Parish Officer*, none of which left the husband responsible for his wife's debt.[45]

Wives' complaints about their husbands' refusal to provide within marriage and separation paint a bleak picture of married women's economic dependence and men's economic autonomy. This was only partially true, because it was countered in two ways: firstly, by men themselves, and secondly, by married women. Male self-sufficient economic mastery was marked by independent status in a trade, craft or profession, by marriage, and by householding status, in terms of property ownership. Alexandra Shepard's excellent study of manhood between 1580 and 1640 concludes that few men could achieve this influential ideal. Numerous men fell short of such independent economic status, including young men who were financially dependent on their parents, servants, wage labourers and apprentices, who as the early modern period progressed were increasingly unable to follow the route from apprentice to journeyman to master. Furthermore, at the beginning of the period, significant numbers of men never married, and though age at marriage lowered with more men marrying in the eighteenth century, this did not automatically provide economic independence. As Shepard and Anna Clark show, such men demonstrated their masculinity through other means like drinking and violence.[46]

This sort of male counter-culture, which was fraternal rather than patriarchal and excluded women, was not just the prerogative of unmarried men and clashed with the realities of married life. Indeed, Clark's work on the marriages of late eighteenth- and early nineteenth-century male artisans suggests that they found it difficult to reconcile their home life with the male camaraderie and bachelor-orientation of their work environment.[47] Wives certainly did not believe that drinking and fighting denoted much in the way of positive masculinity. Work on nineteenth-century temperance campaigns suggests that men's alcohol consumption created conflict over the distribution of resources, because wives viewed it as an act that impoverished the domestic economy.[48] Similar criticisms existed in the seventeenth and eighteenth centuries. For example, women denounced their husbands' drinking habits in 4% of the secondary complaints (Appendix 8). Husbands were also presented to the quarter sessions for attempting to impoverish their families by drinking, amongst other offences.[49] As well as explicitly coupling

[45] Burn, *Justice of the Peace*, Vol. III, pp. 381–4.
[46] Clark, *Struggle for the Breeches*, p. 30; Shepard, 'Manhood, credit and patriarchy', 102–6.
[47] Clark, *Struggle for the Breeches*, p. 5.
[48] P. Walker, '"I live but not yet I for Christ Liveth in Me", men and masculinity in the Salvation Army, 1865–90' in Michael Roper and John Tosh (eds.), *Manful Assertions: Masculinities in Britain since 1800* (London, 1991), pp. 101–4.
[49] See, for example, NCAS, QSB/42, fol. 1, case against Robert Trumble, 1715.

excessive drinking with wife-beating, wives typically added the complaint to a long list of unacceptable male behaviour, like litigiousness, troublesomeness, lewdness, debauchery and fighting.[50] All denoted dishonesty, which was associated with wasting household resources. In 1707 Mary Halleley directly expressed the link between drunken male-bonding, dishonesty and profligacy. She reported that her drunkard husband had brought other drunk and debauched men into her chamber late at night, setting them to singing, roaring, cursing and swearing at her, and observed that his drunkenness led him to associate with lewd women, which resulted in him wasting £200.[51]

When women evaluated men as husbands it was also through the concept of responsible economic autonomy. Chatting to a friend in the 1760s Jane Allison professed that 'she woud never Marry a Husband without having one to Keep her'.[52] For Margaret Sayer, of York, the failure of her husband to be economically proficient dissolved her commitment to the marriage. In 1711, Arthur Sayer brought a restitution suit against her. As well as alleging specific acts of physical abuse in her defence, she explained that Arthur had played her false to persuade her to marry him. Before showing her his house, he borrowed neighbours' goods to furnish it in order to assure her that his business as a joiner would support him and his family. Having discovered after marriage that he was very poor and unable to provide sustenance for his family, Margaret therefore 'humbly conceived she had lawful cause to absent herself from her husband'.[53] Yet for all they acknowledged men's role as provisioner, both women's actions highlight the contradictions undermining the ideal. In reality Jane Allison refused to hand over her economic independence to her husband. Before marriage she had a successful trade as a mantua maker and after it she fought furiously to keep the funeral palls and cloaks and income that she produced in her business. Arthur Sayer married Margaret, a widow, who described herself as able to live very well and credibly through her own business of selling ale, because she was economically self-sufficient. Indeed after she fled his violence she simply physically and metaphorically dusted herself off and, despite his seizing her goods, started selling ale again.

Secondly, therefore, married women's own activities and attitudes in terms of provision, consumption, material contributions and property ownership contradicted male self-sufficiency. Work by Amy Erickson, Alexandra Shepard, Margot Finn, Margaret Hunt and Maxine Berg on a number of different topics has already demonstrated that married women had considerably

---

[50] This grievance was included in 17% of all cruelty separations. For example, BIHR, CP.H/4505, *Pighells* c. *Pighells*, 1697; UOD, DDR/EJ/PRC/2/1743/12, *Smith* c. *Smith*, 1743.
[51] BIHR, D/C.CP.1707/2, *Halleley* c. *Halleley*, 1707.
[52] UOD, DDR/EJ/PRC/2/1765/3, DDR/EJ/CCD/3/1768/2, *Allison* c. *Allison*, 1765.
[53] BIHR, CP.I/187, *Sayer* c. *Sayer*, 1711, Response of Margaret Sayer to Libel.

more economic and financial agency, in terms of entering contracts and owning property, than coverture permitted.[54] Finn and Berg, for instance, believe that this explains both the explosion of texts condemning female consumption in the eighteenth century and married women's important contribution to industrialisation through their consuming habits. All conclude, to use Finn's words, that: 'coverture is best described as existing in a state of suspended animation'.[55] Nonetheless, except for Hunt's work on London marriages, this basic fact of life in the seventeenth and eighteenth centuries has not entered mainstream work on matrimony, and its consequences for married life and marital relationships are neglected. Ideas about the economic roles of spouses and their relationship to authority continue in the same mould. Thus a very recent text-book, which acknowledges the necessity of married women's labour, still assumes that: 'although the earning ability of men differed considerably across society, there can be little doubt that the primary economic responsibility, and (it must be said) power, was theirs'.[56]

All facets of marital economic roles and their implications for power should be scrutinised in more detail. Modern discussions of provision and consumption in the eighteenth-century household often categorise them as separate gendered activities, the former male, and the latter largely female, which is the implication of most contemporary household and marital prescription. Provisioning in these terms was the act of supplying cash or credit, consumption the utilisation of these means to purchase necessaries. William Whately's *Directions for Married Persons* (originally published in 1617 but current for the next two centuries, because John Wesley included it in *A Christian Library*, which ran to several editions) perceptively recognised that both spouses 'maintain and govern, keep and guide' their families and 'join in making Provision of all necessaries for their children and servants'. Nevertheless, he envisioned husbands as the source of money, describing the specifically male duty of maintenance as earning a 'comfortable living' and ensuring that wives were taken care of in widowhood.[57] Publications generally assigned the role of running the domestic economy to women and therefore encouraged them to be thrifty with, significantly, their husbands' money. This advice spanned centuries; recommended, for example, by John Dod and Robert Cleaver in the early seventeenth century, it was still in force at the end

---

[54] Erickson, *Women and Property*, pp. 150–1; Shepard, 'Manhood, credit and patriarchy', 91; Finn, 'Women, consumption'; Hunt, 'Marital "rights"', p. 125; M. Berg, 'Women's consumption and the industrial classes of eighteenth-century England', *Journal of Social History*, 30, 2 (1996), 415–34.

[55] Finn, 'Women, consumption', 707.   [56] Coster, *Family and Kinship*, pp. 36–7.

[57] W. Whateley, *Directions for Married Persons* in John Wesley, *A Christian Library*, 27th edition, 30 vols. (London, 1819), Vol. XI, pp. 294, 325–8. My thanks to Revd John Job for bringing this to my attention.

of the eighteenth century.[58] The 'Rules and Maxims for promoting Matrimonial Happiness', printed in 1760 in the *Newcastle Journal*, asked women: 'Have you any concern for your own ease, or for your husband's esteem? Then have a due regard to his income and circumstances in all your expences and desires; for if necessity should follow, you run the greatest hazard of being deprived of both.'[59] At the end of the century Thomas Gisborne was still warning the female sex against 'ostentation and prodigality'.[60] Of course, in addition to this literary evidence, married women's right to purchase household stuffs, food, drink, clothing and medicine through the law of agency reinforces the concept that they simply spent men's money.

In practice, provision and consumption were more varied and not seen as entirely distinct activities. The role of provisioner was not a men-only activity. Married women also viewed themselves as provisioners in the seventeenth and eighteenth centuries. The words that they chose to describe their husbands' refusal or neglect of provision reveal that they saw it as a joint effort, for they explained their husbands' role as one of contribution or assistance. Several examples are cited to make the point (all my emphases). In 1740 Elizabeth Bell, of Heworth in the county of Yorkshire, requested that the quarter sessions order her husband to provide sureties 'for his keeping the Peace and being of mild behaviour towards her and that he will continue with and *assist* in the Provision for and maintenance of her... and their said children'.[61] Mary Burrell's advert in 1783 complained that her husband had left her destitute 'without in the least *contributing* to my support'.[62] Barbara Hoppard brought her husband before a justice of the peace in 1785 because he beat her and 'refuses to work and *contribute* towards the support and maintenance of her and her child'.[63] When Susannah Rigsby charged her husband with a breach of the peace for his violence, she also alleged that he wasted the income they received from their business as lace-buyers and dealers in bone lace. She described how, in order to safeguard her family, she dealt separately in the lace trade, earning enough to pay the rent of their house and provide clothes and necessaries for her and their children, 'without his *assistance*'.[64] The type of provision described by wives is also informative. Within marriage, complaints tended to focus on food, drink and clothing, and the denial of provision took the form of locking them away, as much as refusing to provide them. This makes the original source

[58] J. Dod and R. Cleaver, cited in Shepard, 'Manhood, credit and patriarchy', 75.
[59] *N.Jour*, 16–23 August 1760, p. 2.
[60] T. Gisborne, *An Enquiry into the Duties of the Female Sex*, 9th edition (London, 1796), p. 152.
[61] NYA, QSB/1741, Information, 30 August 1740, MIC 133.
[62] *N.Chron*, 1 November 1783, p. 3.   [63] NYA, QSB/1785/003092.
[64] CBS, QS Rolls 1775.

or provisioner ambiguous, as can be seen in Margaret Story's description of her husband's malicious acts: 'when she p[ro]vided him meat [he] did dash it about her head and…did give it to ye dogs whereas he would not allow his said wife necessary food for her selfe and childe'.[65] Women's complaints about lack of maintenance in separation also indicate that they saw male provision as contributory, not a sole endeavour. They described it as partial support, rather like poor relief, which was only intended to assist women in gaining a livelihood.

Consumption was also more complex in practice. To put the gendering of consumption in perspective, Margot Finn reminds us that men purchased mundane household goods as well as luxury items.[66] Yet it is likely that married women made most of these purchases. Indeed, husbands' public announcements, which are superficially examples of male economic superiority and female economic disability, actually demonstrate that wives exercised a degree of economic autonomy. Wives could purchase a range of goods with cash, but the bulk of purchases in this period were made on credit. Under the law of agency, married women were only permitted to purchase basic necessaries in their husband's name. Yet it is likely that wives purchased a wider range of goods than permitted under the law of agency. In the first place, women legitimately bought goods other than necessaries in both their single and widowed states, and during marriage when local customs allowed them to trade as if they were single women.[67] These experiences may have inclined wives to buy what they needed, without interrogating whether or not the goods could be categorised as necessaries. Secondly, retailers used their own judgement about selling goods on credit to wives. This is evident in debt litigation, when creditors sued married women over unpaid debts on luxuries rather than necessaries.[68] Finn's analysis of debt litigation in small-claims courts, which grew up in the later eighteenth century, provides numerous examples of married women purchasing a variety of goods from creditors who viewed them as possessing economic autonomy.[69] Alexandra Shepard found that many debt cases nominally brought by men to the Cambridge University Courts in the late sixteenth and early seventeenth centuries involved transactions independently made by their wives, often as the result of their autonomous business concerns.[70] As we will see in the next chapter, wives also contributed the money that eventually settled the debts.

---

[65] NCAS, QSB/5, fols. 14–15, Information of Margaret Storey.
[66] M. Finn, 'Men's things: masculine possession in the consumer revolution', *Social History*, 25, 2 (2000), 138, 139, 153.
[67] Erickson, *Women and Property*, p. 30.
[68] For more detailed discussion see, Bailey, 'Favoured or oppressed?' 8–9.
[69] Finn, 'Women, consumption', 715.
[70] Shepard, 'Manhood, credit and patriarchy', 90–5.

Married women's participation in both provision and consumption meant that they established their own credit networks and reputation, before and during marriage, as the debt litigation shows. This is implicit in another financial obligation that husbands took on when they married. All moneys owing to women at marriage, as well as the goods from their business or occupation, became the property of their husbands, who in turn were responsible for the debts their wives owed before the ceremony.[71] Creditors understood the financial consequences of marriage and descended upon newly wed couples to collect debts, no doubt hoping that the pooling of resources would benefit them, and because men could be sued to satisfy their wives' ante-nuptial obligations.[72] Samuel Finch, a seventy-year-old house carpenter from Crossgate in Durham, wrote to his wife during their separation suit, on 9 January 1779, reminding her that he had been frightened to walk in the street after marriage because people came to him seeking payment of her debts. His formal legal response to Elizabeth's allegation of faculties (a wife's estimate of her husband's worth, in order to set alimony) stated that he had been sued for her debts, amounting to the hefty sum of £28.[73] The pursuit of husbands to settle their wives' debts was not restricted to remarriages, or to unions with women who were in some form of business. John Harris of Long Handborough, Oxfordshire, advertised in 1759 that his wife had eloped and 'hath caused... [him] to be arrested for a large Sum of money pretended to be due for her Maintenance, Lodging, and Education, before her Intermarriage'.[74] Strikingly, as this example demonstrates, men suggested that their wives had acted malevolently and strategically used this feature of coverture to their own ends. Creditors were not discriminatory, also seeking out husbands who were in debt in their own right at marriage, in the conviction that the wife had brought some property to the union.[75]

Complaints about female extravagance and financial mismanagement, which made up 10% of the complaints (Appendix 8), show that wives' personal credit continued to be important during marriage and that wives' consumption was broader than legally permitted, since women were involved in both domestic and business economies. Such complaints were made by men in public announcements, usually to explain the denial of credit, in separation suits in response to allegations of faculties, and in restitution suits to explain why they refused to cohabit with their wives. These complaints had two themes. One was female extravagance. All the adverts that attempted to

---

[71] Anon., *Laws Respecting Women*, pp. 148–52.
[72] Sir T. E. Tomlins (ed.), *The Law Dictionary*, by T. Colpitts Granger, 4th edition (London, 1835), Vol. I, pp. v, vi.
[73] UOD, DDR/EJ/PRC/2/1779/3, *Finch c. Finch.*   [74] *JOJ*, 29 September 1759, p. 3.
[75] For example, see NCAS, QSB/1730, fol. 22, Petition of Henry Hendry.

stem women's use of credit within marriage implied extravagant spending. Thus William Sampson, a tallow chandler and soap boiler from Pontefract, denied his wife the use of his credit in the *York Courant* in 1756 because she 'seems entirely bent to ruin her said Husband'.[76] Words like 'extravagance' and 'wasteful' emphasised that the women were acting beyond their means and were potentially or actually economically damaging.

The second form of the complaint extended past wives' consumption of necessaries for the household, or propensity to purchase unnecessary luxuries. Using words like 'embezzled', 'squandered', 'robbed', 'mismanaged', and 'destroyed', husbands suggested that their wives mishandled business as well as domestic concerns, either through deliberate embezzlement, or through inadequacy. On many occasions husbands made the complaints in response to wives' estimates of their worth. In these circumstances most men rejected the suggested sums in the hope of paying lower maintenance, by explaining that it was their wives' profligacy or mismanagement that made the sums lower than calculated. In 1697 John Pighells, the rector of Patterington, Yorkshire, argued that his personal and real estate were worth nought once he paid off the debts accumulated by his wife's extravagances. A farmer from Burley, Joseph Walker, claimed that his stock was worth no more than £40, not £100, due to the mismanagement of his wife.[77] Such grievances covered several ranks and urban and rural couples. Both the gentleman Roger Manwaring in 1761, and Thomas Wood, a sea-faring man from Whitburn, in 1708 claimed that their wives wasted their estates.[78] Charges made by the gentry simply involved much larger sums of money.

In a society dominated by the threat of bankruptcy, wives' commonplace activities in family businesses, the tendency for household and business accounts to be lumped together, and the lack of a legal distinction between personal and business liability led to the common link between women's financial activities and men's business failure.[79] The public denial of credit was sometimes accompanied by the claim that the advertisers had been bankrupted by their wives' activities. According to Samuel Rutter of Eynsham, Oxfordshire, his wife had involved him in debt 'to his utter Ruin'.[80] The claim was by no means restricted to adverts. In 1700 Ebenezer Robson defended himself in a restitution case by explaining that, until his marriage fourteen years before, he was a tailor with a good trade and ten or more journeymen and apprentices. After about seven years, however, his wife had

---

[76] 3 February 1756.

[77] BIHR, CPH/4505, *Pighells* c. *Pighells*, 1697; BIHR, CPI/812, *Walker* c. *Walker*, 1723.

[78] BIHR, Trans.CP.1766/2, *Manwaring* c. *Manwaring*, 1761; Trans.CP.1709/2, *Wood* c. *Wood*, 1708.

[79] P. Langford, *A Polite and Commercial People: England 1727–1783*, 2nd edition (Oxford, 1989), p. 76; Muldrew, *Economy of Obligation*, p. 158.

[80] *JOJ*, 24 October 1778, p. 2. Also see William Peacock's enigmatic advert, which was followed by the notice that his shop and its stock were for sale (*Y.Cour*, 21 November 1769, p. 3).

wasted his fortune, run him into debt, and lost him his credit and trade. He was forced to turn to the quarter sessions bench for relief and still struggled to keep himself on the post of under-mace-bearer to the mayor at £8 per annum, and then great-mace-bearer at £12 per annum. The claim also had wide cultural purchase. According to Daniel Defoe, "tis a common cry that is rais'd against the woman, when her husband miscarries, namely, that 'tis the wife has ruin'd him'.[81] The *Newcastle Courant* reported, in 1767, that 'many industrious Tradesmen are ruined, from the Extravagance of the Wife': the results of husbands' inability to prohibit their wives from contracting debts without their knowledge or consent.[82] The extravagant wife was such an easily recognisable female stereotype that she was used in the didactic lessons warning against the perils of excessive consumption, which were a common feature of the eighteenth century.[83]

In sum, men's economic position was more fragile than is sometimes assumed when it is compared to women's. Law and culture endowed men with superior economic status but, ironically, wives' economic activities and good credit status influenced their husbands' economic independence. It was undermined by wives' involvement in provisioning and commercial activities, so that the ideal of the male provisioner was as untenable in most seventeenth- and eighteenth-century families as was the concept of the male breadwinner in the nineteenth century.[84] Men's economic autonomy also depended upon their wives' good credit as much as their own. Work on the early modern credit system concludes that male credit depended upon both wider community trust and the individual reputations of the household.[85] However, men's credit did not just depend on their wives' sexual probity, or ability to spend their money wisely, it was also related to their wives' economic reputation. It is true that wives tended to be attributed status for their 'skill in controlling consumption' rather than their work in providing household resources.[86] Yet we have seen that this was contradicted in practice, and if men perceived their access to credit as providing 'independence and self-sufficient mastery' it is not implausible to propose that women's personal credit also accumulated from their own commercial activities.[87] The truth of men's allegations about their wives' extravagance and mismanagement might be questionable, given their desire to reduce the costs of alimony, but they confirm that men's fortunes were recognised to depend upon their wives' credit as much as their own.

[81] D. Defoe, *The Complete English Tradesman in Familiar Letters Directing him in all the Several Parts and Progressions of Trade*, 2nd edition, 2 vols. (London, 1727), Vol. I, p. 132.
[82] *N.Cour*, 3 January 1767, p. 2.
[83] For example, *GM*, 2 (1732), 753; 3 (1733), 645; 4 (1734), 130–1.
[84] E. Ross, '"Fierce questions and taunts": married life in working-class London, 1870–1914', *Feminist Studies*, 8, 3 (1982), 576.
[85] Finn, 'Women, consumption', 719–20; Muldrew, *Economy of Obligation*, pp. 148–59.
[86] D'Cruze, 'Care, diligence', 319.   [87] Shepard, 'Manhood, credit and patriarchy', 88.

Married men's credit was not just undermined by women's activities and their failure of reputation; it may have been contingent to some extent upon their goodwill.[88] For wives apparently recognised their ability to damage their husbands' financial status. The slater and plasterer Soloman Hall probably regretted the advert that he placed on 28 May 1774 denying credit to his absconded wife. Catherine Hall indignantly responded three weeks later, stating that he had turned her out and 'hath now got another Woman in my Place, by the Name of his House-keeper'. At the heart of her advert was a latent threat: 'as for People not trusting me, I think he might have let that alone till I had contracted any Debt – Such Usage was then a hidden Thing to me; but Time discovers many things'.[89] The phrasing in some husbands' adverts even implied that their eloped wives threatened to use the law of agency as if it were a weapon.[90] Occasionally men also alleged that their imprisonment for debt was due to their wives' spiteful actions. John Colston was unable to appear to respond to his wife's suit for separation for cruelty, in 1726, because he was in Kingston upon Hull gaol for debt. He had been committed over debts of £10 to his wife's brother and £40 to her son-in-law, which he eventually claimed were contracted by his wife who then got her relatives to bring actions against him for the sums.[91] One can only guess whether the wife of Thomas Truelove, a laceman, of Castlethorpe, Buckinghamshire, was deliberately acting against him. Imprisoned in Aylesbury gaol for debt in 1743, he produced a schedule of his estate and a list of his debtors. The amounts were inexact because, as it noted on the schedule, his account book was left in his house and 'as he verily believes taken away and conceal[e]d by Catherine Truelove his wife so as he can't come at ye sight of them'.[92]

MANAGING THE HOUSEHOLD

If spouses' activities in the household economy were not separate or gender-specific, those concerning household government were far more distinct. It is possible to glimpse the workings of the middling-sort household through the complaints about wives' management thereof, made in 6% of all the

---

[88] Muldrew makes this point, although he tends to stress that overall household reputation, rather than specifically male reputation, depended upon wives' honesty, modesty and fidelity (Muldrew, *Economy of Obligation*, p. 158).

[89] *JOJ*, 28 May 1774, p. 2; 18 June 1774, p. 3.

[90] For instance, *N.Cour*, 12 June 1731, p. 3, William Morrison's advert.

[91] It is feasible that she did engineer his imprisonment for debt in order to punish him, if her allegations that he was adulterous, violent and denying her maintenance were true (BIHR, CP.I/855, *Colston c. Colston*, 1726).

[92] The note ended with his request to refer himself to his wife, for her to give the best account she possibly could of the book of accounts and notes (CBS, QS Rolls 165/2, Schedule of estate of Thomas Truelove).

secondary complaints (Appendix 8). It was mainly wives who brought separations on the grounds of cruelty who made this complaint, and over
one-third included this grievance. They complained in their libels that their
husbands prevented them from governing the household, an act symbolised
by the removal of the household's keys, and/or by substituting a servant
in their place. Esther Bowes of Staindrop, County Durham, alleged that in
September 1717 her husband had publicly discharged her from 'acteing or
doeing any Matter or thing Relateing to the Managem[en]t of his House'.[93]
Men also portrayed women as bad wives, often in self-defence, by accusing
them of negligence in household duties and mothering (Appendix 8). John
Laughton responded to his wife's allegations of cruelty in 1721 by claiming
that her behaviour changed after her brother came to live with them for a
year. Amongst other characteristically bad behaviour, such as scolding, railing and exposing his circumstances, his wife became negligent in managing
the house and caring for their children.[94] In 1729 James Currie of Carlisle
claimed that his wife had not even shown 'natural and motherly affection' to
the children she had in her first marriage.[95] Moreover, it was not uncommon
in separation cases to demonstrate that wives failed in their other household
function of caring. When William Idelle's wife was supposed to keep him
company and comfort him during his illness, which confined him to bed, she
abused him with her tongue, and disturbed him by playing loudly upon her
violin and other musical instruments.[96]

Husbands' self-defences also often attempted to illustrate that their household followed the recommended model. In 1696 Robert Shaw smugly as-
serted that: 'Ann Shaw had her owne Will in the management of her said
House and was seldome or never contradicted or disturbed by her said
Husband'.[97] As this implies, the role was somewhat more than a deputising
one. The terms both men and women used – management, government and
command – convey power. People expected wives to command the household
without husbandly interference. Margaret Green, the Allensons' household
servant and carer for their children, for example, remarked disapprovingly
in 1676 that her mistress, Grace, worked like a servant and that Charles constantly enquired what she did.[98] On the one occasion when the management
of a household was represented in court as a struggle between a wife and
husband, it is noticeable that the mistress' orders were given greater weight.
Elizabeth Stephenson recalled Robert Shaw grumbling to her that 'it was a

[93] UOD, DDR/EJ/PRC/2/1717/2, *Bowes c. Bowes*, 1717.
[94] BIHR, CP.I/631, *Laughton c. Laughton*, 1721.
[95] BIHR, Trans.CP.1730/6, *Currie c. Currie*, 1729, James' personal response.
[96] BIHR, CP.I/154; CP.I/241; CP.I/2735, *Idelle c. Idelle*, 1706, John Idelle's deposition, 1707.
[97] BIHR, Trans.CP.1697/2; D/C.CP.1696/3, *Shaw c. Shaw*, 1696.
[98] BIHR, CP.H/3264, *Allenson c. Allenson*, 1675.

hard case that he cu'd have no sway in the management of his owne house'. However, this was due to her ignoring his order to buy a joint of meat at Selby market, instead following Ann Shaw's that she must not.[99]

Women's right to govern the household was promoted by advice for women and married couples, which in this respect altered little over the centuries in question. Hannah Woolley pointed out in her 1675 publication, *The Gentlewomans Companion*: 'To govern an House is an excellent and profitable employment; there is nothing more beautiful than an Houshold [*sic*] well and peaceably governed'.[100] In a popular work, first published in 1688, the Marquis of Halifax informed his married female reader that her duty was 'the Government of your House, Family, and Children', whereas the 'Oeconomy of the House' was indecent to a husband whose 'Province is without Doors'.[101] Thomas Gisborne's message at the end of the eighteenth century was identical: '[t]o superintend the various branches of domestic management, or, as St Paul briefly and emphatically expresses the same office, "to guide the house" is the indispensable duty of a married woman... The task must be executed either by the master or the mistress of the house: and reason and scripture concur in assigning it unequivocally to the latter.'[102] In one sense this literature was descriptive, for the matrimonial cases confirm that a domestic double-standard prevailed with husbands' involvement restricted to emergency situations like illness, their wives' lying-in, or periods of male unemployment.[103] Husbands did perceive themselves as undertaking domestic activities, but such were generally different, like 'making or repairing'.[104] There is little evidence here to support Alice Clark's theory that the pre-industrial household, in which productive work occurred, allowed many women to escape housekeeping.[105]

Invariably men were happy to leave the onerous and time-consuming jobs to their wives. Joseph Watson summed it up in his letter persuading his wife to return to him and their inn in Wolsingham, County Durham, after she left him in January 1799, unable to cope with his violence and adultery. He

[99] BIHR, Trans.CP.1697/2; D/C.CP.1696/3, *Shaw c. Shaw*, 1696.
[100] H. Woolley, *The Gentlewomans Companion; or, a Guide to the Female Sex: containing directions of behaviour, in all places, companies, relations, and conditions from their childhood down to old age* (London, 1675), p. 108.
[101] Halifax, *The Lady's New Year Gift: or, Advice to a Daughter* (1688) cited in V. Jones (ed.), *Women in the Eighteenth Century, Constructions of Femininity* (London, 1990), pp. 21, 22.
[102] Gisborne, *Duties of the Female Sex*, pp. 148–9.
[103] For emergencies when spouses swapped roles see Hufton, *The Prospect Before Her*, pp. 151–60; C. Davidson, *A Woman's Work is Never Done: A History of Housework in the British Isles 1650–1950* (London, 1982), p. 186; D'Cruze, 'Care, diligence', 322.
[104] Ben Shaw's comment on his contribution to his household and family (D'Cruze, 'Care, diligence', 322).
[105] Alice Clark, *Working Life*, p. 5.

griped, 'I wish as I all ways Did to leave to thy self and every thing Else that belongs to a woman as I do not like womans work but I am some what more acquainted with it then I wish'd to be.'[106] Women's household labours were many and varied and differed according to rank, life-cycle and urban or rural lifestyle. Nonetheless, wives typically managed or carried out the organisation of the household's contents, cleaning, cooking, preserving, washing, providing water and heating, producing clothes and household goods, making and dispensing medicine, nursing various family members, providing hospitality, and consumption.[107] The range of women's household governance was potentially extensive. Sarah Walton, of Lanchester, accused her husband in 1718 of hiring a married couple and delivering the keys of his house, chests and trunks to the female employee.[108] Information from instances when wives were accused of conveying away goods shows that such keys were access not just to the fabric of the household and its movable goods, but to financial papers, bonds, securities and cash.[109] These time-consuming responsibilities were additional to married women's bearing and raising children, and in many cases working for wages. Mary Collier's poem, of 1739, expressively explains what rural labouring women faced, after completing long hours of monotonous female work like charring, or during the harvest:

> We must make haste, for when we Home are come,
> Alas! we find our Work but just begun;
> So many Things for our Attendance call,
> Had we ten Hands, we could employ them all.
> Our Children put to Bed, with greatest Care
> We all Things for your coming Home prepare:
> You sup, and go to Bed without delay,
> And rest yourselves till the ensuing Day;
> While we, alas! but little Sleep can have,
> Because our froward children Cry and rave[110]

Given its pervasiveness in their lives, wives gained their sense of self-identity from organising and caring for their households and families, as well as, despite what many historians would have us believe, from their occupational identity. All were essential jobs from which they derived pride and status.[111] *The Ladies Dictionary* of 1694 declared:

[106] UOD, DDR/EJ/CCD/3/1801/15, *Watson v Watson*, 1801, Letter presented as exhibit C.

[107] See C. Hole, *The English Housewife in the Seventeenth Century* (London, 1953); Davidson, *A Woman's Work*; Vickery, *Gentleman's Daughter*, chapter 4; D'Cruze, 'Care, diligence', 323.

[108] UOD, DDR/EJ/PRC/2/1718/3, *Walton c. Walton*.   [109] See chapter 5, pp. 99, 101–2.

[110] *The Woman's Labour: an Epistle to Mr Stephen Duck in answer to his late Poem, called The Thresher's Labour* in Jones, *Women*, pp. 154–8.

[111] G. Walker, 'Expanding the boundaries'.

Keeping a house well ordered, and the family affairs well managed and regulated, is no such easy matter as some ladies imagine it and therefore there is a great reputation to be gained in the prudent performance and discharge of such a care and trust, more especially incumbent on those that are entered into a married state; for it not only turns to advantage but procures a true respect and esteem.[112]

On the other hand, men's reputation derived in part from not working in the household and not interfering in their wives' jobs, for it was undermined by their unnecessary intervention in household affairs. Jane Ballantine, the 30-year-old friend of James and Jane Currie, warned James that his removal of household command from his wife was a 'usage...too cruel and unbecoming a Husband'. This criticism was not gender-specific, or due to any sense of female solidarity. The Curries' 64-year-old neighbour John Twentyman told James that he must turn away his servant, who now held the keys, 'for that it was a reproach and scandal to live in the manner yt He did with his wife'. James realised that his reputation was threatened, because he accused his wife of traducing and blackening his name amongst his neighbours by reporting that he had taken the keys from her.[113]

Household management also provided women with a sense of superiority over their husbands. This can be glimpsed in popular literature, which satirised relationships between the sexes. In 1732 the *Gentleman's Magazine* printed a poem called 'The Pig: A Tale', in which a group of husbands who were drinking together began competing to claim the most obedient wife. One of the drinkers wagered that none of their wives were obedient, and devised a test to prove his theory. Each husband was to send a message to his wife that he wanted to invite his friends to dine on a boiled pig that evening. The wives all failed, each in a different manner, but in ways that preserved their own territory, authority and superior female knowledge. The financially independent wife refused to listen to the message; when the worldly wife heard that food was to be prepared she asked: 'Sir, do you take me for your cook?' The wife known for housewifery would only roast the pig, commenting 'I hope you'll give me leave to know / My business better, sir than so.' The wife who had a 'spirit brook'd not to obey' rebuffed the request saying

> The Kitchen is the proper sphere,
> Where none but females should appear,
> And cooks their orders, by your leave,
> Always from mistresses receive.

---

[112] Quoted in N. H. Keeble (ed.), *The Cultural Identity of Seventeenth-Century Woman: A Reader* (London, 1994), p. 190.

[113] BIHR, Trans.CP.1730/6, *Currie c. Currie*, 1729.

The mild wife answered that she would freely boil the pig if he would 'Prove but that ever woman did it', and the plain wife, unused to refusing her lord's commands, agreed to boil a pig, 'to hinder squabble', but refused to eat it herself.[114] No doubt, women's sense of indispensability and their recognition that men were dependent upon them helped make patriarchy bearable.

Women felt that the removal of this integral feature of their lives represented physical and emotional cruelty in a number of ways. It was an injury to their self-identity and public reputation. Perhaps, considering some of the words used to describe the function, like 'trust' and 'care', it also symbolised that their husbands no longer trusted or loved them. This was explicitly intended in a couple of cases when husbands committed the care of household affairs to their mistress. For example, in 1720 when Elizabeth Mills had her husband bound over for beating her, she also complained that he 'gave the trust of all the keys belonging to this Informant to Margaret Hall' with whom William Mills was having an affair.[115] The elevation of servants also denied women their social status. After all, the control of servants was an undisputed source of authority for middling-sort married women.[116] As Anne Bowness stated in 1745, her husband made her wait upon their maid 'in order to Insult and affront' her.[117] In extreme cases this became an act of physical abuse, because in addition to instructing their servants not to obey their wives, men allegedly ordered them to insult their spouses verbally or show physical disrespect by spitting or hitting.[118] The extent to which this represented excessive disorder in household government was symbolised by the few wives who alleged that their husbands conspired with their servants to injure them. Some wives worried about being murdered, and one believed that plans were afoot to drive her mad in order to confine her in a madhouse.[119]

The question that usually follows analyses of married women's unpaid work in the household is whether it supplied them with any authority. It is easier to see the power that was attributed to this role in negative ways. For example, women's control of the household could be viewed as providing dangerous freedoms. Mary Greenwood apparently persuaded her ill husband to go to Matlock for his health for a month, and arranged for her lover, John's saddler, to sleep every night in the house under the auspices of guarding it

[114] GM, 3 (1733), 375–6.
[115] NCAS, QSB/54, fol. 39. See also BIHR, CP.H/3230; CP.H/4662, Currer c. Currer, 1673.
[116] Servants were used to threaten wives' gender and class identity in nineteenth-century marriage breakdown (Hammerton, Cruelty and Companionship, p. 116).
[117] UOD, DDR/EJ/CCD/3/1745/1, EJ/PRC/2/1745/5, Bowness c. Bowness.
[118] For example, BIHR, CP.I/88, Greaves c. Greaves, 1704.
[119] CBS, Q/SO/24, Catherine King's Article of the Peace, 1796; UOD, DDR/EJ/CCD/3/1773/3 and DDR/EJ/PRC/2/1773/4, Greenwell c. Greenwell.

from intruders. The control of servants had similar potential. Susannah Carr convinced her husband to go away for his health in June 1796 and during his absence sent their servants off to a play starring Mrs Siddons and entertained her lover at home.[120]

The most negative sign that wives' activities carried some degree of power was that their roles in provisioning and preparing food were culturally associated with poisoning, seen as a 'female' crime. In a couple of separation cases wives were accused of attempted poisoning (Appendix 8) and they were occasionally brought before the quarter sessions for that reason. Though rare in reality, female poisoning conveyed powerful messages about female empowerment.[121] Laura Gowing argues that female poisoning, unlike male violence, 'had nothing to do with the establishment, or abuse, of hierarchical household power'.[122] Yet it did represent power, simply female rather than male. James Currie's three physicians were sceptical about his belief that his wife was trying to poison him during his illness. Discussing the circumstances at one of their shops in Carlisle, they humorously agreed that they would have little credit of their patient, unless they could cure him of a bad wife, and attributed his distemper to grief and family problems. Whatever the physicians thought, James was undeniably frightened of his wife. His farrier, David Saul, recalled a visit with him at Christmas, 1728, during which Jane brought her husband a posset. James ate a little and then put his finger to his lips, 'and bringing something upon the End of his Finger said Here is a Spider, I am ruin'd I am poisoned'. David persuaded James to eat a little more because his notion was fanciful, but he still vomited later.[123] Women must have recognised their potential to exercise power in the household since they sometimes withheld their work in order to resist what they felt to be unreasonable husbandly behaviour.[124]

Another way to assess the degree of power that women held is to consider the extent to which other people relied upon them. It is no exaggeration to describe women as the social infrastructure of seventeenth- and eighteenth-century England. That might not confer formal authority, but,

---

[120] BIHR, CP.I/2486, *Greenwood c. Greenwood*, 1796; BIHR, Cons.CP.1800/1; CP.I/2569–2571, *Carr c. Carr*, 1800.

[121] G. Robb, 'Circe in Crinoline: Domestic Poisonings in Victorian England', *Journal of Family History*, 22, 2 (1997), 179–80, 186–7.

[122] Gowing, *Domestic Dangers*, pp. 228–9.

[123] BIHR, Trans.CP.1730/6, *Currie c. Currie*, 1729. Mary Huthart, his thirty-year-old spinster niece, to whom he gave charge of the house instead of his wife, supported the allegations. She said he was skeletal since marrying, and that Jane occasionally put white powder in his food.

[124] When Lady Sarah Cowper did this she was rewarded by her husband asking her to return to her role as housekeeper and promising to behave better (Kugler, 'Constructing wifely identity').

as the complaints about household management illustrate, it meant that husbands' dependence upon their wives was considerable. It is significant that it was middling-sort women in households with a female servant who complained that their husbands had prevented them from managing the household. In effect, the sheer extent and intensity of women's household government meant that its denial could only occur when husbands had a substitute for their wives. They gave household government to their servant as if replacing their wives with a version over whom they had a more clearly drawn authority. Though men of lower ranks also needed their wives in the same way, they did not have a ready alternative for their wives in the shape of a servant.[125] Gentry concerns were slightly different. Elite wives held a supervisory position in households that had a greater number of servants. Consequently their struggles over household management were about the authority held over types of servants. William Ettrick complained in his personal answer to his wife's libel in 1765 that Catherine interfered in his dealings with servants, tenants and work-people. On those occasions 'he always told her to dictate to her Maids that was her Province the other his'.[126] Anne Kugler observes that 'the main bone of contention' between the unhappily married Lady Sarah and Sir William Cowper was household power and especially authority over servants. In Sarah's opinion, not only did her husband withhold household management from her, he was inadequate at controlling their servants.[127]

CONCLUSION: MARITAL CO-DEPENDENCY

The everyday life of a household was a demanding one. Each day brought the pressures of feeding a household, caring for family members' needs, attempting to ensure their physical well-being and managing incomings and outgoings, all with an eye to preserving social and economic status. Some of these activities varied in the detail according to the local economy, occupation, level of income, size of residence and number of children. Nonetheless, in the majority of marriages, these demands involved both spouses' work and led to a marital relationship of co-dependency. Co-dependency manifested itself in several ways. Both spouses engaged in provisioning and consumption. In contrast, wives organised and controlled the household, with men participating little in those activities deemed domestic. As a result, men were dependent upon their wives for the everyday running of the household and

---

[125] In times of crisis, lower-ranking men usually relied upon the assistance of female relatives to run the household.
[126] BIHR, Trans.CP.1765/4, *Ettrick c. Ettrick.*
[127] Kugler, 'Constructing wifely identity', 309.

child care. Wives and husbands obtained many elements of their self-identity and public reputation, and even a sense of superiority, from marriage and the household. However, the positions of both were unstable and dependent on each other's goodwill. As the next chapter demonstrates, spouses' material contributions in marriage and perceptions about the ownership of property within matrimony deepened and complicated marital co-dependency.

5

'With all my worldly goods I thee endow': spouses' contributions and possessions within marriage

MATERIAL CONTRIBUTIONS TO MARRIAGE

Women made their first major material contribution when they entered marriage. All women except the vagrant poor brought a portion to their union.[1] The portion, which was also commonly referred to as a fortune, varied in size from a tiny accumulation of ready cash or household goods to thousands of pounds in bonds, securities and mortgages and many acres of land. Details about wives' portions were given in fifty instances of marital difficulties.[2] Most of the detailed descriptions of portions were contained in church court separation suits, where the type of personal or real property was briefly outlined and given a value and/or its annual income was estimated.[3] Nearly two-thirds of the fifty couples fall within the wealthiest social groups in this book and include its few gentry and titled married folk. Still, the portions of women lower down the social scale can be glimpsed, usually through the quarter sessions records. Ann Tomlinson married a Northumberland weaver in the early eighteenth century. A widow, she brought thirteen head of beasts, household goods to the value of £20 and £3 10s per annum dower.[4]

The values of portions can be broadly correlated with social status. Amy Erickson analysed the value of early modern portions and found that women from the upper gentry and the lowest order of the titled aristocracy had portions between £1,000 and £5,000; those from the county gentry £100 to £1,000; those from the ranks of clergymen, merchants and wealthy yeomen and tradesmen £100 to £500; from prosperous yeomen, tradesmen and craftsmen £50 to £100; and husbandmen's daughters had between £10 and

---

[1] Erickson, *Women and Property*, p. 85.
[2] This information was included in separation and restitution suits, wives' petitions to the quarter sessions justices for maintenance, wives' and parishes' requests that men's goods be seized to support their families, and a few advertisements.
[3] Real property was land, personal property movable goods.
[4] NCAS, QSB/50, fol. 57.

£15 and labourers' daughters £1 to £5.[5] The portions documented in the records of marital difficulties fit fairly well with the values that Erickson noted for the four lower social ranks, even though they are from a later period. Given the later date, however, and inflation of portions, wealthy manufacturers and professionals appeared in the 'county gentry' category, many of whom were in Erickson's highest bracket, and some titled couples exceeded the upper limit that she described.[6] The value of portions was not always given. It was simply stated, for instance, that Eleanor Weald, the wife of a husbandman in Oxfordshire, brought a 'considerable fortune'.[7]

The law of coverture took immediate effect on the property women brought to matrimony unless it was protected by separate estate. Husbands owned their wives' personal property (movable goods) outright, their lease-hold land for the duration of the marriage (unless husbands had already disposed of it, it reverted to wives at their husbands' death), and received the profits from their wives' freehold and copyhold land, although they were un-able to dispose of it without their wives' consent.[8] Given this legal context, it is easy to view portions as the means by which husbands entered business, stabilised an existing concern, paid debts and, in some cases, made their fortune.[9] This has some truth. In the 1750s the gentleman William Ettrick used his wife's portion to pay off £2,000 from the mortgage on his mansion at High Barnes, County Durham.[10] Sir Peter Vavasour subsisted on his wife's portion (either £1,000 or £2,000, depending upon which of their claims was correct) until he inherited his father's estate.[11] Lower down the social scale Henry Giles bought a house in the 1740s at Slaley in Northumberland cost-ing £130, partly funding it with his wife's £50 portion, and in the first quarter of the eighteenth century Anthony Storey bought several messuages, lands and tenements in the township of Coundon, County Durham, with part of his wife's portion.[12]

Some men ended courtship if their future bride's financial status was not what they anticipated. Elizabeth Dodshon of Durham City sued Thomas Haswell of Pittington, in 1727, for failing to honour the declaration he made at two Quaker meetings that he intended to marry her. Thomas had courted

---

[5] Erickson, *Women and Property*, pp. 86–9. Also O'Hara, *Courtship and Constraint*, pp. 205–6.

[6] For inflation see O'Hara, *Courtship and Constraint*, pp. 190–2, 207–11.

[7] OA, QS/1697/Ep/6.   [8] Erickson, *Women and Property*, pp. 25–6.

[9] Male diarists, for example, were prone to describing wives in terms of the size of their portions (ibid., pp. 89–90).

[10] BIHR, *Ettrick c. Ettrick*, CP.I/1543, Allegation and exhibits in proof of the allegation of faculties, 1766.

[11] BIHR, CP.I/458, CP.I/661–2, *Vavasour c. Vavasour*, 1715.

[12] UOD, DDR/EJ/PRC/2/1744/11, *Giles c. Giles*; DRO, Q/S/OB/8, p. 461, Petition by Sunder-land churchwardens and overseers, 4 October 1727.

Elizabeth, a widow, in the belief that she was a person of good substance, with enough effects to pay her debts, make a portion for her children, and still have a considerable overplus. Quaker practice permitted the accounts of prospective marriage partners to be examined by an appointed committee, who discovered that Elizabeth was in great debt. Thus Thomas immediately withdrew from the relationship. Apparently Elizabeth absconded to London to escape her creditors and set up a boarding house to raise money.[13] Yet monetary motivations for marriage were increasingly criticised in this period and men were reluctant to give the impression that they had married just for gain.[14] James and Jane Anderson went so far as to place an advert in 1768 to counter gossip that he had left her because he had expected more with her at marriage, or had wasted what she brought him. Explaining that the rumours disadvantaged his character, James set the record straight by explaining that Jane, a housekeeper, was possessed by 'melancholy Apprehensions about the State of her Soul' at marriage. When all his attempts to help her with argument from scripture, reason, prayers, tears and advice failed, he had given her leave to stay with any of her friends. James pointed out that they would confirm his account. He ended by declaring that if Jane were 'not likely to recover, [I] will deliver every Thing she brought me that she can call hers; and if it please God to recover her, will receive her again with every Degree of Love and Tendernesse, if all she has should be spent'.[15]

As Amy Erickson points out, focusing on husbands' economic gains at marriage through their wives' portions is one-sided, because it ignores women's involvement as brides and brides' mothers in the financial arrangements of unions and men's material contributions to matrimony.[16] Some of the wives for whom portions can be identified had them organised by their parents and were invariably from gentry or titled families. Sixteen women (just under one third), however, were widows at marriage and no doubt heavily involved in organising the property that they supplied. Even those whose settlement was organised by a parent would act if its conditions were not fulfilled. Elizabeth Pighell's letter in the late 1690s to the Archbishop of York shows her efforts to ensure that she received the proper return for her £500 portion, which had been arranged by her father. She appealed that the Archbishop refuse to grant her husband, the rector of Patterington, a licence to be non-resident in his rectory, as she believed his request was made in order to abscond and

---

[13] UOD, DDR/EJ/PRC/2/1727/4, *Dodshon c. Haswell*.

[14] For an examination of this discourse see I. H. Tague, 'Love, honor, and obedience: fashionable women and the discourse of marriage in the early eighteenth century', *Journal of British Studies*, 40 (2001), 76–106.

[15] Jane Anderson confirmed her husband's account in a second part to the advert (*N.Jour*, 4–11 June 1768, p. 2).

[16] Erickson, *Women and Property*, pp. 93–4.

evade a bill that she had preferred in Chancery to compel him to arrange her jointure.[17]

It is possible to consider the relative value of male and female contributions to wedlock. In some of the suits calculations were made of husbands' annual income from various forms of land holding, occupation and inheritances, the estimated annual value of the house in which they lived, and the value of their personal property in terms of household goods, tools, livestock, ready cash, and money lent out and the interest it achieved. Wives' earnings from an occupation were not stated and only the value of property is considered in the following discussion. This type of evidence is problematic. Wives often provided details when they attempted to gain alimony during a court case, or to achieve maintenance in separation, and it was in their interests to over-estimate the value of their husbands' income and personal estate, since alimony was determined by husbands' means.[18] According to an information contained in one separation suit on the grounds of cruelty in 1779, which cited various legal authorities, alimony should be one third of the husband's estate, beginning on the date of the primary citation.[19] In turn, husbands rejected the calculations of their personal property and income, often specifying much lower amounts, and sometimes claiming that they had received smaller portions with their wives, or failed to get full payment. One of the most extreme disparities can be seen in the cruelty separation case brought by Martha Brooke against her husband Timothy, in 1683. Martha claimed that she brought £200 to the marriage, and that her husband earned £100 annually from real estate and possessed a personal estate worth £500. While Timothy agreed about her portion's value, he denied that he had any real estate at all, and claimed that his personal estate only amounted to £4 10s after deductions of debts. Probably the deponents were most accurate; they estimated that his real estate raised between £60 and £80 per annum.[20] In most cases, however, the figures are useful because the proportions of the wives' portions to the value of their husbands' property remain similar, whether at their highest or lowest estimates.

It is not always easy to determine relative values because of the process by which estimates were made. The union of Jonathan Bowes, a farmer of County Durham, with Elizabeth, in 1712, brought him household goods, livestock, corn, hay, a farm, and land held by lease for a further nineteen years. Her contribution was calculated by multiplying her yearly rent from the leased land of £20 by the years it had to run, plus the value of the goods. This meant that she brought £645 5s to marriage, in addition to a freehold estate worth £8 per annum. At the time of marriage Jonathan

[17] BIHR, CP.H/4505, *Pighells* c. *Pighells*, 1697.
[18] Stone, *Divorce*, p. 210.   [19] BIHR, Trans.CP.1779/1, *Finch* c. *Finch*.
[20] BIHR, CP.H/3516, *Brooke* c. *Brooke*, 1683.

had a freehold estate worth £48 per annum.[21] In general, however, a large disparity between spouses' contributions to marriage was fairly uncommon. In three instances wives' portions were substantially less than their husband's worth, and when a few husbands were worth considerably less than their wives it was unusual enough to be remarked upon.[22] The seventh article of Elizabeth Stradling's libel outlining her cruelty separation case against her husband Thomas in 1713 specifically stated that he had no fortune or substance at marriage, and that all the estate in lands had come to him by her. A childless widow, she brought a fortune of £1,900 to their union, plus land that Thomas was renting to farmers.[23] Even when the sums were not equal, the gap was usually much closer. For instance, Richard Harding already had an annuity of £70 secured to him during his life when he came into possession of a freehold estate of the yearly value of £40 at marriage in 1737.[24] In many cases wives contributed a sum at marriage that was equivalent to their husbands' personal estate, and occasionally an annuity from land of similar value to their husbands' income. In the later seventeenth century both Elizabeth Day's portion and her husband's personal estate were valued at £100.[25] Barbara Dobby brought £95 worth of household goods and money, while she calculated that her husband was worth £100 in personal estate and £36 per annum.[26] Similarly, using evidence from early modern women's writings and the practice of bequeathing equivalent amounts of property to daughters and younger sons, Erickson concluded that 'it was always the case that the groom's fortune had to be of comparable value to the bride's'.[27]

Legal and informal descriptions of women's portions kept them separate from the estimate of their husbands' worth, regardless of the fact that they came under men's ownership or control at marriage. This emphasises that husbands were recognised to make a contribution on entering matrimony, but was primarily to illustrate wives' input in comparison with their husbands'. This was influenced by a relationship between women's portions and their maintenance during widowhood and/or marriage.[28] One aspect of the link is apparent in the way that a wife's portion was used to provide an income or jointure for her in life or widowhood. It is most obvious in the marriage settlements of wealthy couples. Thus in consideration of Mary Manwaring's hefty portion of £4,500 in 1745, her marriage settlement

---

[21] UOD, DDR/EJ/PRC/2/1717/2, *Bowes c. Bowes*.

[22] For instance, Hooker Barttelot explained that, despite his considerable estates in Kent, his wife only brought £500 (BIHR, CP.I/2366, *Barttelot c. Barttelot*, 1793).

[23] He claimed he did have an estate at marriage, although he did not give its value (BIHR, CP.I/291, *Stradling c. Stradling*, 1713).

[24] UOD, DDR/EJ/PRC/2/1742/5, *Harding c. Harding*.

[25] BIHR, D/C.CP.1699/1, *Day c. Day*.   [26] BIHR, CP.I/581, *Dobby c. Dobby*, 1719.

[27] Erickson, *Women and Property*, pp. 91–2.   [28] Ibid., p. 100.

stipulated that a dower or jointure of lands be settled upon her at a yearly income of £307.[29] There were numerous ways to organise such provision. The woman's cash portion was often used to purchase land to provide the annuity.[30] Some of the other ways to do so are illustrated by Elizabeth Pighell's complaint to the Archbishop of York that her husband was failing to make provision for her. Originally, John Pighells was supposed to settle lands on her of the yearly value of £30 for her widowhood in return for the portion her father supplied. Instead John promised to make provision out of Mr Appleyard's estate for money that Appleyard had of him. When he did not follow this through either, he gave a bond to one of Elizabeth's relations promising that he would pay £70 yearly during his life into the trustee's hands, to be put out at interest to provide for her future maintenance. Despite the bond's £500 penalty John was not paying the annual sum, so that Elizabeth presented a bill at Chancery, in the attempt to force him to fulfil his obligations.[31] A portion might be used to secure an income in addition to jointure. For example, Margaret Lees brought £500 to her marriage with James Lees, a cotton manufacturer in Saddleworth, at the close of the eighteenth century. It was settled for the duration of her life in widowhood, and at her death was to go to the issue of the marriage. If the couple had no surviving children, it would be paid to her in widowhood; if James survived her it was subject to her disposition, and in default it went to her kin. This arrangement was secured on a small real estate of James' and was additional to any dower or jointure that she might receive. In effect, James did not own the £500, though he could manage the sum, invest it and enjoy its profits.[32]

The records of marital difficulties offer several examples of such provision being arranged for women of more modest means. Mary Giles brought a portion of £50 to her marriage in 1741 and had a jointure of £4 10s settled upon her on an estate called the Bush, which generated a yearly income of £6 10s.[33] Erickson brought to our attention the fact that ordinary women organised marriage settlements in simple forms, where husbands entered bonds obliging them to pay the inheritance of children from a previous marriage, to pay wives a specified sum at their death, or to pay a third party a sum of money for their wives' use.[34] A slightly less equitable version was negotiated between Jane and Charles Allison. Their expectations clashed

[29] BIHR, Trans.CP.1766/2, *Manwaring c. Manwaring*, 1761.
[30] The terms were set in a pre-marital settlement with a trust to protect the annuity, as it would otherwise be lost under coverture (Erickson, *Women and Property*, pp. 25–6).
[31] BIHR, CP.H/4505, *Pighells c. Pighells*, 1697.
[32] BIHR, Chanc.CP.1803/3, *Lees c. Lees*.
[33] UOD, DDR/EJ/PRC/2/1744/11, *Giles c. Giles*, Allegation of faculties, 2 November 1744.
[34] Erickson, *Women and Property*, pp. 129–30.

over the money that Jane brought to marriage in 1764. Charles expected her to bring a portion of £85, but discovered that its constituent parts, debts and securities for money due to Jane, had been made payable to her brother William Stokeld, presumably to prevent Charles gaining control of the sums. Consequently, Charles filed a bill in Chancery against his brother-in-law. Learning this, Jane was forced to have the securities for money delivered to him, and thereafter all moneys due were paid to him. Nonetheless, Jane persisted and succeeded in having Charles enter a bond to pay £85 to William Stokeld after her death.[35] It is not clear what was meant to happen to the sum if she survived Charles: whether it was intended as a jointure or not; nevertheless, even if Jane failed to keep the money for her own use during marriage or widowhood, she did ensure that it would return to her natal family.[36]

A direct connection between male provision and female portions was also frequently expressed in attempts to gain maintenance for wives. Parishes equated the two when they sought an order from the magistrates' bench to allow them to seize the goods or rents of husbands to maintain their wives and children. They usually began such requests by outlining what the wives had brought to the union. An entry in Durham Quarter Sessions order book in October 1735 first recorded that Anthony Burn had 'a considerable fortune' with Elizabeth, a widow, at matrimony, before going on to state that he would still not maintain his family after having had his goods seized the previous year.[37] Wives who petitioned the quarter sessions about their husbands' refusal to maintain them also commonly began by stating what they brought to marriage. Elizabeth Hilton, of Bishop Wearmouth, County Durham, explained in 1679 that her violent husband had turned her and one of their children out of the house, leaving another two children to themselves without maintenance, and emphasised that he would not allow them anything despite having gained a portion with her of £150.[38] In 1673 Anne Foster, of Startforth, York, petitioned that her husband had received £100 with her (described here as a competent portion), but had left her and their two children in a poor and deplorable condition.[39] Mary Giles made

---

[35] UOD, DDR/EJ/CCD/3/1765/2, *Allison c. Allison.*

[36] If a husband converted his wife's *choses* in action into money it became his property and was treated like personal property after her decease. It was only if he permitted her to make a will that she could pass on this property after her death; otherwise it remained her husband's to the exclusion of her children or family (Holcombe, *Wives and Property*, pp. 22–5).

[37] DRO, Q/S/OB/9, pp. 98–9; for more of their marital conflict see UOD, DDR/EJ/PRC/2/1736/3, *Burne c. Burne.*

[38] DRO, Q/S/OB/6. The court ordered that she get the yearly profit from his real estate, which made £45 per annum.

[39] The greater part of the portion remained in the hands of her father-in-law. He was ordered to pay 12d a week to maintain his son's family (J. C. Atkinson (ed.), *The North Riding Record Society, Quarter Sessions Records* (London, 1888), Vol. VI, p. 182).

a connection between her contribution at marriage and her husband's financial obligations to her children from a previous union in her advert in the *Newcastle Journal* in 1744. She declared 'that upon Marriage she paid to her said Husband a competent Fortune, in consideration whereof he, by Articles, agreed to secure her two Children the Fortune left them by her late husband'.[40] These examples indicate that, for many couples, husbands' and wives' resources were intended to be pooled for the duration of wedlock for the best interests of them and their children.

This economic interdependency was strengthened by married women's material contributions to the household economy throughout wedlock in the form of unpaid work in family crafts, trades, shops and farms, and paid work carried out both in and outside the home. The records of marital difficulties allow some features of women's work to be reconstructed in 234 instances. The variety of sources provides a somewhat biased picture. Much of the information is derived from the descriptions of the marital conflict, rather than occupational labels. Inevitably, the range and scope of women's work makes the task of categorising and recovering it particularly difficult. Their employment in a variety of agricultural and manufacturing processes, trades and service industries fluctuated according to the level of skill or capital required, and through the exclusion or inclusion of female labour according to regionalisation, specialisation, professionalisation and industrialisation.[41] Nonetheless, women's work was marked by continuities. Firstly, a marked sexual division of labour existed. Secondly, they were paid less than men and accorded less status. Thirdly, most women's work fell within the typical 'female categories' of domestic service, retailing (especially of food and drink), making clothes, charring and washing, and nursing.

The range of female employment described in the records of marital difficulties confirms the extent to which women's working lives were determined by their life-course, shifting according to their marital status: single, married or widowed.[42] Thus, most of the single women were servants. Married women's work, which can be glimpsed in fifty cases, fitted round the demands of pregnancy, nursing, child-rearing and household labour. Their activities included taking in lodgers and wet-nursing, convenient alongside raising children, and midwifery, which suited older women who had fewer dependent children. Other work like washing, keeping shops, alehouses, public houses and inns could be started and stopped according to need. A humorous account in the *Newcastle Chronicle* in 1764 captures the versatility and scope

---

[40] *N.Jour*, 2 June 1744.

[41] For an overview of female employment, see Shoemaker, *Gender*, pp. 145–208.

[42] The nature of the cases produces large numbers of unmarried domestic servants, because they had an important function as witnesses; and since children were often involved, particularly in office adultery cases, midwives and wet-nurses regularly appear.

of women's work. In it a husband complained that his wife was so religious that she neglected her 'Domestic concerns'. This term nicely demonstrates that, while wives were described in domestic and familial terms, this did not preclude other types of work, for the husband bemoaned the loss of his wife's shop-keeping along with her household management and child care.[43]

Forty-one examples of wives' work also record their husbands' occupation (Appendix 21). Albeit on a very small scale, this makes it possible to reflect upon the question of how far wives and husbands shared the same employment, which is sometimes used as an indicator of the quality of married life. Determining the extent to which couples' work was related is not straightforward. Firstly, the use of broad all-inclusive titles like 'gentleman', 'yeoman' and 'labourer' mask the specific occupations of many men.[44]

Secondly, social status played a significant role, as highlighted by Peter Earle's influential study of women's employment between 1695 and 1725.[45] The London consistory court asked female witnesses how they got their living and were maintained. Analysing their responses, Earle found that 256 of the 427 married women stated that they were employed. He categorised 139 of them as wholly maintained by their own employment and 117 as partly maintained by their own work. Only 26 of the working wives stated that they worked with their husbands. The extent of their employment was determined by their social status, because the fully employed wives who worked separately from their husbands in Earle's study were the poorest of the sample, which was already biased towards female artisans and working-class women. From the 41 couples in this book's sample, many of the 23 wives who seem to have worked separately from their husbands were also of modest means. For example, a labourer's wife washed linen, and three other washer-women were married to a husbandman, a cordwainer and a tailor, respectively. Significantly, none of these male occupations guaranteed a regular or substantial income, and the last two did not make use of female assistance. Poorer men's occupations were far more varied than their job title might indicate. Those who participated in other tasks to supplement their household income often continued to use their primary employment as their job title, disguising whether any of their activities were related to their wives' work. Nonetheless, being less wealthy did not guarantee that spouses worked separately, since the mobile poor sometimes carried out the same work; in one case both spouses sold ballads.

---

[43] N.Chron, 8 September 1764.

[44] For an example of the difficulties in categorising male occupations according to wealth and status, see Weatherill, Consumer Behaviour, p. 100.

[45] P. Earle, 'The female labour market in London in the late seventeenth and early eighteenth centuries', Economic History Review, 2nd series, 42, 3 (1989), 328–53.

Thirdly, definitions of related work can be a matter of opinion. It is debatable perhaps how to categorise the work of wives of agricultural labourers who maintained a vegetable plot to provide for the family.

One repercussion of Earle's conclusions is the assumption that the other 40% (171) of the wives in his study, who did not profess to wholly or partly maintaining themselves, had no paid employment.[46] Most of them were married to men of better incomes; as he comments, '[n]o woman whose husband was described as a master said that she worked for her living. The same holds true for the wives of most of the gentlemen, the professionals, the more skilled artisans and the more distinguished and better paid generally.'[47] The records of marital difficulties show, however, that it is unwise to assume that such wives either did not work at all, or did not work in a field related to their husband's occupation. For example, a wife was often involved in her husband's work during his absence. This occurred across the social divide. Elizabeth Seardison was handed the keys and money of the public house owned by her husband (whose job title was recorded as 'miller') when he went away on business.[48] Elite women, as Linda Pollock has demonstrated, routinely ran their husbands' estates and business concerns in their absence.[49] When William Ettrick, justice of the peace, landowner in Sunderland and Bishop Wearmouth, collector of customs, and lender of considerable sums of money upon bottomry, took a lucrative post as a purser in the Royal Navy, he gave his pregnant wife power of attorney during his absence. Catherine Ettrick handled the rents from properties and land, repayments from debts, fees from ferry-crossings, and payment of various annuities, fines, repairs, taxes and tolls for four years. This became a point of dispute in her separation suit against him a few years later in 1765. She felt considerable pride at her 'careful Management and Frugality', which saved him £1,000 out of the rents of his estate. From this sum she gave him £650 on his return and with the remainder renewed a lease and paid several sums on his account. In addition she supported herself, their two children, their servants, and paid the rents of the two houses in town and country in which the family lived during his absence. Despite all her hard work, no doubt Catherine would describe herself as wholly maintained.[50]

At least 44% of the forty-one wives in this study worked, if not alongside their husbands, then in servicing the family concern. Susanna Rigby of Newport Pagnell provided her husband with lace to sell in London, collecting it from out-workers. She was knowledgeable enough to take up dealing in

[46] Ibid. 337–42.   [47] Ibid. 332, 338.
[48] BIHR, CP.I/1975, *Seardison c. Seardison*, 1785.   [49] Pollock, '"Teach her"'.
[50] Contrarily, William claimed that Catherine only raised £500 (from the duplicitous and callous sale of furniture, paintings, stock, crops and husbandry instruments, rather than expertise), did not pay his debts, and impoverished his land. Information contained throughout cause papers: see, for instance, BIHR, CP.I/1535, CP.I/1543, CP.I/1480, *Ettrick c. Ettrick*, 1765.

lace herself when he started wasting the money he received in payment.[51] As discussed above, the fact that spouses worked in related fields is not always apparent from the husband's title. The records reveal that men who were described respectively as a mason, a miller and a joiner also owned alehouses and public houses, in which their wives worked.[52] It is likely that the wives who let out rooms had husbands for whom this was the second string to their bow, like a flax-dresser whose house was used for flax-dressing and as a lodging house.[53] Wives of shopkeepers frequently dealt with retail sales. This was common practice, as one man made clear in his recollection of purchasing some cork from Joseph Avern's shop, when he commented that 'as his wife' Mary Avern received the money. As Margaret Hunt observes, these women would fall outside Earle's category of working wives because they were not earning money independently. Hunt also found that married women in trade-related activities often failed to define themselves as independent traders, instead using the title 'wife of', probably because the low status of women's work caused them to define themselves by their spouse's trade.[54]

The same hidden quality would apply to the numerous wives who kept accounts, and collected and paid debts on behalf of their husbands. Mary Hoggit, the wife of a Sunderland master mariner, explained in 1766 that when her husband went to sea she managed his quarterly payments on a sum borrowed to finance a ship. Furthermore, she paid the money not to the agent who had organised the debt, but to his wife.[55] There is even a tantalising hint that wives participated in their husbands' duties as parish officials. Robert Johnson, a husbandman and overseer of the poor in Hawksar, near Whitby, gave evidence in a bastardy case in 1751. He had persuaded John Harland to return home with a baby that he believed another man had fathered. Johnson explained that, when John returned a few days later during his absence, Mrs Johnson made the decision to put the child out to nurse.[56]

Identifying the working practices of spouses is helpful because historians have associated working conditions with the quality of the marital relationship. Several have suggested that working separately could cause

---

[51] CBS, QS Rolls Michaelmas 1755, examination.

[52] For example UOD, DDR/EJ/CCD/3/1801/15, *Watson c. Watson*. For the importance of wives in attracting and serving customers in the family tavern, inn or shop, see P. Earle, *The Making of the English Middle Class: Business, Society and Family Life in London, 1660–1730* (London, 1989), pp. 162–3.

[53] Samuel Hawkridge, information contained in BIHR, CP.I/1376, *Wentworth c. Wentworth*, 1756.

[54] M. Hunt, *The Middling Sort: Commerce, Gender, and the Family in England, 1680–1780* (Berkeley and London, 1996), pp. 128–9.

[55] BIHR, CP.I/1495, *Ettrick c. Ettrick*, 1765, Mary Hoggit's deposition, 18 November 1766. For other examples, see Hufton, *The Prospect Before Her*, pp. 149, 152, 162–3.

[56] NYA, QSB/1751, examination, 14 October 1751, MIC 137.

marital disharmony. In Alice Clark's 'Family Industry' model, the family was the unit for the production of goods, and wives actively contributed to their husband's trade, craft, shop or farm. The proceeds of work were the joint property of the family unit, which Clark argued provided women with greater status and independence. During the seventeenth century, capitalism pushed poorer wives into factory work and wealthier ones into idleness. Crucially, it denied married women access to the means of production and introduced individual wages rather than a household income, forcing wives into abject dependence on their husbands and bringing family members into conflict.[57] Alice Clark's chronology has been criticised and similar claims for working conditions have been made for other periods. John Tosh, in his study of the effects of domesticity upon nineteenth-century masculinity, proposes that 'friendship between spouses was more likely to be the by-product of a working partnership in the [pre-industrial] home', which was destabilised by the separation of home and work in the nineteenth century.[58] Anna Clark analysed the occupations of men charged with wife-beating in Lancaster between 1799 and 1835 and in Glasgow between 1813 and 1835. She found that artisans in traditional apprenticed trades (like carpenters, tailors and shoemakers) were over-represented in these cases compared to their proportion in the general population, whereas male textile workers were under-represented. She concludes that the separate work of artisan couples and the misogynist male artisan work culture caused marital tension. In contrast the shared tasks of textile workers and their wives created more harmonious relations based on economic partnership, and made men reluctant to damage their economic livelihood by abusing their wives and losing their valuable skills.[59]

The link between spouses' employment and the quality of the marital relationship is appealing but by no means proven. There is no reason to suppose that working together was less stressful than working apart, as anyone who has actually worked with a husband or wife will testify. Indeed the greater willingness of artisans' wives to prosecute their husbands that Anna Clark notices might have more to do with their greater freedom to seek formal assistance. It is as plausible that wives who worked alongside their husbands and whose income was indivisible from theirs, had less financial means and less opportunity to prosecute their abusive husbands.

The occupations of 246 wife-beaters were recorded in this study, though they are not comparable with Clark's figures (her tables 5 and 6).[60] Firstly, it is not possible to measure them against their proportions in the population, because this type of information is unreliable in the pre-census period, and,

[57] Alice Clark, *Working Life*, pp. 6–11, 294–8.   [58] Tosh, *A Man's Place*, pp. 25–6.
[59] Clark, *Struggle for the Breeches*, pp. 74, 87.   [60] Ibid., pp. 76–7.

crucially, because the bulk of wife-beating cases were dealt with by informal means or justices of the peace acting outside of sessions. Different regional specialisations and rates of industrialisation also make direct comparisons difficult. For example, wife-beaters in rural and agriculture-related occupations were quite common, a feature which stems from this book's inclusion of three predominantly rural counties. The counties examined had only small pockets of textile manufacture, thus only 1% of the men worked in this occupational sector. Indeed, the figures demonstrate that the relationship between wife-beaters and their occupations may simply reflect the sources used. For example, one third of the 246 wife-beaters in this book, for whom occupations can be identified, were tradesmen, craftsmen and retailers and another 16% were labourers (Appendix 22), because the bulk of the records providing information about wife-beaters comes from the records of the quarter sessions, which were primarily used by these social groups (Appendix 6). There are a higher proportion of wife-beaters who were professional, mercantile and gentlemen (13%) than in Clark's study, because the wife-beaters include those who were brought to the ecclesiastical courts for separation on the grounds of cruelty. The husbands in Clark's book appeared before the quarter sessions and police courts. The greater number of higher-status men therefore reflects the level of wealth needed to use the church courts, rather than an increased tendency for men of this social and occupational status to beat their wives in the northern and southern counties examined. Further, the prosecution of wife-beaters was influenced by the proximity of prosecutors and plaintiffs to a court or justice of the peace, as much as by the propensity of men with particular occupations to be any more or less conflictual. In sum, spouses' labour and earnings forged interdependence, but have no clear correlation with the quality of married life.

SPOUSES AND PROPERTY OWNERSHIP

Spouses' material contributions to marriage raise questions about their attitudes to movable goods and wealth while it endured. Some work on men's and women's wills proposes that their attitudes to the property that they owned were gendered and it is worth considering how this manifested itself within matrimony.[61] Women entered wedlock with a variety of cash and goods and they earned money in the course of married life, yet coverture transferred possession of both to their husbands. Middling-sort single women and widows had profound emotions about their possessions, and the gentlewoman Elizabeth Shackleton's diaries, written in both wedlock

[61] Berg, 'Women's consumption', 428.

and widowhood, demonstrate similarly strong feelings about her domestic artefacts.[62] The intensity of their feelings raises some questions. Did women switch on and off their emotions about possessions according to marital state? How far did men think about property in terms of coverture: did they adopt the concept of total possession over goods and cash or was there any complexity about the way they perceived them to be owned? The secondary complaints offer insights into these issues.

Men accused their wives of conveying away goods from the marital home in 15% of all the secondary complaints (Appendix 8). These grievances indicate that spouses' feelings of ownership were more multi-layered during wedlock than coverture might imply. Men from a wide range of occupations made the complaint. Few gave the goods they described a value as John Smith, wife-beater and Newcastle attorney, did in 1743. He valued at £50 the bed, bedding, linen and household furniture which his wife took when she left him.[63] This was a very considerable sum of money, given that an annual income of £40 gained inclusion in the lower reaches of the middling-sort. The discrepancy between the values of personal and real estate was not so pronounced in this period as later and both were fairly equivalent in value up to the mid eighteenth century.[64]

There is enough evidence to illustrate that, when wives removed property, they cost their husbands dearly, emphasising that economic interdependency had real meaning for husbands as well as wives. Husbands claimed that their wives' actions left them in difficulties. Samuel Finch wrote to his wife after she left him, resentful that when she removed goods she did not leave him with as much as a towel to dry himself with.[65] According to John Colston in 1726, his wife, with the help of her son-in-law, conveyed away his household goods, plate and linen while he was imprisoned for debt. As a result he had neither the goods nor effects that belonged to his wife before marriage, nor any estate of his own to subsist on; only a small allowance from his mother provided him with necessaries during imprisonment.[66] In 1768 Joseph Fleming, of Sunderland, advertised that after seven months of matrimony his wife had removed all the pewter, linen, a clock and things of value that she had supplied at marriage. Having 'taken all she could' out of the house, along with 'wronging' him of £80, she eloped leaving him in a 'distressed' condition.[67] The value of goods is also indicated by husbands' efforts to regain them. Henry Meadley offered a reward of one guinea for the brown gelding that his wife took in 1765.[68] The attorney John Ridgeway,

---

[62] Ibid., 420–7; Vickery, *Gentleman's Daughter*, pp. 183–94.
[63] UOD, DDR/EJ/PRC/2/1743/12, *Smith c. Smith*.
[64] Erickson, *Women and Property*, pp. 64–7.
[65] UOD, DDR/EJ/PRC/2/1779/3, Letter to Elizabeth dated 9 January 1779.
[66] BIHR, CP.I/855, *Colston c. Colston*, 1726.   [67] *N.Chron*, 4 February 1769, p. 3.
[68] *N.Chron*, 31 August 1765, p. 3.

of the Strand in London, announced in *Jackson's Oxford Journal* that he had revoked the power of attorney, which gave his wife the right to sell and dispose of his goods on his behalf and receive debts due to him. His advert also sought information about goods he believed she had disposed of for her own use, and offered a reward upon recovery at 12% of their value.[69] Husbands like Samuel Morgan, in 1778, also tried to redeem the goods their wives had pawned by requesting information about who had received the property.[70]

It is also possible to explore spouses' attitudes to ownership through the descriptions of wives' removal of goods and the types of goods themselves. Men's descriptions of the ownership of property varied. They generally described the act of conveying as taking away. Many accused their wives of removing their husbands' property. Thus in 1729 John Mercer announced that his wife had taken moneys belonging to him, in 1756 the blacksmith Thomas Tildlsey reported that his wife had removed his goods and moneys, and in 1785 Michael Foxton claimed that his wife had broken open his desk and removed gold and silver.[71] Some husbands neutrally claimed that their wives had removed household items, without ascribing possession to either themselves or their wives. Other husbands differentiated between their own and their wives' goods and the use of the possessive pronoun is frequent enough to rule out such incidents being accidental. According to her husband, a sail-cloth weaver in Yorkshire, Anne Selby took her clothes and all his shirts, silver spoons, several pairs of sheets and many other goods.[72] In 1729 James Currie complained that his wife conveyed away all her own clothes and wearing apparel, plate, linen, goods of value and papers, writings, securities and money, which were her own before marriage 'but also several goods which belonged to [him] before the said marriage'. Fifty years later, Samuel Finch observed that his wife had removed all that she brought to marriage except two tables, a clock and case, and an old tea-board, 'together with other goods and Linnen of considerable Value which belonged to and were in the Possession' of him before and at marriage.[73] A minority of husbands, however, described their wives' actions as 'plundering', 'robbing' or having 'stolen' items; one imaginatively commented that his wife had 'lavishingly, wantonly, and expensively made waste, pawned, destroyed and pledged' the goods.[74]

[69] *JOJ*, 12 January 1757, p. 2.   [70] *JOJ*, 24 October 1778, p. 2.
[71] *Y.Cour*, 13 March 1729; 20 July 1756; 4 January 1785.   [72] *Y.Cour*, 22 December 1761.
[73] BIHR, Trans.CP.1730/6, *Currie* c. *Currie*, Personal response; UOD, DDR/EJ/PRC/2/1779/3, *Finch* c. *Finch*, Personal answer to allegation of faculties.
[74] See *N.Ad*, 29 September 1792, p. 3, George Nicholson's advert; *N.Jour*, 24 December 1768, p. 2, Francis Ayer's advert; *JOJ*, 12 August 1775, p. 3, Thomas Wardington's advert; ibid., 23 August 1777, p. 3, Robert Piercy's advert; *N.Cour*, 2 January 1779, p. 1, Richard Cullen's advert.

In fact, wives were unable to steal from their husbands. This is why the neutral term 'conveying away' was used by the courts. Most legal handbooks remarked that if a wife took her husband's goods it was not a felony, if she took them and delivered them to a stranger, it was no felony in the stranger.[75] Indeed, neither spouse could steal from the other. In her analysis of wives and property, Lee Holcombe comments that larceny

> was legally defined as taking possession of goods without the owner's consent. Since a man became the owner or at least the custodian of his wife's property, then his appropriation of this property did not constitute a crime – he could not steal from himself. A woman who took her husband's goods was presumed to be acting with his consent in her status of wife.[76]

Thus husbands were unable to prosecute those wives who removed property from the marital home. Although Elizabeth Gould, of Eynsham, Oxfordshire, was accused of taking away her husband's goods in 1724, it was the fact that she had deserted her husband and left him chargeable that led to her being bound over on his and the parish overseers' complaint.[77] Wives certainly did not feel that they were stealing the property. Elizabeth Harding, of Seaham, ended her letter to her proctor, in 1742, by explaining that when she left her home to escape her husband's abuse, she took 'my leneng and plate and soum thens of valey tha wer not of hes bying but he sas I sto hes goods' [my linen and plate, and some things of value that were not of his buying, but he says I stole his goods].[78] This remark highlights that the sense of possession was in no way as straightforward as the rules of coverture and reminds us that the act of consumption conferred ownership.

It is of course possible that wives were taking advantage of their ability to remove goods without prosecution, simply because they wanted or needed them, without feeling any particular or conflicting sense of ownership. After all, they had no choice but to convey away goods if they wished to keep them, as husbands continued to own their wives' personal property during separation.[79] Only rarely did wives remove or sell goods and not leave their husbands. In 1791, for example, it was announced that Frances Watson, the wife of a ship-builder from Blyth, 'sold several Articles out of his House',

---

[75] Burn, *Justice of the Peace*, Vol. IV, p. 384. If the wife's lover received the goods, however, it was a felony in him: see Tomlins, *The Law Dictionary*, pp. v, vi.

[76] Holcombe, *Wives and Property*, pp. 28–9.

[77] OA, QS/1724/Ep 4. This is still more unusual in that Elizabeth gave her own recognizance of £20, with two sureties. As a married woman she should have been unable to give such a bond.

[78] UOD, DDR/EJ/PRC/2/1742/5, *Harding c. Harding*.

[79] They also retained their right to manage and gain income from their separated wives' real property and *choses* in action (Holcombe, *Wives and Property*, p. 32).

but no mention was made of her elopement.[80] Possibly this indicates some disagreement about the management of household finances. Often women's actions seem planned; removing goods in the husband's absence, as the foundation for leaving him. As Thomas Nanson, an innkeeper in Bishop Auckland, put it, in 1747, his wife, Eleanor, without his knowledge or consent, did 'convey away, pawn, sell, and dispose of, or deliver to some Person, or Persons, in trust for her own Use' household goods, and 'hath since separated herself'.[81]

To examine spouses' feelings of ownership in more detail, the goods that wives removed have been divided into eleven categories (Appendix 23). Mention was made of 102 different units of goods; of course one wife could take more than one unit. The most common unit of goods taken, at 23%, was described as 'household goods'. This was probably an inclusive term for sundry mundane household objects of minor value, including cooking and brewing utensils, pewter and basic furniture.[82] The next most popular item taken was linen and bedding, at 16%. Wearing apparel and accessories, usually lace (14%), were the third most common items to be conveyed away by wives. Some husbands detailed the clothes their wives took. For example, in 1781, James Kilpatrick of Northumberland listed the two gowns, two cotton gowns, mourning gown, worn callimanco, black silk, white linen gown and two riding habit skirts that his wife removed when she left him.[83] The next items that were most often removed (13% of the 102 units of goods) were described simply as 'things of value', perhaps a phrase applied to objects too diverse to be itemised or detailed. Sometimes this was the only item stated or was appended to a list of specified goods. At 12% of the 102 units, silver was the next item most often taken. Wives also removed cash (10%) from the marital home. When newspapers reported that wives conveyed away goods, it was usually those who had removed cash, in amounts that seem wildly inflated. *Jackson's Oxford Journal* noted in 1773 that a wife had removed £1,500 in cash, and in 1772 the *Newcastle Journal* reported that a pedlar's wife had taken 40 guineas and goods to the value of £60.[84] Perhaps readers found it more interesting to read about wives removing money rather than more mundane goods. The next most common items were household furniture, jewellery, gold, and papers, writings and securities (3% each). Finally, one woman was described as removing her own goods and Ann Meadley took a horse when she left her husband in 1765. She eloped with Christopher Barker, a soldier, and while the tenor of her husband's advert might suggest that she took it to supply Christopher, who was deserting from the First

---

[80] *N.Chron*, 12 February 1791, p. 3.   [81] *N.Jour*, 12 November 1748.
[82] Berg, 'Women's consumption', 427.   [83] *Y.Cour*, 3 July 1781.
[84] *JOJ*, 15 May 1773; *N.Jour*, 9 September 1772.

Regiment of Dragoon Guards quartered in York, it is interesting that it was equipped with a side-saddle.[85]

Undoubtedly pragmatism motivated the removal of many goods. The impression is that women took clothing, linen, bedding and household goods because they were necessary for their future lives. For example, clothing was one of life's three basic necessities along with food and shelter. It was expensive, taking up the greatest proportion of household expenditure after food and was kept for a long time and updated by accessories.[86] Women's need for money to start a new life also prompted them to sell or pawn goods – often those that might be deemed useful in themselves. Elizabeth Hedley, for example, sold her husband's household furniture and wearing apparel in 1787 and then eloped with the money.[87] Women like Ann Hill, in 1761, wife of a carpenter in Bampton, Oxfordshire, pawned household goods and eloped.[88] The need to finance their lives in separation may also have motivated wives' removal of papers, writings and securities. It is not often stated whether these were in the women's name, made out to trustees on their behalf, or in their husbands' name. Yet even the latter could still be useful. As we have seen, wives were routinely involved as agents on their husbands' behalf and the real value of these types of documents is obvious from the advert of John Spencer, a file-smith of Winlaton-Mill. He announced that his wife had taken some writings and requested that no-one should pay her any debts due to him upon them.[89]

Yet it is not fanciful to wonder whether the women felt a sense of possession for the goods that they removed.[90] They were items that they used or wore daily; they were often the same goods that they brought to marriage or purchased. Clothing, jewels and silver, which were defined as 'paraphernalia', may have lent themselves to a quasi-legitimate notion of ownership since, unlike women's other personal estate, this was returned to women at widowhood (although husbands could sell the items during marriage).[91] Certainly, wives seem to have taken gold and jewellery because they were worn or had been owned prior to marriage. There is also evidence that many of the items that they removed were invested with intense emotions for women at other stages of their lives. For Elizabeth Shackleton, clothing, plate, linen, furniture

---

[85] *N.Chron*, 31 August 1765, p. 3.

[86] J. Styles, 'Custom or consumption? Plebeian fashion in eighteenth-century England' in M. Berg and E. Egar (eds.), *Luxury in the Eighteenth Century: Debates, Desires and Delectable Goods* (Basingstoke, 2002); Berg, 'Women's consumption', 421, 423; Weatherill, *Consumer Behaviour*, p. 119.

[87] *N.Chron*, 3 November 1787, p. 3.   [88] *JOJ*, 1 August 1761, p. 3.

[89] *N.Jour*, 18 April 1752, p. 3.

[90] For further discussion, see Bailey, 'Favoured or oppressed?'

[91] Beds were included in some of the definitions of 'paraphernalia' (Anon., *Laws Respecting Women*, pp. 152, 188).

and kitchenware signified different qualities, including dynastic, commemorative and talismanic meaning, and displayed individuality and social status.[92] Maxine Berg's study of men's and women's bequests and inventories in eighteenth-century Birmingham and Sheffield uncovered that these were personal and expressive goods for middling-sort women too.[93] Decorative and luxury items, like china, pictures and looking-glasses, which were considered in these studies, were not often described as removed by wives, but it is likely the catch-all phrase of 'things of value' included some of these items. Berg noticed some gender differences between men's and women's attitudes towards property, with women generally attaching more emotional significance to their possessions than men. Neither sex drew special attention to household goods. Few men attached particular emotions to linen, unlike women for whom it conveyed family connotations. Pertinently, the linen and bedding that wives removed included everyday and old items, particularly linen for child-bed or children, about which they may have felt similarly intense feelings. Berg also found that clothing had more meaning than as an expensive necessity. Women in Sheffield and Birmingham passed on clothing 'as both valuable goods and as personal tokens'. Men did not attach the same personal identity to it.[94] Silver was an item of importance to both sexes because it was regarded as an heirloom and carried family and dynastic meaning.[95] Nonetheless, Berg found that the women who made wills in Birmingham and Sheffield tended to bequeath plate more often than men.[96] Perhaps this is because, as paraphernalia, plate returned to wives at widowhood, and it was certainly often part of women's portions. In turn this might also have motivated women to remove silver when they left their husbands.

More explicit evidence that wives retained some sense of possession towards goods during marriage comes from their complaints that their husbands had disposed of or kept their property (4% of the secondary complaints, Appendix 8). The property ranged from their apparel to livestock. Phillis Dimery, of Brewer's Street, Oxford, mentioned in her advert in December 1781 that her husband had kept a box of her clothes.[97] When Anne Stokoe petitioned the justices at the quarter sessions at Hexham

---

[92] Vickery, *Gentleman's Daughter*, pp. 183–94.   [93] Berg, 'Women's consumption', 421.
[94] Ibid., 421–3, 426–7; A. Vickery 'Women and the world of goods: a Lancashire consumer and her possessions, 1751–81' in J. Brewer and R. Porter (eds.), *Consumption and the World of Goods* (London, 1993), p. 291. Women also stole clothes and household linens over other items more often than men (G. Walker, 'Women, theft and the world of stolen goods' in J. Kermode and G. Walker (eds.), *Women, Crime and the Courts in Early Modern England* (London, 1994), p. 89).
[95] It was commonly recorded in wills studied by Weatherill, *Consumer Behaviour*, p. 207.
[96] Berg, 'Women's consumption', 426.
[97] NCAS, QSB/54, fol. 39; *JOJ*, 24 November 1781, p. 3, and 1 December 1781, p. 3.

in 1766 for relief, she accused her husband of disposing 'of her Goods and Chattels' soon after marriage.[98] Anne Tomlinson complained that her husband 'broke open her Cupboards and disposed of her Linnen and other household goods and her whole stock of Cattle'; then 'after he had Disposed of all her personal Effects' he turned her out.[99]

These claims are problematic, in the legal sense, since there is no evidence of an agreement between spouses that the wife could keep any property for her sole use. It is possible that some had made informal arrangements, since there is evidence that people of modest means and social status arranged to keep property separate for a wife.[100] Charles Allison, according to his wife, promised before their marriage that 'she should have a right and power to dispose amongst her own friends of what money she was worth before the said marriage'. This came to public notice because Charles denied making any such promise and after the ceremony advertised in the Newcastle newspapers that all those who owed debts to Jane must pay him.[101] It is likely that in these disputed instances wives would refer to such arrangements if they existed. Yet Anne Tomlinson's preceding sentences showed that the property she was discussing was brought to marriage as a portion, which therefore came into her husband's ownership.[102] Similarly, Margaret Sayer complained in 1711 that when her husband and his son lived with her they privately conveyed away valuable goods and effects that belonged to her before marriage, and broke open her locks in the night and removed her goods in order to use them for their own support, depriving her of the benefit of them towards her own relief. There is no mention, however, that Arthur had entered a bond securing any property for her use in marriage or widowhood. Nonetheless Margaret felt that she continued to own property after marriage and fully expected York consistory court to disapprove of her husband's behaviour.[103] Some wives, law of coverture or not, even described themselves as the victims of theft. When Mary Payne was committed as a vagrant by an Oxfordshire justice of the peace, her examination explained that three or four years earlier the seaman she had just married 'robbed' her of everything, then left her.[104] It is difficult to know what underlay the committal of Dorothy Metcalfe's husband to Thirsk house of correction 'for robbing and plundering his lawful wife' in 1731.[105]

The records of marital difficulties also offer insights into ideas about male attitudes to property ownership within marriage. They indicate that husbands were supposed to respect their wives' separate property in both its

[98] NCAS, QSB/68, fol. 56.   [99] NCAS, QSB/57, fol. 57.
[100] Informal marriage settlements were common (Erickson, *Women and Property*, p. 145).
[101] UOD, DDR/EJ/CCD/3/1765/2, *Allison c. Allison*, Libel and personal response.
[102] NCAS, QSB/57, fol. 57.   [103] BIHR, CP.I/291, CP.I/187 *Sayer c. Sayer*, 1711.
[104] OA, Ea/1746/1.   [105] NYA, QSB/1731; QSM/1734, 8 October; QSM/1745, 8 April.

simple and elaborate forms. Francis and Jane Gomeldon had lived together for four years until 1739, when Jane's mother died. Isabelle Middleton, a wealthy Quaker, left her estate to Jane for her sole and separate use. In her adverts placed in 1740, Jane accused Francis of using cruelty to force her to give up her estate to him, declaring 'that neither her fortune nor her life was secure', and of keeping her mother's house and goods from her by bringing in armed men. Francis denied coercion, claimed that he merely continued to rent the house that they had lived in since marriage, and demanded that she and her attorney bring firm proof.[106] Significantly, both expected the public to disapprove of a husband's attempts to remove his wife's property. Robert Shaw's self-defence in 1696 suggests that husbands were meant to be tolerant of women having access to some kinds of property. He claimed that Anne 'had always money to lay out and dispose of as she thought fitt and was knowne and observed by all her neighbours to have money besides her and take pledges for money – and did frequently assist and lend money to her said neighbours without her said husbands knowledge or consent'.[107] Moreover, we have seen that some husbands felt that their wives retained some kind of ownership of property during wedlock, for they described their wives' goods as separate. William Eshelby of Ripon, Yorkshire, refused to pay his wife's debts because he declared that she had eloped with all 'her' necessaries and wearing apparel.[108] Thomas Forster of Bywell in Northumberland stated in 1771 that when his wife separated herself she took with her 'such part of the Household Goods as properly belonged to herself'.[109] It is difficult to know how far informal arrangements underlay these statements. It is feasible that, during a functioning marriage at least, some husbands saw their wives' personal property as they did their real property; that is, something which gave them benefit during marriage but reverted to their wives' use afterwards.

Nonetheless, any sense of personal ownership was temporarily over-ruled during marriage by the sense that resources were pooled for familial benefit. This strengthened interdependency. Firstly, the secondary complaints suggest that, in some wives' opinions, they along with their husbands equitably contributed their property and earnings to the union. Thus Anne Shaw countered her husband's claim that she conveyed away goods by stating that she took some necessities of small value, which did not compare to the amount of things he removed eight years before.[110] Women's contributions were

---

[106] N.Cour, 12 July, 26 July 1740; N.Jour, 5 July, 19 July 1740; UOD, DDR/EJ/PRC/2/1740/6, Gomeldon c. Gomeldon.
[107] BIHR, Trans.CP.1697/2; D/C.C.P.1696/3, Shaw c. Shaw, His personal response.
[108] Y.Cour, 18 June 1765, p. 2.   [109] N.Chron, 27 April 1771, p. 2.
[110] BIHR, Trans.CP.1697/2; D/C.C.P.1696/3, Shaw c. Shaw, 1696, Her personal response to his allegation.

familial, not personal. Though the property might go to the husband, it was intended to benefit the family. Mary Taylor of North Shields petitioned the quarter sessions for relief in 1714 and explained that on several occasions she had sold the greatest part of her household goods to clear her husband's debts before he sailed, and once to release him from imprisonment for debt. Clearly this was to allow him to continue to earn money. Since then, however, he had left her and their three children.[111] Jane Liddle complained in 1726 that her husband was bigamous and that this usage was 'to her utter ruine for that she raised some money to buy him tools to work with as a Tinker' and he had then left her after the death of their two children and returned to his first wife in Scotland.[112]

Similar attitudes can be seen in the secondary complaints which have been categorised under the general term 'financial conflict' (Appendix 8). These concerned disputes over property ownership, especially separate estate – a specified property held in trust for the wife's sole and separate use during marriage – and informal versions of it.[113] Catherine Warburton may have given over her separate estate to her husband's use for what might be called familial purposes. A forty-year-old spinster with a separate estate (land, money, linen and plate), Catherine wed Robert Warburton, a fifty-year-old widower, in 1792. They lived happily together in the house she owned at marriage in Moor Monkton, Yorkshire. They then moved and Catherine alleged that Robert's temperament changed, though he denied it at the time, only admitting to 'Family concerns'. In 1797 she agreed to let him have a farm from her separate estate, possibly to assist him in these concerns. For no obvious reason, however, he moved her by a mixture of force and subterfuge to the cottage with its 106 acres at Thorp Arch. She was effectively imprisoned there for three months and prevented from having her own maid-servant. Robert then arranged for her to move into a house in Pontefract with him in April 1798. In all this time he tried to stop her from corresponding with her friends in York. These attempts to isolate her were to persuade her to acquiesce to his demand in December that she release more of her property. She refused because his physical and emotional harassment left her uncertain about his commitment to her well-being and she was afraid that he would spend all her property, leaving her in distress. For five weeks he would not sleep with her or talk to her and then in desperation he locked her in the attic for six days and went away leaving two servants to pass food to her. Eventually she knocked a hole between the bricks in the chimney breast and communicated with her next-door-neighbour's servant, who got a message

---

[111] NCAS, QSB/40, fol. 43.   [112] NCAS, QSB/69, fols. 22–3.

[113] For pre-nuptial agreements see Erickson, *Women and Property*, chapters 6–8; for separate estate, see M. Hunt, *The Middling Sort*, pp. 158–9. For cases concerning disputes over the separate property in Durham Chancery, see Knight, 'Litigants', pp. 347–54.

to her trustees who rescued her.[114] This type of conflict suggests that women were prepared to release property under certain conditions. They needed to feel secure about their husbands' intentions towards them, they wanted to ensure that the property was kept secure and not dissipated or ruined, it had to be put to a good purpose, and they wished to be given a say in its management. Wives refused to transfer their separate property to their husbands when they suspected that they were likely to exploit it.

Secondly, it seems that husbands shared the concept of pooling resources at and during marriage for general household and family benefit. Men who expressed outrage at not receiving their wives' portion, for example, described it as being deprived of something that would assist their family. James Currie framed much of his defence against his wife's cruelty separation suit around Jane's alleged attempt to deny him the £400 he had expected with her at marriage. He claimed that she refused to produce the writings for a mortgage for £35, or give an account of £25 that she had received and £200 that he believed she had invested. He was bitter that he even had to pay £104 plus interest out of the sum that he did receive, as it was due by bond from Jane to her daughter's husband. He also accused his wife of removing a variety of silver items, a gold watch and three rings in order to escape the effects of coverture. Jane Currie admitted only to taking some teaspoons, drainer, tongs and two rings, because, though they were delivered to her by her son while her first husband was alive, they were still her son's property. The couple's predicament was common knowledge. John Twentyman, their neighbour, recalled that it was well known in the town that 'neither had any respect or love for each other immediately after their intermarriage, nor no inveterate Malice or Hatred, but differ'd about her parting with her Fortune to him'.[115] It was also well known that James was given to telling his friends that he had married to gain financial security for his children from a previous marriage. This familial concern may have increased his resentment at not receiving the money he thought Jane was bringing to their union.

Even in contentious break-ups, when men were most likely to assert their full legal rights, these might be defined in familial or relatively equitable ways. Some husbands explained that they kept certain property, which their wives claimed as their own, because they needed it to raise their children or in order to pay alimony. In 1730 Henry Hendry objected to his wife's

---

[114] BIHR, Cons.CP.1800/3; CP.I/2503, *Warburton* c. *Warburton*, 1799.

[115] Deponents favourable to Jane described the mortgages and securities made out to her sons from a previous marriage as perfectly normal procedures following the bequests of their father (BIHR, Trans.CP.1730/6, *Currie* c. *Currie*). It was possible for a husband to have the disposal of his wife's property set aside as a legal fraud if she had disposed of it after having agreed to marry but before the ceremony, without his consent (Holcombe, *Wives and Property*, p. 18).

attempt to have the quarter sessions order that he pay a maintenance to her 'when shee is as able to worke as yo[ur] pet[itioner] who has a child to mentaine otherwise must be left to the parish'.[116] An advert was placed in 1793 denying Thomas Joynson's credit to his wife; instead 'what Money he has in his Wife's Right will be applied for her Support and Maintenance'.[117] In 1719 Zacariah More refused to be assessed for his wife's alimony unless the £39 worth of silver goods she had taken was returned; thus in order to get maintenance, Anne More returned them.[118] This is not to say that ownership was particularly equitable, since wives could bring large portions but end up with small sums of alimony. Nonetheless, there is enough evidence from wills as well as from these complaints to propose that, in marriage, resources were temporarily pooled, to be reorganised at separation, in widowhood, or by bequeathing them to offspring.

CONCLUSION: POWER IN THE HOUSEHOLD

Lyndsey Charles has remarked that a 'complex web of power relationships lies behind' the fact that pre-industrial women were expected to contribute to the household's upkeep through production or wages.[119] The records of marital difference bear this out. Economic interdependence bound couples together in co-dependency, which impacted upon husbands as well as wives. The removal of women's household economic and domestic contributions cost husbands dear. Women's contributions were after all essential to house-hold economic success or continued existence. Although analyses of the real value of women's input to the household economy, whether in cash or kind, are rare, they indicate that it was essential for the household's survival.[120] In eighteenth- and nineteenth-century agrarian labouring families, for example, women's cash earnings provided almost the same income as their husband's wages. Similarly, women in landholding families provided half of household production.[121] Arguably, where wives' contributions allowed more than ba-sic necessaries to be purchased, it is still not the case that this rendered their efforts supplemental. Though women's contributions of goods and earnings did not fall short of their husbands' offerings, it is difficult to judge how far they derived power from them. It seems likely that they conveyed some authority for married women, but that this was only attained in certain

[116] NCAS, QSB/75, fol. 22.   [117] *JOJ*, 19 October 1793, p. 3.
[118] BIHR, CP.I/699, *More* c. *More*, 1719.
[119] L. Charles and L. Duffin (eds.), *Women and Work in Pre-industrial England* (London, 1985), p. 19.
[120] Benjamin Shaw's household depended on his wife's and children's wages (D'Cruze, 'Care, diligence', 321).
[121] Alice Clark, *Working Life*, pp. xix, xxv.

conditions. Equally, if wives gained some sense of power from their instinctive sense of property ownership, it was partial, informal and contingent.

If contributing goods, earnings and labour to the household did not endow married women with institutionalised, formal power, it gave them some sense of entitlement. In return they expected to receive their husbands' assistance in providing for their family and household. This was a very different reciprocity to that suggested by historians like Margaret Hunt, who proposes that in 'the "social contract" between husband and wife, the responsibility to maintain the wife was the *quid pro quo* for her obedience and sexual services'.[122]

It is possible to speculate that wives derived another version of entitlement from their financial investment in marriage. Before allegations of faculties were introduced, which separated out the description of men's ill-usage from the details of their income and personal worth in separate documents, the articles describing spouses' relative property contributions often preceded those detailing violence. Obviously, this confirms the impression that many women brought cruelty separation suits in order to secure maintenance in an existing separation, rather than simply to halt abuse. It is also feasible that wives' material input to marriage was meant to be reciprocated with male respect and honour. In 1734 the *North Country Journal* noted that a wife who had exhibited articles of the peace against her husband in the Court of King's Bench stated that she had been his wife for some years, brought him a very plentiful fortune and was the mother of his several children, yet he was adulterous with a woman he brought into the house, to whom he made his wife act as servant.[123] The order of wording in this statement is perhaps more than accidental. The association was explicit in Samuel Tireman's response to his wife's attempt to have their marriage annulled on the grounds of his impotence, which she alleged also caused him to be cruel. He stated that he had maintained and used her well as his wife 'farr above the fortune he shou[l]d have rece[ive]d with her'.[124] This is not to say that the more money wives supplied, the better they should be treated; nonetheless, perhaps it implies that women felt that they deserved some degree of reasonable treatment in return for their material contributions.

The next chapter examines what was considered unacceptable behaviour within marriage and its implications for the relative power of husbands and wives.

---

[122] Hunt, 'Marital "Rights"', p. 117.   [123] *NCJ*, 7 December 1734.
[124] BIHR, CP.I/169, *Tireman c. Tireman*, 1702.

6

'Wilt thou obey him, and serve him': the marital power balance

WIFE-BEATING CASES AS EVIDENCE

This chapter uses evidence of wife-beating to build a more balanced, dynamic picture of relative power within marriage than those in which men's violence was the result of either their uncontrolled or their frustrated power. It is based on around 600 incidents of domestic violence, 92% of which were carried out by men. Most come to light in the records of justices of the peace and the ecclesiastical courts as primary accusations (458, Appendix 1) and secondary complaints (36, Appendix 8), and an additional 105 reports of wife-beating or spousal murder in the sampled local newspapers are also considered.[1] This evidence reveals attitudes to domestic violence and its perpetrators during a period of change in the expression of theories about social relationships and in legal and popular perceptions of violence. The cases of wife-beating must be carefully placed in their cultural context because ideas about the sexes' capacity for violence were evolving over the course of the sixteenth to nineteenth centuries, despite the fact that it is invariably men who commit the majority of violent offences.[2] The changes are particularly evident in literary portrayals of spousal murder and 'intimate violence'.[3] In the sixteenth and early seventeenth centuries it was wives' violence that was dangerous and frightening in the public's imagination. Frances Dolan demonstrates that representations of domestic crime portrayed the violent wife as the insubordinate dependent who 'abuses intimacy' to kill her husband.[4] Not only were women's forms of physical violence a source of anxiety, their scolding and

---

[1] There were 84 newspaper reports of male cruelty, of which 43 ended in the wife's murder, and 21 press reports of attempted or actual murder of husbands. These are not included in the database.

[2] M. J. Wiener, 'Alice Arden to Bill Sikes: changing nightmares of intimate violence in England, 1558–1869', *Journal of British Studies*, 40 (2001), 184, 186.

[3] These theories are based on relative numbers of popular publications about husband killings and wife killings. See F. E. Dolan, *Dangerous Familiars, Representations of Domestic Crime in England, 1550–1700* (New York, 1994), and Wiener, 'Changing Nightmares'.

[4] Dolan, *Dangerous Familiars*, pp. 2, 30.

swearing were considered to be powerful weapons.[5] Indeed, unruly violent wives were the target of popular rituals displaying community disapproval in the sixteenth and seventeenth centuries.[6]

As the nature and limits of authority came to be questioned in the course of the Civil War, the Restoration and the 1688 Revolution Settlement, men's exploitation of their position of power within marriage became a focus for concern. For example, portrayals of murderous husbands came to outnumber those of murderous wives in pamphlets and ballads after 1650.[7] The shift in attention developed further during the eighteenth and nineteenth centuries, when, in Martin Wiener's words: 'women became perceived... as less dangerous and more in need of protection, and men, complementarily, became perceived as more dangerous and more in need of control'.[8] Thus representations of domestic violence centred on male rather than female aggression and presented women as 'victims'. Novels with a central theme of men's victimisation of women became common. Even murderous women were increasingly portrayed as figures of sympathy, with newspaper reports and court cases describing the personal sufferings that led them to kill their abusive lover/husband.[9] This interest in male cruelty may underlie the shift in the targets of community rituals, which had turned away from cuckolds and aggressive wives to abusive husbands by the late eighteenth century.[10]

The evolution in ideas about the perpetrators of domestic violence had several causes. It was influenced by reassessments of the human body, which in turn impacted on understandings of gender difference. Before the second half of the seventeenth century, the humoral system shaped understandings of human bodies, where the body was believed to consist of four humours, which determined well-being and development. These humours 'created a balance in the individual between hot, dry, wet and cold characteristics'. Men were distinguished by hot and dry, women by cold and wet humours. Women's bodies were thought to seek the characteristics of men's, predisposing them to desire sexual activity with men. When this 'natural' female sexual aggression was combined with ideas that women were less rational than men because of their humoral characteristics, women were designated as dangerously lustful. Elite and professional understandings of the body gradually altered from the 1670s, with findings about the nervous system

[5] Anon., *Poor Robin's True Character of a Scold Or the Shrews Looking-glass* (London, 1678).
[6] M. Ingram, 'Ridings, rough music and the "Reform of popular culture" in early modern England', *Past and Present*, 105 (1984), 79–113; Ingram, 'Ridings, rough music and mocking rhymes in early modern England' in B. Reay (ed.), *Popular Culture in Seventeenth-Century England* (London, 1988); and 'Juridical folklore in England illustrated by rough music' in C. W. Brooks and M. Lobban (eds.), *Communities and Courts 1150–1900* (London, 1997).
[7] Dolan, *Dangerous Familiars*, pp. 12, 89.   [8] Wiener, 'Changing nightmares', 187.
[9] Ibid., 193–5.
[10] E. P. Thompson, *Customs in Common* (London, 1991), pp. 466–538.

and reproduction, new definitions of women's genitalia, and differentiation between female and male skeletons. In the process women and men were redefined as entirely different: the opposite sexes. It came to be believed that men's role in sexual reproduction outweighed women's, who were not given an active role in conception and whose experience of female sexual pleasure began to be questioned.[11] As a result, women were recast as the 'gentler sex'; inherently weak, naturally virtuous and sexually passive, even passionless. Men were redefined as sexual predators.[12] Wiener also suggests that industrialisation and economic change, which encouraged mobility and urban anonymity and loosened social controls on men's behaviour within courtship and marriage, contributed to perceptions of men as threatening.[13] But he singles out the influence in the eighteenth century of the culture of sensibility, which was an engine of change from the 1740s.[14] By elevating feeling and investing it with 'moral value', sensibility powered a number of reforming movements, many of which sought to reform male manners.[15]

Although historians frequently use accounts of domestic violence to explore marital power relationships more broadly, such evidence must be interpreted with caution by establishing in what respects it is representative.[16] Many cases of wife-beating were dealt with informally or by justices of the peace outside sessions and only the most severe cases came before the courts. Most of these beaten wives were terrified of their husbands. Grace Allenson's servant deposed in 1675 that Grace was so afraid of her husband 'that she scarcely durst speake to him or goe to him to dinner or any other place and almost trembled when she saw him'.[17] Therefore the power relationships on view in these court cases are atypical. An analysis of modern domestic violence warns that if it is proposed 'that wife beating mechanically reflects and expresses male dominance', then 'this would lead to the false conclusion that all heterosexual relationships are violent'.[18] Yet this assumption has been made. Roderick Phillips argues that 'women must have expected to be

---

[11] The description of these changes is based on: T. Hitchcock, *English Sexualities, 1700–1800* (London, 1997), pp. 42–9; Fletcher, *Gender, Sex and Subordination*. Historians' debates about the consequences of these changes are critiqued in Shoemaker, *Gender*, pp. 59–86.

[12] Fletcher, *Gender, Sex and Subordination*, pp. 322–46, 376–400.

[13] Wiener, 'Changing nightmares', 203–4.   [14] Ibid., 193–4.

[15] G. J. Barker Benfield, *The Culture of Sensibility. Sex and Society in Eighteenth-Century Britain* (Chicago and London, 1992); Langford, *Polite and Commercial*, p. 481. Men were advised to defend their honour in less violent ways (R. B. Shoemaker, 'Reforming male manners: public insult and the decline of violence in London 1660–1740' in T. Hitchcock and M. Cohen (eds.), *English Masculinities 1660–1800* (London, 1999), pp. 133–50).

[16] For example, Laura Gowing argues that cases of wife-beating reveal the conventions and ideals by which marriage was understood and judged (*Domestic Dangers*, p. 229); Tomes, 'Torrent of abuse'.

[17] BIHR, CP.H/3264, *Allenson c. Allenson*, 1675.

[18] W. Brienes and L. Gordon, 'The new scholarship on family violence', *Signs: Journal of Women in Culture and Society*, 8, 3 (1983), 530.

struck at some time by their husbands', and Nancy Tomes proposes that in nineteenth-century London the behaviour of working-class spouses 'toward one another was shaped by the realization that violence was one possible outcome of a conflict'.[19] The supposition also underlies explanations that patriarchy was the primary cause of husbands' violence to their wives.[20] Susan Amussen remarks, for example, that family violence was sometimes a 'brutal manifestation of patriarchal power'.[21] The role of patriarchy in wife-beating has been described in two related ways. One argument is that wife-beaters expressed the full potential of their authority and beat their wives for failing to carry out their duties through incompetence or disobedience.[22] A second more subtle explanation is that men's own inadequacy, due say to unemployment or the inability to provide for their family, caused them to beat their wives to compensate for their lack of power elsewhere in the marriage.[23] In other words women were beaten when men's power went unchecked or was frustrated. Both approaches imply that wives were required to be submissive in order to avoid being beaten because challenging or disobedient behaviour met with husbands' violence, which was a male tool used to reassert power.[24]

The causes of wife-beating are more complex than these simplified models of unequal power relationships. The hierarchical system of patriarchy did give limited licence to dominant members of relationships to correct their subordinates with moderation in order to maintain order. Most legal, religious and social authorities recognised that patriarchy contained the potential for men to abuse their power and sought to provide means to prevent this. As a recent study of incidents of wife-beating that came before Westminster Quarter Sessions, between 1685 and 1720, concludes, patriarchal authority 'was purchased at the price of granting wives, servants and extended family the right to label certain acts unacceptable and pursue retribution before the courts'.[25] Furthermore, the emotional involvement between spouses and between them and their children complicates family power relationships. Linda Pollock's study of the workings of patriarchy in the Barrett-Lennard family

---

[19] Phillips, *Untying the Knot*, p. 102; Tomes, 'Torrent of abuse', 329.

[20] Tomes, 'Torrent of abuse', 331–3; L. Leneman, '"A tyrant and tormentor": violence against wives in eighteenth- and early nineteenth-century Scotland', *Continuity and Change*, 12 (1997), 40; Hunt, 'Wife beating', 16.

[21] Amussen, '"Being stirred"', 71.   [22] Stone, *Divorce*, pp. 198–9.

[23] J. C. Babcock, J. Waltz, N. S. Jacobson and J. M. Gottman, 'Power and violence: the relation between communication patterns, power discrepancies, and domestic violence', *Journal of Consulting and Clinical Psychology*, 61, 1 (1993), 40.

[24] Stone, *Divorce*, p. 199; Leneman, 'A tyrant and tormentor', 40; L. Abrams, 'Whores, whorechasers, and swine: the regulation of sexuality and the restoration of order in the nineteenth-century German divorce court', *Journal of Family History*, 21, 3 (1996), 267–8.

[25] J. Hurl-Eamon, 'Domestic violence prosecuted: women binding over their husbands for assault at Westminster Quarter Sessions, 1685–1720', *Journal of Family History* 26, 4 (2001), 450.

at the end of the seventeenth century shows that conflict was 'a structural component of family life'. Indeed the dynamics between family members made men's position in the household fairly fragile; thus men did not feel secure in their domination or certain that their demands and wishes would be obeyed instead of ignored, evaded, manipulated or challenged. This does not mean that men's unbridled or thwarted power would automatically culminate in them violently lashing out. Instead, reconciliation and mediation were intended to be bulwarks against marital and familial relations descending into violence. When these failed and wives turned to the courts, the ensuing evidence provides valuable information about spouses' acceptable and unacceptable behaviour and how this was affected by changes in cultural attitudes towards the perpetrators of violence.

DEFINING UNACCEPTABLE MALE BEHAVIOUR IN MARRIAGE

Accounts of violence in women's libels and allegations in cruelty suits and their articles of the peace are depressingly alike, ranging from physical scuffles during quarrels, to sporadic outbursts of brutality where husbands tried to assert control, to systematic acts of appalling abuse. Although they were formulated to fit different legal requirements in each case, the accounts share other common features. In order to secure articles of the peace against husbands, wives had to demonstrate their husbands' past misdeeds and future threat.[26] Thus Katherine Freeman's husband, from Chesham, Buckinghamshire, was committed to the county gaol in 1720 because 'she goes in danger of her life or of some deadly horror to be done to her by her husband'.[27] Surviving informations and examinations suggest that at this level of prosecution wives had been severely beaten as well as suffering verbal and physical threats against their lives. Minor levels of violence and threats were dealt with outside of sessions.[28] Husbands indicted for assault were usually the most violent. For example, in 1763, James Aris beat his wife until he dislocated her elbow and fractured her arm.[29] Until the second half of the eighteenth century, wives who sought a separation from the church courts also emphasised that their life was at risk. Less brutal types of violence were included after this, but the requirements of canon law still made it necessary to stress the continuous nature of husbands' violence since the wives sought permanent separation.[30] Sir Jerome Smithson, of York, beat

---

[26] Burn, *Justice of the Peace*, pp. 247–8.   [27] CBS, QS Rolls 73/12.

[28] At Westminster Quarter Sessions between 1685 and 1720, half the recognizances binding over husbands for assault against their wives implied severe violence, and half offered no elaboration to the formula of assault. It is possible that the latter included only verbal threats (Hurl-Eamon, 'Domestic violence prosecuted', 437–9).

[29] CBS, Q/SO/17, pp. 385, 6, and QS Rolls 1763.

[30] Coote, *Practice*, p. 349; Biggs, *Matrimonial Cruelty*, pp. 62–3.

his wife practically every day, as her libel stated, if he was in health, or at home, sober or drunk, when she was with child or ill. Beaten wives also had to demonstrate that their husbands' behaviour rendered normal life impossible, as well as endangering their health and constitution, in order to gain separation. It is through these descriptions that the sheer viciousness of wife-beaters is glimpsed. John Bowness concluded a quarrel with his wife Anne in the 1740s by striking her on the face until her nose bled. He then asked her to shake hands and be friends and when she put out her hand to him struck her again on the face, swelling her nose and mouth and cutting her lip.[31]

Wives' accusations in all the sources highlighted the same three factors about their husbands' and their own behaviour. Firstly, their husbands' actions were described as barbarous, inhuman, wicked, horrid and unmerciful. From the mid eighteenth century this language of barbarity and inhumanity was imbued with extra meaning by sensibility, for men were now not just lacking in humanity, but in civility too.[32] Secondly, women emphasised that the men's behaviour was irrational, using the terms 'passion', 'fury' and 'rage'.[33] According to his wife in 1781, Francis Spence of Ripon 'ran about the House in an Outrageous manner with a Penknife and Hatchet in his hands threatening Destruction and Vengeance' against her. Deponents used the same language. Charles Allenson's servant described him displaying 'a crosse furious passionate and strange disposition' in 1676, and in 1719 the sixteen-year-old servant of Robert Dobby recalled that he was 'almost like a distracted man Insomuch that it is dangerous to come nigh him'. Isabella Foynes, the wife of a silk weaver, who had been a servant to the Leeses after their marriage in 1796, bluntly stated that James Lees behaved 'more like a madman than anything else'.[34] Newspaper accounts of husbands also equated the acts with madness. *Jackson's Oxford Journal* reported in 1769 that a Slough innkeeper 'being in a State of Insanity' beat his wife to death.[35] Madness was often attributed to drunkenness or jealousy, rather than a psychological condition. In 1761 *Jackson's Oxford Journal* described a greengrocer who had 'drunk himself to a pitch of madness' and beat his wife in a terrible manner.[36] Another man was 'so far hurried beyond his Senses' by finding his wife in bed with her lover in 1739 that he murdered her.[37]

The association of wife-beating with madness had deep roots in the past. Martin Ingram noticed that male violence in five Wiltshire cases of cruelty in

---

[31] BIHR, CP.H/3469, *Smithson c. Smithson*, 1680; UOD, DDR/EJ/CCD/3/1745/2, *Bowness c. Bowness.*

[32] Barker-Benfield, *Culture of Sensibility*, pp. 248, 250.

[33] For example: UOD/DDR/EJ/PRC/2/1712/1, *Ebden c. Ebden*; CBS, QS Rolls 1786, Elizabeth Edgson's article of the peace.

[34] BIHR, CP.I/2013, *Spence c. Spence*, 1782; CP.H/3264, *Allenson c. Allenson*, 1675; CP.I/581 *Dobby c. Dobby*, 1719; Chanc.CP.1803/3, *Lees c. Lees*, 1803.

[35] *JOJ*, 12 August 1769.   [36] *JOJ*, 3 January 1761.   [37] *N.Cour*, 27 January 1739, p. 2.

the early seventeenth century was characterised by mental disturbance.[38] Although Laura Gowing argues that London wife-beaters in the sixteenth and seventeenth centuries emphasised their own rationality in response to accusations of violence, she notes that witnesses described them as irrational. A neighbour of John Farmer, for example, testified in 1586 that she found him beating his wife 'more like a madd man then anie other', using words almost identical to those of Isabella Foynes over 200 years later.[39] The equation of wife-beating with irrationality and madness grew keener as the seventeenth century progressed. Murderous husbands were portrayed as lunatics in popular print after 1650.[40] The association was entrenched in the eighteenth century as concerns about the control of men increasingly over-rode those about women. By the end of the century, educational literature and conduct advice likened anger to madness and specifically associated it with men.[41]

Wife-beaters' irrationality was most forcefully illustrated by their behaviour towards their wives during pregnancy and child-birth and towards their children. For instance, Charles Allenson forced his wife to sit up at nights when she was heavily pregnant.[42] A number of women commented that their husbands' behaviour worsened during their confinements, and a few suffered numerous miscarriages as a result.[43] Husbands were supposed to play an important role during their wives' lying-in period of the four weeks or so after the birth of their child. They were to provide wives with appropriate drink and food, clothing and, importantly, care and time, without making sexual or domestic demands upon them.[44] It was not unusual for abused wives to suffer ill-treatment during their lying-in. A friend of Elizabeth Laughton commented that Elizabeth was afraid to go to bed with her husband in case she got with child because he ill-used her during childbed, refused to let her have a fire in the room, or wine to make cordial, and cursed her 'for laying in Bedd and not Riseing at the Com[m]on hours within a few days after her delivery'. Sixty-year-old Elizabeth Armitage, Elizabeth's midwife during her five deliveries between 1716 and 1720, also catalogued John Laughton's violent and unaccountable passions during these periods.[45] Violence against children provided additional evidence of men's barbarity, madness and lack of love for their families. In a few cases women were beaten

[38] Ingram, *Church Courts*, p. 182.   [39] Gowing, *Domestic Dangers*, pp. 219, 209.

[40] Dolan, *Dangerous Familiars*, pp. 109, 119.

[41] E. Foyster, 'Boys will be boys? Manhood and aggression, 1660–1800' in Hitchcock and Cohen (eds.), *English Masculinities*, pp. 154–5.

[42] BIHR, CP.H/3264, *Allenson c. Allenson*, 1675.

[43] BIHR, Trans.CP.1697/2, D/C.CP.1696/3, *Shaw c. Shaw*.

[44] A. Wilson, 'The ceremony of childbirth and its interpretation' in V. Fildes (ed.), *Women as Mothers in Pre-Industrial England* (London, 1990), pp. 68–102.

[45] BIHR, CP.I/63, *Laughton c. Laughton*, 1721, Depositions of Katherine Arthur and Elizabeth Armitage.

because they intervened to stop their husbands' violence. Henry Gibson attacked his wife because 'she was endeavouring to save her Child whom he...had struck at several times over its Breast'.[46] The account offered by Margaret Sharpe can hardly have failed to move the case against her husband. In 1709 he had threatened her daughter's child and when she begged him for God's sake not to hurt it, he responded: 'Dam the babe, she'd presently see what he'd do to it'.[47] Violence against children was considered worse than wife-beating, despite its inclusion with other forms of cruelty, rather than as a separate prosecution.[48] For example, servants always gave priority to rescuing children and would assist women once the children had been made safe. By the mid eighteenth century this too was bound up with new ideals of behaviour, since sensibility was expressed in protecting children.[49]

Thirdly, wives emphasised that they did not provoke the beating or abuse. This was implicitly addressed by describing the sudden and contextless nature of husbands' abuse; men volcanically erupted into violence without warning. Elizabeth Edgson's account in her article of the peace sworn against her husband, a brickmaker from Burnham, Buckinghamshire, in 1786, is typical in stating that he was moved by a 'sudden transport of Passion' to threaten and cruelly use her.[50] A few years later Sarah Craydon's husband of Great Marlow 'suddenly' rose out of bed to terrorise and abuse her.[51] Men quite literally did all this by themselves: John Greenwell 'worked himself up into great Anger and Passion' in 1766 and James Lees would 'put himself' into his violent passions at the turn of the eighteenth century.[52] These explosions demonstrated that the wives' behaviour had nothing to do with their husbands' abuse. Women in all the legal venues also routinely and explicitly stated that their husbands acted without cause. Cruelty separation cases usually used the term 'provocation', whereas complaints to justices of the peace included other variations on the theme. Margaret Storey's petition to a justice in 1688 noted that her husband frequently beat her for 'light causes', by which she meant reasons that he invented.[53] A century later in North Yorkshire, John Harrison beat his wife 'without any reason or just cause'.[54] Nearly all husbands who responded to accusations of wife-beating commented on their wives' provocation. The comments were invariably brief and simply conveyed that the wives' actions were deliberately and continuously provoking. Even the most explicit statements were not particularly enlightening, like John Pighells' who reported in 1697 that his wife 'has

---

[46] NYA, QSB/1737/film 131.   [47] OA/Ep/1709/8.

[48] There were also no recognizances directed solely at children in Westminster Quarter Sessions between 1685 and 1720 (Hurl-Eamon, 'Domestic violence prosecuted', 443).

[49] Langford, *Polite and Commercial*, pp. 502–3.

[50] CBS, QS Rolls 1786.   [51] CBS, QS Rolls 1791.

[52] UOD, DDR/EJ/CCD/3/1773/3, *Greenwell* c. *Greenwell*; BIHR, Chanc.CP.1803/3, *Lees* c. *Lees*, 1803.

[53] NCAS, QSB/5, fol. 14, January 1688.   [54] NYA, QSB/1786/000873, film 2265.

studied as still she does by all possible means how to disoblige vex and trouble' him.[55]

John Biggs argues that provocation was obviously regarded as capable of affording a defence against allegations of cruelty since all libels stated that cruel conduct was unprovoked. Some legal judgements support this. Sir George Lee made the earliest pronouncement in 1755 in the Court of Arches when he stated, 'I was of opinion a wife was not entitled to a divorce for cruelty, unless it appeared that she was a person of good temper, and had always behaved well and dutifully to her husband, which the appellant had not done.'[56] The law of correction provides further evidence for this view. In the early sixteenth century, for example, Fitzherbert's *The New Natura Brevium* stated that a husband could not do damage to his wife's body 'otherwise than what reasonably belongs to her Husband, for the Sake of Government and Chastisement of his Wife lawfully'.[57] This licence to chastise wives moderately remained in legal texts over the next two centuries but was ambiguously defined. Although extreme violence was described as life-threatening, the degree of force involved in reasonable chastisement was not categorised.[58] Maeve Doggett found that, while Chief Justice Hale ruled in 1674 that reasonable chastisement extended only to admonition or confinement to the house and was not a licence to beat, few eighteenth-century authors denied the legality of wife-beating.[59] It is too easy, however, to get preoccupied by formulaic denials of provocation in beaten wives' accusations. Contemporary thoughts on the matter were infinitely shaded. Indeed, behaviour that constituted provocation was never legally defined and each case was to be considered upon its merits.[60] One nineteenth-century legal authority, commenting on ecclesiastical law before the 1857 Matrimonial Causes Act, acknowledged that a wife's provoking language might push her husband's patience to extremity. While striking out with the hand might be permissible in some circumstances, however, repeated blows were not, nor were deeds out of proportion to the provocation.[61]

In popular opinion, violence could only be justifiably provoked by extreme female behaviour, such as wives' bigamy, adultery, prostitution, or to prevent a vicious attack, though the violent response was not excusable.

[55] BIHR, CP.H/4505, *Pighells c. Pighells*, 1697.
[56] Cited in Biggs, *Matrimonial Cruelty*, pp. 144–5.
[57] Cited in M. E. Doggett, *Marriage, Wife-Beating and the Law in Victorian England* (London, 1992), p. 4.
[58] Biggs, *Matrimonial Cruelty*, p. 23.
[59] For detailed study of the right to beat see Doggett, *Marriage, Wife-Beating*, pp. 3–10.
[60] Bishop, *Commentaries*, p. 476. Provocation was a valid defence in eighteenth-century Scotland, but only 1 husband out of 175 cases succeeded in his use of the plea (Leneman, '"A tyrant and tormentor"', 48–9).
[61] Bishop, *Commentaries*, p. 476.

In 1709, shortly after Anne and Edward Mould were married, Alexander Harrison of York, a 44-year-old brewer, delivered and read a letter to Anne in Edward's presence. Addressed to Mrs Anne Clarke, it revealed that she knew that her former husband was still alive. Alexander handed the letter to Anne who refused to give it to Edward, her bigamous husband. The couple struggled over its possession and Edward threw her on to the bed and tried to retrieve it from the bosom of her dress. This rough treatment made her cry out to Alexander for help, but 'not careing to meddle or concerne himselfe betwixt man and wife' he went downstairs and sent the woman who ran the lodging house to go to them. Perhaps he felt some ambivalence about Edward's violent response.[62] Interestingly, in matrimonial cases before the ecclesiastical courts, men rarely used female infidelity as a reason for lashing out, instead implying that the women were prostitutes, perhaps a more understandable target of violence. Newspapers, however, often reported that wife-killers claimed their wives' adultery drove them to murder. They reported neutrally, without condoning the husbands' action. Indeed the claims could be presented to suggest that the men's jealousy was irrational. This was obvious in the case of John Vickers who was hanged for stabbing his wife. The *York Courant* reported in 1749 that his reason was that he believed she was or soon would be false.[63] Nevertheless, the situation was sometimes described as sad rather than heinous, so when a husband killed his butler and fatally wounded his wife after finding them together in 'a Criminal Way' in 1748, the *Newcastle Journal* called it a 'tragical Affair'.[64]

It is also important to remember that provocation was not gender-specific. Husbands who claimed that their wives had treated them badly also declared that they had not provoked their actions. In 1764 Charles Allison, a master mariner, alleged that his wife frequently 'grossly insulted' him and hit him without provocation. Maria Burbeck, James and Jane Currie's servant, recalled in 1729 that they used to 'taunt and provoke each other, but she can't say which of them were most to blame'.[65] It is also the case that the frequency of descriptions of violence against children complicates concepts about provocation, because they show that male violence did not need a cause. All in all, it is likely that wives' disclaimers and husbands' claims of female provocation were not the key upon which these suits turned, for it was rarely used as a male defence. Some men conceded that they had responded to their wives' provocation in minor ways. John Pighells said that he pushed his wife away to avoid her blows and Francis Spence admitted in 1783 that his wife's temper had 'thrown [him] off his Guard' into using

[62] BIHR, CP.I/542, *Mould c. Mould*, 1709.   [63] *Y.Cour*, 21 November 1749, p. 1.
[64] *N.Jour*, 3 September 1748, p. 2.
[65] DDR/EJ/CCD/3/1765/2, *Allison c. Allison*; BIHR, Trans.CP.1730/6, *Currie c. Currie*, 1729.

'disagreeable language'.[66] One or two husbands were reported by a third party to have claimed they beat their wives because of their provocation. For example, Joseph Walker denied beating his wife in 1723, but her sixty-year-old uncle deposed that when he went to Joseph at Margaret's request to press him not to strike her in future, Joseph 'own'd that he had beate her but said it was her own fault and that she would not obey him'.[67] However, it does not seem to have been a real option for husbands to claim publicly that they physically corrected their wives' provocation.

A breakdown of male responses to accusations of cruelty in fifty-one matrimonial cases before the church courts is suggestive. There are no personal answers to wives' accusations in 37% of them, either because the men refused to respond to the courts' request to provide an answer, or because the document has not survived (Appendix 24). In contrast to Margaret Hunt's declaration, based on ten separation cases from 1710 to 1711, that husbands did not bother to deny allegations of wife-beating, another 37% denied their wives' accusations.[68] In many cases their denials contradicted deponents who supported the wives' claims. Some offered lame explanations for the visible signs of violence. Joseph Watson suggested that his wife got her bruises from falling over when drunk.[69] A few of these men refused to answer the articles that accused them of violence since it was a criminal charge, but then immediately denied it anyway.[70] Of the rest, 18% dealt with the charges in ways that suggest they could not deny them, but were still reluctant to admit them. Four provided a personal answer to the libel but ignored the articles referring to cruelty. For example, in 1682, Timothy Brooke admitted the first article, which outlined the couple's marriage date and proved cohabitation, and responded to the last article by describing his personal estate. He simply ignored the other sixteen articles complaining about his adultery, cruelty, and marital rape of his heavily pregnant wife.[71] Another two husbands side-stepped the issue of violence, by claiming that their marriages were invalid, and three men refused to answer the charge because it was criminal, without then denying it.

On the few occasions that men admitted beating their wives, they usually depicted it as a momentary loss of control. Only four husbands admitted beating their wives (8%, Appendix 24), only one of whom cast the action in terms of moderate correction. In 1697 Robert Shaw's personal response to his wife's libel admitted that on occasion he was provoked to give ill

[66] BIHR, CP.H/4505, *Pighells c. Pighells*, 1697; CP.I/2013, *Spence c. Spence*, 1782.
[67] The wife's behaviour influenced the outcome of this suit. Margaret's uncles, her female cousin and a friend deposed that she was angry, scolding, undutiful and drank too much. The sentence went against her (BIHR, CP.I/812, *Walker c. Walker*, 1723).
[68] Hunt, 'Wife beating', p. 18.   [69] UOD, DDR/EJ/CCD/3/1801/15, *Watson c. Watson*.
[70] For example, BIHR, CP.I/88, *Greaves c. Greaves*, 1704.
[71] BIHR, CP.H/3516, *Brooke c. Brooke*, 1683.

language and once applied 'moderate correction' to his wife, but still denied the specific allegations of abuse. He submitted an explanation in a separate document: his wife 'hath taken him by his members and in a threatening man[n]er endeavoured all she could to dismember and undoe him'. Nonetheless, he insisted that he had struck her without hurting her.[72] The other men mentioned their wives' provocation, but described their own behaviour as a loss of self-control under its strain. The magistrate William Ettrick conceded that on Christmas Day 1765 his wife had 'urged and provoked' him until he 'did give her one box on the Ear only'.[73] In 1713 Thomas Stradling admitted that his wife's unjust behaviour 'has caus'd [him]...to doe such acts to her as otherwise he cou'd not have beene guilty of', that 'there are faults on both sides, and [he] has used such harshness to her...he really thinks the Judge of this Venerable Court may justly by Sentence Sepa[ra]t[e] them'. No such shame was felt by John Smith, an attorney, forty years later, when he admitted that his wife's ill usage 'hath...induced [him] to drink more Strong Liquors than he otherwise should have done and that when he hath come home from Drinking he hath often beat her'. He merely denied beating her as violently as she alleged in her libel, a catalogue of sickening, frenzied abuse between 1738 and 1742. This displacement was no rational correction. Thus even when the spotlight shifted to wives' behaviour in men's self-defences, the emphasis was on appropriate male responses, not on the female behaviour that caused them.[74]

Indeed, rather than stressing female provocation as the cause of violence and their actions as a rational, deliberate response to chastise a disobedient wife, most men claimed that they reacted to it with self-control. In 1729 James Currie claimed that his wife's design to provoke him to anger was not prevented by his 'mild treatment to reclaim her, his good advice and reasoning with her being represented for abuses', so he 'at last resolved and determin'd not to contradict, or Retort, but passively to bear her bitter Speeches'. He described leaving his bed on winter nights to escape his wife's verbal and physical abuse and walking about or lying on the floor wrapped in a quilt. In the 1760s Charles Allison usually 'did get up at midnight and walk in the Streets for hours together to avoid hearing [his wife's] abusive and scandalous Language and the Reflections which she cast upon his Children'. William Idelle proudly declared that he never even lifted a hand to his wife despite her threatening provocation. Witnesses on his behalf offered similar accounts of self-control.[75]

[72] BIHR, Trans.CP.1697/2; D/C.CP.1696/3, *Shaw c. Shaw*, 1696.
[73] BIHR, Trans.CP.1765/4, *Ettrick c. Ettrick*, Personal response to Libel.
[74] BIHR, CP.I/291, *Stradling c. Stradling*, 1713; UOD, DDR/EJ/PRC/2/1743/12, *Smith c. Smith*.
[75] BIHR, Trans.CP.1730/6, *Currie c. Currie*, 1729; DDR/EJ/CCD/3/1765/2, *Allison c. Allison*; CP.I/154, CP.I/241, CP.I/2735, *Idelle c. Idelle*, 1706.

This is a major difference from the sixteenth- and seventeenth-century London husbands that Gowing has examined. They used the law of correction as self-defence and characterised their abuse as a rational, controlled and measured response to wifely provocation. Often the blows were a response to wives' verbal abuse.[76] On the other hand, reason had long been the acceptable alternative to violence. The *Book of Homilies* advised husbands: 'reasoning should be used and not fighting'.[77] By the later seventeenth century, reason was linked to self-control, which was a key feature of manhood. As Elizabeth Foyster shows, men needed to demonstrate that they could manage their superior strength by the use of reason. Men could still physically discipline their wives, but only as long as they did so without losing control and in a rational manner.[78] As ideas about men as the threatening sex, in need of reform and control, developed, male self-control became crucial. Thus, as Foyster notes, by the eighteenth century male self-control was systematically inculcated from childhood as part of the education system. It also came to be associated with civility and politeness so that un-discipline of the passions indicated vulgarity.[79] In this way, wife-beating came to represent dishonour. William Fleetwood's printed sermons dealing with the relative duties of household members, published in 1716, described husbands who used bitter words as 'unmanly and unjust' and when their bitterness went past words 'to personal Outrage, Violence and Hurt' it was 'a thing unworthy any good and honest Man'.[80]

These sentiments were widely shared. In the first decade of the eighteenth century Anne Mould's sister told her brother-in-law that he should be ashamed for abusing his wife.[81] As a result some men abused their wives at night-time or behind closed doors, in order to avoid witnesses and to conceal their behaviour.[82] In general, reactions to wife-beating in witnesses' statements and in press accounts point to a general distaste for domestic violence. It was not considered normal. Some servants deposed in cruelty separation suits that they left their employment when their contract was up, because the domestic violence that they encountered was unacceptable. Martha Copley was a servant to James and Margaret Lees for seven months at the end of the eighteenth century. When her master expressed dissatisfaction with her because she had warned his wife that he was in a foul temper, she informed him that 'she would go immediately if he chose for she had not been accustomed to such quarrelling and it was very disagreeable to her'.[83]

[76] Gowing, *Domestic Dangers*, pp. 219, 222.   [77] DRO, *Book of Homilies*, p. 241.
[78] Foyster, 'Male honour', 216–19, 224.
[79] Foyster, 'Boys will be boys?' in Hitchcock and Cohen (eds.), *English Masculinities*, pp. 152–4, 161–2.
[80] Fleetwood, *Relative duties*.   [81] BIHR, CP.I/542, *Mould c. Mould*, 1709.
[82] UOD, DDR/EJ/PRC/2/1745/9, *Wright c. Wright*.
[83] BIHR, Chanc.CP.1803/3, *Lees c. Lees*, 1803.

Wife-beating was associated with other anti-social ills and condemned as such. Joseph Allenson, for example, was described as 'the terror of all the neighbourhood' in 1761.[84] A justice of the peace jotted on the bottom of Thomas Davy's recognizance in 1734: 'I had many complaints against this Davy for very much beating his wife and the neighbours seemed apprehensive of a dangerous consequence, for which I thought I would do no less than bind him over.'[85] These attitudes were hardened by the perception that violence was a specifically male characteristic, and less a female one. When James Lees' wife sued him for cruelty in the last decade of the century he received an anonymous letter, addressed to 'Thou old whoremonger'. It triumphantly declared: 'I formerly wrote to thee about the sufferings of thy wife. I told thee when thy trial did come on I would bear witness against thee. I did hear the other day that thou art to be tried next week which I am glad of.'[86] The use of 'trial' is interesting because it suggests that by this time people saw a cruelty separation as a way to prosecute a husband.

People used discretion in their attitudes towards domestic violence. Occasional physical struggles or quarrels that ended in a scuffle were dismissed as excusable and not the business of anyone outside the couple. They tried to stop violence when it was one-sided, when men were out of control, when it was against children, or when it was systematic. In 1709 Edward Humphrey and his wife heard their neighbours William and Margaret Sharpe arguing. Edward's wife went next door to ask them to be quiet, in what was probably intended to be a less threatening intervention. When this failed, Edward went himself, warned William Sharpe to be civil, and asked Margaret Sharpe to leave with him. She obviously did not because he quickly returned when he heard William threaten to burn Margaret on the fire. Again he returned home, coming to her assistance once more when he heard her desperately cry out for help. On this third occasion he took a stick, forced open the door and rescued her and her grand-child.[87] Help was also offered in less direct ways. In 1801 Mrs Jones sent her servant Mary Brisco on an errand to a mantua maker in Lever Street, Manchester. While waiting for the door to be answered, Mary looked through the parlour window of the house opposite and saw a 'gentleman' strike the lady sitting there with a child in her arms, dragging her onto the floor. As soon as she got into the mantua maker's house she asked for the couple's name (Lees) and reported what she had seen on her return to her mistress. Mrs Jones immediately sent Mary to Mr Lees' house to ask for a cotton bag, explaining that this might put a stop to further outrage.[88] As many newspaper reports demonstrated, knowledge

---

[84] NYA, QSB/1761/0720, Deposition of Hugh Watson, brother of Anne Allenson, 11 February 1761.
[85] OA/Mi/1734/9.   [86] BIHR, Chanc.CP.1803/3, Lees c. Lees, 1803 (my punctuation).
[87] OA/Ep/1709/8.
[88] BIHR, Chanc.CP.1803/3, Lees c. Lees, 1803, Mary Brisco's deposition.

of and intervention in wife-beating did not always resolve the situation. Indeed it was often the suspicions of servants and neighbours of murdered wives which resulted in their husbands' prosecutions. One neighbourhood managed to instigate a coroner's inquest, and the servants and neighbours of a farmer and tile-man in Worcester had his wife exhumed and examined so that he was accused of her murder and taken into gaol.[89]

This does not mean that only brutal violence was condemned, as some historians have supposed. Legal definitions of cruelty expanded in the second half of the eighteenth century. Little changed in the methods abusive husbands employed against their wives. Most used their fists and feet and threatened their wives with their clasp knives. Others used implements that were close to hand, like sticks, pokers, forks, fire shovels, tongs, bellows and hatchets, as well as throwing fire and coals. Nonetheless, from the mid eighteenth century more types of male behaviour were categorised as cruel in the church courts. Both provincial and London ecclesiastical courts demonstrate this shift. Between 1660 and 1750 the acts described in wives' libels were barbarous, savage, and included attempts on their lives. By the second half of the eighteenth century, libels included violence that was less furious, as well as verbal threats to life.[90] Cases might now involve persistent, numerous, though relatively minor, acts of cruelty and other forms of abuse like locking a wife into an attic to force her to obey an unreasonable demand. The evolution culminated in Lord Stowell's judgement in the 1790s, which allowed wives to use their husbands' threats of violence as sufficient grounds for separation.[91] Biggs and Stone suppose that a more extensive categorisation of cruelty was a sign that wives were coming to be considered less subordinate and more equal to their husbands.[92] There is little evidence that behaviour was affected in this way. It is more plausible that the change reflected the notion that men needed to be subjected to more control in order to prevent violence.

The methods by which wives dealt with their husbands' abuse also seem to have shifted in the same period. As the century progressed, fewer wives brought separation suits on the grounds of cruelty. Of the 47 cases of cruelty separations which came before York and Durham church courts, for which cause papers survive, 77% were heard in the period 1660 to 1750 and 23% between 1750 and the first few years of the new century. Wives were not turning instead to the London courts in the hope of quicker, better services because these courts also experienced a decline in the number of wives suing for cruelty.[93] Of the 98 cruelty cases that came before London consistory court between 1660 and 1800, 76% occurred before 1720. The

[89] *JOJ*, 17 July 1773, p. 1; 19 June 1773, p. 3.
[90] For the Court of Arches see Biggs, *Matrimonial Cruelty*, pp. 21–6.
[91] Cited in ibid., pp. 24–6.   [92] Ibid., p. 21.   [93] Stone, *Divorce*, pp. 41–3.

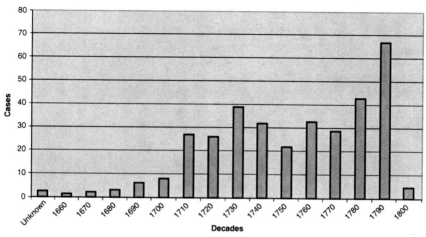

Figure 1. Quarter Sessions wife-beaters per decade

Court of Arches, which also heard appeals from the province of Canterbury, received 90% of its 158 cruelty separation cases before 1750. The Court of Arches was already experiencing a decline from the 1710s, whereas the 1710s and '20s were peak decades in London, Durham and York ecclesiastical courts, with the fall after the 1750s.[94] The change is partly explained by the overall decline in the use of the church courts. For example, numbers of defamation cases at York increased between 1665 and the 1720s but also fell thereafter.[95] It is also plausible that higher-ranking wives used private separation as a replacement for church court separations. Another explanation is offered by Tim Meldrum who argues that the fall in instance business before London consistory court in the eighteenth century is explained by the ineffectiveness of ecclesiastical penalties and cheaper more flexible alternative methods of prosecution available from the quarter sessions.[96]

This is a persuasive theory that may explain the fall in cruelty separations, although it is difficult to provide conclusive evidence that wives turned from the church courts to the quarter sessions in order to deal with their husbands' cruelty. Certainly, instances of wife-beating increased in the quarter sessions studied, as cruelty separations fell in the ecclesiastical courts, peaking in the 1790s (figure 1). However, these rates are problematic. The increase from the

[94] Figures cited in ibid., pp. 425, 428.
[95] J. A. Sharpe, 'Defamation and sexual slander in early modern England: the church courts at York', *Borthwick Papers*, 58 (1980), 27.
[96] He discounts the theory that increasing costs turned people away from the ecclesiastical courts, although he notes that fees were excessive enough to deter lower-rank women from undertaking cases (T. Meldrum, 'A women's court in London: defamation at the Bishop of London's consistory court, 1700–1745', *London Journal*, 19, 1 (1994), 1–5, 15).

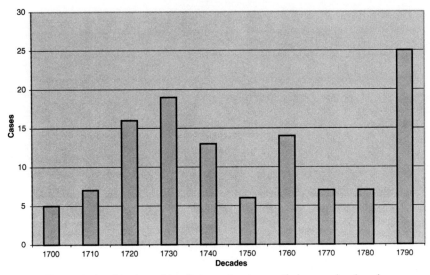

Figure 2. Buckinghamshire Quarter Sessions wife-beaters by decade

1710s is simply a feature of better survival and improvements in record-keeping.[97] Changes in styles of entries in order and minute books probably account for the discrepancies in the decadal rates. In addition, calendars of prisoners appear more frequently and consistently in the later eighteenth century, which is likely to improve the retrieval of wife-beaters from the records. There is also no apparent change in social status of those using the quarter sessions that might indicate that higher-status wives were turning away from the church courts. Nonetheless, when the individual quarter sessions are isolated, all still show a general increase in prosecutions, albeit with different peak decades (figures 2–5). For instance Buckinghamshire experienced a fall in their dealings with wife-beaters in the 1770s and '80s and a peak in the '90s, whereas Oxfordshire had its highest numbers in the '70s and '80s (figures 2 and 3). In North Yorkshire, prosecutions were quite low until the 1780s and '90s (figure 4). Differences in the availability and practices of local justices of the peace may explain these variations, and local circumstances possibly played their part too. The lower decades in Buckinghamshire coincided with their busiest decades in terms of dealing with deserting husbands. It is feasible that poor economic conditions led justices to be more concerned with targeting men who created burdens on parish

---

[97] Quarter sessions with better rates of record survival demonstrate that wives frequently used the courts to prosecute cruel husbands before the 1710s. See Hurl-Eamon, 'Domestic violence prosecuted'.

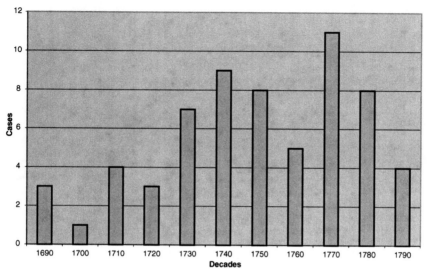

Figure 3. Oxfordshire Quarter Sessions wife-beaters by decade

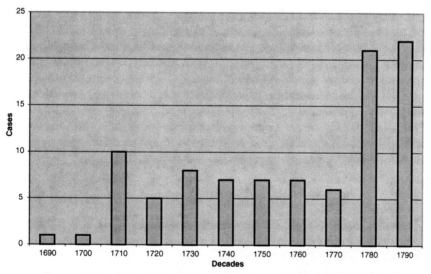

Figure 4. North Yorkshire Quarter Sessions wife-beaters by decade

relief, encouraging mediation for those experiencing domestic violence, with fewer cases reaching the sessions.

The increase in the use of the quarter sessions was perhaps facilitated by the fact that justices of the peace and quarter sessions offered similar

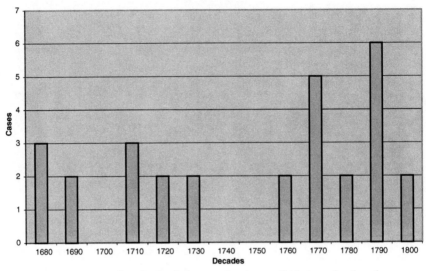

Figure 5. Northumberland Quarter Sessions wife-beaters by decade

outcomes to the church courts by the second half of the eighteenth century, when, in addition to providing mediation and means to halt male violence, they were prepared to organise maintenance and 'legitimise' existing separations. Overall, wives may also have been encouraged to use the quarter sessions to deal with their husbands' violence because of harsher judicial attitudes to violent offenders in general. There was a move away from nominal fines and public whippings to imprisonment for those convicted of assault.[98] Peter King's study of the Essex Quarter Sessions suggests that magisterial willingness to take assault more seriously caused an increase in the numbers of assault indictments brought to those sessions in the 1780s.[99]

DEFINING ACCEPTABLE BEHAVIOUR FOR WIVES

Historians of domestic violence usually dismiss accusations of wives' violence as unrepresentative of power relations in the household and too unusual to deserve much attention. It is true that the incidence of wifely abuse was minuscule compared to male abuse.[100] Although husbands were able to secure articles of the peace against their wives, just as wives could against husbands,

[98] Beattie, *Crime and the Courts*, pp. 457–61, 609, 619, 620.
[99] P. King, 'Punishing assault: the transformation of attitudes in the English courts', *Journal of Interdisciplinary History*, 27, 1 (1996), 70.
[100] For some examples see: J. Sharpe, 'Domestic homicide in early modern England', *Historical Journal*, 24 (1981), 34–6; Robb, 'Circe in crinoline', 176–7.

only a tiny number of husbands did so. Over the period studied the records of the six quarter sessions yield only eleven wives who were brought before a magistrate for a breach of the peace against their husbands and another for threatening to fire her husband's house (Appendix 1). They were brought before the quarter sessions for one-off threats against husbands with knives and pokers and one-off attempts to kill them, whereas wives prosecuted husbands at this level for repeatedly beating them and risking their lives with violence. The number of cases is too small and the record of outcomes too partial to be conclusive, but it seems that violent wives were not treated all that differently from violent husbands, except where arson was involved. Four of the prosecutions included the accusation that the wives threatened and/or attempted to fire their husbands' houses or lodging rooms. The two wives who had set fire to a house were very severely punished. In 1731 Oxfordshire Quarter Sessions committed one wife to gaol for a year and ensured she was also whipped twice until bloody, and Newcastle Quarter Sessions fined another arsonist wife £10 in 1765.[101] Only fifteen men counter-accused their wives of cruelty or attempted poisoning in other matrimonial cases (Appendix 8). The violence was usually minor compared to the wives' equivalent complaints about their husbands. Most accusations centred on wives tearing husbands' clothes, scratching, spitting, striking out and throwing household items at them. In 1675 Charles Allenson described how his wife spat in his face and scratched it, so that he was forced to wear patches and keep to his bed for a week or more.[102] Some deponents supported the husbands. Mary Cross, a servant, deposed in 1697 that she saw Elizabeth Pighells get hold of her husband, a rector, by the collar, tear his cassock, and 'spitt towards him in contempt and scorne of him'. Mary Jenkins reported that when she was a servant to Elizabeth and John, she often heard Elizabeth curse him, pull his wig off and 'bite him by the shoulder'.[103]

For all its rarity in numbers, the evolution in cultural attitudes towards female violence make it worth exploring wives' threatened or committed domestic violence more fully. There were some differences between the cultural images and reality. The most 'female' form of violence in the public mind was poisoning, since it required no strength, and was facilitated by women's role in household provision, consumption and food preparation.[104] Some of the husbands accused their wives of threatening to poison them, among other minor acts of violence, but only two men claimed their wives attempted to poison them (Appendix 8). However, wives often committed acts that were not secretive or covert. It was quite common in the secondary complaints for

---

[101] OA, QS/1731/Ea/1; TWA, QS/NC/1/7, p. 345.
[102] BIHR, CP.H/3264, Allenson c. Allenson, 1675.
[103] BIHR, CP.H/4505, Pighells c. Pighells, 1697, Depositions of Mary Cross and Mary Jenkins.
[104] Dolan, Dangerous Familiars, p. 30; Robb, 'Circe in crinoline'.

wives to have attacked their husbands in more direct ways. Jane Currie was
reported to have kicked her husband in the face when he came to help mend
her broken pillion while she was out riding.[105] Wives also took advantage
of their husbands' incapacity due to illness. In 1706 William Idelle claimed
that his wife struck him on the legs and head with a fire shovel when he was
ill in bed, and his nephew stated that William's legs were bruised and the
skin broken as a result.[106] The sampled newspapers reported on the methods
seventeen wives used to kill their husbands and though nine of them used
poison, another eight used weapons like knives, a poker, a razor, a coal rake
and melted pewter. Cases of husband murder that fascinated the public often
involved a wife who worked with an accomplice, usually her lover, who
boosted the woman's lesser physical strength. The reality of husband murder could be very different, as the desperate, slow struggle that resulted in the
death of William Eagle of Tollerton, Yorkshire, testifies. In 1772, Elizabeth
Eagle and her two sisters Sarah and Mary Penrose were committed to gaol
charged with his murder. Elizabeth and Sarah had followed William into the
field where he was milking and beat him so much that he had to be carried
home. The next day, as the *Newcastle Journal* explained, 'he received from
his wife and her two sisters (none else being with him) a large wound on
the forehead, and another on the back part of his head, of which he died'.
A glimpse of the motivation for this attack is found in the North Riding's
Quarter Sessions records for 1770 and 1771, when William was twice bound
over by his wife Elizabeth to keep the peace towards her.[107]

It is impossible to make any claims about the effect on behaviour of cultural
shifts in perceptions about female violence, but they probably had some
impact on the way that husbands described their wives. Claiming that a
wife was aggressive was never particularly safe because popular literature
equated violent women with weak men. In 1736 an epigram was printed in
the *Gentleman's Magazine*:

> BEN's wife having beat him; his friend *Will* cries, *Nan*!
> Are you not asham'd, thus to fight with a man?
> She reply'd; you poor ignorant son of a wh–re!
> I'll swear I've not *seen* one this hour and more.[108]

While women held their dominance in cultural terms as perpetrators of intimate violence, however, husbands were able to discuss their wives' abuse
and expect it to be taken seriously. Thus in the first part of our period, female
domestic violence was a useful claim for men, because, like male violence, it
signified the disruption of household order. Husbands who counter-accused

[105] BIHR, Trans.CP.1730/6, *Currie c. Currie*, 1729, John Grainger's deposition.
[106] BIHR, CP.I/2735, *Idelle c. Idelle*, 1706.
[107] *N.Jour*, 20 June 1772, p. 3; NYA, QSB/MIC 2182/fr. 003381; QSB/MIC 2182/fr. 004843.
[108] *GM*, 6 (February 1736), 109.

their wives were quite prepared to portray them as openly aggressive. William Idelle also described his wife's response when called over by him; she brought out a sword in an angry and passionate manner, and challenged him to a fight. When he responded by attempting to pacify her, she called him a coward and pitiful fellow.[109] It is also interesting that when a third party described violence between spouses, the relative aggression was more balanced. In 1722 Reverend Shanks' two maid-servants responded to his accusation that they had defamed him, with an information accusing him of ill-treating them following his violent fight with his wife. They described their fight as equal: when he beat his wife with a cane, she took it from him and hid it, and then they 'fell to blows' and she made his face all bloody.[110]

Unfortunately, the evidence is too limited to draw firm conclusions about changes over time, but it is also suggestive. Seven (63%) of the wives were prosecuted for breach of the peace before the mid-century and four (36%) after. This is perhaps made more significant by the facts that most other assaults increased in the latter part of the eighteenth century and that population was increasing. The secondary complaints are also difficult to interpret adequately, because the numbers of cruelty separations declined after the mid eighteenth century and so, therefore, did the opportunities for male defences. It may still be significant that 71% of the husbands counter-accused violence before 1750.

During the second half of the eighteenth century, it seems to have become less viable for men to portray their wives convincingly as abusive. The mid-century was a transition period.[111] George Pearson advertised that he and his wife had mutually separated in 1756 and confirmed that he intended to pay her maintenance as soon as he was able 'in order to prevent, perhaps, shedding each others [sic] Blood; for as she had many Times threatned [sic] me, and once made an Attempt, I have great Reason to be afraid, if I was to give her Opportunity'.[112] There is an impression that the types of violence described in the later eighteenth century were slightly different from those earlier in the period studied. In later cases violence seems to have been a response to a particular situation. John Ferman claimed that his wife struck him with a brush when he refused to let her stay in their house in 1798 after he learned of her adultery. John Greenwell's account in 1773 suggested that his wife tried to poison him for endeavouring to reclaim her from a drunken vicious course of life.[113] Earlier accounts generally had less causation. The response of Robert Northend to his wife's restitution suit in 1702 was of its time and much less tenable sixty years later. This Yorkshire couple appeared before York consistory court when Hannah claimed that,

---

[109] BIHR, CP.I/2735, *Idelle* c. *Idelle*, 1706.   [110] NCAS, QSB/58, fols. 76, 83–6.
[111] Wiener's suggestion ('Changing nightmares', 191).   [112] *Y.Cour*, 21 September 1756.
[113] UOD, DDR/EJ/CCD/3/180/4, *Ferman* c. *Ferman*; DDR/EJ/CCD/3/1773/3, *Greenwell* c. *Greenwell*.

after being married to Robert for several months, he had turned her out of his father's house. She had been Robert's father's housekeeper and was approximately ten years older than him; he used this status and age differential to support his claim that they were not legally married. He did, however, plead that if he had married her, it was because she had intoxicated him and out of fear of being mischiefed by her. He accused her of cutting his forehead and hair with a penknife and warning him that she would 'cutt him as small as flesh to the pott in case he would not marry her'.[114] The increasing 'victimisation' of women in the later eighteenth century probably removed husbands' opportunities to describe their wives as aggressive. Nonetheless, the changes in ideas about women's capacity for violence did not completely disarm them. The culture of sensibility's distaste at wife-beating gave them some rights *in extremis*. In 1799 the *Newcastle Courant* reported that a Derbyshire woman, who had frequently been beaten by her husband, eventually took revenge. While he was asleep she sewed him up in the bed-clothes and then 'thrashed him so soundly that he entered into a treaty of amity, which it is probable, a feeling recollection of his late sufferings will deter him from infringing. When a fellow's heart is so dead to sensibility as to warrant him striking a woman, it is to his shoulders that the remedy should be applied.'[115]

Another way to explore the parameters of acceptable behaviour for wives is through their descriptions of their own character and responses to their husbands. This is most detailed in cruelty separation cases. In them detailed allegations of male violence were preceded with a short relatively formulaic statement about wives' moral worth, virtue, and mild, affable and obliging disposition. Deponents in their favour also supported these personal references, sometimes explicitly spelling out that the women made excellent wives. To some extent these characteristics followed dominant ideals of feminine behaviour that were widely disseminated in printed advice literature, sermons and newspapers. It is worth briefly considering this language of wifely behaviour, which women were familiar with. It was subtle, multi-layered material. Some advice for married women recognised the problems of the marital power relationship for them. The *Book of Homilies* noted that marriage might not appeal to women because 'they must relinquish the liberty of their owne rule'.[116] George Savile, in 1688, commented in the popular *Lady's New Year Gift* that 'obey' 'is an ungenteel word, and less easie to be digested'.[117] While this literature might propose that meek and quiet wives could bear injuries, crosses and hard usage better than those of a violent

---

[114] BIHR, CP.I/3; CP.I/164, *Northend c. Northend*, 1702.
[115] *N.Cour*, 2 February 1799, p. 2.   [116] *Book of Homilies*, pp. 241–4.
[117] Halifax, *The Lady's New Year's Gift: or, Advice to a Daughter* (1688) cited in Jones (ed.), *Women*, p. 18.

temper, it also conceded that female subjection was limited.[118] Wives owed no submission to their husbands when the latter acted against the laws of God or man. Occasionally this went further. In a passage that potentially offered women a great deal of flexibility, William Fleetwood advised, '[w]here Men's Commands are evidently unreasonable, shamefully indiscreet, unusual and unheard of, infamous, or unbecoming their Age, their Credit, Quality and Condition, they may be safely pass'd by; *omitted*, rather *than neglected* or *despis'd*'.[119] The message of wives' subordinate position in relation to their husbands could be cast in persuasive terms. Fleetwood founded his explanation for the duties of wives on the biblical passage: 'Ye Wives, be in Subjection to your own Husbands that if any obey not the Word, they also may, without the Word, be won by the Conversation of the Wives: While they behold their chaste Conversation coupled with Fear.' He employed a rational explanation for its use: the dictate contained the effects of submission, not just the command, 'which is a great Encouragement to the fulfilling it; for when a Law carries its Reason with it, it is more likely to find a good Acceptance and Compliance'.[120]

So by behaving in the proposed way, not only would a wife bring her husband into the ways of God, she would improve his character. Wives were told that they derived power as the corollary of their decision to be subordinate.[121] The motif of female strength lying in weakness was one that dominated the period. In 1688 George Savile informed his female readers, 'You have it in your power not only to free your selves, but to subdue your Masters, and without violence throw both their *Natural* and *Legal Authority* at your Feet.' Later he pointed out, 'You have more strength in your *Looks*, than we have in our *Laws*, and more power by your *Tears*, than we have by our *Arguments*.'[122] In 1745, the *Gentleman's Magazine* printed a poem called 'The Choice, Or the Model of a Wife'. The author's ideal wife, in addition to being virtuous, modest, wise and good-natured, would be adept at appeasing her husband. Through her 'winning art', 'When *most* she rules

---

[118] For example, R. Steele, *The Ladies Library, written by a Lady, 3 vols. Published by Sir Richard Steele*, 6th edition (London, 1714), pp. 50–2.

[119] His only qualification was that impartial people should understand those commands that wives refused to comply with; wives should not oppose simply for mastery (Fleetwood, *Relative duties*, p. 140).

[120] I Peter III, verses 1, 2, in Fleetwood, *Relative duties*, pp. 131–49. See also François Bruys, *The Art of Knowing Women: or, the Female Sex Dissected, in a faithful representation of their virtues and vices, written in French by the Chevalier Plante-amour, published at the Hague, 1729. Now faithfully made English with improvements* (London, 1730), p. 70; Steele, *The Ladies Library*, pp. 37–40.

[121] Law, custom and female privileges further ameliorated this contractual relationship (T. Salmon, *A Critical Essay concerning Marriage* (London, 1724, reprinted 1985), pp. 73, 78).

[122] Cited in Jones (ed.), *Women*, pp. 18–21.

him *seems* t'obey'.[123] By 1759 Thomas Marriott had reached the apotheosis of this style of advice. In verse he explained:

> Hence ev'ry Wife her Husband must obey,
> She, by Compliance, can her Ruler sway;
> Strong, without Strength, she triumphs o'er the Heart,
> What Nature gives not, she acquires by Art;
> Preeminence, herself debasing gains,
> By yielding conquers, and by serving reigns.[124]

Ingrid Tague, in her essay on the relationship between the discourse of marriage and aristocratic women, points out that these texts illustrated 'that the best way for a woman to achieve influence was through abject submission'.[125] Yet in a sense they did give men and women an expectation that wives had access to some forms of power. This could be explicitly recognised to provide authority through women's manipulation of their husbands. For instance, in 1756, Eliza Haywood recommended that a wife should advise her husband about managing his fortune, but 'disguis'd under the softer and more humble appearance of perswasion', in case he felt his prerogative was infringed upon.[126] Nonetheless, the cynicism and hypocrisy underlying the images came under attack. In 1735, in the *Gentleman's Magazine*, 'Mary Rulewell' argued that its advocates were trying 'to make Wives blindly submit to their Husbands, for fear the Good Man shou'd *take Pett*'. In the same volume a letter from 'Martha Love-Rule' acknowledged that some wives made obedience so engaging that their husbands were 'reciprocally Dutiful'. Pertinently, she observed that such manipulation was a disagreeable mixture of liberty and slavery, obedience and government.[127] Perhaps a better description of the message of didactic texts is that they recommended selective and timely deference towards men rather than total submission.

These images lent themselves to being used flexibly by women. Anne Kugler shows how Lady Sarah Cowper adapted them to her personal circumstances.[128] Other recent work provides convincing evidence that women

---

123 *GM*, 15 (June 1745), 327. The message was ubiquitous. See the *Newcastle Intelligencer*, 31 December 1755, p. 4; Steele, *The Ladies Library*, p. 50; *The Matrimonial Preceptor. A collection of examples and precepts relating to the married state, from the most celebrated writers ancient and modern* (London, 1755), pp. 163–5.

124 T. Marriott, *Female Conduct: being an essay on the art of pleasing. To be practised by the fair sex, before, and after marriage. A poem in two books* (London, 1759), pp. 18, 24, 28.

125 Tague, 'Love, honor, and obedience', 84–9.

126 After repeated warnings that wives must not give up trying to reform their husbands, she confided that if all this failed the wife must turn to separation (Haywood herself was separated) (*The Wife, by Mira, one of the Authors of The Female Spectator, and Epistles of Ladies* (London, 1756), pp. 102–3, 276–8).

127 *GM*, 5 (January 1735), 15–16; ibid. (October 1735), 594–5.

128 A. Kugler, 'Prescription, culture, and shaping identity: Lady Sarah Cowper 1644–1720', Ph.D. thesis, University of Michigan (1994).

employed conduct-book rhetoric in their own way. Tague found that aristocratic women drew on this language, which emphasised their obedience to
men, to demonstrate their own virtue and thus their moral authority. It also
provided them with a legitimate framework with which to criticise their husbands in an acceptable manner.[129] The evidence for the responses of women
from the middling sort and ranks of wage labourers to the rhetoric is more
difficult to come by. The records of marital difficulties demonstrate that some
wives employed its objections to husbands who abused their authority and
acted as tyrants. In 1736 the *Gentleman's Magazine* claimed, for example,
that 'Women were never design'd to be *Slaves*, nor Men to be *Tyrants*.'[130]
Thus Catherine Ettrick reported that her husband had insisted, 'Wives should
and ought to be nothing but Vassalls and Slaves to their Husbands', to show
that he was a bad husband. In 1676 Sarah Dawson, the sixteen-year-old
servant of Grace and Charles Allenson, of York, said her mistress' life 'was a
continual slavery'. Yet it has to be said that wives seemed inclined to present
themselves as the unlucky spouses of mad, bad men rather than abject subjects of tyrannical husbands.[131]

The formulaic elements of the legal documents also echoed widespread
literary injunctions to husbands to love their wives. The *Newcastle Journal*
printed advice addressed to widowers, husbands and bachelors in 1760,
suggesting that men 'govern with a gentle sway' and always love and cherish
their wife so that she 'will chearfully [sic] obey so endearing a husband'.[132]
Most wives' libels declared that their husbands beat them because of hatred,
in effect a lack of love. Esther Bowes' libel of 1718 to Durham consistory
court alleged 'That notwithstanding the p[re]misses and the Laws divine and
Humane...every Husband is willed charged and Com[m]anded to Love his
Wife as himself to cherish and comfort her and not to be bitter ag[ains]t her
yet the s[ai]d Jonathan Bowes hath [behaved to her] with great disdain and
outragious Cruelty.'[133]

Despite research that suggests that images of wifely submission were somewhat ambiguous in both content and reception, historians still occasionally
suggest that in order to succeed in court women had to present themselves as
'passive victims' thereby gaining sympathy.[134] Actually, 'passivity' is a problematic term and its connotations of subordination and limitation need to be

[129] Tague, 'Love, honor, and obedience', 95, 96. [130] See *GM*, 8 (1738), 591.
[131] BIHR, CP.I/1503, *Ettrick c. Ettrick*, Answer to William Ettrick's Allegation, 10 April 1767; BIHR, CP.H/3264, *Allenson c. Allenson*, 1675.
[132] *N.Jour*, 16–23 August 1760, p. 2; 6–13 September 1760, p. 1.
[133] UOD, DDR/EJ/PRC/2/1717/2, *Bowes c. Bowes*, 1718.
[134] It is misleading to talk about 'success', for it is impossible to be certain what wives perceived to be the successful result of a cruelty separation. They sought a variety of outcomes, from stopping violence, to legitimising an existing separation, to organising maintenance (M. Hunt, 'Wife beating', p. 24; Shoemaker, *Gender*, p. 107).

set in historical context. Linda Pollock has shown that women were educated
to perform a dual role of 'subordination and competence'. Thus their upbringing 'was intended to ensure adult women were deferential to men, but
not to preclude the possibility of independent thought or action'.[135] There
is ample personal evidence that while wives understood that they needed to
conciliate and appease their husbands, this did not preclude a wide range of
behaviour. For Amanda Vickery, the correspondence of Georgian wives confirms that the 'deferential utterance is not an unerring sign of a deferential
spirit'.[136]

Thus comments about passivity in records of marital difficulties take on
subtler hues. For example, while it served a purpose in court by highlighting
the cruelty of men, it failed as an effective model for wider marital relations
since it was demonstrated that abject female submission also ended in violence. Lucas Mawburne of Craike, a 38-year-old rector, deposed that if Grace
Allenson had not been an 'obedient wife and submitted and complyed with
all his ill humours', Charles Allenson would have done her a mischief.[137]
This is exactly what he did. Beaten women understood the pointlessness of
submission, even when reduced to it as a coping tactic. Catherine Ettrick
said that despite her 'most submissive Behaviour and Affection in doing and
complying with every thing her . . . Husband directed her and to submitting to
what none even the lowest Servant would have submitted to, that would not
prevent his Cruel Barbarous and Brutish Treatment and usage of her'.[138] The
futility of such behaviour appeared in other media. The *Newcastle Journal*
reported in August 1772 that a husband isolated his wife from her friends
and family until she was 'entirely at his mercy' and then poisoned her. The
account's observation that 'She seems to have resigned herself with great
patience and even to have wished for death' can hardly have been exemplary
behaviour for its married female readers since it resulted in her murder.[139]
Indeed, there is scattered evidence that people thought women should leave
abusive partners rather than act submissively. Mary Foster was a widow,
but cohabited with Robert Wilkinson as his wife. Having failed in his own
business, he lived with Mary in her house and brandy shop in Durham City.
According to the newspaper report of her murder in 1743, he drank the
stock and became abusive,

which increas'd by his giving Way to his Passion, and from Words proceeded to
Blows, till it became the Surprise of the whole Neighbourhood, that she did not leave
him, and seek her Bread where she might obtain it with more Peace and Satisfaction,

[135] Pollock, '"Teach her"', 233, 250.   [136] Vickery, *Gentleman's Daughter*, p. 83.
[137] BIHR, CP.H/3264, *Allenson c. Allenson*, 1675.
[138] BIHR, C.P. I/1503, *Ettrick c. Ettrick*, 1765, Answers to William Ettrick's Allegation,
   nos. 11, 13.
[139] *N.Jour*, 29 August 1772, p. 1.

than she might be sensible she could do with him; but such was her Infatuation, that, notwithstanding the many Wounds and Bruises he had lately given her,...she still continu'd with him.[140]

In such a small sample it is impossible to be conclusive about the effects of the changes in ideals of femininity upon marital roles and upon wives' self-representations. Nevertheless, there is a sense that wives were able to present themselves in slightly broader ways in the first part of the period studied. For example, in the face of her husband's repeated defence that she was provoking, Anne Shaw admitted that she was naturally of an unquiet temper, but pointed out that for the last twenty years she had just cause to be passionate because of the intolerable abuses received from her husband.[141] A forceful nature does not seem to have prevented women from being con- sidered a good example of womanhood. In 1719, the 24-year-old friend of Barbara Dobby, who had known her since childhood, responded to the sug- gestion that she was provoking, by explaining that Barbara was a woman 'of a pritty high spirit but...is a person of a civil and vertuous behaviour'.[142] Though the number of cruelty separations declined, reducing the body of evidence, the impression remains that women's self-representations became more restricted in the second half of the eighteenth century. In tandem with men's reluctance to present their wives as physically abusive, wives were less inclined to admit to being disobliging themselves. Yet the language of sensibility also provided a fresh way to express existing ambivalence about men's 'rights' to physically correct their wives. For example in 1785 the *York Chronicle* listed types of behaviour that prevented men from being regarded as men of feeling. It explained that the 'husband who uses his wife as a menial servant, who is never less at home, than when at home with her; and who beats and abuses her, cannot be a *man of feeling*'.[143] Also, in the end, wives' self-representations in court cannot be taken as mirrors of female behaviour elsewhere. Whatever the strategic use of such 'ideas' of behaviour, in less nar- rowly defined situations women provided broader self-descriptions based on many of the characteristics by which men defined themselves, including their civic role, charitable activities and occupational status.

CONCLUSION: A BATTLE OF THE SEXES?

When evidence of wife-beating is considered alongside other evidence from marital difficulties, there emerges a more dynamic picture of marriage than

---

[140] *N.Cour*, 19–26 March 1743, p. 2.
[141] BIHR, Trans.CP.1697/2, D/C.CP.1696/3, *Shaw* c. *Shaw*, Personal response to Robert's allegation.
[142] BIHR, CP.I/581, *Dobby* c. *Dobby*, 1719.   [143] *Y.Chron*, 14 January 1785.

stereotyped models of marital power. Patriarchal ideals were pervasive and partly the cause of wife-beating, for a few men held flawed versions of their dominant position. Joseph Watson told his wife that 'he thought it no sin to kill her that she being his wife he had a right to do with her what he pleased'. A servant deposed that Joseph often declared that 'being his wife he had a right to whip her like a spaniel Dog'.[144] In 1796 Catharine King stated that her husband, Thomas, a dairyman, told her that he did not want to be hanged for her, 'But that he might kick her, and spit in her face or Tread on her Toes, there was no one could hurt him for that.'[145] Patriarchy contained too many checks on this sort of behaviour to make it more than the key-stone of men's exploitation of their position. Indeed, men who attempted to exert too much control over their wives were described as irrational in their demands.[146] In the later seventeenth century, Charles Allenson's behaviour was roundly condemned. For example, he would respond to his wife's enquiry in the evening about what he wanted for dinner the next day by damning her and telling her to ask him in the morning. Grace would then go to him in the morning, so he would curse her for waking him and throw a bed staff at her; if she listened until he stirred he would still curse her.[147] John Greenwell, a Northumberland surgeon, was also presented as unreasonably controlling. He tried to stop his wife leaving the house without his consent and would only intermittently allow her to attend church in the years 1766 to 1768. When he did so, he stood in the street brandishing his stick at her while she left and returned, to signal that she should not talk to anyone.[148]

Changing ideas about the perpetrators of violence also made it more difficult for such men to justify their behaviour as a rational response to wifely transgressions of patriarchy. Even though these shifting gender constructions 'victimised' women, there is little evidence that in reality wives were submissive in order to avoid violence. Women's ability to leave their violent husbands was severely curtailed by having to leave their children and by their economic inter-dependence, but we should not confuse this with passivity. Indeed, economic co-dependency may have affected the power balance in marriage, making wives aware of their importance, privileges and rights. Thus married life contained struggles for control; sometimes men won, sometimes women did. This echoes another literary model of marriage that was widely available to contemporaries: the battle of the sexes. A 'well-known'

---

[144] UOD, DDR/EJ/CCD/3/1801/15, *Watson c. Watson.*   [145] CBS, QS Rolls 1796.

[146] Foyster argues that control over women was one way to gain honour. Therefore men could treat minor misdemeanours as gross errors, in their urge to gain control – although this simply destroyed household order ('Male honour', 216–19).

[147] BIHR, CP.H/3264, *Allenson c. Allenson*, 1675. See also BIHR, *Laughton c. Laughton*, 1721. John Laughton caused quarrels because of his 'unhappy and uneasy temper and finding fault with trifles or where no fault really was' (Deposition of Ann Petty).

[148] UOD, DDR/EJ/CCD/3/1773/3, *Greenwell c. Greenwell.*

tale in 1795, for instance, involved a husband and wife quarrelling and trading blows. At a knock on the door the 'contest' was stopped and the husband went to the window. The caller informed him that he had business with the master of the house. 'That point is not yet settled', said the husband, and shutting the window renewed the fight. 'Within five minutes, the wife gave out; and the husband running to the door, told the stranger, "that he might walk in, for that he had the pleasure of informing him with certainty, that he was the *master of the house*"'.[149] Accounts of this nature represented women as eager combatants in a battle whose victor should preferably be, but not always was, male. The latter situation was a fairly common claim in humorous commentary. The *Newcastle Chronicle* printed 'The Matrimonial Creed' in 1779, which humorously stated that those who married must hold the 'conjugal faith'. In this 'there were two rational beings created both equal, and yet one superior to the other, and the inferior shall bear rule over the superior'. Wives ruled, because 'there is one dominion nominal of the husband, and another dominion real of the wife'.[150]

Perhaps it is not surprising that there was an element of truth in these images when, as the last two chapters demonstrate, female functioning authority could undercut male theoretical authority. The next chapter proposes that the sexual double-standard, like patriarchal ideals of power, acted in less stereotyped ways for spouses than is sometimes imagined and was also influenced by changing cultural attitudes about femininity and masculinity.

---

[149] *N.Cour*, 17 October 1795, p. 4.   [150] *N.Chron*, 16 October 1779, p. 4.

7

'Forsaking all other': marital chastity

CHANGING UNDERSTANDINGS OF ADULTERY

It is well known that a sexual double-standard was rooted in English law and institutions. It was apparent in, amongst other things, conduct books, the law relating to divorce with remarriage and the suing of defamation cases for sexual slander. In them women's pre-marital and extra-marital sex would appear to be punished far more harshly than men's and carried far greater social consequences.[1] However, it is dangerous to presume that this sexual double-standard was so pervasive that the demand for female chastity wholly determined married women's lives and shaped married men's through the fear of cuckoldry, while, conversely, wives tolerated and even ignored male adultery. This is particularly so in the long eighteenth century when definitions of adultery and assessments of culpability were remodelled and complicated by a variety of social and gender shifts.[2] For one thing, the regulation of sexual immorality was changing. Individuals were increasingly unlikely to be prosecuted for the crime of adultery. After the Restoration the volume of cases correcting fornication and adultery in the ecclesiastical courts decreased.[3] There is still evidence that while individuals were prepared to ignore formal action against them, they were not always successful in evading punishment. In 1684 William Addison, a yeoman, petitioned the Bishop of Durham and justices of the peace to intervene in a correction case he had promoted against the gentleman Thomas Ashmall. Thomas was living in adultery with his maid, who was also William's daughter, Mary Addison. William explained that he did not have the financial means to pursue the suit, which Thomas could afford to defend and thereby stall. In the meantime Thomas was refusing to remedy his lifestyle and protecting

---

[1] K. Thomas, 'The double standard', 195; for other examples see Shoemaker, *Gender*, pp. 72–3.

[2] These opening paragraphs are indebted to Turner, 'Representations of adultery'.

[3] Ibid., pp. 6–7. Moral regulatory business had almost disappeared in the early eighteenth-century London consistory court (Meldrum, 'A women's court', 3).

Mary who had been excommunicated by the church court for her offence. William's petition succeeded in getting his daughter committed to the house of correction as an idle person and lewd liver, which he hoped would force her to mend her ways. Official action was not restricted by the sexual double-standard, since the quarter sessions also caught up with Thomas Ashmall and he was committed in September 1685 for refusing to pay the suit's costs or do penance, even after excommunication.[4]

By the 1730s presentments of adulterers in correction cases to York and Durham ecclesiastical courts had dwindled away to nothing.[5] This was due to a combination of popular scepticism and the effect on ecclesiastical authority of the Toleration Act of 1689, which gave licence to those who did not wish to attend church and meant that the church courts were unable to reverse the decay of traditional methods of disciplining the laity.[6] Adultery was not simply decriminalised, however, nor were attitudes to it relaxed. Various sections of society continued to be concerned about immorality and in the 1680s there were worries that religious and moral values were collapsing and offenders such as adulterers were escaping punishment too easily.[7] There is some evidence that the ecclesiastical authorities were indeed losing their power of moral discipline. William Cresswell, esquire, of Cresswell in Northumberland, and Dorothy Stafford, the wife of a local clergyman, were accused of adultery at least four times from 1699 to 1725. On the last occasion their son was married and had a child of his own. William obviously had the means to pay his substantial bonds, which stipulated that if he broke them by cohabiting with Dorothy again, the money would be used for charitable purposes.[8]

The desire for firmer policies against immorality was met in several ways. As the actions taken against Thomas Ashmall and Mary Addison demonstrate, secular authorities offered alternative ways to church court correction for dealing with sexual irregularities. The quarter sessions pursued cases of bastardy and were prepared to prosecute cases against adulterers. Private initiatives offered another route to achieve social discipline. The Reformation of Manners campaign sprang up in London and provincial cities between the 1690s and into the 1730s. These societies, often consisting of tradesmen,

---

[4] UOD, DDR/EJ/OTH/3, Petition by William Addison.

[5] This is based on the number of cases surviving with cause papers.

[6] Meldrum, 'A women's court', 5; G. S. Holmes, *The Making of a Great Power: Late Stuart and Early Georgian Britain, 1660–1722* (London, 1993), p. 361.

[7] Hitchcock, *English Sexualities*, p. 99.

[8] BIHR, Trans.CP.1702/3, *office c. Dorothy Stafford*; UOD, DDR/EJ/PRC/2/1705/4, *promoted office c. William Cresswell*; UOD, DDR/EJ/PRC/2/1724/2, *mere office c. William Cresswell*. One of the bonds survives and was for £200. For other examples of lack of respect for church courts, see Meldrum, 'A women's court', 4.

used voluntary and paid informers to bring prosecutions against lewdness, Sabbath-breaking and blasphemy through the criminal justice system.[9] Thus the 'lewd and disorderly' were committed to houses of correction, thereby punishing immorality more severely than public penance.[10] David Turner persuasively argues that criminal conversation actions were another private initiative that emerged to ensure that adultery was dealt with more effectively. By developing existing laws for redress for the loss of a wife's services, these civil actions provided a further route for individuals to punish adulterers more harshly.[11]

New formulations of ideas about manners, class and status in the eighteenth century also complicated the way adultery was perceived. Politeness was a system of manners and conduct, which determined appropriate behaviour for different social occasions.[12] It was promulgated in advice literature, and emphasised the necessity of standards of manners and civilised sociability in all social relationships, including marital ones. Turner shows how civility and politeness developed as alternative moralities so that adultery came to be seen as a breach of civility. This is exemplified in the strategy at the centre of criminal conversation actions, which was to prove not just adultery but also the manner in which it was committed. Thus they often focused on the way that male lovers had breached codes of polite sociability.[13] The actions were also implicitly an example of the dangers of too much familiarity between the sexes. This was one of the problems inherent in polite culture, which was predicated upon social mixing between the sexes. In the first half of the eighteenth century, hetero-social company was encouraged as a way to refine men through the improving nature of women's conversation. Excessive and easy social mixing between men and women was also thought to risk women's virtue as well as endanger masculinity by encouraging effeminacy.[14]

Throughout the period, marital infidelity also became increasingly associated in the public mind with the aristocracy. Turner shows that while elite men had long been considered to shoulder more blame for adultery, particularly because they were supposed to set an example to others, the notion was strengthened during the first half of the eighteenth century.[15] The explosion of publicity surrounding criminal conversation cases, in the press as

---

[9] Hitchcock, *English Sexualities*, pp. 102–3.
[10] Turner, 'Representations of adultery', pp. 8–9; Meldrum, 'A women's court', 3.
[11] Turner, 'Representations of adultery', pp. 221–3.
[12] For civility and politeness in practice, see Vickery, *Gentleman's Daughter*, pp. 195–223.
[13] Turner, 'Representations of adultery', pp. 243–4.
[14] M. Cohen, 'Manliness, effeminacy and the French: gender and the construction of national character in eighteenth-century England' in Hitchcock and Cohen (eds.), *English Masculinities*, pp. 44–61.
[15] Turner, 'Representations of adultery', pp. 240, 247.

well as specialised journals and pamphlets, inevitably concentrated on cases involving the elite. Between 1770 and 1809 the public discussion of adultery and divorce found another forum in the London debating societies and was joined by campaigns in parliament to restrict divorce and punish adultery more harshly. For instance, a London scandal about aristocratic adultery found its way into the *Newcastle Chronicle* in 1771, along with the comment: 'if no divine ordinances can restrain this infamous inundation of fashionable adultery, the human laws against it should be rendered more severe, as it is big no less with a thousand scandals, than a thousand dangers to community'.[16] Donna Andrew concludes that this focused public antipathy on 'the privileged morality of the upper classes', so that, by the end of the eighteenth century, the aristocracy were believed to follow their own unacceptable separate code of morality, in which adultery took pride of place amongst several other vices.[17]

MALE ADULTERY AND THE SEXUAL DOUBLE-STANDARD

The existence of a sexual double-standard would imply that men, unlike women, were not punished for infidelity, in either law or marriage, or in reputation.[18] The records of marital difficulties include over 207 instances and reports of male and female adultery, as separation and correction cases (80, Appendix 1), as secondary complaints (31, Appendix 8), as the central feature of 13 breaches of the peace that came before the quarter sessions (categorised as miscellaneous, Appendix 1) and in provincial newspaper reports.[19] They show that provincial experiences of infidelity, and opinions expressed about it, diverged considerably from the stereotyped views of the sexual double-standard. It was not just women who were the focus of criticisms of adultery.[20] In religious teaching, adultery broke the conjugal vows and therefore male and female adulteries were considered to be offences of equal weight. The secular and ecclesiastical courts penalised adulterous men as well as women. Turner's analysis of conduct literature between 1660 and 1740 confirms that female adultery was considered more 'blameable' because of the problems it could cause for property inheritance through illegitimate children. He shows that writers also emphasised the dangers of

[16] *N.Chron*, 18 May 1771, p. 2.
[17] D. T. Andrew, '"Adultery a-la-mode": privilege, the law and attitudes to adultery 1770–1809', *Historical Association* (1997), 5–7.
[18] Phillips, *Untying the Knot*, p. 106; Gowing, *Domestic Dangers*, pp. 2–4, 180, 189; Shoemaker, *Gender*, p. 107.
[19] Sampled newspapers contained 83 references to adultery, as reports of criminal conversation actions, comments on divorce bills and 'society' infidelities, and in a range of humorous and didactic accounts.
[20] Gowing, *Domestic Dangers*, p. 180.

male adultery for household order. In turn, some murder and trial pamphlets emphasised this point by regaling their readers with the dire consequences of male infidelity.[21] Commentators also noted that male infidelity severed emotional ties between spouses. The author of 'The Repository on Marriage' in the *York Chronicle*, 19 February 1773, did not distinguish between the sexes when observing that disloyalty destroyed marriage, because it 'dissolves the cement of the relation, weakens the moral tye [*sic*], the chief strength of which lies in the reciprocation of affection'.[22] Furthermore, a variety of sources suggest that people did not automatically apply gender distinctions in considering adulterous relationships. When the Reverend John Thomlinson commented on local suspicions about the infidelities of both sexes, in his diary in the early eighteenth century, he did so without overtly criticising one sex more than the other.[23] The records of marital difficulties show that adulterous men met disapproval from onlookers, not unlike unfaithful women. Elizabeth Vason, a 58-year-old of Newark-upon-Trent, Nottingham, was midwife to the child of Joseph Seardison and Leah Harvey. She often discussed Joseph's adultery with him, with a view 'to prevail on him to forsake . . . Leah Harvey and to return to his Wife'.[24]

The fact that separation suits on the grounds of adultery, which were available to both spouses, tended to be brought by men has been interpreted as yet another example of the sexual double-standard in action. Laura Gowing concludes that gendered suing symbolises that 'Sexual conduct, the entire foundation of women's honour, became also the only measure of their marital conduct.'[25] Yet not all ecclesiastical courts demonstrate this pattern of use. An analysis of adultery separations brought before the Court of Arches, the appeal court for the province of Canterbury and first instance court for peculiars outside the jurisdiction of the Bishop of London, finds that wives initiated 43% of the ninety-two cases brought between 1660 and 1740. When cases on the grounds of cruelty and adultery are added, women brought 53% of all cases involving adultery.[26] There is a discrepancy between the Court of Arches and Durham and York ecclesiastical courts, where women brought only two of the twenty-five adultery separation cases for which cause papers survive (Appendix 2). The difference is partly explained by the fact that this book does not make a record of *all* adultery suits initiated at these courts and is also due to economic factors. In Turner's opinion the high social status of the London women who used the Court of Arches meant they could use their own or their families' wealth to sue for separation.[27] Northern

21 Turner, 'Representations of adultery', pp. 41–50.   22 *Y.Chron*, 19 February 1773, p. 4.
23 Hodgson (ed.), *Six North Country Diaries*, entries for 1718, pp. 126, 135.
24 BIHR, CP.I/1975, *Seardison c. Seardison*, 1785.
25 Gowing, *Domestic Dangers*, p. 180.   26 Turner, 'Representations of adultery', pp. 184–5.
27 Ibid., p. 186.

women's reluctance to bring such suits therefore probably reflects the over-whelming problems they faced in supporting themselves and their children without their husbands' financial contribution. For women of more limited means, it was perhaps more pressing to rid oneself of a cruel husband than an adulterous husband, who at least was not life-threatening. Nevertheless, like their London counterparts, provincial wives found male infidelity un-palatable and it was a fairly common additional accusation in other cases of marital difficulties (Appendix 8).

One noticeable feature of these complaints about husbands' adultery was that it was often equated with husbands' violence. Out of twenty-eight such complaints, 64% (eighteen) were made in cruelty separations and complaints to the quarter sessions about wife-beating (Appendices 8 and 25). There are two main reasons for this association. In the first place, male adultery improved a cruelty separation's chance of success, as it would come to do formally in the nineteenth century. A draft libel sent to Jane Gomeldon's attorney by her proctor, during her cruelty suit against her husband, in 1742, advised 'if you could prove any Instances of his having Criminal conversation with any other woman before her [Jane's] departure it would be a great strengthning [sic] to her case'.[28]

Secondly, male infidelity was believed to spark disagreements so severe that they could end in violence, reflecting the perception in various forms of print that male adultery disrupted patriarchy. The correction case against Ellen Lambe for adultery and fornication in 1694 stated that her actions caused 'great disatisfaccon and difference betweene Joseph [Hornby] and his wife in so much that he hath of late times frequently beaten and abused her with-out any cause or reason'. Typically, the husbands' abuse began when their wives discovered their infidelity.[29] Possibly contemporaries believed that men lashed out from guilt, or the frustration of being unable to escape an unsat-isfactory marriage. In her separation case on the grounds of cruelty in 1798, Lady Mary Shafto claimed that Sir Cuthbert Shafto was more cruel than normal to coerce her to leave Barington Hall in Northumberland, thereby leaving him free to install his mistress there instead.[30] Most obviously the correlation between male adultery and wife-beating reveals that wives were not expected to tolerate male infidelity resignedly, since it was their com-plaints that led to violent tussles. A deponent in Ellen Lambe's presentment, for example, recalled that when Joseph's wife turned up at Ellen's house late one night in order to force him to leave, he threatened to beat her when they got home. Yet once the matter was resolved, the Hornbys lived 'very quietly

[28] UOD, DDR/EJ/PRC/2/1740/6, *Gomeldon c. Gomeldon*.
[29] For example, NCAS, QSB/58, fol. 40, Michaelmas 1722, Information of Anne Taylor.
[30] BIHR, CP.I/2568, *Shafto c. Shafto*, 1800.

and comfortably together'.[31] It is not the case, however, that male adultery was considered reason for complaint only when it caused men to beat their wives.[32] Echoing conduct literature, male adultery was understood to damage the emotional and material foundations of marriage. An article in Anne Fletcher's libel in 1687 noted that in order to 'disturb, or disquiet and vex the minde of' Anne more grievously, her husband had repeatedly bragged before her that he lay with Jane Snawden and would keep, love and maintain Jane as long as he lived.[33]

It is possible to discover the status or occupation of twenty-five of the fifty-eight women who were named as having affairs with married men. Eighteen of them were servants (Appendix 26). It is common for historians to comment on the way that men took advantage of their superior position in patriarchy to exploit their servant sexually.[34] Cissie Fairchilds' book about domestic service in France shows that French female servants entered relationships with their masters out of loneliness and sexual frustration, for affection and the reward of protection or money, or in fear of a withheld salary or dismissal. They also literally had nowhere to hide.[35] The records of marital difficulties contain some servants who accused their masters of such callous coercion. In 1693, York church court prosecuted William Burton, a beer brewer in the city of York, for adultery with his 38-year-old servant Agnes Hunter. Agnes deposed that William had forced her to consent to sex with him when she had to attend him in the night-time during his wife's lying-in period. Once she was pregnant he told her not to worry because he frequently got his servants with child. Presumably his solution was to send them away to have their babies, since Agnes had been brought before two justices of the peace at Kendal for bearing a bastard, at which point she confessed that William was its father.[36]

Yet not all cases of adultery between masters and their servants conform to this model of exploitation. The economic disparity between master and servant in some regions and ranks was not extreme enough to suggest economic and social exploitation in all cases.[37] Nor were all women victims.

---

[31] BIHR, CP.H/4349, *office c. Lambe*, 1694, Depositions of Anne Harwood and Mary Rawnforth.
[32] For other examples of women responding assertively to their husbands' adultery see Capp, 'The double standard revisited: plebeian women and male sexual reputation in early modern England', *Past and Present*, 162 (1999), 73.
[33] BIHR, Trans.CP.1688/3, *Fletcher c. Fletcher*.
[34] J. Barber, '"Stolen goods": the sexual harassment of female servants in West Wales during the nineteenth century', *Rural History*, 4, 2 (1993), 123–36.
[35] C. Fairchilds, *Domestic Enemies: Servants and Their Masters in Old Regime France* (London, 1984), pp. 164–81, 188–92.
[36] BIHR, CP.H/4587, *office c. Burton*, 1693.
[37] T. Meldrum, *Domestic Service and Gender 1660–1750: Life and Work in the London Household* (London, 2000), p. 105; R. Adair, *Courtship, Illegitimacy*, p. 86.

Occasionally, relatively informed decisions lie behind their claims about their masters' deception. Elizabeth Lupton told the quarter sessions that her master, the husbandman Joshua Nicholson, of Tollerton, North Yorkshire, had inveigled her to lie with him for some years on 'pretence that his wife was an old woman and could not last long, and then he would marry' Elizabeth.[38] It was not unknown for housekeepers to marry their masters.[39] This occurred when the master was single or widowed, but cohabitation was an informal equivalent for married men. Ann Watson obtained a separation on the grounds of cruelty from her husband Joseph, an innkeeper in Wolsingham, in 1803. Only passing comment was made about the involvement of a third party in their conflict. Jane Kirkley, their servant, remembered that on a summer's day in 1800, Joseph cut his wife's head by throwing an earthenware pot at her. A surgeon was sent for to dress the wound, and Joseph then threatened his wife's life if she would not bring Sarah Ayton back into their house. We have to wait for Joseph's will to get further information. When he died in 1822 he left his copyhold house and appurtenances in Headhope Street to his daughter. He also left £20 per annum to his 'housekeeper' Sarah Ayton, to be paid as long as she remained unmarried and behaved herself to the satisfaction of the trustees. After her decease the residue was to be shared between all of Joseph's children: the three born in wedlock and the five 'natural' children he had by Sarah.[40]

Another break with the stereotype of the actions of the sexual double-standard on married men is shown by their awareness that their personal sexual behaviour could have a profound impact on their reputation. David Turner's case-study of the evidence from a promoted correction case against the clergyman Robert Foulkes for adultery and the material produced by his indictment and execution for murdering his illegitimate child shows that men employed gossip about sexual immorality against other men 'as a means of erasing dignity and undermining claims to respect on which honour and status depended'.[41] Indeed, as Bernard Capp has shown, male sexual reputation in the late sixteenth and seventeenth centuries was so vulnerable that women could manipulate it for their own ends.[42] For example, some servants falsely claimed that their masters had fathered their illegitimate children. These allegations were common enough to cause concern. At the turn of the seventeenth century Ellen Sakeshaft, the wife of an innkeeper, advised

[38] NYA, QSB/1733, deposition, 1 December 1733, MIC 130.
[39] Adair, *Courtship, Illegitimacy*, pp. 83–6.
[40] UOD, DDR/EJ/CCD/31/1801/15, *Watson c. Watson*; DPR, 1822, Joseph Watson, Wolsingham.
[41] D. Turner, '"Nothing is so secret but shall be revealed": the scandalous life of Robert Foulkes' in Hitchcock and Cohen (eds.), *English Masculinities*, p. 191.
[42] Capp, 'Double standard revisited'.

her servant, eighteen weeks pregnant, to be very careful about naming its father, because 'it was a very ill thing in her to charge a marryd man with such a fault in case hee was not really faulty' and 'p[er]haps some young man might have had dealings with her'.[43] The reason for falsely accusing masters was simple. Mary Page laid her child upon her master, Thomas Mewburne, in 1716. However, a deponent overheard Thomas Hughill, a fellow servant, admit to his wife that he was the father, and explain that Mary was laying the baby on those that had more money to keep it.[44]

Men were extremely anxious about the repercussions of such accusations. In 1737 Francis Nicholls, justice of the peace, wrote to John Perkins expressing his fears about Mary Horne, who was being considered for committal because of her 'railing and malice' against her husband. He explained that she was declaring that Francis had fathered fourteen children on her, and intended to announce this if brought before the bar, 'in order to Revenge her self, by Blasting my Creditt; or keeping me in Awe, for her owne further advantage and profitt'. Although he took pains to spell out to Perkins that her claims were exaggerated, since she did not even have that many children, he mentioned that he had supported and educated her fourteen-year-old daughter from birth to date. His footnote leaves the question of his paternity of the girl open to speculation:

If any thing should be offerd to ye Court in Relation to the Child, I thinke it will properly not be fitt for them to heare it, or take notice of any action or Passages of Life, yt were acted or done fourteen years by Past, but that they should make Enquiry into the Informations against her without otherwise troubleing them selves about what is so long past, of this pray informe yr Counsell; to Try if they can divert it.[45]

The susceptibility of men's reputation perhaps accounts for their violent outbursts and agonised responses to allegations of infidelity. When the married Reverend James Robertson's maid told him she was pregnant in 1754, he threw himself on the bed, cried bitterly and wrung his hands, saying he would be ruined.[46] Men often denied accusations of adultery in the attempt to protect their reputation, perhaps because there was too much at stake simply to confess and do penance. John Davison of Treswell, Nottinghamshire, denied that he had committed adultery with his servant, Mary Barthroy, when York chancery court prosecuted him in 1665. He claimed that she retaliated to his giving 'her some blowes' during a quarrel by getting a justice of the peace

---

[43] BIHR, Ex.CP.I/141, *office c. Slainhead*, 1700.

[44] The practice could backfire on the women; this case ended up at the North Riding Quarter Sessions (NYA, QSB/1716, depositions, 20 August to 24 September, MIC 124).

[45] DRO, DIST/C2/3/18 (2). Many thanks to Adrian Green for bringing this document to my attention.

[46] UOD, DDR/EJ/PRC/2/1755/1, *office c. Robertson*. For other examples, see Capp, 'Double standard revisited', 72–3.

to issue a warrant against him for adultery with her.[47] Other men put rumours down to misunderstandings. John Jopling was presented in 1674 for
adultery with Elizabeth Myres, the widow of an alderman of Durham City.
His defence explained that Elizabeth's late husband had entrusted him with
the management of her affairs. Therefore gossip had only arisen when he was
obliged to visit her house in order to carry out his duties after her husband's
death.[48] Men continued to reject charges in the face of evidence as suggestive
as the birth of illegitimate children whom they were maintaining.[49] Some
took their denials to elaborate lengths. In 1705 Kirkby-in-Ashfield's church-
wardens presented William Newton to Nottingham's archdeaconry court for
adultery and getting his servant Catherine Donnelly with child. He claimed
that another man had fathered the baby and then fled into the army. He also
blamed the local rector, with whom he was in dispute about tithe hay, for
inciting rumours and threatening to destroy the 71-year-old midwife who
delivered Catherine's baby, unless she swore that Catherine had confessed
during labour that her master was the father.[50]

Men also brought defamation prosecutions against those who accused
them of adultery.[51] George Smith, a gentleman of Trimdon, County Durham,
sued Isaac Steer in 1746 after Isaac shouted during a quarrel, 'George makes
as much use of Jane Gowland...as you do of your own wife'. According to
George, a married man, this accusation injured his good name among his
neighbours.[52] It is important to remember that men's business affairs were
affected by their sexual behaviour. The manager of a York station-wagon
line placed an advert in the press in which he denied having been found 'in
some unlawful and scandalous familiarity' with another man's wife. He was
attempting to restore his good name because the gossip was damaging his
business.[53]

FEMALE ADULTERY AND THE SEXUAL DOUBLE-STANDARD

By re-examining female adultery outside the framework of the sexual double-
standard it is possible to see that opinions about women's infidelity were
more varied than demands for chastity imply. We have already seen that

[47] When he appeared before the justice he promised to pay her £4 to end the differences. The
church court prosecution arose from this action (BIHR, CP.H/2797, *office c. Davison*, 1665).
[48] BIHR, Trans.CP.1674/3, *office c. Elizabeth Myres*; UOD, DDR/EJ/PRC/2/undated/11, *office
c. Jopling*.
[49] BIHR, CP.H/2843, *office c. Duning*, 1668.
[50] BIHR, Trans.CP.1707/1, *office c. Newton*, 1707.
[51] Of a random selection of fourteen defamation cases brought before Durham consistory court
citing accusations of adultery between the 1740s and 1780s, married men brought five and
married women brought nine. For the theory that male interest in bringing such defamation
cases declined after the mid eighteenth century, see Morris, 'Defamation', p. 605.
[52] UOD, DDR/EJ/CCD/3/1746/7, *Smith c. Steer*.
[53] Looney, 'Advertising and society', p. 218.

women's reputations were multi-faceted and not solely determined by their chastity.[54] In this context, damage to reputation was not necessarily irrevocable. For one thing, it is possible that women's repentance alleviated their offence. In 1685 Daniel Ottie admitted turning his wife out because she was adulterous; he refused to accept her back because 'she has not as yett made any submission or declared any sorrow or pentenance [*sic*]' for her faults and continued to live a 'lewd life'.[55] Both infidelity and separation affected women's lives, but it seems that there were degrees of female adultery, some more acceptable than others. Thus, for instance, a stable long-lasting relationship following an existing separation was less likely to incur criticism than a short-term affair carried out while a woman was living with her husband. Women who were still cohabiting with their husbands found it difficult to get temporary lodgings with a lover when their relationship was known. Some of those in longer-term relationships following separation, however, found it less of a problem. Admittedly this was often because the couple moved to where they were unknown and passed as husband and wife. Yet even where a relationship was known, lodgings were available, though they might not be suitable to the woman's social status.

Thus women whose marriages ended due to their infidelity might face a lower standard of living and in many cases their social circles narrowed and changed.[56] Higher-status women, for example, lost access to their usual social circle. Dorothea Wentworth, wife of Godfrey, esquire, and daughter of Sir Lionel Pilkington, Baronet, found that in separation 'few of the better sort of people in Knaresborough would admit of any visits from her'.[57] Securing a living was also difficult since husbands were not obliged to maintain wives who had eloped or were proven to be adulterous. It is possible that some areas of work were restricted to them. Mary Ferman left her husband, a Newcastle confectioner, in July 1796, after a long affair with Isaac Dixon, a spirit merchant, and went to Ripon where she kept a school under the name of Miss Richmond. According to John Ferman, however, the people there, hearing of her 'bad character and who she was, withdrew their children from her' after a couple of months.[58] Yet, even so, the situation for women could be more flexible. Not all unfaithful wives lost the support of family or friends.[59] Susan Staves found occasions where adulterous wives negotiated

---

[54] Chapter 4, pp. 78–80.
[55] BIHR, CP.H/5734, D/C.CP.1685/8, *Ottie/Ottey* als. *Awtie/Awtey* c. *Ottie/Ottey* als. *Awtie/Awtey*.
[56] Chapter 8, p. 180.
[57] BIHR, CP.I/1376, *Wentworth* c. *Wentworth*, 1756, Robert Pulman's deposition.
[58] UOD, DDR/EJ/CCD/3/1801/4, *Ferman* c. *Ferman*.
[59] For an example of a wife going to live with her mother after adultery and receiving support from her sister and various friends see UOD, DDR/EJ/CCD/3/1789/4, *Smith* c. *Smith*.

private separation contracts, which included financial support.[60] For some women, a lover replaced the loss of maintenance by restoring them to a double-income household.

There is no doubt, nevertheless, that the harshest penalty incurred by an adulterous wife whose husband would not forgive her was that she could be legitimately denied any access to her children. Thus, even if the likelihood of socio-economic downturn was bearable, the problems women faced in retaining contact with their children raise vital questions about their motivation in committing adultery. On the rare occasions when historians consider women's motivation for entering an extra-marital affair, they usually explain it in two ways: women were either calculating or exploited. Robert Shoemaker and Faramerz Dabhoiwala, for example, argue that married women calculatedly provided sexual favours to advance the social or economic status of their husbands, or in return for a variety of leisure entertainments. While this implies that higher-ranking men took advantage of such an availability of married women, more obviously victimised were the women who were blackmailed into an affair to avoid detrimental effects for their spouse.[61] As they are seen through the lens of a rigid sexual double-standard and rely on a limited set of sources, these interpretations are both simplistic and narrow. For instance, both Shoemaker and Dabhoiwala use Samuel Pepys' diary to explore married women's reasons for adultery. This is a questionable source, because Pepys may well have explained his own and the married women's actions in ways that alleviated his own conscience or absolved him from moral or social responsibility. Ultimately, one man's explanations for his married lovers' motivation and conduct are inadequate. While it may be futile and even presumptuous to try to understand individuals' reasons for having affairs, it is possible to use the adultery correction cases and separation suits to explore the background to women's infidelity in a far more woman-centred way. On this evidence, women entered relationships for a variety of reasons – mostly more prosaic than the proposals above, with little evidence of calculation or victimisation.

While in general there is little evidence that unfaithful married women were exploited, it is important to note that a handful of wives defended themselves from accusations of adultery by claiming that they were coerced by force or threat to have sex. In 1699, Peter Poole was bound over to appear at the quarter sessions to answer the information of Margaret Metcalfe, the wife of a weaver in Ebberston. She claimed that he was lewd and disorderly and

[60] Staves, 'Separate maintenance contracts', 82.
[61] Shoemaker, Gender, pp. 74–5; F. Dabhoiwala, 'The pattern of sexual immorality in seventeenth- and eighteenth-century London' in P. Griffiths and M. S. R. Jenner, Londinopolis. Essays in the Cultural and Social History of Early Modern London (Manchester, 2000), pp. 89–90.

several times had tempted her to lie with him. Eventually, 'with p[er]swacons and Threats [he] p[re]vailed with her' to have carnal knowledge of her body and continued to solicit her to commit the 'detestable' act with him.[62] The plea was also used less directly in correction cases and occasionally in adultery separation suits. Studies have revealed the existence of coercive sex in the period.[63] Perhaps it can be acknowledged that the plea of unwillingness also may have allowed women to save face while admitting to a sexual liaison outside marriage. Rachel Harland's husband refused to maintain her child because he was not its father. The case ended up before the justice of the peace. Rachel explained to him that Richard Jackson, an innkeeper, had visited her house several times in 1750, during her husband's absence at sea, and tried to induce her to lie with him. She always refused until she was returning home from Whitby one evening after Lammas when Richard forced her into a coal house where they had sex. Like some other cases, it is not specified whether the intercourse itself was forced. Richard visited Rachel three more times in the following three weeks when they continued their physical relationship. Richard apparently explained that she should not be uneasy if she proved to be with child, for he would not let them be in want.[64] It is also perhaps significant that ravishment could be a bar to being sued for adultery.[65]

The explanation that married women committed adultery to obtain an amusing life or their husbands' preferment collapses when the social status or occupation of husbands is compared with that of the lovers.[66] Both were specified in thirty-two instances of infidelity (Appendix 27). Husbands were of lower status than their wives' lovers in only 16% of these cases and of similar status in 19%, whereas 62% were of higher status than their wives' lovers. In some cases the lovers were employed by the husbands as, for example, domestic servants, estate workers or clerks, or temporarily hired as builders or, in one case, a painter of miniature portraits. Work on domestic service touches on this type of relationship, but still stereotypes the women involved as victims. Tim Meldrum, for instance, views them as the sexual prey of their male servant-lovers, largely because they stood to lose so much by participating in such a relationship. As he points out, an 'affair

62 NYA, QSB/1700, film 119, deposition and recognizance, 27 December 1699.
63 For a discussion of early modern ambivalence about coercive sex and 'public cultures of nonconsensual intercourse', see R. F. King, 'Rape in England 1660–1800: trials, narratives and the question of consent', MA dissertation, University of Durham (1998), pp. 83–120, 141.
64 NYA, QSB/1751/ MIC 137, examination, 6 January 1752.
65 M. Nevill, 'Women and marriage breakdown in England, 1832–1857', Ph.D. thesis, University of Essex (1989), p. 148.
66 Earlier London separation suits also show the same differences in rank between lover and wife (Gowing, *Domestic Dangers*, p. 142).

between mistress and manservant was not just a sexual but also a social inversion': it attacked the hierarchical structure of patriarchy and presaged social as well as gender disorder.[67] This was indeed a popular theme in early modern print. Representations of crime between 1550 and 1700, which were intended to illustrate the numerous social ills that resulted from moral irregularity, often showed wives conniving with their male servant-lovers to murder their husbands.[68] Such cultural unease may have been waning during the eighteenth century, as only one of the adultery separation suits remarked on the socially unbalanced relationship between wife and lover. The articles describing Mary Manwaring's affair in the late 1750s dwelled on the physical signs of her relationship with John Read, a tenant farmer. They listed the cow dung and filth that dirtied the back of Mary's clothes, her upturned soiled hat, the grass that stained her sleeves and the back of her cloak, and proposed that John's dirty leathern breeches caused the turned-up, soiled and greasy lower part of Mary's shift. The libel even claimed that Mary replied to friends' comments by explaining, 'That Love was a Levellar and that...John Read was a Clean sweet Man and had that which would recommend him before any Gentleman'.[69]

Though the case of Mary Manwaring was somewhat ambiguous, since most of the protagonists seem to have been manipulating each other for various ends, there is little evidence that lower-status lovers exploited their married mistresses. More mundanely, the relationships resulted from the legitimate close contact that occurred between such men and socially superior married women in work situations or when women's circle of acquaintances narrowed after separation. Henrietta Stapylton and her father-in-law's butler, John Muskiet, were well aware of the dangers of their affair. When Lucy Lockton, the house-maid, told John, who had also courted her, about the rumours, he became agitated and swore that she was mad – after all, 'Did she think that he would be Guilty of such a crime as that with his Master's Daughter in Law and that too in Sir Martin's own House No he loved Mrs Stapylton as his own Brother.' The evidence suggests that, against their better judgement, they fell in love. When Henrietta was sent away in her father-in-law's carriage, John, who had been dismissed earlier, leapt over a hedge into the lane to stop the carriage, about a quarter of a mile from Myton. Both bitterly weeping, they made their farewells.[70] It is

---

[67] He refers to the male servants' 'predatory sexuality' directed at mistresses (T. Meldrum, 'London domestic servants from depositional evidence, 1660–1750: servant-employer sexuality in the patriarchal household' in T. Hitchcock, P. King and P. Sharpe (eds.), *Chronicling Poverty: The Voices and Strategies of the English Poor, 1640–1840* (London, 1997), pp. 60–1.

[68] Dolan, *Dangerous Familiars*, pp. 56–7.

[69] BIHR, Trans.CP.1766/2, *Manwaring c. Manwaring*, 1761.

[70] BIHR, CP.I/2245–75, *Stapylton c. Stapylton*, 1786.

Dorothea Wentworth's smaller social circle that explains her unlikely relationship with Samuel Hawkredge, a flax-dresser. His family circumstances make it extremely improbable that he, or she, exploited the other. If her surviving letters are anything to go by, they too fell in love, for she observed that no-one could love more than they did.[71]

Another way to consider female motivation is to examine the context of wives' infidelities. Four common themes emerge. In 27% of the cases for which enough details are available, the extra-marital affairs occurred after the married couple had already separated (Appendix 28). Since husbands initiated the suits, existing separations were blamed on the wives' faults. Godfrey Wentworth explained that he and his wife Dorothea had separated in 1749, after twenty-one years of marriage, due to several disputes and misunderstandings resulting from her 'unsociable Temper and behaviour'. Although the libel accused her of adultery with diverse unnamed men from 1749, it is relevant that the specific affair cited did not begin until summer 1755.[72] Some couples may have felt that a long separation justified a new relationship. The Siddalls lived together for five years after their marriage in November 1697 in Pontefract. In January 1708 the parish overseer presented Sarah to the justice of peace, where she swore that Thomas Sickling was the father of her fourteen-week-old baby and explained that she had not seen her husband for three years. Indeed the overseer deposed that Sarah had planned to marry Thomas until she heard that her husband was still alive and living at Bridlington.[73]

Uncertainty about the validity of the marriage itself provided others with different vindication for entering an adulterous relationship. The Agars cohabited between March 1764 and January 1768 when the Reverend William Agar probably went to North America, since he initiated the separation suit in 1773 from Virginia. Elizabeth Agar began a relationship in July 1768 and went to Scotland to get married, well aware that her first husband was alive. Perhaps she believed her existing marriage was null and void, for she told a servant that she had never consummated the union with William.[74]

Secondly, 19% of the couples had experienced lengthy or regular separations during marriage due to the husbands' occupation or business (Appendix 28). Eleanor Smith's husband, a vicar, regularly travelled to minister to his other parish. John Taylor, of Bridlington, an attorney, frequently left his wife to travel on business between 1775 and 1776, when she had an affair with the labourer John Bentley. Elizabeth Dent had an affair with her

---

[71] BIHR, CP.I/1376, *Wentworth c. Wentworth*, 1756.   [72] Ibid.

[73] BIHR, CP.I/2759, *Siddall c. Siddall*, 1707.

[74] BIHR, CP.I/1647, *Agar c. Agar*, 1773, Ann Matson's deposition. Adultery was categorised as a breach of the marriage contract, so the ambiguous contracts at the heart of clandestine marriage, popular between 1660 and 1753, may also have challenged ideas about adultery (Turner, 'Representations of adultery', pp. 57–63).

husband's brother during John Dent's ten-month absence, between 1720 and 1721, in London on business.[75] Rachel Harland travelled with her husband John, a mariner, from Shields on his trip carrying coal to London, but stayed at Whitby when they called there on their return, about Candlemas 1749. John only saw her again for a few weeks in January 1751 and went to sea again without realising that she was pregnant. On his return in August he discovered that she had given birth to a son in May, which could not be his.[76] One husband's illness seemed to facilitate an infidelity. Mary and John Greenwood were married in 1781, when he was nineteen and she eighteen years old. Thirteen years later, Mary embarked on an affair with Charles Wrigglesworth, a twenty-year-old saddler and innkeeper. Mary's defence to John's separation suit associated her infidelity with John's incapacity from illness; for example, her interrogatories asked whether John was not 'a person of Weak Habit or Constitution frequently out of Health'. The deponents confirmed this, as well as, poignantly, her affection and care for him when he was indisposed. Indeed, John's death brought an end to the suit.[77]

Thirdly, adultery separation suits sometimes gave the age of spouses, and overall 15% of the husbands were considerably older than their wives (Appendix 28). The affair typically occurred many years into wedlock, which was perhaps when the age difference was most pronounced. John and Ann Taylor of Bridlington, for example, were nineteen years apart in age, at forty-one and twenty-two respectively when they married, and her infidelity occurred in 1775, when she was thirty-eight. William Chaworth was forty when he married Alice Colly, twenty years his junior, in December 1747. After eleven years they separated and the following year Alice became involved with William Heppenstall, a cordwainer.[78] It is also feasible in some cases that marital sexual relations had stopped by the time infidelity occurred. Eleanor Smith, for example, could state with certainty that her youngest son was her lover's child, not her husband's.[79]

The fourth common factor relates to whether the couples had children or not. It is tempting to suppose that married women's affairs took place after some years of marriage, when children were older and women less likely to have infants removed from their care if their infidelity was discovered. For example, two of Dorothy Cunliffe's young children were already boarded at a country house in Lancashire in 1700 when her affair allegedly began. Though Lady Jane Vavasour tried to take her children with her when she eloped, it

---

[75] UOD, DDR/EJ/CCD/3/1789/4, *Smith c. Smith*; BIHR, CP.I/1817, *Taylor c. Taylor*, 1776; BIHR, CP.I/697, *Dent c. Dent*, 1722.

[76] John took the baby to the overseers in order to insist that its real father maintain it (NYA, QSB/1752/ MIC 137, examinations, 6 January 1752).

[77] BIHR, CP.I/2486, *Greenwood c. Greenwood*, 1796.

[78] BIHR, CP.I/1817, *Taylor c. Taylor*, 1776; BIHR, CP.I/1414, *Chaworth c. Chaworth*, 1760.

[79] UOD, DDR/EJ/CCD/3/1789/4, *Smith c. Smith*.

is unlikely that this included all of her four children, since two of her sons were put to school in Osmotherley, North Yorkshire. Alice Chaworth and her husband William separated from 10 August 1758 after nearly eleven years of marriage. By 1760 their only son was at Chesterfield School and possibly out of her daily care.[80] These examples cannot be taken as representative, given the considerable time-span over which women bore children, so that even those who had been married for some time might still have young children. A more persuasive reason to consider this factor is indicated by the fact that eight (and probably ten) of the twenty-five couples involved in adultery separation suits were childless by the time of the conflict (Appendix 28).[81] In some of these cases one of the partners went on to have children in another relationship.[82] This is not to say that childlessness caused adultery – though Roger Manwaring seems to have sought a parliamentary divorce, which would free him to remarry and gain a legitimate heir – but it certainly gave a couple more freedom to separate and the women less to lose by entering an extra-marital affair.[83]

Opinions about women's adultery can also be considered in broader ways than the sexual double-standard. Disparate studies, for example, have inferred from court cases against female adulterers that at various times and places communities have practised informal social policing on married women in order to control their behaviour. According to Laura Gowing, wives in sixteenth- and early seventeenth-century London were scrutinised by their neighbours.[84] Sara Mendelson and Patricia Crawford claim that seventeenth-century labouring men were unable to 'safeguard their wives' chastity' in person, 'but the local community generally deputized for them, using such popular group rituals as charivari or Skimington'.[85] Lynn Abrams concludes that in nineteenth-century Germany 'husbands relied upon village community structures to regulate their wives' behaviour when they were away'.[86] Lawrence Stone argued that servants served a similar purpose in elite eighteenth-century households, by opportunistically storing up information about their mistresses, waiting for the right time to reveal evidence of sexual immorality for their own greatest benefit.[87]

There are a few examples in the records of marital difficulties where community members acted in a deliberately intrusive manner to enforce

---

[80] BIHR, CP.I/54, *Cunliffe* c. *Cunliffe*, 1701; BIHR, CP.I/458, and BIHR, CP.I/661–2, *Vavasour* c. *Vavasour*, 1715; BIHR, CP.I/1414, *Chaworth* c. *Chaworth*, 1760.

[81] For example, BIHR, CP.I/1647, *Agar* c. *Agar*, 1773; C.P. I/2366, *Barttelot* c. *Barttelot*, 1793.

[82] For example, BIHR, C.P. I/1710, *Mitchinson* c. *Mitchinson*, 1775; C.P. I/2366, *Barttelot* c. *Barttelot*, 1793.

[83] BIHR, Trans.CP.1766/2, *Manwaring* c. *Manwaring*, 1761.

[84] Gowing, *Domestic Dangers*, pp. 189–92.

[85] Mendelson and Crawford, *Women in Early Modern English Society*, p. 146.

[86] Abrams, 'Whores, whore-chasers, and swine', 274.

[87] Stone, *Divorce*, pp. 211–15, 220–5.

or maintain propriety. John Bridges, the rector of Tateham, deposed in 1687 that he had called on Gervase and Mary Pigot as soon as he had heard rumours that Mary was previously married to a gold- (or silver-) smith still living in London. He left them alone when Mary denied being in an adulterous relationship and insisted that she was married to no-one but Gervase.[88] In one case where community policing is apparent, it was directed at a single woman, Ellen Lambe, and she, at least, rejected it. Ellen owned and lived alone in her house in New Malton, North Yorkshire. She was subjected to a correction case at York consistory court in 1694 after the church wardens presented her. This was followed by the petition of fourteen male inhabitants of New Malton that she was of lewd life. Her female neighbours also reproved her because she was in a relationship with a married man. The scandalous reports about 'Bonny Nell' even encouraged several people to break her windows, according to one neighbour. Ellen rejected this moral supervision, keeping a pistol and threatening to discharge it in the face of anyone looking in or listening at her windows.[89]

It is also true that servants were ordered to check on a wife's behaviour if suspicions were stirred. However, such activities were often far more complex than a cursory reading suggests, for servants also had their own agendas for monitoring other people's behaviour. At his request in the late 1780s, Sir Martin Stapylton's servants at Myton House watched his daughter-in-law Henrietta's activities with his butler John Muskiet. Lady Stapylton's maid, Martha Bromley, initiated this action because of her concerns about John Muskiet's courtship of his fellow servant, Lois (Lucy) Lockton. Convinced that John and Lucy were meeting after the family had gone to bed and fearing that John would debauch Lucy, Martha kept watch late one night. To her surprise she discovered that John was actually meeting Henrietta Stapylton and reported this to her master. Thus when Henrietta's husband was away in York, Sir Martin ordered Lucy and a fellow maid, Ann Gill, to keep watch. Yet Lucy obviously had her own reasons for spying; indeed she was so agitated that she had to be physically restrained from forcing open a chamber door to confront John with his lover.[90] It is too simplistic to characterise servants as routinely spying on their mistresses and then reporting suspicious behaviour to a male hierarchical figure.

Indeed servants were as likely to be confidantes and reluctant deponents.[91] Though the evidence may have been given to emphasise their own morality, some servants would seem to have used intimate knowledge merely to warn their mistresses about the consequences of their behaviour. Anne Metcalfe,

[88] BIHR, Trans.CP.1688/2, *office c. Elizabeth Cowley* als. *Cowland* als. *Mary Pigot.*
[89] BIHR, CP.H/4349, *office c. Ellen Lambe.*
[90] BIHR, CP.I/2245–75, *Stapylton c. Stapylton,* 1786.
[91] For other examples of the dilemmas faced by servants whose mistresses were adulterous, see Meldrum, *Domestic Service,* p. 94; Stone, *Divorce,* pp. 220–4.

a 37-year-old maid, apparently cautioned Lady Jane Vavasour against meeting William Parker, Sir Peter Vavasour's steward, in York because she was concerned that her mistress would have carnal relations with him.[92] Relationships between servants and mistresses could be quite close in less well-off households, which had smaller numbers of servants, often only one.[93] Francis Place, for example, recalled that his family's maid often sat at table with them when they took short lunches.[94] Indeed, women were assisted by their servants to gain privacy. Elizabeth Myres' servants knew that when the married John Jopling visited, they were to keep out of the chamber. Her maid promised not to betray her mistress about the affair.[95] Perhaps such bonds between servants and their employers were only broken when they were required to give evidence under oath.

Frequently it is the collation of evidence in depositions that gives the impression that neighbours, work-mates, employees or servants systematically watched married women whenever their husbands were away. Yet these conclusions are to some extent shaped by the structure of adultery separation suits and the legal requirements of proof. In order to avoid the risk of collusion between spouses, at least two deponents were required to depose that they had witnessed intercourse.[96] Being caught in the act was simply too unlikely, and proof of adultery was therefore mostly established by circumstantial evidence. As one treatise explained, three links needed to be established: the criminal intent of the defendant; the intent of their alleged lover; and their opportunity for adultery.[97] This emphasis on female demeanour and behaviour evokes methodical surveillance. A closer reading indicates, however, that many extra-marital relationships became public property after the adultery, once all the 'public' elements of it were collected within a suit. In many cases, deponents were required to piece together their recollections and suspicions after the event, not be ever-vigilant, acting as a store of information to aid the policing of married women.

In general, many instances of 'spying' on married women were opportunistic, occurring after suspicious behaviour, and were not organised checks. The

---

[92] BIHR, CP.I/661–2, *Vavasour c. Vavasour*, 1715.

[93] For the ambiguous categories of domestic service, see Meldrum, *Domestic Service*, p. 31.

[94] B. Hill, *Servants: English Domestics in the Eighteenth Century* (Oxford, 1996), p. 11.

[95] BIHR, Trans.CP.1674/3, *office c. Myres and Jopling*, 1674.

[96] A spouse's confession was ranked as evidence but was not enough to prove adultery because it could also be the result of collusion between spouses. Definitive evidence included a pregnancy which could not have been the result of the conjugal relationship and evidence that one spouse was living with another partner following separation. Other admissible evidence included visiting a brothel and venereal disease that began long after the wedding. Letters from a wife to her lover could be admitted as proof if they indicated 'gross familiarities', but were insufficient if they did not imply physical adultery (Coote, *Practice*, pp. 315, 362; Bishop, *Commentaries*, pp. 333–410; Burn, *Ecclesiastical Law*, Vol. II, p. 42).

[97] Bishop, *Commentaries*, pp. 422–7.

clergyman's wife Eleanor Smith's openly flirtatious manner stimulated gossip in the late 1780s. Two young men, Thomas Telfer, an apprentice plasterer, and James Stevenson, a husbandman, who were working on the rectory, took the opportunity during her husband's absence to try to see her with a lover. They positioned themselves in a high part of the garden at nine o'clock in the evening and looked into her chamber on the second floor. They saw very little and when Eleanor put out the candle and got into her press-bed, they decided to look more closely. Failing to find a ladder, they put a hand-barrow under the window and climbed on it, noticed a hat and jacket and concluded that she was with John Smith, another workman.[98] Their activities were not carried out to prevent her behaviour, but to amuse themselves.

There is evidence that attitudes to adulterous women varied greatly. Family relationships coloured responses and some records vividly evoke angry scenes. Samuel Hawkridge, a flax-dresser in Knaresborough, his wife and their children shared a house with his parents. As well as flax-dressing, they also took in lodgers. One Thursday morning in 1756, Samuel's father, George Hawkridge, found his wife, Samuel's mother, in a 'great flutter and concern' and at her direction went into a chamber set aside for storing yarn. He was shocked to find his son in bed with Dorothea Wentworth, whom he knew because she had lodged nearby. Unable to force her to leave immediately because she could not hire a post-chaise, he had to let her stay another night. However, he described himself as 'so very angry and amazed that he would not see her after'. Alice Hawkridge, Samuel's mother, was equally stunned and on discovering the couple she asked Dorothea 'how she could have the Impudence to come here in that manner and used other angry Expressions'. Samuel confessed to his mother that Dorothea had come to the house four nights before, unknown to everyone, and promised that he would have nothing more to do with her.[99] More stable relationships also created turmoil. Joseph Avern and Mary Ellison were presented to the church courts in 1718 for adultery because they had married while Mary's first husband was still living. Joseph Avern's daughter clearly objected to this relationship and was affronted by the way that Mary wore her mother's clothes and rings and took 'upon her to behave her self as her father's wife'.[100]

People outside the family circle expressed more conventional disapproval about women's adultery. Those whose own reputation might be affected were most vehement. For example, Richard Pape, a 51-year-old gardener, who also kept a public house in Newton, Wakefield, gave a room for a night to Dorothy Cunliffe and John Wheatley at his pub, in 1701. When he was

[98] UOD, DDR/EJ/CCD/3/1789/4, *Smith c. Smith*.
[99] BIHR, CP.I/1376, *Wentworth c. Wentworth*, 1756.
[100] BIHR, Trans.CP.1721/3, *office c. Joseph Avern*, William Woods' deposition, 1718.

told who the gentlewoman was, he informed John 'what a Shame and Sin it was to lye with other men's wives and bid him gett one of his owne and live honestly'.[101] Lady Jane Vavasour stayed for four or five nights at a lodgings house in York owned by Mr and Mrs Horncastle. William Parker stayed in the room adjoining hers. She returned a fortnight later and Mr Horncastle was reluctant to give her lodgings in case William arrived as well. Indeed, he did just that the next day after she was cried down by a common bellman. Mrs Horncastle therefore told Lady Jane that William could not have a room. This infuriated her so that she left the next day.[102] Landlords and innkeepers no doubt sought to protect their public reputation, though there are also examples of women and their lovers staying in lodgings as well as living together where their status was known.[103] Servants also feared for their own reputation when working for spouses with marital difficulties.[104] Ann Shanks wanted to quit the Smiths' service, at Martinmas 1786, because she worried that her own character would suffer from her mistress' adultery. Francis Metcalfe left Sir Peter Vavasour's service in 1713, after witnessing the intimacies passing between Lady Jane and William Parker, Sir Peter's steward. He realised that her behaviour would ruin Sir Peter, and we can perhaps infer that he thought it might also affect his own reputation. Alisimon Booth of Broughton, Lincoln, was maid from 1758 to 1759 to Alice Chaworth, when she lodged in Newark after her separation. Alice would order Alisimon to sit up at nights in another room, in order to get time alone with her lover William Heppenstall, because the lodgings only had one bed. Alisimon quit Alice's service, not only because she disapproved of her mistress' lewdness, but also because the nights sitting-up made her ill.[105]

Unchaste married women were not automatically thought of as common whores, but a few correction cases brought against adulterous women described them as a common whore or stated that they had the reputation of one. The adultery separation initiated against Anne Tindal in 1731 did not just accuse her of adultery with John Thompson, who fathered one of her children, but included an article claiming that she had the reputation of a whore in Gateshead for the last two to three years. It also claimed that she had been salivated for the French disease in that time (a reference to the physical result of being treated with mercury for venereal disease), which was important evidence since venereal disease that began long after

[101] BIHR, CP.I/54, *Cunliffe* c. *Cunliffe*, 1701.
[102] BIHR, CP.I/661–2, *Vavasour* c. *Vavasour*, 1715.
[103] BIHR, CP.H/4729–30, CP.H/4737, CP.H/4740, *Silvester* c. *Silvester*, 1675.
[104] Meldrum, *Domestic Service*, p. 59.
[105] UOD, DDR/EJ/CCD/3/1789/4, *Smith* c. *Smith*; BIHR, CP.I/661–2, *Vavasour* c. *Vavasour*, 1715; BIHR, CP.I/1414, *Chaworth* c. *Chaworth*, 1760.

the wedding was admissible proof of adultery.[106] Mostly, however, there was a generalised statement in the libel, one of the most formulaic parts of the proceedings, that the women lived a lewd debauched life. Occasionally it also claimed that they had the carnal use of the bodies of diverse strange men, though it usually proceeded to name one lover. While this can give the impression that there was a lack of clear distinction between forms of sexual immorality, adultery separation suits reveal that provincial people did distinguish between common whores and adulteresses.[107] For instance, deponents were unlikely to make the same generalised claims as the libels. They might refer to a woman's loss of reputation, but did not equate this with whoredom. One deponent did comment that Ann Spink was reputed a common woman of the town and to live in a bawdy house. She was married in 1786, eloped in 1795, and was accused of having lewd and adulterous correspondence with several persons thereafter, though two men were named as her lovers between 1795 and 1804 when the case was brought. Yet two female neighbours simply understood that Ann and Francis Harper lived together as man and wife.[108] Indeed the statements about lewd lives were so much a formulaic element of the suits that the two adultery separations brought against men in the second half of the eighteenth century used exactly the same language. George Shafto was accused in the libel of adultery with different strange women and of leading a 'vicious lewd debauched life and conversation'.[109]

CHANGES IN THE PERCEPTIONS OF ADULTERESSES, THEIR HUSBANDS AND THEIR LOVERS

The shifts that occurred in ideas about male and female sexuality between the 1670s and 1820s are reflected in attitudes towards the main protagonists in a woman's infidelity. These shifts can be detected in several ways. Representations of unfaithful wives' responses to the discovery of their adulterous behaviour differed over the period studied. In the late seventeenth century they responded in a brazen, confrontational manner that ignored their precarious position. In 1666, Mary Babb's neighbours interrupted her during sex with her brother-in-law, Richard Babb. He looked 'shameful' and was

---

[106] UOD, DDR/EJ/PRC/2/1731/12, Tindal c. Tindal.

[107] It has been argued that adultery, prostitution and other types of sexual immorality should not be analysed in isolation, because they were part of one interconnected pattern of social and sexual relations. The church simply defined relationships as either chaste or unchaste, sexual immorality was defined very broadly in law, and fluid relational patterns made it difficult to determine a basic distinction between chaste and unchaste relationships (Dabhoiwala, 'Pattern of sexual immorality').

[108] BIHR, Cons.CP.1804/5, Spink c. Spink.   [109] BIHR, CP.I/2568, Shafto c. Shafto, 1800.

unable to speak 'he was so amazed'. Mary, however, nonchalantly said 'Lord Blesse me' and 'sett a bold face on it'.[110] According to deponents in 1675, Anne Silvester boasted about her adultery with Joseph Oakes and was indifferent to any criticism. When Joseph claimed that he was Anne's husband, Anne contradicted 'by God he was not nor never should bee', and on another occasion swore bitterly that she and John would lie together in a bed at Barnsley Cross 'that all the world might see them'.[111] A century later, wives were portrayed expressing shame and even remorse. A servant recalled that Eleanor Smith told her that she was 'ashamed' to visit Admiral Roddam, who normally received her and her husband with civility, respect and friendship, after discovering that there was a rumour that Eleanor had been found in bed with a lover. When Eleanor confessed to her husband in 1788 that she had committed adultery with George Fettis, who had fathered her youngest child, it was with great sorrow. The libel and depositions described her feeling shamed, asking forgiveness, and spending much of the time crying.[112] The next year, in 1789, Henrietta Stapylton was reported to have cried until she was almost sick when she was confronted with the discoveries about her. Ordered to leave her father-in-law's house and her husband, she replied to her maid's reminder that she had a gown at the mantua makers: 'well you may take it your self and remember every time you put it on what a vile wretch used to wear it'.[113] Mary Fortnam managed a fairly cool response in 1775 when two of her mother's male servants confronted her with knowledge of her affair with her mother's shepherd. On being reproached again she threatened to hang or drown herself.[114] Of course both brazen and shamed responses were intended to show that the women were admitting to their behaviour, but the way that this was depicted had changed substantially by the end of the eighteenth century.

Criminal conversation actions reveal the extent to which the shift was taking root. They were predicated upon the belief that men were naturally sexually aggressive and that women were passive victims of either male sexual and emotional neglect or attention.[115] They offered two versions of adulterous wives, which depended on whether they were presented by the counsel for the plaintiff or for the defendant. The former portrayed adulteresses as women seduced by sexually aggressive men, the latter as women led by romantic folly

[110] BIHR, CP.H/2688, CP.H/2807, CP.H/2741, *office c. Babb*, 1666.
[111] BIHR, CP.H/4729–30; CP.H/4737; CP.H/4740, *Silvester c. Silvester*, 1675.
[112] UOD, DDR/EJ/CCD/3/1789/4, *Smith c. Smith.*
[113] BIHR, CP.I/2245–75, *Stapylton c. Stapylton*, 1786.
[114] OA, Mss.Oxf.dioc.papers c.92, *Fortnam c. Fortnam*, 1775.
[115] For this point see Turner, 'Representations of adultery', pp. 222, 237–9; for the 'theatrical' elements of the actions, see Staves, 'Money for honor'.

into inappropriate relationships with lovers through husbandly neglect. Thus in 1791, the defendant's counsel in the criminal conversation trial between Mr Moresome, gentleman, and Mr Clarke, a magistrate for the county of York, charged Mr Moresome with negligence and inattention. Conversely, the plaintiff's counsel stated that the Moresomes were happy until Mr Clarke carried off, dishonoured and ruined Mrs Moresome.[116] Both were images of women as passive. An examination of parliamentary debate about adultery shows that both sides in the debate during the 1800 bill to restrict adultery perceived women to be swayed by impulse and passion.[117] Yet this differed substantially from earlier ideas about active female sexual voraciousness, because these women were victims of male seduction.[118] Perhaps this explains why wives seem to have been given second chances more often in the later eighteenth century. Mary Winham, a maid, was wary about going into the service of the indecorous Eleanor Smith. Her mother accompanied her on a visit to one of Eleanor's neighbours, to enquire about her before agreeing to work for her. The neighbour confirmed that there had been gossip about Mrs Smith and John Hall; but that he was leaving and she would perhaps do better after he was gone.[119] By the later eighteenth century adulterous wives were even depicted acting honourably. In a widely reported aristocratic marital breakdown, the Marchioness of Abercorn's conduct was described as 'irreproachable' and 'meritorious' because she had confessed to her husband that her feelings for another man were contrary to 'conjugal duty', without first committing adultery. One newspaper reported that as a result those who knew her looked on her 'imprudence with pity and tenderness, rather than with the asperity of censure'.[120]

Attitudes to men whose wives were unfaithful were also shifting. In the sixteenth and seventeenth centuries cuckolds were scorned and derided in popular culture; figures of bawdy mockery, their sexual inadequacy was blamed for causing their wives' adultery.[121] There was some continuity through the eighteenth century. For example, Turner observes that criminal conversation actions reported in the press offered a fresh venue for mocking cuckolds, as did new genres that emerged in the late eighteenth century, like the journal the *Cuckold's Chronicle*.[122] Sexual neglect continued to be inferred in the first half of the eighteenth century. In a pamphlet published in 1746, 'Lady Traffick' informed her husband:

---

[116] The jury awarded £3,500 damages for the plaintiff (*N.Chron*, 25 June 1791, p. 4).
[117] Andrew, '"Adultery a-la-mode"', 21.   [118] Turner, 'Representations of adultery', p. 23.
[119] UOD, DDR/EJ/CCD/3/1789/4, *Smith c. Smith.*   [120] *Y.Her*, 17 November 1798, p. 3.
[121] E. A. Foyster, *Manhood in Early Modern England. Honour, Sex and Marriage* (London, 1999), pp. 66–72; Foyster, 'A laughing matter? Marital discord and gender control in seventeenth-century England', *Rural History*, 4 (1993), 8, 11.
[122] Turner, 'Representations of adultery', pp. 112–14.

> If you the threaten'd dread Divorce pursue,
> Think, from your own Neglect, 'tis but your Due:
> When Vigour, ev'n in Youth, exhausted grows,
> The Shallow Stream in *frigid Channels* flows;
> The disappointed Wife in Secret pines,
> and curses Matrimony many Times[123]

In 1722 Elizabeth Dent illustrated that her husband had neglected her, by stating that when he lived in Beverley he spent all days and most nights at Samuel Dalton's house.[124] However, it was becoming less common for husbands in this situation to be seen as failing sexually. Commentary increasingly highlighted the emotional aspects of a husband's neglect. The breadth of the concept was expressed in legal treatises. *The Laws Respecting Women*, published in 1777, argued against preventing adulteresses from marrying their lovers following divorce, since some 'modern breaches of chastity in women may be excited, by notorious, avowed, and long persisted in, acts of indifference and neglect in the husband'.[125] As we have seen, a frequent defence in criminal conversation actions was that husbands neglected their wives, and in this genre too it incorporated emotional features.[126] For instance, in 1798, the *York Herald* reported that the Marchioness of Abercorn turned to Captain Copley for affection because she had long been 'prey to hopeless dejection, and mortified by neglect'.[127]

Contempt for men with unfaithful wives was never universally applied, and there was a noticeable inclination in the eighteenth century to sympathise with them.[128] In 1739 the *Gentleman's Magazine* printed 'Mr Spectator's' response to a cuckold who requested consolation and advice. He conveyed his pity, but observed that 'it is too common a Case to affect the Generality of the World'. Indeed, it was so common that 'it ought to be esteem'd as nothing; for it brings no real Injury to a Man's Reputation or Fame, since it depends not on his Will or Consent'. He concluded that the correspondent was in the same society as kings, dukes, earls, bishops and numerous other worthies.[129] A less positive version of this sentiment was pity. The wife of Eleanor Smith's lover, talking about Reverend William Smith in 1788, remarked, 'Poor Man I pity the Priest, little does he know what sort of a Wife he has.'[130] Accounts of cuckoldry did not focus on the weakness of husbands, particularly if they took the initiative in dealing with the aftermath of their wives' adultery. In 1751 the *Newcastle Courant* reported on a Banbury

123 Anon., *Adultery A-la-Mode. An Epistle from Lady Traffick to Sir John* (London, 1746), p. 12.
124 BIHR, CP. I/697, *Dent c. Dent*, 1722.   125 Anon., *Laws Respecting Women*, p. 93.
126 Also see Andrew, '"Adultery a-la-mode"', 19.
127 *Y.Her*, 17 November 1798, p. 3.   128 Turner, 'Representations of adultery', pp. 85–9.
129 *GM*, 9 (October 1739), 530–1.   130 UOD, DDR/EJ/CCD/3/1789/4, *Smith c. Smith*.

dealer, who returned home unexpectedly and found his wife in bed with another man. Getting some assistance he took them out of bed, tied their arms together and sat them on the floor in front of a large fire. He then had tea, coffee and punch provided and invited his neighbours round on the pretext that his wife was ill. Thus 'he exposed his Wife and her Gallant for some Hours, which seem'd a greater Mortification to them than any Thing else he could have done; and at the same Time the Husband appear'd perfectly contented'.[131] Husbands such as these were also shown to be honourable in their dealings with their adulterous wives. The *Newcastle Journal* admired Lord Grosvenor's generosity to his wife in 1772, when he stopped the proceedings of his separation suit against her in Doctors Commons, after her seducer deserted her and left her destitute. In doing so, he showed kindness and 'rescue[d] her from insult'.[132] Other husbands were congratulated for granting access to children, against their right of sole custody. For this reason, the *York Herald* celebrated the Marquis of Abercorn's '*liberality* as a man'.[133]

The shift in representations of those involved in an extra-marital affair was particularly noticeable in the way that culpability was reassessed. By the later eighteenth century, adultery was often blamed on parents who forced their children into loveless marriages. There was also an undoubted shift across the board from blaming wives for their adultery to blaming their male lovers, which is apparent from the mid eighteenth century.[134] In the 1760s Peter Wilkinson, a 68-year-old yeoman, deposed that John Read, who was in debt to him, had informed him that he would have enough money to pay him if he claimed to have had criminal conversation with Mary Manwaring. John's implication was that Mary's husband would pay him for stating that he had an affair with her. Peter and his wife were shocked. Peter told John that if he had been 'great with Mrs Manwaring you are a Rogue to tell it and if you have not you are a Damnable Rogue to say or swear so'. Mrs Wilkinson responded: 'Oh! Mr Read if you do such a thing I wou'd have you tied to a Post and pulled Limb from Limb by Women and I'll help to pull the first Limb.'[135] Debating societies in the 1780s often decided that the seducer was more to blame than the adulteress was.[136] By the later eighteenth century, male lovers were routinely portrayed as manipulative seducers exploiting ties of friendship with husbands to gain access to their

[131] *N.Cour*, 9 March 1751, p. 2.   [132] *N.Jour*, 29 February – 7 March 1772, p. 1.
[133] *Y.Her*, 17 November 1798, p. 3.
[134] For an unusual view of this shift, see R. Trumbach, *Sex and the Gender Revolution* (Chicago and London, 1998), pp. 12, 393–5.
[135] BIHR, Trans.CP.1766/2, *Manwaring c. Manwaring*, 1761.
[136] Andrew, '"Adultery a-la-mode"', 13.

wives.[137] This was the import of the libel of Captain Hooker Bartellot who brought an adultery separation suit in 1793 against his wife, as part of the process of gaining a divorce by act of parliament. It stated that after three years of apparently happy marriage, Hooker became acquainted with Samuel Hawker, a lieutenant in the sixteenth Regiment of Light Dragoons who 'so ingratiated himself into the Good Opinion of... Hooker Bartellot by his hypocrisy and pretensions of Friendship' that he was frequently invited to their house. He then took advantage of Hooker's unsuspecting disposition to alienate Amelia's affections from her husband.[138] The notion of the artful seducer was particularly effective in criminal conversation actions. As Lord Kenyon remarked in 1794, damages were awarded in criminal conversation cases to punish 'the Libertine who violates the Law of God, of Social Duty, and Religion'.[139]

It is possible that representations of the female lovers of married men underwent change, in tandem with ideas about female sexuality, but there is not enough evidence to be conclusive. In the first part of the period female lovers were blamed for the affairs in ways that fit with the idea that women took the sexual initiative. Thus neighbours criticised Ellen Lambe for keeping company 'with another woemans [*sic*] husband' because she kept him from and alienated his affections from his wife.[140] When Margaret Gordon went to a justice of the peace in 1695 because her husband Adam was beating her, she stated that his mistress Margaret Roullish was 'the great occasion of all this dissention [*sic*]' between them.[141] Female lovers were also accused of verbal and physical violence against the wives. Much of this information comes from correction cases in the ecclesiastical courts, which had all but disappeared by the mid eighteenth century. Thus further research would be required to chart whether female lovers were portrayed differently when women were thought to be sexually passive.

CONCLUSION: FUTURE RESEARCH

There is no doubt that historians must take account of the sexual double-standard in more multi-faceted ways. This is underway where men's experiences are concerned, but more work needs to be done on women's experiences too. This chapter's findings about the state of their marriage when they committed adultery and their motivation and timing in doing so are by no means conclusive, as they are based on such a small sample of cases. Nonetheless, they suggest ways to analyse this issue. Further work of this

---

[137] This was a feature of debates about adultery (ibid., 17).
[138] BIHR, CP.I/2366, *Barttelot c. Barttelot*, 1793. [139] *Y.Her*, 1 March 1794, p. 3.
[140] BIHR, CP.H/4349, *office c. Ellen Lambe*. [141] NCAS, QSB/7, fol. 4.

nature on adultery separation suits and criminal conversation suits from the central court of King's Bench would be welcome. Some clues are also provided in this chapter about the attitudes of provincial ordinary men and women towards infidelity in the eighteenth century. Again, more work could be profitably carried out on this subject and the findings compared with attitudes in the capital. One useful source for this would be criminal conversation actions that came to trial in local assizes around the country. For example, *Jackson's Oxford Journal* reported that an action was brought at Bedford Assizes by a plumber and glazier against a fishmonger, both of Windsor.[142] The next chapter is devoted to another area of married couples' lives that is rarely assessed in great detail: their experience of life after total marital breakdown.

[142] *JOJ*, 19 July 1777, p. 2.

8

'Till death us do part': life after a failed marriage

Couples who stopped cohabiting when they were unable to resolve their marital difficulties became part of a sizeable minority of individuals who lived outside a marital relationship in the later seventeenth and eighteenth centuries. Early in this period 15% of adults never married, though their numbers had declined to 7% by the nineteenth century.[1] Frequent widowhood forced many others to live without a spouse for a period of time, and it became less likely for the widowed to remarry by the later eighteenth century.[2] The numbers of separated spouses joining these groups are difficult to estimate. Pamela Sharpe concludes that 10% of marriages that took place in Colyton, Devon, between 1725 and 1756 ended in separation, but detailed parish reconstitutions of this nature are few and far between.[3] Studies have also counted the numbers of desertions found in the material generated by the settlement laws.[4] Yet this is no indication of total desertion rates within a population, never mind separations not caused by absconding husbands. In general, the types of records which contain information about marriages ending in separation and/or desertion neither are directly comparable nor do they reflect the total incidence of temporary and permanent separations. Though it is impossible to count separated spouses, the records of marital difficulties provide valuable information about the circumstances leading to marriage collapse and the living and working arrangements of spouses thereafter.

[1] E. A. Wrigley and R. S. Schofield, *The Population History of England, 1541–1871* (London, 1981), p. 265.
[2] For examples of the proportion of widows heading households in the period see Mary Prior (ed.), *Women in English Society 1500–1800* (London, 1985), p. 105; S. J. Wright, 'The elderly and the bereaved in eighteenth-century Ludlow' in Pelling and Smith (eds.), *Life, Death*, p. 104; O. Hufton, 'Women without men: widows and spinsters in Britain and France in the eighteenth century', *Journal of Family History* (1984), 358; J. Boulton, 'London widowhood revisited: the decline of female remarriage in the seventeenth and early eighteenth centuries', *Continuity and Change*, 5, 3 (1990), 325–55.
[3] P. Sharpe, 'Marital separation in the eighteenth and early nineteenth centuries', *Local Population Studies*, 45 (1990), 67.
[4] Kent, 'Gone for a soldier', 29–39; Snell, *Annals*, p. 360.

THE REASONS FOR IRRECONCILABLE MARRIAGE BREAKDOWN

Numerous factors, like the individual dynamics of a relationship, personal character, and levels of wealth and financial independence, determined whether specific marriages with difficulties continued or ended in separation. Even so, it is possible to outline general reasons from the fairly detailed records of separation. Inevitably, these records were generated by the more substantial middling sorts, professionals and gentry, but the background of the lower middling sort's and wage labourers' failed marriages can sometimes be glimpsed in the 608 records arising from husbands' desertion and refusal to contribute to their families' maintenance. As might be expected, emotional, physical and economic problems could be insurmountable. Some spouses simply felt that they were incompatible with each other or fell out of love. Others fell in love with another person. In some cases spouses were unable to forgive infidelity and in others they had no choice because unfaithful wives and husbands left to be with their lovers. William Adkins, a boot-catcher and postilion at the Red Lion Inn in Banbury, in 1789, and 35-year-old James Piercey, in 1793, according to *Jackson's Oxford Journal*, both abandoned their wives and families to go away with 'young' women.[5]

Intolerable cruelty forced wives to terminate matrimony; even women without financial or familial support might do so despite its dangerous economic repercussions. Elizabeth Tongue, a 26-year-old, was married in 1761 and lived with her husband for about three years in Oxford until 'her Husband being unkind she thought she might do better by beging [*sic*]'. In 1767 she was apprehended for wandering and begging in Leachlade, Gloucestershire, and removed to Oxford.[6] Nor was it uncommon for male desertions to be preceded by violent conflict. Like the wife of John Cripps, a miller of Thrupp, Oxfordshire, in 1695, many wives stated that their husbands had beaten them and then left them. Cripps added insult to injury by leaving his wife and child without habitation.[7] Occasionally the stages of such a collapsing marriage can be traced through the entries in quarter sessions' records. Benbrook Watson, a butcher of Iver, Buckinghamshire, was bound over in July 1737 to answer his wife's complaint and to keep the peace towards her. At the Epiphany session in 1746 a warrant was issued to take him to Aylesbury Gaol for turning out his wife and infant child, leaving them chargeable. After being discharged at the Easter sessions, he was committed again in September 1748 for having run away from his family. He remained in the house of correction, until at least summer 1749, for not reimbursing the £2 16s spent by the parish on his family's upkeep.[8]

[5] *JOJ*, 6 November 1789, p. 2; 17 August 1793, p. 2.
[6] OA, Par 213/5/A1/1/St Peter in the East.   [7] OA, QS/1695/Ea/4.
[8] CBS Q/SM/2 Midsummer 1737; QS Rolls 173/10; Q/SM/3 Michaelmas 1748; QS Rolls 185/32.

Some separations were not necessarily caused by conflict. The wife of William Saunders placed an advert in *Jackson's Oxford Journal* in 1772, seeking information about her husband who had absconded from her and his large family because he was 'deprived of his senses'.[9] Men also left their families to escape specific problems. Jane Herrison's husband ran away from her and their baby in 1694 because he was suspected of stealing two oxen.[10] No doubt, coerced marriages were particularly susceptible to ending prematurely. Men who were pressured by parish officers to marry the women they had made pregnant had little incentive to stay in the marriage.[11] George Colsell married his wife Sarah in order to make money. Unable to maintain herself because she was an epileptic, she was taken into the workhouse for twelve months. The overseers of Chipping Wycombe, Buckinghamshire, entered an arrangement with George that they would give him £5 if he married her. Sarah agreed to the union and was married on 1 May 1796, when the officers told her that George was to take her away and she was not to be troublesome to them again. Having engineered a way to avoid paying for Sarah's long-term care, the parish officers must have been disappointed when George abandoned her after six weeks. He was apprehended and opted for entering the marines rather than staying around for any other punishment.[12]

Direct evidence about husbands who abandoned their families is rare, and since most information about desertion is found in poor-relief material it is tempting to characterise them as more hard-hearted and irresponsible than other social groups of men, and as members of the lowest social ranks. This image is partly shaped by the reasons for the records being produced, which were to force husbands to take on their financial obligations to their families and to obtain relief for their wives and children. Therefore, those emanating from local authorities emphasised that men had rejected their responsibilities, highlighting their senselessness and callousness. Equally, abandoned wives' testimony stressed their husbands' motiveless, even deliberately cruel behaviour, to demonstrate their eligibility for assistance. Mary Craske's pain and contempt for her husband pervades her letter to Reverend Wise in Rochford, requesting his assistance in getting her poor relief paid in 1803. She described her children as 'discarded' by their father and, without mentioning his name, commented, 'I hear Southampton harbours the Author of Our destiny.' She also admitted that she 'shou'd like to know what atonement he has made to (Almighty God) from [*sic*] his Great Crimes and think one step towards forgiveness wou'd to remit all he could possibly spare to

[9] *JOJ*, 22 February 1772, p. 3.
[10] NCAS, QSB/7 fol. 40, petition by the overseer of Bywell St Peter, July 1695.
[11] P. Sharpe, 'Marital separation', 67.
[12] The parish disputing Sarah's settlement probably failed in its attempt to show that Chipping Wycombe's parish officers were acting illegitimately, because it was unable to provide proof (OA, Mss.D.D.Rotherfield Greys/C.11/Item b.1).

his Inquir'd Parish'.[13] It is, of course, difficult not to see deserting men as irresponsible, given that they so often left young children as well as their wives. Admittedly, some men might have absolved their conscience about abandoning them by leaving a sum of money for their upkeep. In 1687 Thomas Smith left his wife and baby to go to France. Nonetheless, he left £10 for them with Mr Walter, a collier of Witney. Susan Munday, his wife, revealed this when she was forced to give the name of her child's father, after being prosecuted for bearing a bastard child and committed to the house of correction in January 1688. Her statement, given at the Easter sessions, also explained that she had married Thomas, a university student, in 1680, when she was a servant at an Oxford inn. This was an irregular ceremony and they did not live together, since she remained a servant for another eighteen months, although their relationship continued until after their daughter's birth in 1687.[14]

There is good reason to believe that poor men left their wives and young children when these families were under the most economic stress. Rural families which broke up in the south of England between 1700 and 1880, for example, had more young children than those who stayed together.[15] The deserted families considered in this analysis have similar characteristics since they were predominantly from the agricultural and rural counties of North Yorkshire, Oxfordshire and Buckinghamshire.[16] Thus, 78% of husbands who had left their wives also abandoned children. The numbers of children were given in 193 instances (Appendix 29) and nearly 40% of the couples had three or more children (10% of them had five or more children), and approximately 61% had one or two.[17] In many cases, the children were described as nurse children, infants, or were five and under; testimony to the pressing life-cycle poverty which was caused when children were too young to be economically productive and wives had to focus on child-rearing rather than earning.[18] These separated rural families were larger than equivalent urban ones in the Westminster parish of St Martin-in-the-Fields. David Kent wonders if this was caused by lower rates of marital fertility in London and suggests that the poverty cycle was reached sooner there than in the countryside.[19] Not that childlessness was any guarantee of marital security. Of 403 desertions in St Martin-in-the-Fields in the second

---

[13] T. Sokoll (ed.), *Essex Pauper Letters 1731–1837*, Records of Social and Economic History New Series, 30 (Oxford, 2001), p. 585.

[14] OA, QS/1688/Ea/1.

[15] Taken from 289 sample settlement certificates (Snell, *Annals*, p. 360).

[16] This study did not, however, compare deserted families with other families coming under the poor laws and settlement laws.

[17] In 232 instances children were mentioned without specifying their number.

[18] Kent, 'Gone for a Soldier', 33.

[19] In the Westminster parish, 80% of the deserted families had one or two children, 19% had three or four, and only 0.5% had five children (ibid., 35–6).

half of the eighteenth century 43% involved childless couples, probably because childlessness made husbands' decision to leave easier and the consequences of their actions less injurious.[20]

Recent literature on the survival strategies of paupers' households also stresses that poverty frequently fragmented families, although it shows that it was not always a unilateral male decision.[21] For instance, some of the separations in Colyton were parish-approved tactics to lessen poverty, where couples split up to live in shared houses with other people of similar age and sex, their children boarded out or apprenticed.[22] Jeremy Boulton's study of London's West End demonstrates that children might be temporarily left on the parish, in the workhouse, or placed with relatives in order to increase their chances of survival. Still, when circumstances improved, families were intended to be reconstructed.[23]

Boulton comments, thought-provokingly, that the 'desertion of wives and children by hard-pressed husbands could even be said to be an extreme example of [such] rational and calculating behaviour on the part of poor families'.[24] The husbands in this study, however, acted less rationally and more desperately, taking the easiest option by running away from their insurmountable economic problems. A number of men left in fear of being arrested for debt.[25] Limited employment opportunities and the resulting economic hardship pushed many others on their way. Sharpe notes that the background of separations in Colyton was limited agricultural employment opportunities and declining textile industries.[26] It was Ralph Mather's opinion, in 1780, that technological changes restricted work opportunities and forced families into hardship, causing over 4,000 poor men to enlist.[27] Statistics back him up. Desertions in the Westminster parish of St Martin-in-the-Fields, for example, increased during war or preparation for war when recruitment into the army or navy was available.[28] Contemporaries were well aware of the link between enlistment and limited work. It was even used by men as a strategy to obtain poor relief. In 1826, 44-year-old David Rivenall wrote from London to the overseer of Chelmsford requesting relief for his wife and family (five children between seven and fifteen years old),

---

[20] Ibid., 34.
[21] J. Boulton, '"It is extreme necessity that makes me do this": some "survival strategies" of pauper households in London's West End during the early eighteenth century' in L. Fontaine and J. Schlumbohm, *Household Strategies for Survival 1600–2000: Fission, Faction and Cooperation*, International Review of Social History, 45, Cambridge, 2000, p. 66.
[22] P. Sharpe, 'Marital separation', 67.
[23] Boulton, 'Extreme necessity', pp. 53–5, 66.   [24] Ibid., p. 66.
[25] For example, OA, St Peter in the East/C.3/72, settlement certificate about Hesther Bourton, and CBS, QS Rolls 105/73, Epiphany 1729, Mary Mulfield.
[26] P. Sharpe, 'Marital separation', 66, 67.
[27] Quoted in Clark, *Struggle for the Breeches*, p. 20; Sharpe, 'Marital separation', 66.
[28] Kent, 'Gone for a soldier', 30.

warning him that if it was not forthcoming 'they will be on the parish as I [sic] is my wish to go to Sea for I cannot bear to see my Children want as well as my Dear partner'. While he did not actually desert them, he was well aware of the force of his threat.[29] Although outside the period studied in this book, it is possible that Rivenall's threat that he would leave his family because he could not watch them suffer was a real motive behind some eighteenth-century men's desertions. Mather, for example, described husbands leaving 'to escape the cries of their starving wives and children'.[30] When Mary-Ann Smith applied to the overseer of Upminster, Essex, for relief in 1814, she stated that she had 'nothing but what I work for and my Husband through distress has diserted [sic] from home'.[31] His distress may have been emotional as well as economic. Of course, the fact that such men were ineffectual rather than malicious in intent or inherently irresponsible was cold comfort for their wives and children.

There is information about the occupations of 196 of the 608 men who deserted their families (Appendix 30) and it provides further evidence that desertion was often associated with economic factors. Nevertheless, it also shows that abandonment was not just a habit of the lowest social ranks. We need to adjust our preconceptions that it was only men without property who deserted their families because they were less encumbered by property and financial obligations.[32] For a start, parishes often seized the goods, rents and profits of men who had absconded or refused to contribute towards their families' maintenance.[33] Secondly, the occupations show that 2% of deserting husbands were described as gentlemen, or were professionals, and that a few in agriculture-related occupations were farmers and yeomen. More significantly, one third of the deserting husbands were tradesmen, craftsmen and retailers, some of whom were likely to have owned a little real property and certainly some personal property. Yet these were also social and occupational groups that were subject to factors causing poverty such as economic cycles and seasonal fluctuations; the consequences of warfare, taxation and demobilisation; environmental problems, disease and infirmity; the loss of a spouse and the financial strain of numerous young children.[34] Over half of the deserting husbands were even more susceptible because they came from poorly paid, seasonal and less secure occupational groups. Labourers made up 38% and, since many of them lived in Buckinghamshire, were probably agricultural labourers; 3% were servants, a few of whom were servants in

[29] Sokoll, *Pauper Letters*, p. 240. For an account of the Rivenall family, see T. Sokoll, 'Negotiating a living: Essex pauper letters from London, 1800–1834' in Fontaine and Schlumbohm, *Household Strategies*, pp. 25–8.
[30] Clark, *Struggle for the Breeches*, p. 20.   [31] Sokoll, *Pauper Letters*, pp. 622–3.
[32] Stone, *Divorce*, p. 141.   [33] Chapter 3, p. 37.
[34] Fontaine and Schlumbohm's observation (*Household Strategies*, p. 1).

husbandry. Another 6% of the men were in agricultural occupations and 4% were unskilled craftsmen. The rest were in river- or sea-related occupations (4%), were soldiers or militia-men (7%) or pedlars (2%).

The precarious nature of these employment sectors is reflected in the way that families routinely broke up when men left to seek work. This is illustrated by the examination of Nathaniel Cole, who was committed as a vagrant to Northallerton house of correction in 1788. A shipwright who came to England from South Carolina, he was married in Westmoreland, Cumbria, and then worked for eight years at Lancaster and four years at Hull. Unfortunately, he developed dropsy and left Hull, presumably because he was unable to work at his regular job, and travelled in Yorkshire, picking up work. In the meantime his wife and three children were with her widowed mother in Perth, Cumberland.[35] The process of seeking work made it all too easy for husbands to fail to return home or contribute to their families' support when communication broke down or they failed to find employment. There was a fine line between searching for temporary work and desertion. In the early nineteenth century, a parish officer responded to a newspaper advertisement seeking the whereabouts of a runaway husband. He informed his recipient that the absconder was in Rochford, which he described as a 'remote place where A many of our Essex chaps especially Runaways fly too [sic] when they desert their families'.[36] Though the 'not-guilty' pleas used by some husbands accused of desertion are rarely detailed, searching for work might have served as a plausible explanation for being away from home. It was used by Ben Castle whose petition is a rare example of a deserting man's self-defence. A labourer from Wilcot, Oxfordshire, he was committed to hard labour in the house of correction, in January 1702, for leaving John Sellman's employment without his consent, after being hired at harvest to cut corn, and for leaving his wife and two children on the parish. He was also accused of being about to marry a 'lewd idle' woman, thus bringing a further charge on the parish. Ben petitioned that he had simply gone to Berkshire to get harvest work; while he was there his wife had died and the parish officers had removed his two children and pulled down his house. His petition went on, therefore, to request that he be provided with a house in order to avoid becoming a vagrant.[37]

The connection between economic difficulties and abandonment is supported by the apparent increase in numbers of desertions during the second half of the eighteenth century, when average food prices rose and probably

[35] NYA, QSB/1788 MIC 001297.
[36] P. Sharpe, "The bowels of compation": a labouring family and the law, c. 1790–1834' in Hitchcock, King and Sharpe (eds.), *Chronicling Poverty*, p. 97.
[37] OA, QS/1702/Ep/44.

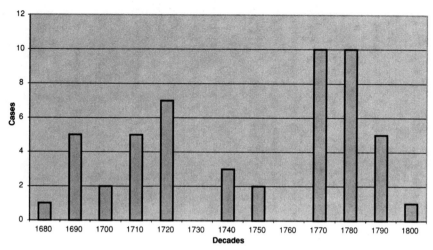

Figure 6. Northumberland desertions by decade

outstripped wage rates.[38] This 'placed a greater proportion of the work-ing population closer to the fear of want'.[39] Problems were exacerbated by harvest failures, the impact of enclosure, and the disruption to some trades caused by warfare and demobilisation.[40] Contemporaries certainly felt that the numbers of runaway husbands were escalating in the later eighteenth century. When reporting on the offences dealt with by Oxfordshire County Sessions in July 1787, *Jackson's Oxford Journal* noted that desertion was 'an Offence now become so common; that the Magistrates seem determined to punish Offenders of that Class with due Rigour'.[41] The majority of the desertions in this study occurred after the mid eighteenth century, particu-larly from the 1770s, with different peak decades according to counties.[42] For example, the 1770s and '80s in Northumberland saw the highest num-bers of desertions coming to the attention of the justices of the peace and, similarly, the 1780s was the peak decade in the North Riding of Yorkshire (figures 6 and 7).[43] The desertions recorded in Oxfordshire's quarter sessions

---

[38] B. A. Holderness, 'Price, productivity and output' in G. E. Mingay (ed.), *The Agrarian History of England and Wales*, Vol. VI, *1750–1850* (Cambridge, 1989), p. 92.

[39] D. Hay and N. Rogers, *Eighteenth-century English Society: Shuttles and Swords* (Oxford, 1997), p. 72.

[40] Hay and Rogers, *Eighteenth-Century English Society*, pp. 71–83; J. Black, *Eighteenth-century Britain 1688–1783* (Basingstoke, 2001), pp. 104–9.

[41] *JOJ*, 14 July 1787, p. 3.

[42] This refers to the total of 608 desertions. Four counties have been selected in the following discussion encompassing 477 desertions.

[43] 1772 and 1782–3 were years of high food prices due to dearth. Hay and Rogers, *Eighteenth-Century English Society*, p. 71.

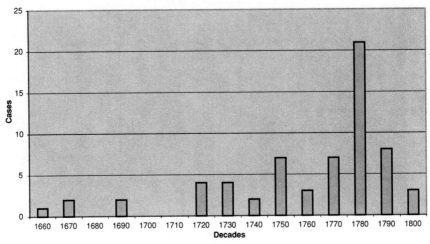

Figure 7. Yorkshire desertions by decade

records, however, appear fairly consistent from the 1740s to '60s, falling thereafter until a peak decade in the 1790s (figure 8). Unfortunately it is difficult to compare counties or be conclusive about the correlation between the numbers of deserters coming before the quarter sessions and economic conditions, because each of the counties studied had different methods of recording desertion, and variations in the survival rates of records.[44]

However, one example of fairly consistent record-keeping can be found in Buckinghamshire, whose practice was to indict deserting husbands for misdemeanour or, if repeated offenders, for felony. Rates of prosecution of deserting husbands in Buckinghamshire were higher in the 1770s and 1780s, with a slight fall in the 1790s that might be related to the county's practice of making up labourers' wages when under-paid (figure 9).[45] It seems possible that these higher rates correlated with declining agricultural employment. After all, by 1802 Buckinghamshire was amongst those rural counties in England with the highest proportions of paupers in the population.[46] However, it is still inconclusive whether the higher rates of prosecution indicate a higher number of desertions. The punishment of deserting husbands certainly suggests that the authorities in Buckinghamshire were very concerned about the problem. Convicted men were rigorously punished in the houses of correction. In the 1750s and 1760s, at the height of the popularity of using

---

[44] Snell concluded that deserted wives in rural southern England and Wales, as a percentage of numbers, remained reasonably constant over the eighteenth and nineteenth centuries, except for a slight rise after 1781 which could be explained by soldiers going to war (Snell, *Annals*, p. 361).

[45] CBS, Q/SM/10, Epiphany 1795.   [46] Sokoll, *Pauper Letters*, p. 28.

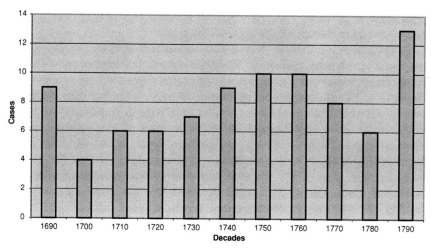

Figure 8. Oxfordshire desertions by decade

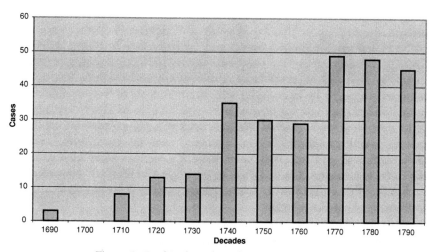

Figure 9. Buckinghamshire desertions by decade

transportation as a punishment, men who had repeatedly left their families were transported to America as incorrigible rogues.[47] This extreme punishment was probably intended to dissuade other like-minded men and, if removing the worst offenders through transportation did not cut demand on

---

[47] The American Revolution stopped transportation to the American colonies in 1776. For the development of transportation as a form of punishment, see Beattie, *Crime and the Courts*, pp. 451–73, 500–13, 538–48.

poor relief, it probably reduced surplus labour supply, leaving employment opportunities to those considered more worthy.

Sharpe points out that the poor economic conditions besetting the labouring poor in eighteenth-century Colyton caused 'loosely structured and short term household arrangements partially dependent on poor relief payments'.[48] True enough; but we must not move a further step and characterise the marriages of the lower ranks as inherently transient. Not every desertion by a low-earning husband was the result of economic pressures. The marriages of wage labourers were not automatically inclined to collapse because of economic difficulties. In fact, it could be argued that they might be stronger *because* of the potential economic problems faced by people in this social group. Diane O'Hara has demonstrated that people in the lower reaches of society in sixteenth-century Kent exercised extreme care when planning matrimony. Material considerations were all-consuming, for couples needed to ensure that they could accumulate the resources necessary to set up a household and bring in enough money to run it thereafter.[49] Moreover, the repercussions of marriage failure for those with few means were likely to be more serious than for those with financial support. Thus there is little reason to suppose that seventeenth- and eighteenth-century poor people were less careful about making, and, by extension, breaking, marriage. Though the marriages of the poor were not naturally transient, it is feasible that some husbands were subject to different cultural controls. One avenue for research might be to consider whether the ideals of 'responsible' manhood had less purchase for men who were unlikely to be able to achieve any of its necessary fundamentals. We have seen that sub-cultures of manhood existed, which repudiated the 'mainstream' elements constituting responsible manhood, and they may have made it easier for some men to reject the cultural pressures that tied them to marriage and family.[50] Nevertheless, such men often entered other relationships, so they were not spurning the institution of marriage itself.

LIVING ARRANGEMENTS

The living arrangements of separated spouses were similar to those of other individuals outside of the conjugal unit. Peter Laslett estimated that only 1% of the population lived on their own in pre-industrial England.[51] Studies of demography, the poor, the widowed and the single have gone on to reveal the range of relationships within which 'lone' people outside of the conjugal unit lived. As well as remarrying, the widowed might live with their offspring

---

[48] P. Sharpe, 'Marital separation', 69.
[49] O'Hara, *Courtship and Constraint*, pp. 219–20.   [50] Chapter 4, pp. 68–9.
[51] Peter Laslett, *Family Life and Illicit Love in Earlier Generations* (Cambridge, 1977), p. 199.

or unrelated people, or as lodgers; other lone individuals clustered together into groups with similar individuals.[52] In other words, all adopted strategies aimed at constructing a viable household and/or pooling of resources. Even separated husbands with some means would reconstruct their household with female servants or relations as 'surrogate' wives, in the terms of household manager, child-carer and, sometimes, sexual partner. Reverend James Robertson, curate of Holy Island, whose wife had lived 'from him at a great Distance' (Alnwick) for several years, for example, employed two maids to care for his house and children.[53] In this sense, separated husbands were no different to long-term bachelors or widowers. In Ludlow, for example, three-quarters of the widowers who were bereaved between 1710 and 1749 and did not remarry for a decade or more usually had another woman in their household, variously an unmarried daughter, kinswoman or female servant.[54] The reputation of such men living without wives could be vulnerable. In 1664 the chapel warden of Lower Peever in Chester promoted a correction case against an elderly widower for sleeping with his maid. Thomas Dean's defence was that his maid stayed with him because of his illness. Until his incapacity, he had organised his living arrangements to prevent local rumour. Dean used to send his maid to sleep with the daughters of the Kinsey family, who lived in the other end of the house to him and his children, because 'hee would not give occasion to people to talke of them'.[55]

A degree of social decline may also have followed hot on the heels of a broken marriage, even for middling-sort men cushioned by relative economic comfort. In 1705 John Greaves insisted that his trade as a Beverley shopkeeper was bad, 'by reason of his wife's Character of him, her elopement from, and deserting of him'.[56] Other husbands did not attempt to continue as before, once they separated.[57] John Carr, the owner of a dye-works in Leeds, with a large house and gardens nearby, married in 1788. In 1795 he employed Henry Johns, a painter of miniature portraits, to paint his and his wife's portraits. Sarah Carr admired more than Henry's painting skills and they embarked on an affair. As soon as John discovered his wife's infidelity, he dismantled the household. The maids lost their places shortly after Sarah

---

[52] For various arrangements, see Pelling and Smith (eds.), *Life, Death*, p. 85; Pelling, 'Who most needs to marry? Ageing and inequality among women and men in early modern Norwich' in Botelho and Thane, *Women and Ageing*, p. 34; and S. Ottaway, 'The old woman's home in eighteenth-century England' in Botelho and Thane, *Women and Ageing*, p. 126. For single women, see A. M. Froide, 'Old maids: the lifecycle of single women in early modern England' in Botelho and Thane, *Women and Ageing*, p. 96.

[53] UOD, DDR/EJ/PRC/2/1755/1, *office c. Robertson*.

[54] Wright, 'Elderly and the bereaved' in Pelling and Smith (eds.), *Life, Death*, p. 121.

[55] BIHR, Trans.CP.1665/4, *office c. Dean*, 1665.

[56] BIHR, CP.I/88, *Greaves c. Greaves*, 1704.

[57] Old men who lacked a spouse showed a greater tendency to live as lodgers and in institutions (Laslett, *Family Life*, p. 200).

left; John Thomas, Carr's apprentice, who had lived with the Carrs for eight of his nine years of apprenticeship, had to board with John Carr's brother for the final year, his master 'having given up housekeeping on parting from his wife'.[58] Similarly, John Winks, the master of a brigantine in North Shields, advertised in 1791 that his wife's behaviour had obliged him 'to decline house-keeping'.[59]

Husbands who were inclined, able or obliged to, would maintain two 'households'; paying towards the lodgings and upkeep of their separated wives in addition to their own upkeep. As well as these separated wives who had financial support from their husbands, those who had access to a separate income, or could earn a living, might be able to live in their own lodgings, with a servant or some of their children, depending on their rank, wealth and the extent of amicability of their marital breakdown. Those who were unable or unwilling to act as the nucleus of a 'new' household could, as we have seen, go to stay temporarily or permanently with their natal family or other relations.[60] Middling-sort and elite families routinely assisted women without husbands. This could be mutually convenient, as financial outlay remained within the family and the women 'paid' for their keep by providing caring services.[61] Such assistance was not restricted to the wealthier social ranks. There are examples of deserted wives taking their children to live with their widowed mothers, which was of reciprocal benefit to both women.[62] Indeed, recent work on poor relief emphasises that familial aid was crucial to many people who had problems making ends meet.[63] Grace Featherstone, the wife of Ralph, a miner of Stanhope, went to live with her parents when her marriage deteriorated in 1776. Grace's parents were also involved in the negotiations for her to return to Ralph, and, when that failed, her maintenance. Ralph demanded the return of his daughter, whom Grace had taken with her to her parents, and offered £4 a year towards Grace's maintenance. Some compromise was reached because the restitution cause initiated by Grace was dismissed and when Ralph died in 1797 he bequeathed £280 to his daughter, by then a married woman, and £6 a year to Grace.[64]

---

[58] BIHR, CP.I/2569, *Carr c. Carr*, 1800, John Thomas' deposition. For the report on Carr's criminal conversation action, heard at York Assizes in 1797, see *Y.Cour*, 27 March 1797, p. 3.

[59] *N.Cour*, 22 January 1791, p. 1.   [60] Chapter 3, p. 33.

[61] Hufton, 'Women without men', 368.

[62] For examples of unmarried women and their illegitimate children in similar circumstances, see Sokoll, 'Negotiating a living', p. 38.

[63] T. Wales, 'Poverty, poor relief and the life-cycle: some evidence from seventeenth-century Norfolk' in R. M. Smith (ed.), *Land, Kinship, and Life-Cycle* (Cambridge, 1984), pp. 383–4; S. King, 'Reconstructing lives: the poor, the Poor Law and welfare in Calverley, 1650–1820', *Social History*, 22, 3 (1997), 336.

[64] UOD, DDR/EJ/PRC/2/1776/2, *Featherstone c. Featherstone*, 1776; DPR, 1798, Ralph Featherstone.

Unfortunately, in many cases alimony was neither a substantial nor secure income. We have seen that a few men ensured that they ended any financial commitment to their separated wives by using evidence that they were adulterous to sue them for separation in the ecclesiastical courts.[65] Yet even wives who fulfilled all the criteria for receiving alimony or the law of agency frequently faced difficulties in obtaining either.[66] Obviously, in the case of deserted wives, many husbands were just not around to offer financial assistance or credit. If alimony was forthcoming, wives often found that payments were too low and infrequent. In the first place evidence from a variety of sources demonstrates that the amounts paid were small; falling within the range of late seventeenth- and early eighteenth-century London women's wages of between 4s and 10s a week, which Earle established would be inadequate to support a lone woman with children.[67] The private separation agreement between Francis Spence and his wife, for example, stipulated that he pay her and his child £10 a year during their separation between 1763 and 1772.[68] This was not a large sum, though it is not clear from these agreements whether wives had any other income or support. Certain criteria determined the sums set by quarter sessions and ecclesiastical courts for alimony and maintenance. Quarter sessions' orders for sums of maintenance for wives and children varied considerably, probably according to the husbands' ability to pay, the wives' ability to work, and the numbers and ages of children. For example, in Northumberland, husbands were ordered to pay 2s a week to a wife and child in 1698, 9d a week for a wife in 1719, and 7s 6d weekly for a wife in 1722.[69] Ecclesiastical courts used similar criteria. In 1737 the maintenance of Elizabeth Bowes, wife of a gentleman, was fixed at 6s 8d per week, and in 1745 John Bowness, who held land worth £60 per annum, was ordered to pay his wife the weekly sum of 5s.[70] Wives frequently considered such payments insufficient and their status might determine what they felt were fit sums for their and their children's upkeep. Lady Mary Shafto described her alimony of £40 per annum as a 'scanty pittance', when she complained in her cruelty separation suit at the end of the eighteenth century that her husband was being awkward about paying it.[71]

Secondly, as Cuthbert Shafto demonstrates, it was not unknown for husbands to delay or refuse to make payments. Charles Eades, a leather

---

[65] Chapter 3, p. 49.   [66] Holcombe, *Wives and Property*, pp. 31–2.
[67] Earle, 'The female labour market', 342–3.
[68] BIHR, CP.I/2013, *Spence* c. *Spence*, 1782.
[69] NCAS, QSO 3, Midsummer 1698, p. 39; QSO 6, Midsummer 1719, p. 4; QSO 6, Epiphany 1722, p. 227.
[70] BIHR, Trans.CP.1737/2, *Bowes* c. *Bowes*, 1737; DDR/EJ/PRC/2/1745/5, *Bowness* c. *Bowness*, 1745.
[71] BIHR, Trans.CP.1798/1; D/C.CP.1798/3, *Shafto* c. *Shafto*, 1797.

officer, tricked his wife Ann in January 1715 into going to London to claim an inheritance. On arrival, she found out that she had been fooled, but by the time she had got back home to Leeds, Charles had apparently gone to Ireland. In reality, as Ann accidentally discovered, he had moved to Morpeth, where he told everyone that he was a widower. She tracked him down and after a violent outburst he agreed to give her £10 per annum. By January 1716, however, she was compelled to petition the Northumberland Quarter Sessions to force him to fulfil his promise.[72] This was no guarantee of a steady income, for some men simply evaded the quarter sessions' orders. Thomas Yates, a blacksmith, ignored the maintenance order imposed on him by Northallerton Quarter Sessions to pay for his wife and son's upkeep for a year between 1796 and 1797.[73] Anthony Burn, a yeoman of Billingham, refused to pay for his wife, their twins and her children from a previous marriage until the justices of the peace ordered that his estate, goods and chattels be seized in 1734. A year later, however, he was still declining to contribute to his family's upkeep. Perhaps he contributed to their upkeep when he and his wife were temporarily reconciled. Then things went wrong again and it was not until February 1737, after his wife initiated a restitution suit at Durham consistory court, that he announced that he was ready to receive his wife at bed and board, and pay costs.[74]

Enforcing the payment of alimony was difficult. Under common law a court would assign maintenance, but could only compel the husband to pay it by ecclesiastical censures, which were restricted to excommunication.[75] Wealthier women who had a separate maintenance contract could attempt to have it enforced by the courts of equity. The situation for ordinary women was alleviated by the Poor Relief (Destitute Wives and Children) Act of 1718, which permitted the goods, chattels or annual rent of absconding husbands to be seized as a source of maintenance for their wives and children under the warrant of two justices.[76] Thus wives with less financial independence could initiate proceedings to get their husbands' property seized and directed towards their maintenance. Parish overseers also routinely used this route to reimburse their expenditure on abandoned women and children in need, collecting a range of sums. In 1738 Thomas Gooding of South Shields had his goods seized to the value of £2 19s to keep his wife until the next quarter

---

[72] NCAS, QSB/42, fol. 4.
[73] NYA, QSB/1796, MIC 002532; QSB/1797, MIC 002633, 002909; QSM/1797, pp. 117, 128.
[74] UOD, DDR/EJ/PRC/2/1736/3, *Burne c. Burne* [sic], 1736, Letter to John Pye. See also DDR III, 23 April 1726 to July 1737.
[75] J. E. Hovenden, *Commentaries on the Laws of England by Sir William Blackstone*, Vol. III, 19th edition (London, 1836), p. 94.
[76] The overseers were required to submit their accounts for approval by the quarter sessions (Nicholls, *English Poor Law*, Vol. II, pp. 5–6).

sessions.[77] When John Fawcett, a husbandman of Darlington, went into another county in 1743, his rent from land in Carlton, to the sum of £10 a year, was seized for his wife and six children.[78] In 1780 the annual income of £70 from William Vernall's real estate was seized to pay towards the upkeep of his wife and three children.[79] This could be a regular event. Benjamin Finch's real-estate rents were seized annually for at least eight years to reimburse the parish for his wife's support.[80]

Perhaps the most obvious way for widowed people to form a new household and avoid poverty was through remarriage.[81] Similarly, though less legitimately, separated men and women attempted to establish another viable household unit through cohabitation or bigamy. John Pink's advert in 1766, which warned people not to 'harbour, entertain, or succour' his wife after 27 January, also stated that she had eloped from him and now lived with Thomas Gunnyman, a sackcloth weaver in Ashingdon, Berkshire.[82] It is likely that, when eloping women travelled or lived with their lovers, they passed themselves off as man and wife. Thus John Ferman's wife and Isaac Dixon, a spirit merchant of Newcastle, pretended to be married when they eloped in 1796 and lived at Ferryhill and Hartlepool.[83] Perhaps such pretence made it easier to find lodgings. Bigamy served similar public and private interests and, like cohabitation, is 'strong evidence of the resilience of people's attachment to matrimony in all classes'.[84] The speed at which William Scott of Bellingham remarried surely demonstrates that people escaped one marriage in particular, not the institution itself. He left his wife in March 1724 and by 1725 had married the widow Jane Forster.[85] As well as gaining emotional involvement and support, there were sound practical reasons for entering new relationships. For instance, it seems that work and cottages were allocated to married rather than single men in Essex, obviously an incentive to remarry.[86]

While it is often taken for granted that the situation of women who left their husbands was improved by already being in a relationship or forming another one, a new relationship undoubtedly benefited men too.[87] This was especially so for men who abandoned their wives, because they became outcasts of the relief system unless they were prepared to support their

---

[77] DRO, Q/S/OB 9, p. 166.   [78] DRO, Q/S/OB 9, p. 401.   [79] OA, QS/1780/Tr/6.

[80] For one entry, DRO, Q/S/OB 13, 15 July 1767, p. 129.

[81] Wright, 'Elderly and the bereaved' in Pelling and Smith (eds.), Life, Death, p. 106.

[82] JOJ, 25 January 1766, p. 3.   [83] UOD, DDR/EJ/CCD/3/1801/4, Ferman c. Ferman.

[84] G. Frost, 'Bigamy and cohabitation in Victorian England', Journal of Family History, 22, 3 (1997), 291.

[85] NCAS, QSB/66, fol. 41.

[86] P. Sharpe, 'Bigamy among the labouring poor in Essex, 1754–1857', Local Historian, 24, 3 (1994), 144.

[87] Stone, Divorce, p. 142.

neglected families.[88] Any subsequent request for poor relief would force them to acknowledge their act of desertion and suffer the consequences. Absconding husbands were punishable under the Vagrancy Acts, and subject to being whipped, committed to hard labour in the house of correction and, in Buckinghamshire later in the century, solitary confinement in a dark cell.[89] Following punishment the men would be returned to their parish of settlement and were expected to reimburse it for money laid out on the support of their families and then resume assisting in their maintenance. Obviously another relationship would provide men who were unwilling to do this with more stability. Bigamy was not even an especially risky alternative, because its definition was somewhat ambiguous. Though it was a felony punishable by execution, this did not apply to people whose spouses were absent or constantly overseas for seven years or more, or to 'any person that shall be at the time of such marriage divorced by any sentence in the ecclesiastical court', or whose marriage was declared null and void.[90] Furthermore, during the eighteenth century, the availability and use of benefit of clergy (exemption from capital punishment) mitigated sentencing.[91] Pamela Sharpe analysed cases of bigamy in Essex between 1754 and 1857 and discovered that penalties were not severe for bigamists who were caught. Overseers even occasionally validated an illegal marriage when it saved them from providing a woman with financial support.[92]

Communities also seem to have accepted bigamy up to a point. Ginger Frost's study of nineteenth-century bigamy reveals that it was tolerated as long as several criteria were satisfied. Bigamists needed reasonable vindication for leaving their spouses, it was preferable for the second spouse to be aware of the situation, and both families had to be supported by the bigamous spouse.[93] Eighteenth-century communities seem to have exercised similar 'rules'. For instance, spouses used sexual incompatibility, as well as adultery and cruelty, to justify leaving their partners. John Taylor explained that he separated from his first wife, whom he had married in 1781, because she would not receive his embraces. His second marriage, in 1790, landed him on trial at the Old Bailey in 1794. He was found guilty, but there was a measure of sympathy for him because he was only sentenced to a fortnight's confinement and then discharged after paying one shilling.[94] In many people's eyes, long-term separation also justified bigamous relationships, echoing the

[88] Snell, *Annals*, p. 363.   [89] CBS, Q/SO/24, Epiphany 1796.
[90] Burn, *Justice of the Peace*, Vol. III, pp. 312–13. Nonetheless, church courts still counted such bigamous unions as null and void.
[91] Stone, *Divorce*, p. 143.
[92] P. Sharpe, 'Bigamy among the labouring poor', 140–3. For nominal punishments in the nineteenth century, see Frost, 'Bigamy', 298–302.
[93] Frost, 'Bigamy'.   [94] *Y.Her*, 22 November 1794, p. 2.

legal formulation that the absence of a spouse for seven years or more meant that their partner could not be prosecuted for bigamy. William Lipscomb of Kidlington, Oxfordshire, and Elizabeth Harris were together from their marriage in 1754 until Elizabeth eloped from him in 1774. He may well have decided after a few years that Elizabeth was dead, for, in October 1778, he married Mary Jones of Windsor, Berkshire. Unfortunately, the new couple's peace of mind was soon unsettled by reports that Elizabeth was still alive. The following month Mary advertised in *Jackson's Oxford Journal* for Elizabeth Harris, described as forty to fifty years old and a pedlar, to appear to her, or for information about her.[95] Not surprisingly, periods of war were notorious for resulting in bigamy. The *Newcastle Courant* commented in 1763, at the end of the Seven Years War, on the numerous bigamous marriages that had occurred after wives whose husbands had gone into the navy or army remarried assuming that they were dead. Interestingly, the paper noted that, even where children had been born to the second husband, all situations were 'amicably settled'.[96] Arrangements could be surprisingly flexible. Sometimes the bigamous wife simply returned to her first husband. One sailor husband came back to find his wife remarried, but 'frankly and generously overlooking all that's past, he took her to his arms . . . and 'tis thought they'll now be a happy couple'.[97]

The other criteria for the toleration of bigamy identified by Frost are evident in the eighteenth century. There are several instances in which the second wife knew that the first was still alive. Denby Hartwell, a soldier in the second regiment of the Foot Guards, married Margaret Smith in 1707 and they lived in Flanders until they separated when Margaret returned to London to run her brandy shop. Denby returned later and though Margaret was still alive he married Christiana in 1710. Ten years later Christiana sought an annulment from Denby on the grounds that their marriage was bigamous. Whatever motivated her to bring the suit, it was not the sudden discovery of her status. Their friends knew both wives; Christiana's aunt and mother were acquainted with Margaret and knew that she was still alive.[98] The punishment of John Taylor, discussed above, may have been mitigated by the fact that his first and second wives were great friends.[99] Bigamous husbands' financial commitment to both marriages was also crucial in the eighteenth century. Indeed it was often the discovery that husbands had remarried when they were failing to support their 'first' wives and families that prompted these wives to prosecute their husbands. About a year after their marriage, and just before the birth of their twins, John Scott left his wife,

---

[95] *JOJ*, 7 November 1778, p. 3.   [96] *N.Cour*, 29 January 1763, p. 2.
[97] *N.Chron*, 11 August 1764, p. 2.   [98] BIHR, CP.I/619–20, *Hartwell c. Hartwell*, 1720.
[99] *Y.Her*, 22 November 1794, p. 2.

Alice, at Gateshead, claiming he was going to the country to get work to support her. It was thirteen years before she brought her husband's bigamy to the attention of the quarter sessions at Morpeth in 1714. Alice simply stated in her petition that he had since married another women, with whom he had three children, and requested that the magistrates do her justice 'in this unlawfull and unlegal Way of Matrimony'. Though her motivation is not explicitly stated, it is likely that having tracked him down, she wanted him to be forced to maintain her.[100]

Bigamous unions falling outside these criteria were unacceptable. Men who deliberately duped their second wives were roundly condemned. In 1738, the *York Courant* criticised the tendency to accept bigamy, arguing 'Crimes of this Nature, howsoever frequently committed, and to the Scandal of our Country suffered to pass with Impunity, are of the blackest Nature.' Bigamy was evil because, in addition to ruining the peace of families, it was especially harsh on innocent second wives. The unwitting second wife in this case was described as 'totally deprived of all Hopes of Happiness in this World, and doom'd to a Life worse than Death itself'.[101] Other factors offset the degree to which bigamy was tolerated. Disreputable behaviour did not help. A defendant in a church court office suit in 1700 excepted against Richard Walker, a deponent, because he had no credit, was beggarly, a liar, a profaner and reputedly a bigamist.[102] There may also have been less toleration of higher social ranks practising bigamy, perhaps because they could afford divorce. In 1767 a newspaper report about a bigamist who had been charged and taken into custody at Southwark, to be tried at the next assizes, stressed that he was a young gentleman of fortune.[103] Certainly higher-ranking men were sometimes given longer sentences at trial in the nineteenth century because they were setting a bad example.[104] It is difficult to tell whether male and female bigamists were treated similarly because most of the detailed cases involved bigamous husbands. It is unclear how much attention to pay to the fact that one union involving a bigamous wife was not accepted. The relationship between Thomas Suttell, a wine merchant, and the bigamous Elizabeth Agar created animosities between Thomas and his friends in the city of York.[105]

Given some bigamous husbands' proven ability to run away, they were hardly a safe bet for other women. William Powell, a joiner and cabinet maker, married Margaret Griffit [*sic*] in 1761 and deserted her after one and a half years. She attempted to track him down by going to his last settlement

---

[100] NCAS, QSB 39, fol. 74.
[101] *Y.Cour*, 6 June 1738, p. 3. See also *N.Cour*, 10–17 October 1747, p. 4.
[102] BIHR, EX.CP.I/141, *office c. Slainhead*, 1700.   [103] *N.Cour*, 21 February 1767, p. 2.
[104] Frost, 'Bigamy', 299.   [105] BIHR, CP.I/1647, *Agar c. Agar*, 1773.

in the Strand, London. The parish officer there could not tell her where her husband was, but could tell her that he had already abandoned a first wife and two children.[106] Such husbands may have found it difficult to decide which family took precedence. George Shafto left his wife, Hester, after four years of marriage in 1789, and from 1791 lived as the husband of Anna Powell who kept a milliner's shop near Leicester Square, London. From 1792 to 1797 they were put in the Fleet and King's Bench Prisons for debt. On liberation he got a lieutenancy in the Second Northumberland Regiment of Militia and returned to Alnwick to live with Hester again. After living together for a short time at Newcastle and Sunderland, George explained to Hester that he was under obligations to Anna and had sent for her. George then lived with Anna in Sunderland from late 1798 until 1799, when he obtained another lieutenancy in a different regiment and moved with her to Liverpool. At this point Hester sued him for restitution.[107] Patrick Liddle also shuttled between wives. He married his first wife in 1711 and lived with her for ten years. He then left her and married Jane, his 'second wife', as he called her, in September 1723. They had two children. Nonetheless he left her and returned to his first wife, until Jane found him after a few months and persuaded him to come back to Newcastle with her. In January 1726, after cohabiting for about ten months during 1725, Patrick again left her for his first wife. Whether his first wife found this unacceptable is unknown, but Jane's patience ended and she complained about him to the justice of the peace. Patrick's departure from Jane seems to have followed the death of their two children, which perhaps caused stress in their relationship or, in his opinion, freed him from obligation.[108]

WORKING ARRANGEMENTS

Many of the records do not reveal spouses' living arrangements after separation or desertion. An alternative way to consider such spouses' experiences, therefore, is to examine their employment. Below the gentry, most people who found themselves in this situation continued to work. For absconding husbands and deserted wives, in particular, employment remained essential but became even more precarious than usual. The former faced the usual vagaries of insecure or seasonal employment without the support network of poor relief and the latter found that any problem that stopped them working quickly pushed them into poverty. Records related to the poor demonstrate

---

[106] OA, QS/1763/Ep/2.
[107] BIHR, Trans.CP.1798/1; D/C.CP.1798/3, *Shafto c. Shafto*, 1797.
[108] NCAS, QSB/69, fols. 22–3.

the extent to which deserted wives faced an insecure future, for the majority of those defined as paupers were women, typically without a spouse.[109] Abandonment could leave wives in extreme poverty and at risk. Mary Payne was forced to become a vagrant in the 1740s after her husband, a seaman, robbed her of all she owned and absconded three weeks into marriage.[110] Isabel Macintosh was taken up as a vagabond with her four children in Yorkshire in 1768. Originally from Dalkeith in Scotland, her husband, a tailor, had 'lately left her pretending he was going to work in Yorkshire'. Not hearing from him, she set out from Scotland with her children to trace him. They arrived in Yarm but could not find him and were forced to beg when they ran out of money. Isabel and her children were conveyed back to Dalkeith.[111] Some wives were prepared to take to the road to find their husbands even after several years. Elizabeth Hill, who had married in Wiltshire in 1732, had no communication about her husband, Thomas, for two years after he abandoned her. On hearing that he was in Upton in Buckinghamshire she set off to find him. Indeed she may have caught up with him, for Upton then entered a wrangle with another parish about her and her husband's settlements.[112] Taking to the road in this way was not only dangerous in itself, it was also likely to exacerbate poverty and lead to prosecutions for vagrancy.

It is a mistake, however, to type-cast deserted wives as victims. Poor-relief records provide ample evidence that they took on paid labour for lengthy periods, basically for as long as they could, to support themselves and their families. In 1726, Mary White explained that she had used her utmost endeavours by hard labour to sustain herself and her children for the sixteen years since her husband left her.[113] They certainly fall within Thomas Sokoll's characterisation of the labouring poor as people who held 'a deeply rooted positive attitude to work and a firm belief in its social function'.[114] Women were only expected to stop paid employment while their children were totally dependent upon them. Deserted women who worked to support themselves were praised. The *Newcastle Journal* reported in 1752 that a 'bad husband' unexpectedly came across his wife after leaving her to live with another woman. He was drinking outside a London alehouse when

---

[109] For seventeenth-century Norfolk parishes where women formed around 60% of parish paupers see Wales, 'Poverty, poor relief' in Smith (ed.), *Land, Kinship*, p. 380; for the eighteenth century, see R. Connors, 'Poor women, the parish and the politics of poverty' in H. Barker and E. Chalus (eds.), *Gender*, pp. 136–8.

[110] OA, QS/1746/Ea/1.

[111] NYA, QSB/1768, MIC 002322, poor-law examination, 24 May 1768; MIC 002532, removal order.

[112] CBS, Q/SM/2 Ep 1737.   [113] NCAS, QSB/67, fol. 18.

[114] Sokoll, 'Old age in poverty: the record of Essex pauper letters, 1780–1834' in Hitchcock *et al.*, *Chronicling Poverty*, pp. 144–5.

he spotted her ironing in a house opposite. In response to his swearing and claims that he would murder her, the people around him demanded that he let her alone because she 'worked very honestly for her Living'. The report triumphantly concluded that his continual blaspheming startled his horse, so that it threw him off the cart he was sitting on and under its wheel, where he was crushed to death.[115]

The employment available for such women was limited and low-paid. A few more comfortable middling-sort lone women may have taken in lodgers or rented out property to gain a living. Elizabeth Myres, the widow of an alderman of Durham City, for example, had a married couple as her tenants.[116] Earning a living for most lone women consisted of casual labour, often archetypal 'female' jobs such as petty retailing, charring, nursing and clothes-making, which formed the lowest-paid, lowest-skilled parts of the economy and provided inadequate wages on which to support children.[117] Thus, while deserted wives may well have been successful for substantial periods of time, they slid all too easily into poverty through a combination of low wages and any factors that temporarily prevented them from working. According to women's requests for relief, the most common factors that stopped them working were personal infirmity due to age or illness, and young or ill children. Frances Goffe of Headington petitioned Oxfordshire Quarter Sessions for relief in 1711 because she was sixty-eight years old and unable to get her own maintenance, and Jane Milburn did the same in 1718 because she was eighty-two years old and infirm. Elizabeth Ferguson had supported herself and three children for four years until she was sick with an ague for nine months in 1719.[118] Rebecka Roberts of Elsfield, Oxfordshire, could no longer provide for herself on becoming lame in 1692.[119] Even when they got sick, women first sold their goods for subsistence before seeking relief. Mary Amble's petition explained that she had sold her goods to keep her and her small children while she was ill, and now that resource was exhausted she needed relief or a pass to Leeds where her husband had gone.[120]

Women's resources were particularly drained by having young, ill or disabled children since it was difficult for women to work and/or to afford treatment for them. One of Mary Taylor's three small children was blind and therefore unable to work and contribute to the family's income; Mary's problems were exacerbated by having sold all her goods to get her husband out of prison before he absconded.[121] Margaret Parsley's petition explained

---

[115] N.Jour, 23–30 May 1752, p. 1.   [116] BIHR, Trans.CP.1674/3, office c. Myres, 1674.
[117] For examples of work see Hufton, The Prospect Before Her, pp. 56–7; Earle, 'The female labour market', 342–3.
[118] OA, QS/1711/Ep/11; NCAS, QSB/48, fol. 38; NCAS, QSB/51, fol. 83.
[119] OA, QS/1692/Tr/20.   [120] NCAS, QSB/61, fol. 48.   [121] NCAS, QSB/40, fol. 43.

that one of her children was blind and she was 'noe way able to maintain her great charge'.[122]

Again, deserted women who requested poor relief, either through petitions or letters, were no more passive victims of individual men or the poor laws than any other poor petitioners. All exercised tactical methods to ensure that their applications were successful.[123] One particular position that they adopted was to express their entitlement to receive relief.[124] Mary White from Allendale claimed a pension in 1726 on the grounds that her husband had lived at Howsley for several years, farmed at £5 or £6 per annum, paid all neighbourhood 'assesses' and served as constable.[125] Ruth Goodson of Hampton Gay opened her petition in 1693 by observing that she and her husband had lived well in previous times and relieved others. She gained an order for relief for her and her three small children, though she was obliged to petition the justices twice more in 1694 when her landlord turned her out, leaving her without habitation, and when her parish officers suspended her 2s 6d, which had been ordered by the justices.[126]

Deserted wives were as determined as any other people who were forced by their circumstances to demand public-funded assistance and, like them, had no compunction about seeking relief from a higher authority. Anyone who felt that their overseer was unjust to them, by supplying inadequate relief or refusing their plea, could appeal to a justice or quarter sessions bench and wives did just that. Northumberland Quarter Sessions ordered that Elizabeth Grant be paid 6d a week in 1725, to assist in supporting her and her three younger children. The churchwardens and overseers of Acomb paid it for some time, but then stopped and 'though they saw her ready to starve they w[ou]ld give no ear to her miserable Complaints daily made'. Consequently she directed her claims to the quarter sessions bench.[127] Richard Connors remarks that by appealing to the justices, such women challenged their local parish authority and frequently had the justice side with them.[128] Deserted women also applied strategies that were unavailable to other petitioners. Catherine Pinkering used notions about responsible manhood in her information to the Christmas sessions at Morpeth, held in January 1697/8. She emphasised that when John married her the previous July he had promised to take, care and provide for her, but had deserted her after getting her with child and refused to afford her any relief.[129]

---

[122] OA, QS/1718/Tr/9.   [123] Sokoll, 'Negotiating a living', pp. 42–6.
[124] For an explanation of paupers' belief that they had a right to relief, see Hitchcock *et al.*, *Chronicling Poverty*, pp. 5–11.
[125] NCAS, QSB/69, fol. 18.   [126] OA, QS/1693/Mi/4; 1694/Ea/1; 1694/Mi/3.
[127] NCAS, QSB/69, Petition of Elizabeth Grant, 14 July 1726, fol. 21.
[128] Connors, 'Poor women' in H. Barker and Chalus (eds.), *Gender*, p. 144.
[129] NCAS, QSB/10, fol. 51.

The relief that women gained was usually less than the most basic subsistence and not intended to be a living wage.[130] Quarter sessions orders to Northumberland parishes to support deserted women ranged from 1s in 1721, to 1s 6d in 1695 and 1714, and 2s 6d in 1713. An unusually descriptive overseers' account book for the parish of St Nicholas in Newcastle, from 1786 to 1794, shows that, like alimony, the support given to deserted families varied according to the number of children. Jane Scott who had seven children was given approximately 4s a week in 1789, while Mary Chipchase, who had one son, was paid 2s a week in 1790.[131] Of course, children themselves contributed to family income. In 1726, Elizabeth Grant was assisted by her daughter who could work for her own meat and Elizabeth's input was to provide her with clothes.[132] Thus once children were able to help, their family's parish dole was lowered since their need was no longer as great. Similarly, Jane Liddell's 8d weekly allowance was halted by Benwell in 1738, because her children were grown up and she could maintain herself.[133] Given its limitations, deserted wives adopted other strategies in addition to poor relief; for example, moving to cheaper accommodation, gaining extended credit, and being assisted by friends, kin and, occasionally, neighbours.[134] In 1743 Lois Miller included a petition for relief, dated from her husband's desertion, in the letter to her proctor instructing him about her restitution suit at Durham consistory court. It concluded that only the charity of her good neighbours prevented her from starving, even '[t]ho I endeavour to the utmost I possibly can with my hands, being never brought up with hard labour'.[135]

CONCLUSION

The majority of individuals suffered some sort of socio-economic decline once they stopped living with their spouses. Though this impacted hardest on women of all ranks and upon men who absconded, even relatively wealthy men claimed that their households and/or businesses were damaged by their wives' absence. The poor laws recognised that a wife's elopement could lead husbands into poverty. In 1730 Bedfordshire Quarter Sessions heard that Mary Barnett of Biddenham had absented herself several times from her husband and wandered abroad 'by reason whereof the said William Barnett has been rendered incapable of supporting his family' and was forced to ask for

---

[130] For contrasting views about the value of poor relief, see P. Rushton, 'The Poor Law, the parish and the community in north-east England, 1660–1800', *Northern History*, 25 (1989), and King, 'Reconstructing lives'.
[131] TWA, EP.86/118. [132] NCAS, QSB/69, fol. 21. [133] NCAS, QSO 7, pp. 344, 352.
[134] Boulton, 'Extreme necessity', pp. 55–9; Sokoll, 'Negotiating a living', p. 19.
[135] UOD, DDR/EJ/PRC/2/1744/12, *Miller c. Miller.*

relief.[136] In general these cases demonstrate that provision became a female responsibility when husbands were ill. Mary Chadwell was committed to the house of correction in November 1705 for running away and leaving her aged impotent husband and five children on the parish, despite being able to work and maintain herself, and help towards their maintenance.[137] In 1773, Oxford's guardians of the poor placed an advert, which stated that 27-year-old Hannah Morse's elopement from her husband, a writing master, had left him in a bad state of health, their three small children in a miserable condition, and all liable to be chargeable. Treating her as they would her male counterparts, they requested information about her whereabouts and warned that they would prosecute anyone who harboured her.[138]

These findings suggest that husbands relied a great deal on their wives and are doubly significant when they are set alongside figures demonstrating that fewer elderly men lived alone than elderly women. For example, more widowers than widows in eighteenth-century Ludlow remarried, and Richard Wall estimates that before 1800, in rural and small-town England, 2% of elderly men lived alone compared to 16% of elderly women.[139] Indeed recent studies of the rates and reasons for the widowed remarrying question the automatic assumption that it was widows who would be most likely to remarry out of necessity, rather than widowers. Remarriage was influenced by rank, occupation, age, life-cycle and wealth as much as by gender. In sixteenth-century Norwich, for instance, many more spouseless elderly women lived alone than elderly men, who, in Margaret Pelling's opinion, were less able to be self-sufficient than their female counterparts.[140] The likelihood that widowed and probably separated men were less inclined to live alone lends further support to the model of extensive co-dependency within marriage.

---

[136] *Bedfordshire County Records*, pp. 10–11.
[137] OA, QS/1706/Ep/56.   [138] *JOJ*, 1 May 1773, p. 3.
[139] Wright, 'Elderly and the bereaved' in Pelling and Smith (eds.), *Life, Death*, p. 106; R. Wall, 'The residence patterns of elderly English women in comparative perspective' in Botelho and Thane, *Women and Ageing*, p. 143.
[140] Pelling, 'Who most needs to marry?' in Botelho and Thane, *Women and Ageing*, pp. 34–5, 38.

9

'Mutual society, help and comfort':
conclusion

In the late 1660s a clerk scribbled in the front of York Chancery Court's act book, 'Marriage frees a man from care for when hee's wedd his wife takes all upon her.'[1] A chance jotting, it powerfully captures the marital relationship described in this book, far more than any of the genteel, polite phrases of male superiority that are common in published advice for wives and husbands in the long eighteenth century. In these few words the material and emotional ties binding husbands and wives are succinctly conveyed. We have seen that married women did indeed take many things upon them and that their labour was not limited to household management, child care and nursing.[2] Though these were mainly wives' work, the division of household labour and duties was not as utterly gendered as is often stated.[3] Contemporary household prescription and some historians recognise this when they describe pre-industrial women as their husbands' helpmeets. Yet the extent to which wives assisted in provisioning the household, as suppliers as well as consumers, is not always fully appreciated. Rosemary O'Day helpfully observes that 'wives were helpmeets not dependents' and it is essential to avoid using 'helpmeet' as a synonym for a more subsidiary, supplementary role than wives understood it themselves.[4] They knew that the maintenance of the family was a dual activity and described their husbands as contributors to the household economy, not its primary providers.[5] We have also seen that both spouses made material contributions to the household economy at and throughout wedlock, which encouraged wives and husbands to view their wages, labour and property as pooled for familial benefit for the duration of wedlock. Such attitudes contradicted the common law doctrine of coverture, which specified that husbands gained outright possession of all their wives' movable goods and wages during marriage.[6]

---

[1] BIHR, Chanc.Act Book 29, Court Book, 1667–70.
[2] See chapters 4 and 5, pp. 70–6, 92–6.   [3] Shoemaker, *Gender*, p. 122.
[4] R. O'Day, *The Family and Family Relationships, 1500–1900: England, France and the United States of America* (Basingstoke, 1994), p. 204.
[5] Chapter 4, pp. 71–2.   [6] Chapter 5, pp. 105–8.

All these material factors forged co-dependency between wives and husbands, which could be intensified by their emotional needs. Men's emotional ties to their wives are most often explored in work on nineteenth-century masculinity. John Tosh, for example, has worked on the marriage of Edward Benson (1829–96), first master of Wellington College and later Archbishop of Canterbury, and explains that Benson's public posture of self-reliance and command was underpinned by his emotional dependence on his wife.[7] This is perhaps a line of enquiry that could also be developed by those interested in eighteenth-century marriage, using male diaries, memoirs and letters.

Co-dependency has many implications for our understanding of the power balance between wives and husbands and it is necessary therefore to compare it to the pessimistic and optimistic approaches discussed in the introduction.[8] Pessimistic interpretations of marriage would insist that men held ultimate power in the household, because in law they controlled material resources and profits from work. In this approach, household hierarchy was entirely predicated upon male power, not female. Pessimists are right to suggest that wives derived no wider institutional, political or legal power from their household activities, but this is not the full story. Indeed O'Day observes that historians are 'misled by late-twentieth-century preoccupations with the position of women and the whole issue of equality'; for contemporaries would have followed household prescription in thinking 'that the essential division in the family was that between the "Governours" (husband and wife together) and "those that must be ruled" (children and servants)'.[9] Thus by integrating the economic, power and emotional aspects of marriage with the household, a more subtle, dynamic picture of power in marriage emerges in this book.[10] In it, authority in the household was central to women's personae as wives. In 1685, a deponent before York Dean and Chapter court explained that he understood that his master and mistress, Thomas Bullock and Ellen Turner, were married to each other, because while he lived with them as a servant, 'he called him [Thomas] Master, and the said Ellen Dame, and . . . she ruled and comanded [*sic*] as such in the said house'.[11]

Women's role in managing the household and material resources also gave them a sense of their own rights in marriage, as Margaret Hunt has pointed out. She describes the four beliefs about marriage held by London wives in the early eighteenth century: at separation or widowhood they were entitled to

---

[7] J. Tosh, 'Domesticity and manliness in the Victorian middle class. The family of Edward White Benson', in Roper and Tosh (eds.), *Manful Assertions*, p. 56; Tosh, *A Man's Place*, pp. 68–71.

[8] Chapter 1, pp. 8–11.   [9] O'Day, *Family*, pp. 40, 161.

[10] This is a methodology aimed at by current work on family history, see ibid., pp. 137–63. For historiography of methodologies, see ibid., Chapter 1, and Coster, *Family and Kinship*, Chapters 1 to 5.

[11] BIHR, D/C. CP.1685/7, *office promoted by Stockdale c. Bullock and Turner* (marriage within prohibited degrees).

money equivalent in value to their portion; they had a right to maintenance; it was unjust for husbands to coerce them to give up their money; and they believed they had a right to go to law to deal with abusive husbands. This book resoundingly answers 'NO' to Hunt's concluding question '*Was it the case that metropolitan women were "not [as] easily to be imposed on" as other women?*' by showing that this type of 'female marital economy' was by no means restricted to London women; nor was it particularly 'female' for that matter.[12] Similarly, Shani D'Cruze demonstrates that working-class women in Victorian Lancashire, Cheshire and Suffolk gained identity and status from their household role, providing them with the personal resources to use the courts to get redress for their husbands' violence.[13]

Moreover, wives' and husbands' descriptions of incidents of wife-beating indicate that few people thought wives should be submissive in order not to be beaten. Wives themselves expected to be able to resort to a variety of active responses to their husbands and to control their situation in 'normal' marriages, without incurring danger. They were supported in their belief by the fact that wife-beating was not considered acceptable and in the way that more forms of male behaviour were categorised as cruel over the course of the eighteenth century.[14] The pessimistic vision of power in marriage and the household in the long eighteenth century is also challenged by the findings that the sexual double-standard was not rigidly applied in everyday life. Husbands were subjected to criticism for infidelity from their wives and peers and their personal sexual behaviour had an impact on their reputation. Equally, women's honour was defined by their labour, household position and charitable works, as well as by their sexual reputation. Realistic interpretations of female adulterers' motivation also move us away from a male-centred approach, which casts such wives as victims or manipulators of exploitative male lovers.[15]

The picture of married life for the middling sort and wage labourers presented in this book has more in common with optimistic models of early modern marriage. After all, optimists emphasise the economic importance of wives and correlate it with their practical authority. Thus Keith Wrightson concludes that marriage between 1580 and 1680 was most likely to be 'a practical and emotional partnership' and in Jim Sharpe's opinion husbands and wives were more or less equal partners in seventeenth-century plebeian marriages.[16] Nonetheless, although they think many relationships may have

---

[12] Hunt, 'Marital "rights"', pp. 118–21, 125.

[13] S. D'Cruze, *Crimes of Outrage: Sex, Violence and Victorian Working Women* (London, 1998), p. 80.

[14] Chapter 6, pp. 122–4, 135–7.   [15] Chapter 7, pp. 143–6, 147–9, 151–6.

[16] Wrightson, *English Society*, p. 104; J. A. Sharpe, 'Plebeian marriage in Stuart England: some evidence from popular literature', *Transactions of the Royal Historical Society*, fifth series, 36 (1986), 84.

been egalitarian in everyday life, many optimists concede that men had the
'upper hand' in the final analysis.[17] Thus O'Day describes the household
as a 'benevolent' monarchy.[18] To a greater or lesser extent this is true in
individual cases. Wives' authority was indeed vulnerable because it was not
particularly well defined in law or supported institutionally.[19] Moreover, men
could undermine their wives' household position and public status on a personal level by interfering in household government against general opinion
or by impugning their credit reputation.

Men's role as husbands was far more complex than either the pessimists'
view of them as autocrats or the optimists' view of them as benevolent masters. Indeed what distinguishes the model of marriage in this book from the
'optimistic' model is its emphasis on husbands' dependence on their wives.
Simply put, co-dependency afforded wives a functioning authority because
their activities in the household economy, household management and child
care were indispensable to their husbands. Surprisingly few historians have
used Shani D'Cruze's theory of 'hidden dependences'. She found that married
middling-sort men's position in public life in eighteenth-century Colchester
was facilitated by the labour and support of their wives and children. Her
study of Ben Shaw, a mechanic of Preston, Lancashire, and his family, c.
1770 to c. 1840, also reveals that working-class men's reputation involved
'the work and conduct of wives and daughters', particularly their successful
management of the household economy.[20] This book has also found that
men in the later seventeenth and eighteenth centuries depended upon their
wives' abilities as consumers and provisioners. All this did indeed free men
from cares, but it also had its negative aspects for them. Co-dependency
undercut male autonomy. It is vital to note that men's power in the household was not just destabilised by their inability in many instances to un-
dertake provisioning alone, but because their material life and credit was
dependent on their wives' economic goodwill and good sense. For example, husbands' announcements, which first appear to be simply about male
economic power, since husbands were denying their wives the use of their
credit, actually illustrate how much their superior economic position rested
upon women's activities. Male control over material resources was neither

---

[17] For example, Shoemaker, *Gender*, p. 112; Wrightson noted the primacy of male authority
although felt that this was less likely to take the foreground (*English Society*, p. 104).
[18] O'Day, *Family*, p. 151.
[19] Wives' role in household provisioning and consumption did allow them to participate in
politics through rioting in the eighteenth century, see J. Bohstedt, 'Gender, household and
community politics: women in English riots 1790–1810', *Past and Present*, 120 (1988),
88–122.
[20] D'Cruze, 'Care, diligence', 336; S. D'Cruze, 'The middling sort in eighteenth-century Colchester: independence, social relations and the community broker' in Barry and Brooks, *The
Middling*, pp. 182, 207.

automatic nor guaranteed, consequently men's socio-economic status rested upon their wives' economic conduct, credit status and access to credit, reputation and goodwill.[21]

Given the emphasis on the material features of married life in this book, the question that follows is how far the economic and occupational status of spouses influenced the quality of their marital relationships.[22] Alice Clark's theory that women's status in the household was determined by their economic role continues to reverberate into the twenty-first century. Some features of marital co-dependency described in this book have much in common with her conclusions that spouses were economically mutually dependent and that wives had a vital role in the domestic economy in the seventeenth-century 'Family Industry' household. However, the decline she identified in middling-sort and poorer women's position due to capitalism or industrialisation, which forced many married women to work outside the home for wages, removing their independence and downgrading their status, is not very apparent in the records of marital difficulties. There is no doubt that wives' earnings were essential for survival in most cases, whether they worked with their husband or worked outside the home, though the extent to which they were accorded value for this is still open to debate.[23] Anna Clark concludes that industrialisation in the later eighteenth century only exacerbated existing chronic sexual conflict in plebeian life, which was 'endemic to an economy where women's labor was necessary yet undervalued'. In her opinion this caused widespread domestic violence in such communities and 'the sense of independence wives gained by wage-earning clashed with husbands' desire to dominate, resulting in a "struggle for the breeches"'. Nevertheless, she suggests that spouses' shared labour rendered their relationships less conflictual than those in which husbands and wives worked separately.[24]

This line of thought has been developed by studies of nineteenth-century marriage to take account of the cultural influence of social class on married life. Nancy Tomes, for example, argues that industrialisation may have increased women's economic dependency on their husbands, but suggests that this did not automatically lead to their worse treatment by men. Instead she observes that there were 'two forms of female economic dependency' in nineteenth-century working-class households: '[i]n one, women had more power but endured a high level of physical abuse; in the other, women were more passive but enjoyed greater physical comfort'. The latter was, she

---

[21] Chapter 4, pp. 71–6.
[22] For a sensible critique of historians' claims that family life altered in response to economic change, see O'Day, *Family*, pp. 191–6.
[23] Alice Clark, *Working Life*, pp. 12, 290, 297–9.
[24] Clark, *Struggle for the Breeches*, pp. 265, 64.

argues, ushered in by improvements in the standard of living and the adoption of notions of middle-class respectability.[25] In contrast, A. J. Hammerton believes that this middle-class respectability 'where the worlds of men and women were more rigidly separate, where women's economic dependence and marginality were entrenched' simply made women more vulnerable to male abuse.[26] As far as the long eighteenth century is concerned, there is no firm evidence for the theory that the pre-industrial household or cooperative labour encouraged greater harmony and friendliness than industrial households or separate employment, for there was no correlation between any one work pattern and good or bad marital relations.[27]

Perhaps a more convincing model of the causes of conflict in marriage can be built on the contrast between reality and ideals in marital roles. Historians of the nineteenth century notice the tensions caused by the difference between the concept of the male breadwinner and everyday life, explaining that men were unable to provide for their households without their wives' and children's financial support. It has been argued that the politicised notion of breadwinner carried more exclusive connotations of single-handed male support than the earlier notion of the male provisioner, which envisaged wives as supplementary financial contributors.[28] Whatever the subtle distinctions between the situations in the pre-industrial and industrial contexts, both had the potential to cause marital conflict. Martin Ingram suggests, for example, that in the later sixteenth and early seventeenth centuries, 'menfolk clung to their wives for economic reasons, while at the same time resenting and ill-treating them'.[29] Men in the long eighteenth century probably found the situation difficult too. Despite a greater acceptance of female contributions, co-dependency did not fit well with received wisdom in common law, concepts of work, advice literature and scripture, all of which promoted men as the heads of household and economic providers. Robert Shoemaker suggests that it was men's attempts to retain decision-making powers in the face of married women's autonomy in the household, which was bolstered by the Evangelical movement's emphasis on the moral influence of women, which created marital conflict.[30]

Conflict may have been more complex and deep-seated than men demanding their 'rights' and wives challenging them.[31] For example, the claim that eighteenth- and nineteenth-century men expected female obedience in return

---

[25] Tomes, 'Torrent of abuse', 341–2.
[26] Hammerton, *Cruelty and Companionship*, p. 33.
[27] Chapter 5, pp. 95–7.   [28] Tosh, *A Man's Place*, p. 14.
[29] Ingram, *Church Courts*, p. 184.   [30] Shoemaker, *Gender*, p. 122.
[31] See Hunt, 'Marital "rights"', pp. 114–16. A later example is found in Ross, '"Fierce Questions and Taunts"'.

for male maintenance is not supported by the wives in this book who were unaware of any such concept of marital obligations.[32] In their opinion, their material contributions to marriage entitled them to maintenance.[33] We have seen that emotional and material co-dependency worked against male autonomy in the households and that men needed their wives to facilitate their private and public lives. This book suggests therefore that many people understood and accepted wives' practical authority and contributions. Rather than a consistently adversarial relationship, it was only when the intrinsic ambivalence between the ideal of manhood and realities of marital material life could not be accommodated that conflict could arise. Thus issues in which both spouses had a vested interest, like child care and upbringing and finances, were those most likely to create power struggles, leading men to express and attempt to implement patriarchal ideals.

It is crucial, however, not to describe this conflict as if it were a social anomaly. Though patriarchy was very flexible and accommodated women's participation in certain spheres, such tensions were unavoidable and thus marital difficulties were accepted as part of the process of married life. This is apparent in the tone of much advice for spouses. The Book of Homilies, still widely heard in our period, noted 'few Matrimonies there bee without chidings, brawlings, tauntings, repentings, bitter cursings, and fightings'.[34] Perhaps the most widely held aphorism was a variation on the theme: 'women very seldom make bad wives, when they have got good husbands'.[35] The Newcastle Journal in 1760 concluded, 'In a word, the likeliest way for a man to obtain a good wife, or keep one so, is to be good himself.'[36] The concept informed the enduring warnings that spouses should choose wisely before entering marriage. As a collection of writings about marriage pointed out in 1755: 'Matrimony ought to be considered as the most important step a man can take in private life, as it is that upon which his fortune, his credit and his peace must depend.'[37] Thus in order to illustrate that people should choose their partners wisely and not just for fortune or beauty, the Newcastle Chronicle published an 'Essay on Marriage' in 1768 posing the rhetorical question: 'How many husbands and wives do we see, who, after being married a twelvemonth, have nothing in common, but their name, their quality, their peevishness and their misery?'[38] The routine discussion of marital conflict occasionally took on a tone of heightened concern. Many

---

[32] Hunt, 'Marital "rights"', p. 117; Tomes, 'Torrent of abuse', 334.
[33] Chapter 5, pp. 89–93.
[34] Book of Homilies, The second Tome of Homilies, of such matters As were Promised and Entituled in the former part of Homilies (London, 1633), p. 240.
[35] N.Chron, 12 August 1769, p. 3.   [36] N.Jour, 6–13 September 1760, p. 1.
[37] The Matrimonial Preceptor, p. 221.   [38] N.Chron, 3 September 1768, p. 3.

genres in the early eighteenth century, for example, expressed particular anxiety about mercenary matches and the marital difficulties that ensued.[39] In the main, such concern did not simply represent a fear that society was about to collapse under the weight of moral irregularities, it promoted the idea that conflict was fairly normal and allowed diverse forms of reconciliation to be offered to couples in difficulties.

Indeed there were far more sophisticated ways of dealing with conflict in the long eighteenth century than is sometimes assumed.[40] Even people of relatively modest means employed a variety of forms of reconciliation in similarly informed ways to those who used civil and state separation in the second half of the nineteenth century. Olive Anderson's detailed examination of separation and divorce reveals that private separation and forms of separation available through the local magistrates' courts were used more extensively than judicial separation, which was available from the divorce courts set up by the Matrimonial Causes Act of 1857. The former methods were quicker, cheaper, more reliable, and brought equal or greater financial benefits. These patterns had their roots in the eighteenth century. Like their nineteenth-century counterparts, couples who could agree turned increasingly to forms of private separation drawn up by local lawyers. While wives with cruel husbands sought church court separations less often later in the eighteenth century, husbands continued to seek adultery separations because this was the most successful way to avoid paying maintenance to their wives and for a few it was the route to divorce by act of parliament. Similarly, nineteenth-century husbands with adulterous wives selected divorce over judicial separation because it allowed them to remarry.[41] Battered women in the second half of the eighteenth century were probably turning to justices of the peace in greater numbers for quicker, cheaper solutions to domestic violence, as their nineteenth-century counterparts would turn to local magistrates' courts because they offered better routes to alimony and allowed equivalent property rights to those under judicial separation. Also already in existence in the eighteenth century was the practice of shifting between various forms of resolution, as one or the other was of more benefit.[42] In one case, for example, a wife abandoned a suit for judicial separation once a private separation was achieved, then initiated a restitution suit when that in turn failed to meet her needs.[43]

It will be noted that the experience and expectations of married life described in this book do not fit easily into the standard narratives of change in

---

[39] Tague, 'Love, honor, and obedience', 76–81.
[40] For a more negative view of options open to unhappy wives see Mendelson and Crawford, *Women in Early Modern English Society*, pp. 141–5.
[41] Anderson, 'State, civil society', 167–8, 173–6.   [42] Ibid., 195–8.
[43] For example, DDR/EJ/CCD/3/1765/2, *Allison c. Allison*, 1765.

marriage during the long eighteenth century. There is little hard evidence for a general long-term social and economic decline in women's status within marriage as the result of changing work patterns in the wake of industrialisation. Indeed, this book has emphasised continuity in spouses' roles in household production and consumption across the seventeenth and eighteenth centuries, regardless of local economic conditions.[44] Nor is there much evidence that supports the controversial theory that the emotional character of marriage was transformed during the second half of the eighteenth century.[45] Amanda Vickery has convincingly argued that, although practice probably varied little, there was indeed a change in the way marriage was described, and the period 'saw a sustained, secular celebration of romantic marriage and loving domesticity'.[46] Interestingly, however, there is little evidence of spouses' heightened use of affectionate or sentimental language to characterise their marriage or marital difficulties in line with this cultural shift. Perhaps it is most evident in published material and the personal reflections and correspondence of the educated elite. Nonetheless, there is evidence that many wives of all social ranks continued to exploit the conventional language of subordination and deference in order to gain their ends.[47] Moreover, though the concept of domesticity, which flourished in the nineteenth century, was developing in the eighteenth century, it was restricted to print rather than spouses' self-representations. Thus no spouses adopted the rhetoric of the *York Chronicle*'s 'Repository on Marriage' in 1773, when it noted that men in business grow 'stern and severe' or 'peevish and morose' because of pressures of work, making female meekness 'requisite to soften their severity, and change their ill-humour into domestic tenderness'.[48] Nonetheless, this book has shown that representations of married life responded to other cultural shifts in the eighteenth century.

The 'polarising of sexual difference in science and arts', demographic shifts, changes in working patterns due to industrialisation and the consequent effects of urbanisation have all been shown to have contributed to changing definitions of femininity and masculinity.[49] They profoundly altered English cultures of sex and domestic violence, which in turn seem to have influenced the way that some features of married life were

---

[44] Wrightson, *Earthly Necessities*, pp. 42–50, 296–300; Muldrew, *Economy of Obligation*, pp. 148–71; S. Parker, *Informal Marriage, Cohabitation and the Law, 1750–1989* (London, 1990), p. 11.
[45] Stone, *Family, Sex, Marriage*.   [46] Vickery, *Gentleman's Daughter*, p. 285.
[47] For an example of elite women's use of such prescriptive language, see Tague, 'Love, honor and obedience', 81, 95–6.
[48] *Y.Chron*, 19 February 1773, p. 4.
[49] Quotation from J. Tosh, 'The old Adam and the new man: emerging themes in the history of English masculinities, 1750–1850' in Hitchcock and Cohen (eds.), *English Masculinities*, p. 22.

conceptualised. For instance, Tim Hitchcock shows that one consequence of changes in elite views of the role of men and women in reproduction was that 'men were liberated from the obligation to be [sexually] responsible, while women were redefined as sexual victims, whose main interest should lie in reproduction rather than pleasure'.[50] The records of marital difficulties suggest that this had some impact on perceptions of adulteresses, their lovers and husbands over the course of the eighteenth century. Adulterous wives were presented more sympathetically, and with some understanding, as the victims of male sexual urges, rather than their own. Their husbands were less likely to be scornfully dismissed as cuckolds. Though the term never escaped its derisory connotations, men with unfaithful wives were viewed compassionately in some circles. Culpability for female infidelity shifted away from sexually lustful women and sexually inadequate husbands, to male lovers who seduced innocent wives and betrayed male friendships.[51]

Changing ideas about gender difference also led to new attitudes to domestic violence and its perpetrators, which influenced images of spouses' aggression and responses to violence. In the sixteenth and seventeenth centuries, husbands who used violence against their wives could describe it as a rational act in the pursuit of correction and household order. By the second half of the eighteenth century, husbands' abuse of wives was less a question of the proper or improper application of status, than a demonstration of men's baser 'natural' urge to dominate by using their greater physical strength. Wife-beating was described as a raging madness risking the loss of identity and manhood, rather than dispassionate correction. With the increasing emphasis on reforming male manners in the second half of the eighteenth century, self-control was promoted as the key to preventing men's propensity for causing cruelty.[52] The shifts also made it less convincing for eighteenth-century men explicitly to blame their wives' conduct for their violence and the men emphasised their self-control in the face of female provocation. While female violence was always rejected, it was clearly a more plausible counter-accusation for men to make before the 1750s. In turn, though the 'victimisation' of women in the later eighteenth century was hardly liberating, it was a useful way for beaten wives to emphasise the unprovoked cruelty of their husbands.

These changes are surely a precursor to A. J. Hammerton's findings that ideas about the culpability of husbands and wives for marital difficulties were redefined in the nineteenth century. Before the 1857 Divorce Act 'the spotlight was on women's domestic failures' whereas 'men's failings [were] viewed as subsidiary and often the consequence of women's factiousness'. Thereafter 'a parallel critique of men's conduct in marriage', which focused

---

[50] Hitchcock, *English Sexualities*, p. 111.   [51] Chapter 7, pp. 161–6.
[52] Chapter 6, pp. 121–2.

on working-class wife-beating and middle-class male tyranny, grew in importance so that by the late nineteenth century 'men's unreasonable and selfish behaviour was being identified and debated as the chief cause of ailing marriages'.[53] This phenomenon had its roots in the wider cultural concern in the eighteenth century that men were dangerous, predatory and threatening. Interestingly, reports in provincial newspapers about wife-beating and husbandly tyranny were already emerging into the social-class pattern that became entrenched in the second half of the nineteenth century. The development may have focused some attention on men's roles specifically as husbands. Writers did not just criticise husbands' cruelty.[54] For example, the *Gentleman's Magazine* sometimes included pieces that criticised husbands who were overly jealous of their wives. One poem in 1735 observed that jealousy was the 'Source of domestick misery'.[55]

Entering marriage for women in the seventeenth century has been described by Sara Mendelson and Patricia Crawford as 'a violent discontinuity', a break from their previous life that 'was felt in sexual, emotional, and physical terms', particularly by elite women. In this as in many other aspects 'Marriage was a different kind of institution and experience for women and for men in early modern times'.[56] It is difficult to find such an aversion to marriage in the records of marital difficulties, though this is not to deny that some spouses suffered disillusionment after the ceremony. Instead there is more evidence that people favoured marriage, entering illegitimate relationships when barred from legitimate versions. This attachment to the institution itself, if not specific examples, even entered humorous accounts of spouses' attitudes towards each other. Thus *Jackson's Oxford Journal* reported in 1773 that a lady near Windsor asked her husband what he would do if it was necessary for him to marry again. He dashed his wife's hopes that he would re-affirm his conjugal bliss with her and declare that he would marry her again. Instead he replied that he would indeed marry again 'but I don't tell you who should be my wife'.[57] Nor was there any sense in the records of marital difficulties, as we have seen, that the experience and culture of married life was totally gendered. Some tasks were different and others were shared, but co-dependency breaks down the crude assignment of differently gendered ideas and expectations to these activities.

Even the living and working arrangements of many spouses after complete marriage breakdown underline the extent to which marriage was a relationship of co-dependency.[58] The predicament of wives without their

[53] Hammerton, *Cruelty and Companionship*, pp. 166–7.
[54] For some examples of this from the *Spectator* and the *Tatler*, see the *Matrimonial Preceptor*, 19, p. 83, and 32, pp. 130–3.
[55] *GM*, 3 (1733), 90; 5 (1735), 270, 471; see also *GM*, 8 (1738), 85.
[56] Mendelson and Crawford, *Women in Early Modern English Society*, pp. 129, 147.
[57] *JOJ*, 5 June 1773, p. 1.   [58] Chapter 8, pp. 191–2.

husbands is well known, but without their wives, husbands faced the loss of income, property, household management, child care and reputation. In this vein, perhaps historians should be more sensitive to the implications of men's reactions to the loss of their wives when assessing marital relationships. Thomas Turner (1729–93), a Sussex shopkeeper and schoolmaster, married Peggy Slater in 1755 and was widowed in 1761. Two months after his wife's death, he wrote in his diary: 'Almost distracted with trouble: how do I hourly find the loss I have sustained in the death of my dear wife! What can equal the value of a virtuous wife? I hardly know which way to turn, or what way of life to pursue. I am left as a beacon on a rock, or an ensign on a hill.' In later entries he complained about problems of household management and dealing with servants.[59] The benefits of marriage for both men and women, therefore, outweighed any of its disadvantages. Husbands and wives were not puppets of an unfair gender order, but reacted to and against the circumstances of life-cycle, social and financial status, and changing ideologies. They determined themselves whether they had quiet lives.

[59] Cited in O'Day, *Family*, pp. 201–2.

Appendices

The data used for this book were entered onto a relational database. The database has two main tables. One ('Couple') has biographical information about the married couples, and the other linked table ('Conflict') has details about the types of marital difficulties experienced by these couples. As a result, the first table contains 1,403 married couples, and the second 1,583 instances of conflict, because some couples experienced more than one type of difficulty. There are nine additional related tables. 'Secondary Complaints' categorises secondary grievances and is linked to the 'Conflict' table. The other eight are linked to 'Couple': 'Types of Informal Intervention', 'Type of Goods Conveyed', 'Sum Bound Over', 'Sureties for Wife-Beaters', 'Role of Children', 'Reason for Adultery', 'Context of Adultery' and 'Lovers' Status/Occupation'.

Evidence about other couples' marital difficulties was collected and used in the book, but not entered onto the database because not enough information was available about them or their conflict. For example, accounts and reports of attempted or actual wife/husband murder in newspapers. When these couples are discussed, it is stated in the references that they are not included in the database.

The data were derived from the following sources (see bibliography for information about archives):

(A) ECCLESIASTICAL COURTS

All matrimonial and correction cases from:

Durham: UOD DDR/EJ/CCD/3 (1678 and 1716–1868); UOD DDR/EJ/PRC/2 (1608–1853)
Oxford: Mss.Oxf.dioc.papers c. 91 – c. 101
York: CP.H/2446–6009 and CP.I/1–3122 (1663–1800); Cons.CP and Chanc.CP (1800–1990); Trans.CP, indexed in W. J. Shiels, *Ecclesiastical Cause Papers at York: Files Transmitted on Appeal 1500–1883*, Borthwick Text and Calendar,

9 (1983); D/C.CP, indexed in K. M. Longley, *Ecclesiastical Cause Papers at York I: Dean and Chapter's Court 1350–1843*, Borthwick Text and Calendar, 6 (1980)

(B) QUARTER SESSIONS COURTS

All cases relating to marital difficulties from:

Buckinghamshire: Q/SO/1–26 (1678–1800); Q/SM/1–11 (1727–1800); QS Rolls (1732–1800)
Durham: Q/S/OB 5–16 (1660–1810)
Newcastle: QS/NC/1/2–8 (1665–1802)
Northumberland: QSB/1–87 (1680–1742); QSO 1–15 (1680–1800)
North Yorkshire: QSB (1685–1800); QSM (1703–1800); DC/SCB VI 2/1/1/1–4 (1696–1723, 1778–1821); DC/RMB III 3/1/3 (1627–1822)
Oxfordshire: QS/ (1687–1830)
Bedfordshire County Records

(C) JUSTICES OF THE PEACE

All references to marital difficulties in:

DRO D/X 730/1 Journal of Reverend Edmund Tew, 1750–64
Crittal (ed.), *Justicing Notebook of William Hunt*
Paley (ed.), *Justicing Notebook of Henry Norris*
Silverthorne (ed.), *Deposition Book of Richard Wyatt*

(D) NEWSPAPERS

All advertisements relating to married couples in sampled newspapers (every fifth year):

JOJ, N.Ad, N.Chron, N.Cour, N.Jour, NCJ, *Newcastle Gazette* (1744–52), *Newcastle Intelligencer* (1755–9), *Newcastle Weekly Mercury* (1722–3), Y.Chron, Y.Cour, Y.Her.

(E) PARISH RECORDS

All references to desertion or separation in material dealing with poor relief, settlement laws and vagrancy:

Durham, Northumberland: EP/ Church of England parish records
North Yorkshire: PR/ parish records
Oxfordshire: Mss.D.D.Par/parish collections

All appendices' references to sources use A, B, C, D or E to refer to the above information.

Appendix 1. *Types of marital conflict*

Types of conflict	Numbers of conflict
Desertion	608
Wife-beating	447
Public announcements	278
Correction cases against adulterers	55
Threatened use of law of harbouring	36
Miscellaneous	34
Restitution of conjugal rights	26
Separation on grounds of adultery	25
Private separations	18
Bastardy	17
Annulment cases	11
Women charged with breach of peace against their husbands	11
Bigamy	7
Jactitation	5
Criminal conversation actions, actual and threatened	4
Divorce on the grounds of sodomy	1
Total	**1,583**

Sources:

Wife-beating: husbands bound over by justices of the peace to keep the peace in (B) and violent husbands in (C). Also separations on the grounds of cruelty (47) in (A). Total includes references to constables dealing with domestic violence.

Desertion: all references to desertion and husbands who were accused of failing to maintain their wives and families, without necessarily having left the vicinity in (B), (C), (D), (E).

Announcements: references to bellmen and newspaper advertisements in (A), (B), and advertisements in (D).

Correction cases: mere and promoted office cases from (A).

Law of harbouring: collected from (A), (B), (D).

Miscellaneous: variety of misdemeanours and breaches of the peace (other than domestic violence and desertion), which included information on marital difficulties, from (B), and a correction case against a clergyman dealt with by York ecclesiastical court (A).

Restitution: from (A).

Adultery separation: from (A).

Private separations: collected from (A), (B), (D).

Bastardy: selected cases containing references to marital difficulties in (A), (B), (C).

Annulment: instance cases from York and Durham ecclesiastical courts (references in 'Wife-beating', above).

Breach of peace against husbands: from (B).

Bigamy: from (A), (B), (D).

Jactitation: selected because it was alleged that the couple had lived together for some time, from (A).

Criminal conversation: collected from reports in (D), matrimonial cases in York and Durham ecclesiastical courts (A) and UOD Baker Baker vouchers DPR/Ref. 92/83.

Sodomy divorce: BIHR, CP.I/2364 in (A).

Appendix 2. *Initiator of instance matrimonial cases before York, Durham and Oxford ecclesiastical courts*

Type of instance case	Wife	Husband	Family	Unclear	Total
Cruelty separation	47	—	—	—	47
Adultery separation	2	23	—	—	25
Restitution of conjugal rights	22	4	—	—	26
Annulment	7	2	1	1	11
Jactitation	—	3	2	—	5
Total	78	32	3	1	114

Sources: (A).

Appendix 3. *Initiator of wife-beating and desertions coming to the attention of JPs and parish authorities*

Type of case	Wife	Husband	Parish	Other[1]	Total
Desertion	84	1	518	5	608
Wife-beating	442	—	1	4	447
Total	526	1	519	9	1,055

Sources: (B), (C), (E).
[1] Community, neighbours, unclear.

Appendix 4. *Initiator of public announcements*

	Wife	Husband	Parish	Other[1]	Total
Announcements	9	261	2	6	278

Sources: (A), (B), (D). Does not include advertisements for absconded husbands.
[1] Includes the couple themselves, a father, a son, and unclear.

Appendix 5. *Occupations, estimated wealth or income of husbands who came before York, Durham and Oxford ecclesiastical courts as parties in matrimonial cases*

Category	Number within category
Titled/gentry or annual income over £200 and/or worth over £500	49
Professional	20
Substantial middling-sort occupations[1]	20
Annual income over £50 and under £200 and/or worth over £200 and under £500	7
Unskilled and/or annual income under £50 and/or worth under £200[2]	18
Rural/agricultural	5
Total	**119**

Sources: (A).
[1] Includes dye-works owner, cotton manufacturer, mill owner, gold-smith.
[2] Includes soldiers, cork-cutter, carpenter.

Appendix 6. *Occupations of husbands who came to the attention of quarter sessions because of marital difficulties*

Category	Occurrences of occupation
Tradesmen, craftsmen and retailers	135
Labourers	99
Rural/agricultural	76
Unskilled	37
Gentlemen	9
Soldiers/militia-men/sailors	9
Petty retailers[1]	9
Professionals	7
Unclear	4
Total	**385**

Sources: (B).
[1] Includes higglers, hawkers, pedlars.

Appendix 7. *Occupations of advertising husbands*

Category	Occurrences of occupation
Tradesmen, craftsmen and retailers	75
Rural/agricultural	28
Labourers	24
Unskilled	13
Professionals	11
Sea-related[1]	9
Titled or gentry[2]	8
Servants	3
Total	**171**

Sources: (A), (B), (D).
[1] Includes mariners and a pilot.
[2] Includes a cotton manufacturer who described himself as a gentleman.

Appendix 8. *Secondary complaints*

Grouped category of complaint	Specific complaint within category	No. of specific complaints within category
Provision	Husband's refusal to provide	78
Property	Wife conveyed away goods	55
	Husband kept property of wife	14
		Sub total 69
Household/ business management	Female extravagance	25
	Inverting household order	14
	Female financial mismanagement	10
	Denial of household management	5
	Female inadequate household management	2
		Sub total 56
Adultery	Male adultery	28
	Female adultery	3
		Sub total 31
Male violence	Male physical cruelty	21
	Male mental cruelty	3
	Marital rape	2
	Infected wife with VD	2
	Attempted to poison wife	1
		Sub total 29

Appendix 8. *(cont.)*

Grouped category of complaint	Specific complaint within category	No. of specific complaints within category
Financial conflict	Complaints of financial nature[1]	25
Children[2]	Husband denied provision for own	10
	Husband denied step-children	7
	Wife denied step-children	3
	Wife provided inadequate child care	2
	Wife denied own child	1
		Sub total 23
Drinking	Male drinking	14
	Female drinking	6
		Sub total 20
Female violence	Actual violence	13
	Attempt to poison husband	2
	Threatened violence	1
		Sub total 16
Bigamy	Male and female	14
Jealousy	Male	3
Religion	Religious disagreement	1
	Total	365

Sources: (A), (B), (C), (D), (E). Complaints expressed by spouses as *secondary* grievance to primary reason for bringing marital difficulties to public attention. One couple could express several different types of secondary complaint.

[1] Includes general complaints about assignment of property, other than specific claims about conveying or keeping movable goods.

[2] Includes denials of provision and attempts to remove property of, or failure to allot property to, children, as well as failure to care for them physically.

Appendix 9. *Types of informal intervention*

General category of intervention	Specific types of intervention within category	Numbers of type of intervention
Intervention in violence		38
Advice/reconciliation	Attempted/actual reconciliation	18
	Offer of advice	12
	Negotiated separation	4
		sub total 34
Refuge offered to wives	Place to live	19
	Place to stay	10
		sub total 29
Material aid for wives	Provide necessaries	16
	Financial help	5
		sub total 21
Exacerbated marital difficulties	Caused quarrels	10
	Assisted in violence	2
	Informed husband of wife's infidelity	2
		sub total 14
	Total	**136**

Sources: (A), (B), (C), (D), (E). There could be more than one type of intervention per couple.

Appendix 10. *Types of husbands' sureties*

Category of husbands' relationships with sureties	Number within category
Husbands with one surety with same surname	56
Husbands with two sureties with same surname	8
Husband with one surety who was a widow with a different name	1
	sub total 65
Husbands with one surety with same/related occupation	55
Husbands with two sureties with same/related occupation	10
	sub total 65
Husbands with one surety with same residence	29
Husbands with two sureties with same residence	33
	sub total 62
Husband with lower social status than one or more sureties	19
Husbands where insufficient information about husband and/or surety	18
Husbands whose sureties do not fall into any other categories	13
Husbands with higher social status than one or more sureties	5
Total	**247**

Sources: 189 husbands who were bound over by justices of the peace, for whom details about both sureties were recorded, in (B), (C). Husbands could fall into more than one of the categories.

Appendix 11. *Types of sources of information about desertion*

Type of source	Number
Vagrancy laws[1]	361
General poor law relief[2]	100
Settlement papers[3]	86
Newspaper advertisements[4]	58
Other[5]	3
Total	**608**

Sources: (B), (C), (D), (E).
[1] Husbands who were classed as vagrants because they threatened to or did leave wives and families chargeable to the parish. Figure includes 114 men who were described as leaving families chargeable, since available cross-referencing indicates that this term was often used in practice to denote wife and family.
[2] Includes requests by or for wives to receive relief or have husbands' goods seized to pay maintenance, and complaints that husbands were failing to maintain families.
[3] Information about desertion mentioned in settlement papers or parish disputes over settlement of wives and their children.
[4] Newspaper advertisements seeking whereabouts of absconding husbands.
[5] Includes desertions referred to in other sources.

Appendix 12. *Types of cases before justices of the peace concerning marital difficulties, which resulted in an individual being bound over by recognizance*

Type of case[1]	Number of cases
Wife-beating	188
Desertion	10
Wife charged with breach of peace against husband	3
Wife prosecuting man for attempting to commit adultery with her	2
Husband prosecuting man for committing adultery with his wife	2
Trespass and adultery	1
Husband prosecuting man for harbouring his wife and causing quarrels between them	1
Total	**207**

Sources: (B), (C).
[1] The actual number of people who entered recognizances was higher, because these figures do not include those who went on to be indicted, though they would also have been bound over to appear, or those who were prosecuted by recognizance, but failed to get sureties.

Appendix 13. *Duration or outcome of recognizances*

General category of outcome		Numbers
Recognizance discharged	at next sessions	75
	after two sessions	2
	after one year	1
	on condition	1
	by request/consent of wife	5
	by proclamation	2
	due to no complaint	4
Recognizance duration unknown		66
Recognizance for specified duration	one year	4
	two years	1
	three years	1
Recognizance continued	at next sessions	30
	for one year	1
	for over one year	1
Recognizance respited		13
	Total	**207**

Sources: (B), (C).

Appendix 14. *Indictments by type of marital difficulty*

Category of conflict	Number within category
Desertion[1]	81
Wife-beating	35
Wife charged with breach of peace against husband	5
Bigamy	2
Other[2]	2
Not clear	1
Total	**126**

Sources: (B), (C).
[1] Includes two husbands indicted for leaving wives/families on parish.
[2] Violent married couple indicted as part of a servant's complaint; husband indicted for violence against his wife's alleged lover.

Appendix 15. *Outcomes of indictments for wife-beating*

Outcome		Number
Unknown[1]		12
Innocent		11
Guilty		9
Recognizance respited		3
	Total	35

Sources: (B), (C).
[1] Includes at least three husbands who pleaded not guilty.

Appendix 16. *Outcomes of indictments for all marital difficulties*

Outcome		Number
Guilty[1]		71
Innocent		20
Unknown		17
No indictment preferred, therefore discharged		14
Recognizance respited		3
Released by husband		1
	Total	126

Sources: (B), (C).
[1] Includes twelve husbands indicted for felony and transported.

Appendix 17. *Types of correction case against adulterers*

Type of case		Number
Mere office[1]		39
Voluntary promoter[2]		16
	Total	55

Sources: (A)
[1] Office cases that were brought by the office of the judge.
[2] Promoted by a third party through the office of the judge. Figures include five promoters who were husbands of the named women, two fathers and one relation of the women, and one neighbour.

Appendix 18. *Outcomes of separation cases on the grounds of cruelty and adultery, and restitution of conjugal rights and annulment cases before the ecclesiastical courts*

Outcome	Cruelty	Adultery[1]	Restitution	Annulment	Total
Unknown	6	3	4	3	16
Abandoned	13	1	5	1	20
Agreed	6	—	3	—	9
Appealed by defendant	6	5	7	1	19
Appealed by plaintiff	4	1	—	2	7
Defendant excommunicated	6	—	—	—	6
Sentence in favour of defendant	2	—	1	—	3
Sentence in favour of plaintiff	4	14	5	4	27
Death of plaintiff	—	1	—	—	1
Death of defendant	—	—	1	—	1
Total	47	25	26	11	109

Sources: (A).
[1] Two plaintiffs were female.

Appendix 19. *Outcomes of separation cases on the grounds of cruelty and adultery, and restitution of conjugal rights and annulment cases by sex of plaintiff*

Outcome		Male	Female
Unknown		5	9
Abandoned		1	19
Agreed		1	8
Appealed by defendant		4	15
Appealed by plaintiff		2	5
Defendant excommunicated		—	6
Sentence in favour of defendant		—	3
Sentence in favour of plaintiff		15	12
Death of plaintiff		1	—
Death of defendant		—	1
	Total	29	78

Sources: (A). In addition there was one family who initiated a case, and one case was unclear.

Appendix 20. *Categories of public announcements*

Category	Number
Denying credit due to wife's elopement	157
Denying credit, but no reference to wife's elopement or to separation	68
Denying credit due to mutually agreed separation	34
Miscellaneous[1]	13
Wife's advert in response to husband's	6
Total	**278**

Sources: (A), (B), (D). Table does not include fifty-eight adverts placed by parish authorities seeking whereabouts of absconded husbands.
[1] Includes adverts seeking whereabouts of missing spouses, requesting a husband to come to his wife, adverts refuting accusations and apologising for defamation, and one wife's advert in which she declared that her husband had left her for another woman and was not paying maintenance.

Appendix 21. *List of wives' and husbands' work or means of income*

Husbands and wives doing different work		Husbands and wives doing related work	
Wife	Husband	Wife	Husband
Washed linen	Labourer	Assisting in farm work	Yeoman
Washing	Cordwainer	Coffeehouse owner	Owned stage-coach
Washer-woman	Husbandman	Assisted in public house	Publican
Washer-woman	Tailor	Kept alehouse	Mason / alehouse owner
Wet-nurse	Yeoman	Ran inn	Innkeeper
Wet-nurse	Yeoman	Kept public house	Kept public house
Wet-nurse	Woodworker	Looked after public house in husband's absence	Joiner / kept public house
Wet-nurse	Cordwainer	Ran inn	Innkeeper
Midwife	Linen draper	Ran public house in husband's absence	Miller / public house owner
Midwife	Basket maker	Helped run inn	Innkeeper
Midwife	Labourer	Helped run inn	Innkeeper
Ran alehouse	Seaman	Brandy-shop owner	Brandy-shop owner
Kept alehouse	Yeoman	Shopkeeper	Cork-shop owner
Brandy-shop owner	Gentleman	Looked after lodgers	Flax-dresser, lodgings-house owner

(cont.)

Appendix 21. *(cont.)*

Husbands and wives doing different work		Husbands and wives doing related work	
Wife	Husband	Wife	Husband
Kept lodgers	Gentleman	Supplied husband with lace	Lace buyer/dealer
Let furnished rooms	Fitter	Ballad seller	Ballad seller
Let a shop	Barber / peruke maker	Selling holly	Selling holly
Cork-cutting	Shoemaker	Assisted in husband's overseeing duties	Overseer
Taught children to read	Tailor		
Spinning	Farmer		
Work woman (inn)	Cordwainer		
Carrier	Yeoman		
Quilted petticoats	Cabinet maker		

Sources: all references in (A), (B), (C), (D), (E), where both wives' and their husbands' work was described (includes deponents as well as litigants in ecclesiastical courts). Descriptions are based on the way the activity was described and does not necessarily define the individual's main occupation or means of earning a living.

Appendix 22. *Occupations of wife-beaters*

Category	Number of occurrences
Tradesmen, craftsmen and retailers	82
Rural/agricultural	62
Labourers	40
Titled/gentlemen	20
Unskilled	15
Professionals	13
Miscellaneous	11
Textiles	3
Total	246

Sources: (A), (B), (C).

Appendix 23. *Types of goods conveyed away by wives*

Types of goods	Occurrences of type
Household goods	23
Linen/bedding	16
Clothes/lace	14
Things of value	13
Silver	12
Cash	10
Household furniture	3
Papers/writings/securities	3
Gold	3
Jewellery	3
Miscellaneous[1]	2
Total	102

Sources: all references in (A), (B), (C), (D). The number of occurrences is higher than the number of husbands who made the complaint of conveying away goods since wives could convey away more than one type of goods. The complaint of conveying away goods was also made without describing them.

[1] One horse and one 'her own goods'.

Appendix 24. *Male responses to libels or additional positions accusing them of cruelty to their wives*

Response	Number
No answer given, or has not survived	19
Deny	14
Refuse to answer the articles, but still deny violence[1]	4
Answer, but ignore articles including accusation of cruelty	4
Refuse to answer because criminal charge	3
Admit and claim wife was provoking	3
Deny marriage was valid	2
Deny accusation, claim wife was insane	1
Admit and take partial responsibility	1
Total	51

Sources: Forty-seven cruelty separations, one adultery separation, one jactitation and two restitution of conjugal rights in (A).

[1] Refused to answer because the accusation of violence was a criminal charge, but nevertheless in the process of the statement denied the accusation.

Appendix 25. *Types of marital difficulties that included secondary complaints about adultery*

Type of marital difficulty	Number
Cruelty separations	12
Complaints of wife-beating before a JP	6
Defence in restitution of conjugal rights	5
Miscellaneous[1]	5
Counter-accusation in adultery separation	3
Total	**31**

Sources: (A), (B), (D).
[1] Includes advertisements, desertion and other breaches of the peace.

Appendix 26. *Status or occupation of female lovers of married men accused of adultery*

Status or occupation	Number
Servant	18
Miscellaneous[1]	2
Alehouse keeper	1
Householder	1
Landlady	1
Millinery shop owner	1
Took in lodgers	1
Total	**25**

Sources: selected from fifty-eight allegations of male adultery (where status or occupation can be derived from description given) in (A).
[1] Slightly unclear, but probably an alehouse keeper and a servant who did not live in employer's household.

Appendix 27. *Comparison of status or occupation of husbands with that of male lovers of married women accused of adultery*

	Husband	Lover
Husband higher status:	Apothecary	Butcher
	Gentleman	Butler
	Gentleman	Clerk
	Gentleman	Coachman
	Esquire	Cordwainer
	Esquire	Flax-dresser
	Clergyman	Gardener
	Master weaver	Journeyman weaver / servant
	Officer of customs	Keelman
	Miller	Labourer
	Attorney	Labourer
	Esquire	Lieutenant
	Dye-works owner	Travelling portrait painter
	Gentleman	Saddler
	Mill owner	Saddler and innkeeper
	Confectioner	Seaman
	Clergyman	Servant
	Baronet	Steward
	Esquire	Yeoman
	Gentleman	Yeoman
Husband and lover of similar status:	Attorney	Clergyman
	Mariner	Innholder
	Labourer	Labourer
	Confectioner	Spirit merchant
	Clergyman	Wine merchant
	Cork-cutter	Cork-cutter
Lover higher status than husband:	Clergyman	Esquire
	Clergyman	Gentleman
	Gold-smith	Gentleman
	Keelman	Gentleman
	Labourer	Tailor
Unclear	Labourer	'Gallant'
	Total	32

Sources: incidents of female adultery where both husband's and lover's status or occupation recorded in (A), (B), (D). The decision about whether a particular status/occupation was higher or lower was informed by other information given in the cases.

Appendix 28. *Marital background of female infidelity*

Background	Number
No children when affair occurred	8
Existing separation	7
Absent husband / ill husband	5
Spouses with substantial difference in age between them	4
Spouses with substantial difference in social status between them	2
Total	**26**

Sources: twenty-three adultery separations and correction cases and one detailed quarter sessions case in (A), (B). Some couples experienced more than one of these backgrounds.

Appendix 29. *Number of children in the deserted families*

Number of children	Number of desertion cases
1	60
2	57
3	32
4	24
5	7
6	9
7	2
8	1
10	1
Total	**193**

Sources: (B), (C), (D), (E).

Appendix 30. *Deserting husbands' occupations*

Category	Number within category
Labourers	75
Tradesmen, craftsmen and retailers[1]	64
Soldiers/militia-men	14
Rural/agricultural	12
Unskilled[2]	7
Sea-/river-related	7
Servants	5
Gentry/professional	4
Pedlars	4
Unclear	4
Total	**196**

Sources: (B), (C), (D), (E).
[1] Includes bakers, butchers, cordwainers, blacksmiths, tailors, shopkeepers.
[2] Includes brick-maker, broom-maker, sweep.

BIBLIOGRAPHY

MANUSCRIPTS

Borthwick Institute of Historical Research, York

All matrimonial cases for the period 1660–1804 for which cause papers survive collected from:
Cons.CP and Chanc.CP (1800–1990) Consistory and Chancery court cause papers
CP.H/2446–6009 and CP.I/1–3122 (1663–1800) Consistory court cause papers
D/C.CP Dean and Chapter court cause papers. Indexed in K. M. Longley, *Ecclesiastical Cause Papers at York I: Dean and Chapter's Court 1350–1843*, Borthwick Text and Calendar, 6, York, 1980
Trans.CP Transmitted cause papers. Indexed in W. J. Shiels, *Ecclesiastical Cause Papers at York: Files Transmitted on Appeal 1500–1883*, Borthwick Text and Calendar, 9, York, 1983

Centre for Buckinghamshire Studies, Aylesbury

Q/SM/1–11 (1727–1800) Quarter sessions minute books
Q/SO/1–26 (1678–1800) Quarter sessions order books
QS Rolls (1732–1800) Quarter sessions rolls
All years up to 1718 are calendared in the published volumes:
W. Le Hardy and G. L. Rickett (eds.), *County of Buckingham Calendar to the Sessions Records*, 4 vols., Aylesbury, 1933, 1939, 1951 (comprising Vols. I–IV and unpublished volumes and manuscript)
W. Le Hardy (ed.), *County of Buckingham Calendar to the Sessions Records*, 3 vols., Aylesbury, 1958, 1980, (comprising Vols. V and VII and manuscript Vol. VIII)

Durham Record Office, County Hall, Durham

EP/ Church of England parish records (1660–1800). References to marital difficulties contained in indexes to relevant poor law, settlement and vagrancy material
Q/S/OB 5–16 (1660–1810) Quarter sessions order books

D/X 730/1 Journal of Reverend Edmund Tew, 1750–64. This is published in
G. Morgan and P. Rushton (eds.), *The Justicing Notebook (1750–1764)
of Edmund Tew, Rector of Boldon*, Surtees Society, Woodbridge,
2001
DRO/EP/Wi 72, *Book of Homilies*, London, 1633 (purchased for Winston Church
in 1677)

Northumberland County Archives Service, Morpeth Record Office, Morpeth

EP/ Church of England parish records (1700–1800). References to marital
difficulties contained in indexes to relevant poor law, settlement and vagrancy
material
QSB/1–87 (1680–1742) Quarter sessions bundles
QSO 1–15 (1680–1800) Quarter sessions order books

North Yorkshire Archives, North Yorkshire County Record Office, Northallerton

DC/RMB III 3/1/3 (1627–1822 though 1720s through to 1770s largely missing)
Richmond quarter sessions files
DC/SCB VI 2/1/1/1–4 (1696–1723, 1778–1821) Borough of Scarborough quarter
sessions minute books
PR/ Church of England parish records (1700–1800). References to marital
difficulties contained in indexes to relevant poor law, settlement and vagrancy
material
QSB (1685–1800) Quarter sessions rolls and bundles
QSM Vols. 20–9 (1703–1800) and Vols. 1–3 (1769–1802) Quarter sessions minute
and order books. Up to 1769 the books contain judicial and administrative
work, after 1769 they were entered separately.

Oxfordshire Archives, Oxfordshire Record Office, Cowley, Oxford

Mss.D.D.Par/ parish collections (1700–1800). References to marital difficulties
contained in indexes to relevant poor law, settlement and vagrancy
material
QS/ (1687–1830) Quarter sessions records summarised by Canon Oldfield in
'Calendar of Quarter Sessions Rolls', Vols. I–IX.
All matrimonial cases for the period 1660–1804 for which cause papers survive
collected from:
Mss.Oxf.dioc.papers c. 91 – c. 101 (seventeenth–nineteenth centuries) Consistory
and archdeaconry court papers

Tyne and Wear Archives, Newcastle

QS/NC/1/2–8 (1665–1802) Borough of Newcastle quarter sessions order books

University of Durham, University Library, Palace Green Section

All matrimonial cases for the period 1660–1804 for which cause papers survive collected from:
DDR/EJ/CC 22–7 Court books
DDR/EJ/CCD/3 (1678 and 1716–1868) Consistory court cause papers
DDR/EJ/PRC/2 (1608–1853) Proctors' papers and correspondence for individual consistory court cases
DDR/EJ/PRO Durham Probate Records, wills and administrative material

PRINTED PRIMARY SOURCES

Jackson's Oxford Journal (1753–1800)
The Matrimonial Preceptor. A collection of examples and precepts relating to the married state, from the most celebrated writers ancient and modern (London, 1755)
Newcastle Advertiser (1788–1800)
Newcastle Chronicle (1764–1800)
Newcastle Courant (1711–1800)
Newcastle Gazette (1744–52)
Newcastle Intelligencer (1755–9)
Newcastle Journal (1739–88)
Newcastle Weekly Mercury (1722–3)
North Country Journal: Or, The Impartial Intelligencer (1734–8)
The Wife, by Mira, one of the Authors of 'The Female Spectator', and 'Epistles of Ladies' (London, 1756)
York Chronicle (1773–1800)
York Courant (1728–1800)
York Herald and County Advertiser (1790–1800)
Anon., *Adultery A-la-Mode. An Epistle from Lady Traffick to Sir John*, London, 1746.
  A Treatise of Feme Coverts: Or, the Lady's Law containing all the Laws and Statutes relating to Women, London, 1732.
  Baron and Feme. A Treatise of Law and Equity, concerning husbands and wives, 3rd edition, London, 1738.
  The Laws Respecting Women, as they regard their natural rights, or their connections and conduct, London, 1777.
  Letters on Love, Marriage, and Adultery; Addressed to the Right Honorable The Earl of Exeter, London, 1789.
  Poor Robin's True Character of a Scold Or the Shrews Looking-glass, London, 1678.
Atkinson, J. C. (ed.), *The North Riding Record Society, Quarter Sessions Records*, Vols. VI and VII, London, 1888 and 1889.
Bedfordshire County Records. Notes and Extracts from the County Records comprised in the Quarter Sessions Rolls from 1714 to 1832, Bedford, 1902, Vol. I.
Bishop, Joel Prentiss, *Commentaries on the Law of Marriage and Divorce and Evidence in Matrimonial Suits*, London, 1852.
Blackstone, Sir William, *Commentaries on The Laws of England*, 19th edition, ed. J. E. Hovenden, London, 1836, Vol. III.

Book of Homilies, *The second Tome of Homilies, of such matters As were Promised and Entituled in the former part of Homilies*, London, 1633.

Bruys, François, *The Art of Knowing Women: or, the Female Sex Dissected, in a faithful representation of their virtues and vices, written in French by the Chevalier Plante-amour, published at the Hague, 1729. Now faithfully made English with improvements*, London, 1730.

Burn, Richard, *Ecclesiastical Law*, 2 vols., London, 1763.

The Justice of the Peace and Parish Officer, 15th edition, 4 vols., London, 1785.

Coote, Henry Charles, *The Practice of the Ecclesiastical Courts*, London, 1847.

Crittal, Elizabeth (ed.), *The Justicing Notebook of William Hunt 1744–1749*, Wiltshire Record Society, 37, Stoke-on-Trent, 1981.

Defoe, Daniel, *The Complete English Tradesman in Familiar Letters Directing him in all the several Parts and Progressions of Trade*, 2nd edition, 2 vols., 1727; reprint: New York, 1969.

Dickinson, H. T. (ed.), *The Correspondence of Sir James Clavering*, Surtees Society, 178, Gateshead, 1967.

Essex, John, *The Young Ladies Conduct or Rules for Education under Several Heads; with instructions upon dress both before and after marriage. And advice to young wives*, London, 1722.

Fleetwood, William, *The relative duties of parents and children, husbands and wives, masters and servants; consider'd in sixteen practical discourses with sermons upon the case of self-murther*, 2nd edition, London, 1716.

Fraser, C. M. (ed.), *Durham Quarter Sessions Rolls 1471–1625*, Surtees Society, 199, Newcastle, 1991.

Gisborne, Thomas, *An Enquiry into the Duties of the Female Sex*, 9th edition, London, 1796.

Greene, Douglas G. (ed.), *The Meditations of Lady Elizabeth Delaval, Written Between 1662 and 1671*, Surtees Society, 190, 1975.

Hembry, Phyllis, *Calendar of Bradford-on-Avon Settlement Examinations and Removal Orders 1725–98*, Wiltshire Record Society, 46, Trowbridge, 1990.

Hodgson, J. C. (ed.), *Six North Country Diaries*, Surtees Society, 118, Durham, 1910.

Marriott, Thomas, *Female Conduct: being an essay on the art of pleasing. To be practised by the fair sex, before, and after marriage. A poem in two books*, London, 1759.

Meriton, George, *A Guide for Constables*, 6th edition, London, 1679.

Morgan, Fidelis (ed.), *The Female Tatler*, London, 1992.

Paley, Ruth (ed.), *Justice in Eighteenth-Century Hackney: The Justicing Notebook of Henry Norris and the Hackney Petty Sessions Book*, London Record Society, London, 1991.

Pennington, Sarah, *An Unfortunate Mother's Advice to her Absent Daughters; in a Letter to Miss Pennington*, 2nd edition, London, 1761.

Philogamus, *The Present State of Matrimony: Or, the real causes of conjugal infidelity and unhappy marriages. In a letter to a friend*, London, 1739.

Raine, James (ed.), *Depositions from the Castle of York*. Surtees Society, 40, Durham, 1861.

Richardson, M. A., *The Local Historian's Table Book of Remarkable Occurrences, Historical Facts, Traditions, Legendary and Descriptive Ballads, etc, etc, connected with the Counties of Newcastle-upon-Tyne, Northumberland and Durham*, Newcastle-upon-Tyne, 1861.

Salmon, Thomas, *A Critical Essay concerning Marriage* (1724), London, 1985.
Shephard, William, *A Sure Guide for his Majesties Justices of the Peace*, London, 1663.
Silverthorne, Elizabeth (ed.), *Deposition Book of Richard Wyatt, JP, 1767–1776*, Surrey Record Society, 30, Guildford, 1978.
Steele, Richard, *The Ladies Library, written by a Lady, 3 vols., Published by Sir Richard Steele*, 6th edition, London, 1714.
Summers, Jeremiah William, *The History and Antiquities of Sunderland, Bishopwearmouth, Bishopwearmouth Panns, Burdon, Ford, Ryhope, Silksworth, Tunstall, Monkwearmouth, Monkwearmouth Shore, Fulwell, Hylton, and Southwick*, Sunderland, 1858, Vol. I.
Sykes, John (ed.), *Local Records: or Historical Register of Remarkable Events*, Newcastle, 1865, Vol. I.
Tomlins, Sir Thomas Edlyne (ed.), *The Law Dictionary*, by Thomas Colpitts Granger, 4th edition, London, 1835, Vol. I.
Whateley, William, *Directions for Married Persons* in John Wesley, *A Christian Library*, 27th edition, 30 vols., London, 1819, Vol. XI.
Woolley, Hannah, *The Gentlewomans Companion; or, a Guide to the Female Sex: containing directions of behaviour, in all places, companies, relations, and conditions from their childhood down to old age*, London, 1675.

SECONDARY SOURCES

Abrams, Lynn, 'Whores, whore-chasers, and swine: the regulation of sexuality and the restoration of order in the nineteenth-century German divorce court', *Journal of Family History* 21, 3 (1996), 267–80.
Adair, Richard, *Courtship, Illegitimacy and Marriage in Early Modern England*, Manchester, 1996.
Allan, T. (ed.), *Philip's County Guide: Oxfordshire*, London, 1994.
Amussen, Susan Dwyer, *An Ordered Society: Gender and Class in Early Modern England*, Oxford, 1988.
' "Being stirred to much unquietness": violence and domestic violence in early modern England', *Journal of Women's History* 6, 2 (1994), 70–89.
' "The part of a Christian man": the cultural politics of manhood in early modern England' in S. Amussen and M. Kishlansky (eds.), *Political Culture and Cultural Politics in Early Modern England*, Manchester, 1995, pp. 213–33.
Anderson, O. 'State, civil society and separation in Victorian marriage', *Past and Present* 163 (1998), 161–201.
Anderson, Stuart, 'Legislative divorce – law for the aristocracy' in G. R. Rubin and David Sugarman (eds.), *Law, Economy and Society, 1750–1914: Essays in the History of English Law*, Abingdon, 1984, pp. 412–45.
Andrew, Donna T., ' "Adultery a-la-mode": privilege, the law and attitudes to adultery 1770–1809', *Historical Association* (1997), 5–23.
Armstrong, Alan, *Stability and Change in an English County Town: A Social Study of York 1801–51*, London, 1974.
Babcock, Julia C., Waltz, Jennifer, Jacobson, Neil S. and Gottman, John M., 'Power and violence: the relation between communication patterns, power discrepancies, and domestic violence', *Journal of Consulting and Clinical Psychology* 61, 1 (1993), 40–50.

Bailey, Joanne, 'Breaking the conjugal vows: marriage and marriage breakdown in the north of England, 1660–1800', Ph.D. thesis, University of Durham (1999).
'Favoured or oppressed? Married women, property and "coverture" in England, 1660–1800', *Continuity and Change* 17, 3 (2002), 1–22.
'Voices in court: lawyers' or litigants'?' *Historical Research* 74, 186 (2001), 392–408.
Baker, J. H., *An Introduction to English Legal History*, London, 1979.
Barber, Jill, '"Stolen goods": the sexual harassment of female servants in West Wales during the nineteenth century', *Rural History* 4, 2 (1993), 123–36.
Barker, Hannah, 'Catering for provincial tastes: newspapers, readership and profit in late eighteenth-century England', *Historical Research, The Bulletin of the Institute of Historical Research* 69, 168 (1996), 42–61.
Newspapers, Politics and English Society 1695–1855, Harlow, 2000.
Barker, Hannah and Chalus, Elaine (eds.), *Gender in Eighteenth-Century England: Roles, Representations and Responsibilities*, London, 1997.
Barker, Malcolm, *Yorkshire: The North Riding*, London, 1977.
Barker-Benfield, G. J., *The Culture of Sensibility. Sex and Society in Eighteenth-Century Britain*, Chicago and London, 1992.
Barry, Jonathan and Brooks, Christopher (eds.), *The Middling Sort of People: Culture, Society and Politics in England, 1550–1800*, Basingstoke, 1994.
Bates, Cadwallader J., *The History of Northumberland*, London, 1895.
Beattie, J. M., *Crime and the Courts in England 1660–1800*, Oxford, 1986.
Beckett, I. F. W., *Shire County Guide 13: Buckinghamshire*, Aylesbury, 1987.
Bell, Susan Groag and Offen, Karen M. (eds.), *Women, the Family, and Freedom: The Debate in Documents*, Stanford, 1983.
Bender, John, 'A new history of the Enlightenment?' *Eighteenth-Century Life* 16 (1992), 1–20.
Bennett, J., *Women in the Medieval English Countryside: Gender and Household in Brigstock Before the Plague*, Oxford, 1987.
Bennett, W. Lance and Feldman, Martha S., *Reconstructing Reality in the Courtroom*, London, 1981.
Berg, Maxine, 'Women's consumption and the industrial classes of eighteenth-century England', *Journal of Social History* 30, 2 (1996), 415–34.
Berry, H., 'Prudent luxury: the metropolitan tastes of Judith Baker, Durham gentlewoman' in P. Lane and R. Sweet (eds.), *'On the Town': Women and Urban Life in Eighteenth-Century England*, forthcoming, 2003, pp. 130–54.
Bertelsen, Lance, 'Committed by Justice Fielding: judicial and journalistic representation in the Bow Street Magistrate's Office, January 3 – November 24, 1752', *Eighteenth-Century Studies* 30, 4 (1997), 337–63.
Biggs, J. M., *The Concept of Matrimonial Cruelty*, University of London Legal Series, 6, London, 1962.
Black, Jeremy, *Eighteenth-century Britain 1688–1783*, Basingstoke, 2001.
The English Press in the Eighteenth Century, London, 1987.
Boardman, Carl, *Oxfordshire Sinners and Villains*, Stroud, 1994.
Bohstedt, John, 'Gender, household and community politics: women in English riots 1790–1810', *Past and Present* 120 (1988), 88–122.
Borsay, P., *The English Urban Renaissance, Culture and Society in the Provincial Town, 1660–1770*, Oxford, 1989.
Botelho, L. and Thane, P., *Women and Ageing in British Society Since 1500*, Harlow, 2001.

Bouce, Paul-Gabriel (ed.), *Sexuality in Eighteenth-Century Britain*, Manchester, 1982.

Bouchard, Gerard, 'Through the meshes of patriarchy: the male/female relationship in the Saguenay peasant society (1860–1930)', *History of the Family* 4, 4 (1999), 397–425.

Boulton, Jeremy, ' "It is extreme necessity that makes me do this": some "survival strategies" of pauper households in London's West End during the early eighteenth century' in L. Fontaine and J. Schlumbohm, *Household Strategies for Survival 1600–2000: Fission, Faction and Cooperation*, International Review of Social History, 45, Cambridge, 2000, pp. 47–69.

'London widowhood revisited: the decline of female remarriage in the seventeenth and early eighteenth centuries', *Continuity and Change* 5, 3 (1990), 325–55.

Brant, Clare and Purkiss, Diane, *Women, Texts and Histories 1575–1760*, London, 1992.

Bray, Alan, 'To be a man in early modern society. The curious case of Michael Wigglesworth', *History Workshop Journal* 41 (1996), 155–65.

Brewer, John and Porter, Roy (eds.), *Consumption and the World of Goods*, London, 1993.

Brienes, Wini and Gordon, Linda, 'The new scholarship on family violence', *Signs: Journal of Women in Culture and Society* 8, 3 (1983), 490–530.

Brooks, Christopher W., 'Interpersonal conflict and social tension: civil litigation in England, 1640–1830' in A. L. Beier, David Cannadine and James M. Rosenheim (eds.), *The First Modern Society: Essays in English History in Honour of Lawrence Stone*, Cambridge, 1989, pp. 357–99.

Lawyers, Litigation and English Society since 1450, London, 1998.

Pettyfoggers and Vipers of the Commonwealth: The 'Lower Branch' of the Legal Profession in Early Modern England, Cambridge, 1986.

Brooks, Christopher W. and Lobban, Michael (eds.), *Communities and Courts 1150–1900*, London, 1997.

Burke, Peter (ed.), *New Perspectives on Historical Writing*, Cambridge, 1991.

Capp, Bernard, 'The double standard revisited: plebeian women and male sexual reputation in early modern England', *Past and Present* 162 (1999), 70–100.

Carlson, Eric Josef, *Marriage and the English Reformation*, Oxford, 1994.

Cavallo, S. and Warner, L. (eds.), *Widowhood in Medieval and Early Modern Europe*, London, 1999.

Chapman, Colin R., *Ecclesiastical Courts, Their Officials and Their Records*, Dursley, 1992.

Chapman, Colin, with Litton, Pauline M., *Marriage Laws, Rites, Records and Customs*, Dursley, 1996.

Charles, L. and Duffin, L. (eds.), *Women and Work in Pre-industrial England*, London, 1985.

Chaytor, Miranda, 'Husbandry: narratives of rape in the seventeenth century', *Gender and History* 7, 3 (1995), 378–407.

Chester, Robert and Streather, Jane, 'Cruelty in English divorce: some empirical findings', *Journal of Marriage and Family* 34 (1972), 706–12.

Churches, Christine, ' "The most unconvincing testimony": the genesis and historical usefulness of the country depositions in Chancery', *Seventeenth Century* 11, 2 (1996), 209–27.

'Women and property in early modern England: a case-study', *Social History* 23, 2 (1998), 165–85.

Clark, Alice, *Working Life of Women in the Seventeenth Century*, 3rd edition, London, 1992.

Clark, Anna, 'Humanity or justice? Wifebeating and the law in the eighteenth and nineteenth centuries' in Carol Smart (ed.), *Representing Womanhood: Historical Writings on Marriage, Motherhood and Sexuality*, London, 1992, pp. 187–206.

Men's Violence, Women's Silence: Sexual Assault in England, 1770–1845, London, 1987.

The Struggle for the Breeches: Gender and the Making of the British Working Class, London, 1995.

'Whores and gossips: sexual reputation in London 1770–1825' in Arina Angerman, Geerte Binnema, Annemike Keunen, Vefie Poels, and Jacqueline Zirkzee, *Current Issues in Women's History*, London, 1989, pp. 231–48.

Clark, Peter, *The English Alehouse. A Social History, 1200–1830*, London, 1983.

Clarkson, L. A., *Proto-Industrialization: The First Phase of Industrialization?* London, 1986.

Clay, Michael, Milburn, Geoffrey and Miller, Stuart (eds.), *An Eye Plan of Sunderland and Bishopwearmouth 1785–1790, by John Rain*, Newcastle, 1984.

Cockburn, J. S., 'Early-modern assize records as historical evidence', *Journal of the Society of Archivists* 5 (1974–7), 215–31.

'The work of the North Riding quarter sessions in the early eighteenth century', Master of Law thesis, University of Leeds (1961).

Colley, Linda, *Britons. Forging the Nation 1707–1837*, London, 1992.

Conley, Carolyn A., 'No pedestals: women and violence in late nineteenth-century Ireland', *Journal of Social History* 28 (1995), 801–18.

The Unwritten Law: Criminal Justice in Victorian Kent, Oxford, 1991.

Coster, W., *Family and Kinship in England 1450–1800*, London, 2001.

Cressy, David, *Birth, Marriage and Death: Ritual, Religion and the Life-Cycle in Tudor and Stuart England*, Oxford, 1997.

D'Cruze, Shani, 'Care, diligence and "Usfull Pride" [*sic*]: gender, industrialisation and the domestic economy, c. 1770 to c. 1840', *Women's History Review* 3, 3 (1994), 315–45.

Crimes of Outrage: Sex, Violence and Victorian Working Women, London, 1998.

Dabhoiwala, Faramerz, 'The construction of honour, reputation and status in late seventeenth- and early eighteenth-century England', *Transactions of the Royal Historical Society*, 6th series, 6 (1996), 201–13.

'The pattern of sexual immorality in seventeenth- and eighteenth-century London' in P. Griffiths and M. S. R. Jenner, *Londinopolis. Essays in the Cultural and Social History of Early Modern London*, Manchester, 2000, pp. 86–106.

Davidoff, Leonore, 'The rationalization of housework' in Diana Leonard Barker and Sheila Allen, *Dependence and Exploitation in Work and Marriage*, London, 1976, pp. 121–51.

Davidoff, L., Doolittle, M., Fink, J. and Holden, K., *Family Story: Blood, Contract and Intimacy 1830–1960*, London, 1999.

Davidoff, Leonore and Hall, Catherine, *Family Fortunes. Men and Women of the English Middle Class, 1780–1850*, London, 1987.

Davidson, Caroline, *A Woman's Work is Never Done: A History of Housework in the British Isles 1650–1950*, London, 1982.

Davidson, Terry, 'Wifebeating: a recurring phenomenon throughout history' in Maria Roy (ed.), *Battered Women, a Psychosociological Study of Domestic Violence*, 1997, pp. 2–23.

Davies, N. (ed.), *Paston Letters and Papers of the Fifteenth Century*, 2 vols., Oxford, 1971, 1976, Vol. I.

Davis, Natalie Zemon, *Fiction in the Archives: Pardon Tales and Their Tellers in Sixteenth-Century France*, Cambridge, 1987.

Davis, Natalie Zemon and Farge, Arlette (eds.), *A History of Women in the West*, Vol. III, *Renaissance and Enlightenment Paradoxes*, London, 1993.

de Vries, Jan, 'Between purchasing power and the world of goods: understanding the household economy in early modern Europe' in Pamela Sharpe (ed.), *Women's Work. The English Experience 1650–1914*, London, 1998, pp. 209–39.

Doggett, Maeve E., *Marriage, Wife-Beating and the Law in Victorian England*, London, 1992.

Dolan, Frances E., *Dangerous Familiars, Representations of Domestic Crime in England, 1550–1700*, New York, 1994.

Doolittle, Megan, 'Close relations? Bringing together gender and family in English history', *Gender and History* 11, 3 (1999), 542–54.

Dowdell, E. G., *A Hundred Years of Quarter Sessions, The Government of Middlesex from 1660–1760*, London, 1932.

Duncan, G. I. O., *The High Courts of Delegates*, London, 1971.

Eales, Jacqueline, *Women in Early Modern England, 1500–1700*, London, 1998.

Earle, Peter, 'The female labour market in London in the late seventeenth and early eighteenth centuries', *Economic History Review* 2nd series, 42, 3 (1989), 328–53.

The Making of the English Middle Class: Business, Society and Family Life in London, 1660–1730, London, 1989.

Ellis, J., *The Georgian Town 1680–1840*, Basingstoke, 2001.

Emmison, F. G. and Gray, Irvine, *County Records,* The Historical Association, H.62, London, 1967.

English, Barbara and Saville, John, *Strict Settlement: A Guide for Historians*, University of Hull, Occasional Papers in Economic and Social History, 10, Hull, 1983.

Erickson, Amy Louise, *Women and Property in Early Modern England*, London, 1993.

Fairchilds, Cissie, *Domestic Enemies: Servants and Their Masters in Old Regime France*, London, 1984.

Fawcett, Barbara, Featherstone, Brid, Hearn, Jeff and Toft, Christine, *Violence and Gender Relations: Theories and Interventions*, London, 1996.

Finn, Margot, 'Men's things: masculine possession in the consumer revolution', *Social History* 25, 2 (2000), 133–55.

'Women, consumption and coverture in England, c. 1760–1860', *Historical Journal* 39, 3 (1996), 702–22.

Fletcher, Anthony, *Gender, Sex and Subordination in England 1500–1800*, London, 1995.

'The protestant idea of marriage in early modern England' in A. Fletcher and P. Roberts, *Religion, Culture, and Society in Early Modern Britain*, Cambridge, 1994, pp. 161–81.

Flint, Christopher, *Family Fictions, Narrative and Domestic Relations in Britain, 1688–1798*, Stanford, 1998.

Fontaine, L. and Schlumbohm, J., *Household Strategies for Survival 1600–2000: Fission, Faction and Cooperation*, International Review of Social History, 45, 2000.

Forster, G. C. F., 'The North Riding justices and their sessions, 1603–1625', *Northern History* 10 (1975), 102–25.

Foyster, Elizabeth Ann, 'The concept of male honour in seventeenth-century England', Ph.D. thesis, University of Durham (1996).

'A laughing matter? Marital discord and gender control in seventeenth-century England', *Rural History* 4 (1993), 5–21.

'Male honour, social control and wife beating in late Stuart England', *Transactions of the Royal Historical Society*, 6th series, 6 (1996), 214–24.

Manhood in Early Modern England. Honour, Sex and Marriage, London, 1999.

'Parenting was for life, not just for childhood: the role of parents in the married lives of their children in early modern England', *History* 86, 283 (2001), 313–27.

'Silent witnesses? Children and the breakdown of domestic and social order in early modern England' in A. Fletcher and S. Hussey (eds.), *Childhood in Question: Children, Parents and the State*, Manchester, 1999, pp. 57–73.

Frost, Ginger, 'Bigamy and cohabitation in Victorian England', *Journal of Family History* 22, 3 (1997), 286–306.

Promises Broken: Courtship, Class and Gender in Victorian England, London, 1995.

Gibson, Colin S., *Dissolving Wedlock*, London, 1994.

Gillis, John R., *For Better, For Worse: British Marriages, 1600 to the Present*, Oxford, 1985.

Goldberg, P. J. P., *Women, Work, and Life Cycle in a Medieval Economy: Women in York and Yorkshire c. 1300–1520*, Oxford, 1992.

Gordon, Linda, *Heroes of Their Own Lives: The Politics and History of Family Violence, Boston 1880–1960*, New York, 1988.

Gowing, Laura, *Domestic Dangers: Women, Words, and Sex in Early Modern London*, Oxford, 1996.

'Women, sex and honour: the London church courts, 1570–1640', Ph.D. thesis, University of London (1993).

'Women, status and the popular culture of dishonour', *Transactions of the Royal Historical Society*, 6th series, 6 (1996), 225–34.

Graham, Frank, *Northumberland and Durham: A Social and Political Miscellany*, Newcastle, 1979.

Green, A, '"A clumsey Countrey Girl": the material and print culture of Betty Bowes' in H. Berry and J. Gregson (eds.), *Creating and Consuming Culture in North East England, 1660–1832*, forthcoming.

'Houses and households in County Durham and Newcastle-upon-Tyne, c. 1570–1730', Ph.D. thesis, University of Durham (2000).

Gretton, Mary Sturge, *Oxfordshire Justices of the Peace in the Seventeenth Century*, Oxfordshire Record Society, 16, Oxford, 1934.

Hammerton, A. James, *Cruelty and Companionship: Conflict in Nineteenth-century Married Life*, London, 1992.

'The targets of "rough music": respectability and domestic violence in Victorian England', *Gender and History* 3, 1 (1991), 23–44.

Hanawalt, B., *The Ties that Bound: Peasant Families in Medieval England*, Oxford, 1986.

Harris, C. G., 'Marriages in Oxford before 1754', *Oxfordshire Family Historian* 2 (1982), 278–85.

Hay, D. and Rogers, N., *Eighteenth-century English Society: Shuttles and Swords*, Oxford, 1997.

Helmholz, R. H., *Marriage Litigation in Medieval England*, London, 1974.

Hepple, L. W. and Doggett, A. M., *The Chilterns*, 2nd edition, Chichester, 1994.

Herrup, Cynthia, 'The patriarch at home: the trial of the 2nd Earl of Castlehaven for rape and sodomy', *History Workshop Journal* 41 (1996), 1–18.

' "To pluck bright honour from the pale faced moon": gender and honour in the Castlehaven story', *Transactions of the Royal Historical Society*, 6th series, 6 (1996), 137–59.

Hill, Bridget, *Servants: English Domestics in the Eighteenth Century*, Oxford, 1996.

Hindle, Steve, 'The problem of pauper marriage in seventeenth-century England', *Transactions of the Royal Historical Society*, 6th series, 6 (1998), 71–89.

'The shaming of Margaret Knowsley: gossip, gender and the experience of authority in early modern England', *Continuity and Change* 9, 3 (1994), 391–419.

Hitchcock, Tim, *English Sexualities, 1700–1800*, London, 1997.

Hitchcock, Tim and Cohen, Michele (eds.), *English Masculinities 1660–1800*, London, 1999.

Hitchcock, Tim, King, Peter and Sharpe, Pamela (eds.), *Chronicling Poverty: The Voices and Strategies of the English Poor, 1640–1840*, London, 1997.

Hodgson, J. C. (ed.), *Six North Country Diaries*, Surtees Society, 118, Durham, 1910.

Hodgson, John, *A History of Morpeth* (1832), Newcastle, 1973.

Hodgson, R. I., 'Demographic trends in County Durham, 1560–1801: data sources and preliminary findings with particular reference to North Durham', *University of Manchester School of Geography, Research Papers* 5 (1978).

Holcombe, Lee, *Wives and Property: Reform of the Married Women's Property Law in Nineteenth-Century England*, Oxford, 1983.

Hole, Christina, *The English Housewife in the Seventeenth Century*, London, 1953.

Holmes, G. S., *The Making of a Great Power: Late Stuart and Early Georgian Britain 1660–1722*, London, 1993.

Hoppit, Julian, 'Financial crises in eighteenth-century England', *Economic History Review*, 2nd series, 39, 1 (1986), 39–58.

Horsley, P. M., *Eighteenth-century Newcastle*, Newcastle, 1971.

Houlbrooke, Ralph A., *Church Courts and the People During the English Reformation 1520–1570*, Oxford, 1979.

The English Family 1450–1700, Harlow, 1984.

Howell, Roger, *Newcastle upon Tyne and the Puritan Revolution*, Oxford, 1967.

Hufton, Olwen, *The Prospect Before Her: A History of Women in Western Europe, 1500–1800*, London, 1995.

'Women without men: widows and spinsters in Britain and France in the eighteenth century', *Journal of Family History* (1984), 355–76.

Hughes, Edward, *North Country Life in the Eighteenth Century, The North-East, 1700–1750*, London, 1952.

Hunt, Lynn (ed.), *The New Cultural History*, Berkeley, Los Angeles, London, 1989.

Hunt, Margaret R., *The Middling Sort: Commerce, Gender, and the Family in England, 1680–1780*, Berkeley and London, 1996.

'Wife beating, domesticity and women's independence in eighteenth-century London', *Gender and History* 4 (1992), 10–29.

'Wives and marital "rights" in the Court of Exchequer in the early eighteenth century' in P. Griffiths and M. S. R. Jenner (eds.), *Londinopolis. Essays in the Cultural and Social History of Early Modern London*, Manchester, 2000, pp. 107–29.

Hunt, Margaret, Jacob, Margaret, Mack, Phyllis and Perry, Ruth, 'Women and the Enlightenment', *Women and History* 9 (The Institute for Research in History and The Haworth Press, Inc., Spring 1984).

Hurl-Eamon, J., 'Domestic violence prosecuted: women binding over their husbands for assault at Westminster Quarter Sessions, 1685–1720', *Journal of Family History* 26, 4 (2001), 435–54.

Ingram, Martin, *Church Courts, Sex and Marriage in England, 1570–1640*, Cambridge, 1987.

'Ridings, rough music and the "reform of popular culture" in early modern England', *Past and Present*, 105 (1984), 79–113.

Israel, Kali, 'French vices and British liberties: gender, class and narrative competition in a late Victorian sex scandal', *Social History* 22, 1 (1997), 1–26.

James, Philip S. with Brown, D. J. L., *General Principles of the Law of Torts*, London, 1978.

Jewell, H., *Women in Medieval England*, Manchester, 1996.

Jones, Vivien (ed.), *Women in the Eighteenth Century, Constructions of Femininity*, London, 1990.

Keeble, N. H. (ed.), *The Cultural Identity of Seventeenth-Century Woman: A Reader*, London, 1994.

Kent, D. A., '"Gone for a soldier": family breakdown and the demography of desertion in a London parish, 1750–91', *Local Population Studies* 45 (1990), 27–42.

Kent, Joan R., *The English Village Constable, 1580–1642*, Oxford, 1986.

Kenyon, Olga, *800 Years of Women's Letters*, Stroud, 1992.

Kermode, J. and Walker, G. (eds.), *Women, Crime and the Courts in Early Modern England*, London, 1994.

King, Peter, 'Punishing assault: the transformation of attitudes in the English courts', *Journal of Interdisciplinary History* 27, 1 (1996), 43–74.

King, Rebecca F., 'Rape in England 1660–1800: trials, narratives and the question of consent', MA dissertation, University of Durham (1998).

King, Steve, 'Reconstructing lives: the poor, the Poor Law and welfare in Calverley, 1650–1820', *Social History* 22, 3 (1997), 318–38.

Klein, Lawrence E., 'Gender and the public/private distinction in the eighteenth century: some questions about evidence and analytic procedure', *Eighteenth-Century Studies* 29, 1 (1995), 97–109.

Knight, Marcus, 'Litigants and litigation in the seventeenth-century palatinate of Durham', Ph.D. thesis, University of Cambridge (1990).

Koehler, Lyle A., *Search for Power: The 'Weaker Sex' in Seventeenth-Century New England*, Urbana, Ill., 1980.

Kugler, A., 'Constructing wifely identity: prescription and practice in the life of Lady Sarah Cowper', *Journal of British Studies* 40 (2001), 291–323.

'Prescription, culture, and shaping identity: Lady Sarah Cowper 1644–1720', Ph.D. thesis, University of Michigan (1994).

Lambertz, Jan, 'Feminists and the politics of wife-beating' in Harold Smith (ed.), *British Feminism in the Twentieth Century*, Aldershot, 1990, pp. 25–43.

Landau, Norma, *The Justices of the Peace 1679–1760*, Berkeley, Calif., 1984.

Langford, Paul, *A Polite and Commercial People: England 1727–1783*, 2nd edition, Oxford, 1989.

Lantz, Herman R., *Marital Incompatibility and Social Change in Early America*, Beverly Hills, 1976.

Laslett, Peter, *Family Life and Illicit Love in Earlier Generations*, Cambridge, 1977.

Laurence, Anne, *Women in England 1500–1760: A Social History*, London, 1994.

Lemmings, David, 'Marriage and the law in the eighteenth century: Hardwicke's Marriage Act of 1753', *Historical Journal* 39, 2 (1996), 339–60.

Leneman, Leah, '"A tyrant and tormentor": violence against wives in eighteenth- and early nineteenth-century Scotland', *Continuity and Change* 12 (1997), 31–54.

Alienated Affections: The Scottish Experience of Divorce and Separation, 1684–1830, Edinburgh, 1998.

'"Disregarding the matrimonial vows": divorce in eighteenth- and early nineteenth-century Scotland', *Journal of Social History* 30, 2 (1996), 465–82.

Levine, David and Wrightson, Keith, *The Making of an Industrial Society: Whickham 1560–1765*, Oxford, 1991.

Longley, K. M., *Ecclesiastical Cause Papers at York: Dean and Chapter's Court 1350–1843*, York, 1980.

Looney, John Jefferson, 'Advertising and society in England, 1720–1820: a statistical analysis of Yorkshire newspaper advertisements', Ph.D. thesis, Princeton University (1983).

MacDonald, Michael, *Mystical Bedlam: Madness, Anxiety, and Healing in Seventeenth-century England*, Cambridge, 1981.

MacDonald, Michael and Murphy, T. R., *Sleepless Souls, Suicide in Early Modern England*, Oxford, 1990.

Marchant, Ronald A., *The Church Under the Law: Justice, Administration and Discipline in the Diocese of York 1560–1640*, London, 1969.

Martin, J. P. (ed.), *Violence and the Family*, Chichester, 1978.

Mascuch, Michael, 'Social mobility and middling self-identity: the ethos of British autobiographers, 1600–1750', *Social History* 20, 1 (1995), 45–61.

Mate, M., *Women in Medieval English Society*, Cambridge, 1999.

Maza, Sarah, 'Domestic melodrama as political ideology: the case of the Comte de Sanois', *American Historical Review* (1989), 1249–64.

McCoy, Kathleen, 'The femininity of Moll Flanders', *Studies in Eighteenth-Century Culture* 7 (1978), 413–22.

McGregor, O. R., Blom-Cooper, Louis and Gibson, Colin, *Separated Spouses: A Study of the Matrimonial Jurisdiction of Magistrates' Courts*, London, 1970.

Meehan, Michael, 'Authorship and imagination in Blackstone's commentaries on the laws of England', *Eighteenth-Century Life* 8, 16 (1992), 111–26.

Meldrum, Tim, 'A women's court in London: defamation at the Bishop of London's Consistory court, 1700–1745', *London Journal* 19, 1 (1994), 1–20.

Domestic Service and Gender 1660–1750: Life and Work in the London Household, London, 2000.

Mendelson, Sara and Crawford, Patricia, *Women in Early Modern English Society, 1550–1720*, Oxford, 1998.

Mercer, Sarah, 'Crime in late-seventeenth-century Yorkshire: an exception to a national pattern?' *Northern History* 27 (1991), 106–19.

Mingay, G. E. (ed.), *The Agrarian History of England and Wales*, Vol. VI, 1750–1850, Cambridge, 1989.

Morgan, Gwenda and Rushton, Peter, *Rogues, Thieves and the Rule of Law: The Problem of Law Enforcement in North-east England, 1718–1800*, London, 1998.

Morris, Polly, 'Defamation and sexual reputation in Somerset, 1733–1850', Ph.D. thesis, University of Warwick (1985).

Mueller, Gerhard O. W., 'Inquiry into the state of a divorceless society: domestic relations law and morals in England from 1660 to 1857', *University of Pittsburgh Law Review* 18 (1959), 548–78.

Muldrew, Craig, *The Economy of Obligation: The Culture of Credit and Social Relations in Early Modern England*, London, 1998.

Nevill, Marjorie, 'Women and marriage breakdown in England, 1832–1857', Ph.D. thesis, University of Essex (1989).

Nicholls, George, *A History of the English Poor Law*, 2 vols., 1898 edition.

O'Day, R., *The Family and Family Relationships, 1500–1900: England, France and the United States of America*, Basingstoke, 1994.

O'Donovan, Katherine, 'Wife sale and desertion as alternatives to judicial marriage dissolution' in John M. Eekelaar and N. Katz Sanford (eds.), *The Resolution of Family Conflict: Comparative Legal Perspectives*, Canada, 1984, pp. 41–51.

O'Hara, Diana, *Courtship and Constraint: Rethinking the Making of Marriage in Tudor England*, Manchester, 2000.

Okin, Susan Moller, 'Patriarchy and married women's property in England: questions on some current views', *Eighteenth-Century Studies* 17, 2 (1983/4), 121–38.

Outhwaite, R. B. *Clandestine Marriage in England, 1500–1850*, London, 1995.
  (ed.), *Marriage and Society: Studies in the Social History of Marriage*, London, 1981.

Page, William (ed.), *The Victoria County History of the Counties of England, A History of Durham*, London, 1968 edition, Vol. II.
  The Victoria County History of the Counties of England, Buckinghamshire, London, 1969 edition, Vol. II.
  The Victoria County History of the Counties of England, Oxfordshire, London, 1907, Vol. II.

Papke, David Ray, *Narrative and the Legal Discourse, A Reader in Storytelling and the Law*, Liverpool, 1991.

Parker, S., *Informal Marriage, Cohabitation and the Law, 1750–1989*, London, 1990.

Pedersen, Frederik, 'Demography in the archives: social and geographical factors in fourteenth-century York cause paper marriage litigation', *Continuity and Change* 10, 3 (1995), 405–37.
  Marriage Disputes in Medieval England, London, 2000.
  '"Romeo and Juliet of Stonegate": a medieval marriage in crisis', *Borthwick Paper* 87 (University of York, 1995), 1–31.

Pelling, Margaret and Smith, Richard M. (eds.), *Life, Death, and the Elderly, Historical Perspectives*, London, 1991.

Perkin, Joan, *Victorian Women*, London, 1993.

Peterson del Mar, David, *What Trouble I Have Seen*, Cambridge, Mass., 1996.

Phillips, Roderick, *Untying the Knot. A Short History of Divorce*, Cambridge, 1991.

Phythian-Adams, Charles (ed.), *Societies, Cultures and Kinship, 1580–1850*, Leicester, 1993.

Pleck, Elizabeth, *Domestic Tyranny: The Making of Social Policy Against Family Violence from Colonial Times to the Present*, Oxford, 1987.

Pollock, Linda A., 'Embarking on a rough passage' in V. Fildes (ed.), *Women as Mothers in Pre-Industrial England*, London, 1990, pp. 39–67.

'Living on the stage of the world: the concept of privacy among the elite of early modern England' in Adrian Wilson (ed.), *Rethinking Social History, English Society 1570–1920 and its Interpretation*, Manchester, 1993, pp. 78–96.

'Rethinking patriarchy and the family in seventeenth-century England', *Journal of Family History* 23, 1 (1998), 3–27.

'"Teach her to live under obedience": the making of women in the upper ranks of early modern England', *Continuity and Change* 4, 2 (1989), 231–58.

Porter, Roy, 'Madness and the family before Freud: the view of the mad-doctors', *Journal of Family History* 23, 2 (1998), 159–72.

Porter, Roy and Teich, Mikulas, *Sexual Knowledge, Sexual Science: The History of Attitudes to Sexuality*, Cambridge, 1994.

Poska, Allyson M., 'When love goes wrong: getting out of marriage in seventeenth-century Spain', *Journal of Social History* 29, 4 (1996), 871–82.

Prior, Mary (ed.), *Women in English Society 1500–1800*, London, 1985.

Purvis, J. S., *An Introduction to Ecclesiastical Records*, London, 1953.

Quaife, G. R., *Wanton Wenches and Wayward Wives: Peasants and Illicit Sex in Early Seventeenth-Century England*, London, 1979.

Raven, James, 'Defending conduct and property. The London press and the luxury debate' in John Brewer and Susan Staves (eds.), *Early Modern Conceptions of Property*, London 1995, pp. 301–19.

Read, Donald, 'North of England newspapers c. 1700–1900 and their value to historians', *Proceedings, Leeds Philosophical and Literary Society* 8 (1957), 200–15.

Reay, B. (ed.), *Popular Culture in Seventeenth-Century England*, London, 1988.

Rigby, S. H., 'Gendering the Black Death: women in later medieval England', *Gender and History* 3, 12 (2000), 745–54.

Ritchie, Carson I. A., *The Ecclesiastical Courts of York*, Arbroath, 1956.

Robb, George, 'Circe in crinoline: domestic poisonings in Victorian England', *Journal of Family History* 22, 2 (1997), 176–90.

Roberts, Michael, '"Words they are women, and deeds they are men": images of work and gender in early modern England' in Lindsey Charles and Lorna Duffin (eds.), *Women and Work in Pre-Industrial England*, London, 1985.

Robson, Robert, *The Attorney in Eighteenth-Century England*, Cambridge, 1959.

Roper, Lyndal, *Oedipus and the Devil: Witchcraft, Sexuality and Religion in Early Modern Europe*, London, 1994.

Roper, Michael and Tosh, John (eds.), *Manful Assertions: Masculinities in Britain since 1800*, London, 1991.

Rose, Sonya, O., 'Proto-industry, women's work and the household economy in the transition to industrial capitalism', *Journal of Family History* 13, 3 (1988), 181–93.

Ross, E., '"Fierce questions and taunts": married life in working-class London, 1870–1914', *Feminist Studies* 8, 3 (1982), 575–602.

Rowthorn, Robert, 'Marriage and trust: some lessons from economics', *Cambridge Journal of Economics* 23 (1999), 661–91.

Rule, John, *The Vital Century: England's Developing Economy, 1714–1815*, London, 1992.

Rushton, Peter, 'The broken marriage in early modern England: matrimonial cases from the Durham church courts, 1560–1630', *Archaeologia Aeliana* 5, 13 (1985), 187–96.
'The Poor Law, the parish and the community in north-east England, 1660–1800', *Northern History* 25 (1989), 135–52.
Sabean, David Warren, *Property, Production, and Family in Neckarhausen, 1700–1870*, Cambridge, 1990.
Scott, Joan Wallach (ed.), *Feminism and History*, Oxford, 1996.
Sharpe, J. A. 'Courts, crime and litigation in the Isle of Man, 1580–1700', *Historical Research* 72, 178 (1999), 141–59.
Crime in Early Modern England 1550–1750, London, 1984.
'Debate: the history of violence in England: some observations', *Past and Present* 108 (1985), 206–15.
'Defamation and sexual slander in early modern England: the church courts at York', *Borthwick Papers* 58 (1980), 1–36.
'Domestic homicide in early modern England', *Historical Journal* 24 (1981), 29–48.
'Plebeian marriage in Stuart England: some evidence from popular literature', *Transactions of the Royal Historical Society*, fifth series, 36 (1986), 69–90.
Sharpe, Pamela, 'Bigamy among the labouring poor in Essex, 1754–1857', *Local Historian* 24, 3 (1994), 139–45.
'Marital separation in the eighteenth and early nineteenth centuries', *Local Population Studies* 45 (1990), 66–70.
Shepard, A., 'Manhood, credit and patriarchy in early modern England c. 1580–1640', *Past and Present* 167 (2000), 83–6.
Shoemaker, Robert B., *Gender in English Society, 1650–1850: The Emergence of Separate Spheres?* London, 1998.
Prosecution and Punishment, Petty Crime and the Law in London and Rural Middlesex, c. 1660–1725, Cambridge, 1991.
'Using quarter sessions records as evidence for the study of crime and criminal justice', *Archives* 20, 90 (1993), 145–57.
Simpson, Richard, *North Shields and Tynemouth*, Chichester, 1988.
Skyrme, Thomas, *History of the Justices of the Peace*, Vol. II, *England 1689–1989*, Chichester, 1991.
Slack, Paul, *The English Poor Law 1531–1782*, Basingstoke, 1990.
Poverty and Policy in Tudor and Stuart England, London, 1988.
Smith, R. M. (ed.), *Land, Kinship, and Life-Cycle*, Cambridge, 1984.
Snell, K. D. M., *Annals of the Labouring Poor, Social Change and Agrarian England, 1660–1900*, Cambridge, 1985.
'Settlement, Poor Law and the rural historian: new approaches and opportunities', *Rural History* 3, 2 (1992), 145–72.
Sohn, Anne-Marie, 'The golden age of male adultery: the Third Republic', *Journal of Social History* 28, 3 (1995), 469–90.
Sokoll, T., 'Negotiating a living: Essex pauper letters from London, 1800–1834' in L. Fontaine and J. Schlumbohm, *Household Strategies for Survival 1600–2000: Fission, Faction and Cooperation*, International Review of Social History, 45, Cambridge, 2000, pp. 19–46.
(ed.), *Essex Pauper Letters 1731–1837*, Records of Social and Economic History New Series, 30, Oxford, 2001.

Spufford, Margaret, *Contrasting Communities: English Villagers in the Sixteenth and Seventeenth Centuries*, Cambridge, 1974.

Staves, Susan, 'Money for honor: damages for criminal conversation', *Studies in Eighteenth-century Culture* 11 (1982), 279–97.

'Separate maintenance contracts', *Eighteenth-century Life* 11 (1987), 78–101.

'Where is history but in texts? Reading the history of marriage' in John M. Wallace (ed.), *The Golden and Brazen World, Papers in Literature and History, 650–1800*, Berkeley, 1985, pp. 125–43.

Stone, Lawrence, *The Family, Sex and Marriage in England 1500–1800*, abridged edition, London, 1977.

Road to Divorce, England 1530–1987, 2nd edition, Oxford, 1990.

Uncertain Unions and Broken Lives: Marriage and Divorce in England 1660–1857, 2nd edition, Oxford, 1992.

Stretton, Tim, *Women Waging Law in Elizabethan England*, Cambridge, 1998.

Styles, John, 'Custom or consumption? Plebeian fashion in eighteenth-century England' in M. Berg and E. Egar (eds.), *Luxury in the Eighteenth Century: Debates, Desires and Delectable Goods*, Basingstoke, 2002.

'Print and policing: crime advertising in eighteenth-century provincial England' in Douglas Hay and Francis Snyder, *Policing and Prosecution in Britain, 1750–1850*, Oxford, 1989, pp. 69–73.

Swan, Philip and Foster, David (eds.), *Essays in Regional and Local History*, Beverley, 1992.

Tadmor, Naomi, 'The concept of the household-family in eighteenth century England', *Past and Present* 151 (1996), 111–40.

Tague, I. H., 'Love, honor, and obedience: fashionable women and the discourse of marriage in the early eighteenth century', *Journal of British Studies* 40 (2001), 76–106.

Tarver, Anne, *Church Court Records*, Chichester, 1995.

Taylor, James Stephen, 'The impact of pauper settlement 1691–1834', *Past and Present* 73 (1976), 42–74.

Thirsk, J. (ed.), *The Agrarian History of England and Wales*, Cambridge, 1967, Vol. IV, *1500–1640*; Vol. V. 1, *1640–1750: Regional Farming Systems*.

Thomas, Keith, 'The double standard', *Journal of History of Ideas* 20 (1959), 195–217.

Thompson, E. P., *Customs in Common*, London, 1991.

Tillyard, Stella, *Aristocrats: Caroline, Emily, Louisa and Sarah Lennox 1740–1832*, 2nd edition, London, 1994.

Todd, Barbara J, 'Demographic determinism and female agency: the remarrying widow reconsidered... again', *Continuity and Change* 9, 3 (1994), 421–50.

Tomes, Nancy, 'A "torrent of abuse": crimes of violence between working-class men and women in London, 1840–1875', *Journal of Social History* 11, 3 (1978), 328–45.

Tomlinson, William Weaver, *Comprehensive Guide to the County of Northumberland*, London, 1888.

Tosh, J., *A Man's Place: Masculinity and the Middle-Class Home in Victorian England*, London, 1999.

Trumbach, Randolph, *Sex and the Gender Revolution*, Chicago and London, 1998.

Turner, D. M., 'Representations of adultery in England c. 1660 – c. 1740: a study of changing perceptions of marital infidelity in conduct literature, drama, trial publications and the records of the Court of Arches', Ph.D. thesis, University of Oxford (1998).

Turner, H. L., *Oxfordshire: A Look at the Past*, Derby, 1997.

Velody, Irving, 'Constructing the social', *History of the Human Sciences* 7, 1 (1994), 81–5.

Vickery, Amanda, *The Gentleman's Daughter: Women's Lives in Georgian England*, London, 1998.

'Golden age to separate spheres? A review of the categories and chronology of English women's history', *Historical Journal* 36, 2 (1993), 383–414.

'The neglected century: writing the history of eighteenth-century women', *Gender and History* 3, 2 (1991), 211–19.

'Women and the world of goods: a Lancashire consumer and her possessions, 1751–81' in J. Brewer and R. Porter (eds.), *Consumption and the World of Goods*, London, 1993, pp. 274–301.

'Women of the local elite in Lancashire, 1750 – c. 1825', Ph.D. thesis, University of London (1991).

Wagner, Peter, 'Trial reports as a genre of eighteenth-century erotica', *British Journal for Eighteenth-Century Studies* 5 (1982), 117–21.

Walker, Garthine, 'Expanding the boundaries of female honour in early modern England', *Transactions of the Royal Historical Society*, 6th series, 6 (1996), 235–45.

Watt, Jeffrey R., *The Making of Modern Marriage: Matrimonial Control and the Rise of Sentiment in Neuchatel, 1550–1800*, New York, 1992.

Watts Moses, E., 'The Ettricks of High Barnes', *Antiquities of Sunderland* 20 (1932–43) (1951), 9–21.

Weatherill, Lorna, *Consumer Behaviour and Material Culture in Britain 1660–1760*, Cambridge, 1988.

'A possession of one's own: women and consumer behaviour in England, 1660–1740', *Journal of British Studies* 25 (1986), 131–56.

Webb, Beatrice and Webb, Sidney, *English Local Government from the Revolution to the Municipal Corporations Act: The Parish and the County*, London, 1929.

Wiener, M. J., 'Alice Arden to Bill Sikes: changing nightmares of intimate violence in England, 1558–1869', *Journal of British Studies* 40 (2001), 184–212.

Wilson, Adrian, 'The ceremony of childbirth and its interpretation' in V. Fildes (ed.), *Women as Mothers in Pre-Industrial England*, London, 1990, pp. 68–107.

Wolfram, S., 'Divorce in England 1700–1857', *Oxford Journal of Legal Studies* 5, 2 (1985), 155–86.

In-Laws and Outlaws: Kinship and Marriage in England, New York, 1987.

Wrightson, Keith, *Earthly Necessities: Economic Lives in Early Modern Britain*, London, 2000.

English Society 1580–1680, London, 1982.

'Two concepts of order: justices, constables and jurymen in seventeenth-century England' in J. Brewer and J. Styles, *An Ungovernable People: The English and their Law in the Seventeenth and Eighteenth Centuries*, London, 1980, pp. 21–46.

Wrigley, E. A. and Schofield, R. S., *The Population History of England, 1541–1871*, London, 1981.

INDEX

separation (*cont.*)
  from bed and board on the grounds of
    cruelty 26, 114, 132, 200
  living arrangements of separated couples
    178–87
  mutually agreed 1, 58, 131
  outcome of separation suits 47–8, 49, 51,
    216
servants 26, 146, 152, 160
  as mediators in marital difficulties 32, 33,
    35, 38, 117
  as witnesses in separation cases 115, 122,
    156, 157–8
settlement, law of 36, 184
sex, coercive 151–2
sexual
  double-standard 5, 8, 140, 143–5, 147,
    149, 156, 166, 195
  exploitation 146–7, 151–4
sexuality 184
  changes in understanding of 111–12, 161,
    162, 201
Shepard, Alexandra 63, 68, 69, 72
Shoemaker, Robert 151, 198
social status 2, 3, 6, 12–14, 85–6, 93, 173,
  178, 179, 186
step-children 26, 35, 65–6
Stone, Lawrence 4, 6, 28, 124, 156
Stretton, Tim 9
summary conviction 43
  length of committal 43
sureties, breakdown of 33–4, 212

town criers 13, 22, 57
transportation 177
Turner, David 142, 143, 144, 147, 163
tyranny, *see* husbands

vagrancy, law of 36, 188
Vickery, Amanda 7, 136, 201

violence, changes in attitudes to 110–12,
  202

wife-beating 5, 200, 210, *see also* domestic
  violence; separation, from bed and
  board on the grounds of cruelty;
  violence
attitudes to 45, 122–4, 195, 202
causes of 113
changes in legal definitions of 124
changes in numbers of cases 124–8
defences of wife-beaters 120–2, 219
indicator of marital power relations
  110–14
irrationality of wife-beaters 115–17,
  202
occupation of wife-beaters 96–7, 218
popular rituals against 111
provocation of 117–22, 202
wives
  business concerns of 74
  credit relationships of 73
  economic autonomy of 69, 70, 72,
    196–7
  independence of 16, 96
  self-representations of 132–7
  subordination of 4, 133–4, 136–7, 138,
    194, 195, 201
work
  effect on marital relationships 3–4, 7, 8,
    95–7, 188, 197–8
  husbands and wives shared 93–5, 217
  men's, after separation or desertion 174,
    187
  men's, during marriage 93
  women's, after separation or desertion
    188–90
  women's, during marriage 92–3, 94–5

York 18, 19

Titles in the series

*The Common Peace: Participation and the Criminal Law in Seventeenth-Century England**
CYNTHIA B. HERRUP

*Politics, Society and Civil War in Warwickshire, 1620–1660**
ANN HUGHES

*London Crowds in the Reign of Charles II: Propaganda and Politics from the Restoration to the Exclusion Crisis**
TIM HARRIS

*Criticism and Compliment: The Politics of Literature in the England of Charles I**
KEVIN SHARPE

*Central Government and the Localities: Hampshire, 1649–1689**
ANDREW COLEBY

*John Skelton and the Politics of the 1520s**
GREG WALKER

Algernon Sidney and the English Republic, 1623–1677
JONATHAN SCOTT

*Thomas Starkey and the Commonweal: Humanist Politics and Religion in the Reign of Henry VIII**
THOMAS F. MAYER

*The Blind Devotion of the People: Popular Religion and the English Reformation**
ROBERT WHITING

*The Cavalier Parliament and the Reconstruction of the Old Regime, 1661–1667**
PAUL SEAWARD

The Blessed Revolution: England, Politics and the Coming of War, 1621–1624
THOMAS COGSWELL

*Charles I and the Road to Personal Rule**
L. J. REEVE

*George Lawson's 'Politica' and the English Revolution**
CONAL CONDREN

Puritans and Roundheads: The Harleys of Brampton Bryan and the Outbreak of the Civil War
JACQUELINE EALES

An Uncounselled King: Charles I and the Scottish Troubles, 1637–1641
PETER DONALD

*Cheap Print and Popular Piety, 1550–1640**
TESSA WATT

The Pursuit of Stability: Social Relations in Elizabethan London
IAN W. ARCHER

Prosecution and Punishment: Petty Crime and the Law in London and Rural Middlesex, c. 1660–1725
ROBERT B. SHOEMAKER

The Politics of Court Scandal in Early Modern England: News Culture and
the Overbury Affair, 1603–1660
ALASTAIR BELLANY

The Politics of Religion in the Age of Mary, Queen of Scots: The Earl of Argyll
and the Struggle for Britain and Ireland
JANE E. A. DAWSON

Treason and the State: Law, Politics and Ideology in the English Civil War
D. ALAN ORR

Preaching during the English Reformation
SUSAN WABUDA

Pamphlets and Pamphleteering in Early Modern Britain
JOAD RAYMOND

Patterns of Piety: Women, Gender and Religion in Late Medieval and
Reformation England
CHRISTINE PETERS

Popular Politics and the English Reformation*
ETHAN SHAGAN

Crime, Gender and Social Order in Early Modern England
GARTHINE WALKER

Mercy and Authority in the Tudor State
K. J. KESSELRING

Unquiet Lives: Marriage and Marriage Breakdown in England, 1660–1800
JOANNE BAILEY

*Also published as a paperback

Lightning Source UK Ltd.
Milton Keynes UK
171842UK00001B/118/P